PREDICTING YOUR FUTURE

PREDICTING YOUR FUTURE

This edition published in 1996 by
SMITHMARK Publishers,
a division of U.S. Media Holdings, Inc.,
16 East 32nd Street,
New York, NY 10016.

9 8 7 6 5 4 3 2 1

SMITHMARK books are available for
bulk purchase for sales promotion and
premium use. For details write or call
the manager of special sales,
SMITHMARK Publishers,
16 East 32nd Street, New York,
NY 10016; (212) 532-6600.

ISBN 0-8317-6776-6

Printed in China

All correspondence concerning the
content of this volume should be
addressed to Salamander Books Ltd.

Designer
Rod Ferring

Color artwork
Rod Ferring © Salamander Books Ltd

Filmset
Old Mill Typesetting, England

Color reproduction
Kentscan Ltd, England

CONTENTS

INTRODUCTION

The desire to discover what the future holds is innate in man for he is, by nature, curious and has always been intrigued by the unknown. This has led him, over the centuries, to devise a great variety of techniques to aid him in his search for arcane knowledge. Yet, whatever method is employed, no matter what approach the enquirer takes to the subject, divination is a means of gaining access to the supernormal; it is, by definition, a way of acquiring insight, both to the true nature of man and the universe as a whole.

Divination, in one form or another, has been practised by all cultures and civilisations throughout history. Every society has had its prophet, seer, soothsayer, wiseman or woman, shaman, high priest or priestess, magician, and so on; the title bestowed may have differed according to the time and culture yet the function of such individuals was the same: to advise and guide the community in which they lived in the light of their special knowledge, their ability to read the signs and interpret them accurately.

Nowadays we would probably call such people clairvoyants, mediums, sensitives or psychics, yet their role remains unchanged except that their guidance is more often sought by individuals than by groups, for divination is still prevalent today in every country in the world. The methods used may vary little from those practised centuries ago, others have been adapted or developed to such an extent through the ages that their origins are barely recognisable.

The 20th century businessperson who rolls dice or tosses a coin before making a decision would probably be surprised to learn that he or she was performing an identical act to that of the tribal shaman who consulted his fortune-bones, yet this is so. Similarly, our ancient forefathers who built monolithic constructs such as Stonehenge were as much concerned with the interrelationship between the heavenly bodies and events on Earth as is the modern astrologer who calculates a birth chart using a computer. No matter how simple or sophisticated the technique used may be, the underlying purpose of divination remains the same: to uncover hidden truths.

The object of this book is to provide the reader with the means to fulfil his or her potential in whatever way suits them best. Yet it is eminently practical; a team of experts have provided all the information necessary for someone with little or no knowledge of the subjects covered to discover more about himself and others. Simple, step by step guidelines show the reader how to foresee the possibilities and thus predetermine his own and others' reactions to life's changing patterns. May your voyage of discovery be an enjoyable one.

Selene

CHAPTER ONE

WESTERN ASTROLOGY

Astrology is one of the earliest divinatory arts devised by man. It is easy to picture our cave-dwelling ancestors observing the changing shape of the Moon over its 28-day cycle and the movement of the Sun over the year; eventually divining omens and portents from these changes.

Five planets are visible to the naked eye, and these were called ''wanderers'' because their path across the heavens is so obvious against the more remote background of fixed stars which form the constellations or ''signs'' with which most people are familiar, for these are the 12 signs of the zodiac.

Yet there are, of course, more than five planets in our Solar system, just as there is more to astrology than reading a Sun sign forecast. Astrology can reveal a person's temperament and the way in which he or she is most likely to react in a given set of circumstances, making it a key to self-knowledge.

Early astrology was based upon actual observation of the heavens and, in later years, when people had become mathematically minded, man already knew that the movements of the Sun, Moon, Mercury, Venus, Mars, Jupiter and Saturn were predictable because they followed a regular pattern. The angular relationship between these heavenly bodies was also studied and found to be important. Thus the early astrologers tabulated the movements of the planets and these ephemerides, as they are called, are very similar to the ones in use today.

An elaboration of the early system, which dwelt upon the signs, Sun, Moon and five visible planets, was the use of 12 houses which cover every possible area of life. The arrangement of these is dependent upon knowledge of the subject's birth-time which allows us to know the exact position that was on the Eastern horizon at the moment of birth. This is called the Ascendant or rising sign and often has more effect upon one's personality and life-style than does the Sun sign.

In some ways little has changed in astrology since those early beginnings except that the advent of the telescope allowed us to discover three more planets: Uranus, Neptune and Pluto. But even today more emphasis is usually placed upon the position of the Sun through to Saturn in natal astrology than on these outer planets. The former are termed 'personal' planets whereas the three more recent discoveries, which are slower moving, are mainly considered to be more effective in terms of one's generation.

Once every year the Earth makes a complete journey around the Sun, and the eight planets all revolve around the Sun in approximately the same plane as the Earth's orbit. Astrology is concerned with the relationship between the members of the Solar system and what happens on Earth, therefore the movements of the Sun, Moon and planets, as they revolve in their orbits, are calculated from a geocentric point of view: that is, as if viewed from the Earth.

Although the Sun is the centre of our system, from our viewpoint on Earth it appears as though the Sun and other planetary bodies move through the heavens against the backcloth of the zodiac. The zodiacal circle is divided into 12 sections or segments known as signs: Aries, Taurus, Gemini, Cancer, Leo, Virgo, Libra, Scorpio, Sagittarius, Capricorn, Aquarius and Pisces.

Because of the Sun's apparent journey through the zodiac and our ability to calculate exact times when it will 'enter' and 'leave' each sign in turn, astrology based on the Sun's position alone has come to be called Sun sign astrology. Although popular, as no specialist knowledge or complicated calculations are necessary, Sun sign astrology must, by definition, be rather limited in its application. Also, the Sun's entry into each sign varies slightly from year to year, so the dates quoted for each sign provide only a rough guide; for accuracy, an ephemeris should be consulted to discover the exact time and date of the Sun's entry into a particular sign in any given year.

Natal astrology, however, can give a much fuller picture of an individual's character because all the planetary positions and inter-relationships at birth will be taken into consideration. Unless one has a computer to do the work for you, some calculation will be necessary, though this may be much simpler than imagined and is explained later in this chapter. But the first step towards practising astrology is to learn about the planets, their nature and areas of influence. (In astrological terms, the Sun and Moon are referred to as planets, also lights or luminaries.)

As you can see by the diagram below, the focal point of our system is the Sun and nearest to that is Mercury, followed by Venus, the Earth and Mars. These are all comparatively close together, within the context of the vast distances involved, and are therefore usually referred to as the fast-moving planets.

Next in order from the Sun come the 'giants' of our Solar system, Jupiter and Saturn which, before the advent of the telescope, was thought to be the furthermost planet.

Finally, we come to the newest discoveries, Uranus, Neptune and Pluto; sometimes referred to as the 'transpersonal' planets by astrologers.

Our diagram shows the planetary order and their relative sizes. Of course, the relative distances between planets are not taken into consideration here.

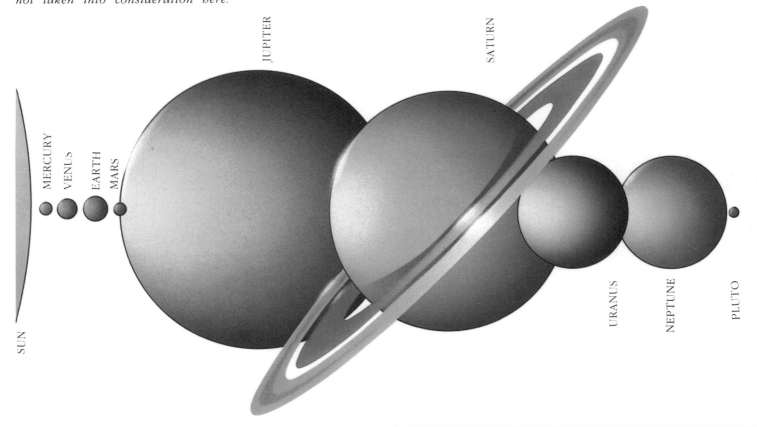

SUN MERCURY VENUS EARTH MARS JUPITER SATURN URANUS NEPTUNE PLUTO

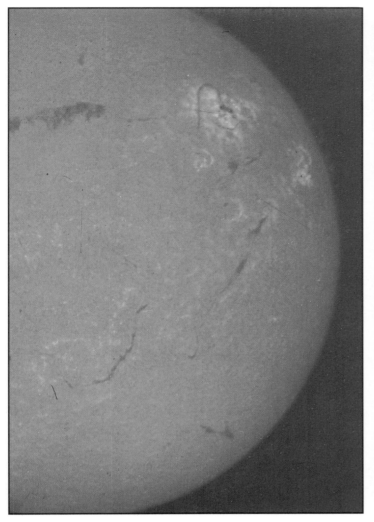

SUN

The Sun is the centre of our Solar system and everything else revolves around it. The light and heat that it generates is responsible for all life on this planet, nothing could exist without it. So, in a birth-chart it equates with the essential self and rules the heart, the central core of the physical body. Without the heart's ability to pump blood around our bodies we, too, could not exist. It is also interesting to note that we should never look at the physical Sun directly. Direct observation with the aid of binoculars or telescope is likely to result in blindness. In much the same way, it is impossible to "see" the whole person from his or her Sun sign alone.

The position of the Sun at birth is important, of course, yet it only reveals one facet of the personality; it is the interrelationship between all the planets that will disclose the complete picture. Apart from needing to pair it with the Moon, for reasons that will be discussed elsewhere, we should pay special heed to the Sun's position in relation to the Ascendant, which represents our birth-place here on Earth.

MOON

The Moon is a natural satellite of Earth and is our closest companion on our annual journey around the Sun, also in our infinite quest through space and time. The Moon is a barren place that has no water nor any light of its own. The light that it appears to emit is reflected from the Sun. This apparent light and changing shape (called phases, which repeat approximately every 28 days) are caused by the Moon's fairly complicated orbital revolution around our planet; this results in a constantly changing angular relationship to the Sun.

From these astronomical facts astrologers have learned that, because it is always with us, the Moon reveals our environment and regular habits; but it is the Moon's different phases which are responsible for our constantly changing moods and feelings. When studying a birth-chart, it is especially important to study the Sun and Moon together for the angular relationship between these two luminaries will reveal much about an individual's character for, in Jungian terms, they represent the anima and animus. Moon phases also play an important role in making predictions.

Qualities
MASCULINE PRINCIPLE □ WARMTH □ SELF-ESTEEM
HONOUR □ DOMINANCE □ STAMINA □ ARROGANCE
CONFIDENCE □ PROCREATION □ PLEASURE
GENEROSITY □ SELF-SATISFACTION □ VITALITY
DIGNITY □ WILL-POWER □ CREATIVITY
ORGANISATION □ CONDESCENSION □ BENEVOLENCE
PRIDE

Qualities
FEMININE PRINCIPLE □ FAMILIARITY □ HOME
MOTHER □ HABITS □ FERTILITY □ SENSITIVITY
EMOTIONS □ MOODS □ NURTURING □ RECEPTIVITY
DIGESTION □ MEMORY □ RESPONSE □ INSTINCTS
DOMESTICITY □ SECURITY □ ANCESTRY
CHANGEABILITY □ FLUCTUATIONS □ CONCEPTION
MOTION

MERCURY

Mercury is the smallest planet in the Solar system and it is also the one that is closest to the Sun. In fact, these two bodies can never be more than 28 degrees apart and it only requires 88 days for Mercury to complete its orbital journey. Its closeness to the life-giving force of the Sun may account for its association with health and well-being. This tiny planet posed problems for the ancients: they could not understand its rapid movement, its talent for seemingly disappearing from view, and were puzzled by its eccentric orbit which made it appear to move up and down, above and below the horizon. When it deigned to be visible for short periods, it was only ever seen in close company with its lord and master, the Sun, either preceding him in the Eastern sky at dawn or trailing not too far behind in the Western sky at dusk. Hence it was thought to be the Messenger of the Gods, with a reputation for agility, speed and trickery, though endowed with considerable mental ability. Perhaps Mercury's connection with short trips rather than long journeys arose because it never rises very far above our earthly horizon.

VENUS

Venus, the second planet from the Sun, has an orbit between Mercury and ourselves. She requires 243 days for her journey, and she can never be more than 48 degrees from the Sun, but Venus does have the ability to rise high above the horizon so that we can observe her in all her glory. As the most beautiful object in the sky Venus easily deserves her reputation as Goddess of Love and Beauty. However, it might be significant that she travels between us and the planet that rules our mental faculties! It also might be worth remembering that the mysteriously beautiful clouds that surround her are said to be largely composed of sulphuric acid. Yet the dense atmosphere that enfolds her prevents us from ever seeing her true surface, which is said to be smoother than that of any other planet.

Sadly, when Venus is at her closest point to Earth, she is totally invisible, so we can only ever covet her beauty from afar. Perhaps that is why this lovely planet also came to be associated with money and possessions, for these, too, so often appear to be unattainable and out of reach.

Qualities
INTELLECT ☐ COMMUNICATION ☐ PERCEPTION ☐ WIT
SPEECH ☐ WRITING ☐ LOGIC ☐ REASON
VERSATILITY ☐ ADAPTABILITY ☐ SARCASM ☐ TRICKERY
DUALITY ☐ SHORT JOURNEYS ☐ FLIPPANCY
INFORMATION ☐ AGILITY ☐ NEIGHBOURS ☐ BRETHREN
VARIETY ☐ DEXTERITY ☐ HEALING ☐ EXPRESSION

Qualities
LOVE ☐ MONEY ☐ POSSESSIONS ☐ VALUES ☐ ART
MUSIC ☐ BEAUTY ☐ GRACE ☐ FEMININITY
SENSUALITY ☐ HARMONY ☐ SOCIABILITY ☐ LAZINESS
VANITY ☐ RELATIONSHIPS ☐ CHARM ☐ POPULARITY
TACT ☐ DIPLOMACY ☐ COMFORT ☐ FECUNDITY
RICHNESS ☐ FULFILMENT ☐ LAZINESS ☐ WARMTH

MARS

The first planet in the Solar system to orbit the Sun outside Earth, Mars takes 687 of our earthly days to complete this journey. Perhaps the fact that we have to turn away from our protective centre, the Sun, to observe him is the reason that Mars has always been associated with initiative and self-assertion: Martian traits always require us to ignore all that is closest, most comfortable and most familiar in order to explore new horizons. Easily visible to the naked eye, its bright orange-red glow has traditional associations with courage, daring and danger. But, in this age of space-probes, it is fascinating to learn that Mars really does have dry, red dust and a salmon-pink sky.

In the same way as the astrological glyph (symbol) for Venus represents the female principle in science, the glyph for Mars represents that of the male; and Mars has always been regarded as the pioneer who seeks adventure and conquest. Thus it seems fitting that it is planned that this should be the first planet to receive a colony of pioneering Earthlings who will study it while living on a space station for up to a year.

JUPITER

Taking twleve years to move around the Sun, Jupiter is the largest planet in our Solar system. Appropriately enough, astrologers have always maintained that Jupiter rules expansion and now scientific exploration has proved that this planet is so huge, it could contain all the others and their satellites together, and still have room to spare. I doubt if our ancestors were aware of this, yet it has always been associated with everything that is larger than life, with amazingly lucky breaks (even winnings), and also the majestic crash of thunder. The latter traditional attribute is especially apt as we now know Jupiter is a stormy place where there are frequent discharges of lightning.

This planet is sometimes connected with great expectations yet, in reality, it is without any sort of solid surface, perhaps indicating that optimism can sometimes be misplaced. The word "jovial" sprang from this planet's apparently friendly image, so one is not surprised to learn that it also has the largest entourage, having more satellites than any other planet in the Solar system.

Qualities
INITIATIVE □ ENERGY □ MASCULINITY □ CONQUEST
AGGRESSION □ COURAGE □ BRAVADO
SELF-ASSERTION □ DIRECTION □ PENETRATION
ANGER □ ACTION □ IMPATIENCE □ IMPULSIVENESS
SEXUALITY □ EXPLORATION □ ENTHUSIASM
CHALLENGES □ SELFISHNESS □ DRIVE

Qualities
EXPANSION □ GROWTH □ OPTIMISM
EXPECTANCY □ EXCESS □ BELIEFS □ MORALS
LONG JOURNEYS □ MATURITY □ LUCK □ OPPORTUNITY
GREED □ PROSPERITY □ PHILOSOPHY
FURTHER EDUCATION □ JOVIALITY □ EXAGGERATION
SPECULATION □ SELF-RIGHTEOUSNESS □ POMP

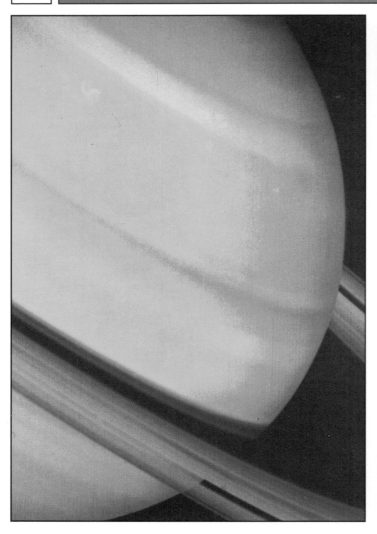

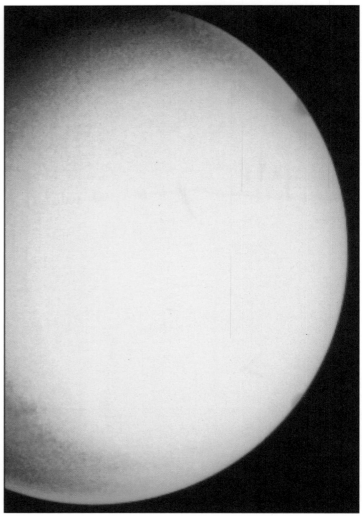

SATURN

Long thought to be the outermost planet of our Solar system, Saturn is the last that can be seen with the naked eye. Not unnaturally, therefore, it was said to rule boundaries, barriers and limitations of every kind. It was also decreed that a Saturnine person was very self-contained, cold and inhibited. Such definitions were laid down by people who had no access to our modern-day telescopes, let alone space-probes, so they could not have known that this planet actually is surrounded by a magnificent system of rings consisting of frozen particles that form a natural barrier.

An extremely cold planet, current scientific investigation suggests that Saturn may have a central core of rock; if true, this would accord well with the ancient definition of a Saturnian character. Saturn takes almost 30 years to journey round the Sun and is second only to Jupiter in size. Such information would seem to falsify its traditional image of small-boned thinness were it not for an odd astronomical fact which reveals that its low density would allow the whole planet to float on water, should such a large ocean be available.

URANUS

Fully justifying its reputation for unpredictability and eccentricity, its discovery caused chaos by utterly destroying the previously held vision of the ideal planetary number, the mystic seven. Next, there was argument over this planet's name. The discoverer wanted to call it Georgium Sidus, in honour of "mad" George III who had given him a pension; others wished to name it Herschel, after its discoverer. Luckily, J. E. Bode suggested Uranus (Saturn's father) and this totally appropriate name found favour.

Not known for its conformity, it should come as little surprise to learn that its axial rotation is different to that of any other planet — by no less than 90 degrees. So, when compared to its fellow travellers, Uranus appears to make its 84-year-long journey round the Sun while lying on its side. As recently as 1977 we learned that it has a number of rings which do not appear to reflect light. Although the Voyager 2 space-probe has added enormously to our knowledge, the tilt of this eccentric planet placed tremendous constraints on the mission, vindicating its astrological reputation.

Qualities
EXPERIENCE ☐ DISCIPLINE ☐ FEAR ☐ RESPONSIBILITY
BOUNDARIES ☐ TIME ☐ OLD AGE ☐ DUTY ☐ ORDER
WISDOM ☐ COLDNESS ☐ PERSEVERANCE ☐ AUTHORITY
PATIENCE ☐ THRIFT ☐ CAUTION ☐ DELAY
INHIBITION ☐ ISOLATION ☐ STABILITY ☐ CONTROL
REVOLUTION ☐ CATASTROPHE

Qualities
CHANGE ☐ REVOLUTION ☐ CATASTROPHE
SUDDENNESS ☐ INDEPENDENCE ☐ ECCENTRICITY
GENIUS ☐ CHAOS ☐ EXCITEMENT ☐ BOREDOM
INVENTION ☐ BRILLIANCE ☐ INSIGHT ☐ REBELLION
UNIQUENESS ☐ ELECTRICITY ☐ TECHNOLOGY
ACQUAINTANCES ☐ ORIGINALITY ☐ UNPREDICTABILITY

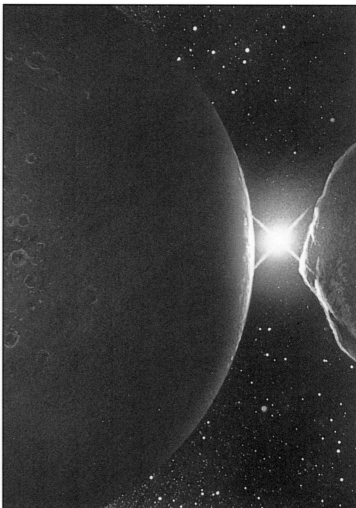

NEPTUNE

Neptune, the planet with weird attributes, takes 165 years to move around the Sun. Obviously eager to live up to its future astrological image, it was discovered independently by two different astronomers at the same time. Mathematical calculations of a hypothetical body were sent to yet another astronomer in a third country, where its position was confirmed by observation. Later it was learned that Neptune had, in truth, been spotted much earlier but wrongly catalogued as a fixed star!

This gaseous planet is not only the outermost giant but often the outermost planet of the Solar system, too, through no fault of its own. While happily following a regular orbit, its path is often crossed by that of pushy Pluto; which would appear to be a fine example of Neptunian good intentions going wrong. Unfortunately, there is little information about these far distant planets at present, although we may learn more from the future Voyager 2 encounter. But, knowing the nebulous image astrologers attribute to Neptune, one wonders if the space probe may get lost on the way!

PLUTO

Pluto is a highly eccentric planet that is believed to take 248 years to travel its vast journey around the Sun. This, too, was discovered mathematically, 14 years before its eventual observation in 1930. As befits a planet concerned with transformation, astronomers are constantly revising their ideas in connection with it. Apart from quarrels about Pluto's size, some even argue that this frozen solid mass is not even a proper planet. But, not being short on willpower, it presses on regardless, even having the audacity to come in from the cold from time to time by crossing the path of Neptune. By tradition, the God of the Underworld makes his journey to and from Hades in the company of the ferryman Charon.

It now appears that planet Pluto does in fact parallel its mythical counterpart, for in 1978 its satellite Moon was discovered. This was named Charon because its revolution exactly equals the rotation of Pluto, making them appear to move in perfect synchronicity. One wonders if these are true planetary soulmates — or could this be a perfect example of plutonic power?

Qualities
ILLUSION ☐ IMAGINATION ☐ INTUITION ☐ IDEALISM
VAGUENESS ☐ CONFUSION ☐ MYSTIQUE ☐ CHARISMA
FANTASY ☐ INSPIRATION ☐ POETRY ☐ SPIRITUALITY
SENTIMENT ☐ DECEPTION ☐ UNREALITY
GLAMOUR ☐ DISSOLUTION ☐ WEAKNESS ☐ PRIVACY
SECRECY ☐ IDEALISM ☐ DREAMINESS

Qualities
TRANSFORMATION ☐ REGENERATION ☐ POWER
COMPULSION ☐ OBSESSION ☐ INTENSITY
RUTHLESSNESS ☐ SUBCONSCIOUS ☐ INTERNMENT
FANATICISM ☐ COERCION ☐ SECRECY
ELIMINATION ☐ REJUVENATION ☐ EXPLOSION
DESTRUCTION ☐ BIRTH ☐ DEATH ☐ REBIRTH

ANGLES OF THE CHART

The Ascendant, rising sign or 1st House cusp, is regarded as very important by astrologers. This point, which represents that which was rising in the East at the moment of birth, is considered to reveal the face we present to the world; the Ascendant sign is in fact often more noticeable in our natures than that of the Sun. Likewise, the planet that rules the rising sign will gain significance, and its house position, sign and aspects will be carefully noted. Sometimes an individual may go through life feeling vaguely puzzled why he or she is so unlike the sensitive Piscean nature that is described in Sun sign books. It may be that such a person has courageous Leo rising, with his or her Piscean Sun hidden in the 8th House which has affinity with forceful Scorpio. Therefore, to understand their nature in its entirety it would be necessary to blend these three factors together. Planets that are close to the Ascendant are termed prominent; these, too, will hold considerable strength in any chart. The opposite point is called the Descendant and this will tell us much about our relationships. The Midheaven represents the place that the Sun would hold if it were high overhead and any planets that are close to this point in a chart are instrumental in the achievement of ambition. This, too, has its opposite, the *Immum Coeli,* and this point may tell us much about our inner self.

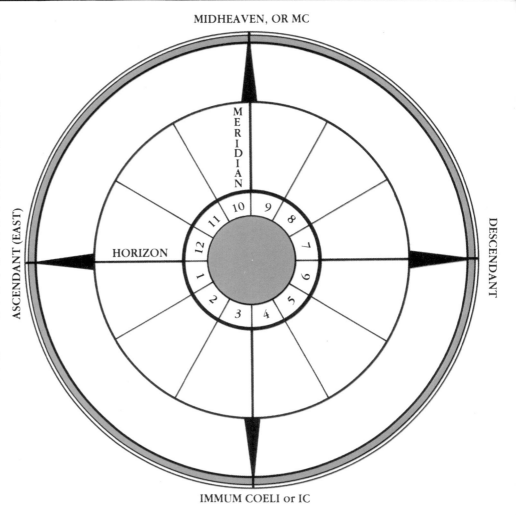

ERECTING A CHART

Now that you have been introduced to the nature of the planets, it is time to discover the other components that make up a chart. The background against which these heavenly bodies circulate is called the zodiac and this is divided into 12 sections called signs. These follow a particular sequence: Aries, Taurus, Gemini, Cancer, Leo, Virgo, Libra, Scorpio, Sagittarius, Capricorn, Aquarius and Pisces.

Astrologers say that planets are 'in' signs, and will interpret each planet slightly differently according to the nature of the sign that it occupies.

Soon you will learn how to calculate a chart and will begin to understand the role each of these planets and signs plays in your own life. You will then begin to understand more about yourself and learn what makes you a unique human being.

In order to construct your own birth chart you will need to know the time, place and date of your birth. In addition you will require an ephemeris (astronomical tables) for the year in question. The most widely used is *Raphael's Ephemeris* which is published annually by W. Foulsham & Co. Ltd. This publication lists the longitudes of the planets; the Sidereal Time for noon each day; notes the aspects; the daily motion of the planets and other phenomena, such as the Moon's phases; the time of the entry of the planets into the zodiacal signs; also the com-

THE SIGNS	THE PLANETS	OTHER	THE MODES
♈ ARIES	☉ SUN	MOON'S NORTH NODE ☊	CARDINAL
♉ TAURUS	☽ MOON	MOON'S SOUTH NODE ☋	FIXED
♊ GEMINI	☿ MERCURY	ASCENDANT OR RISING SIGN — Asc	MUTABLE
♋ CANCER	♀ VENUS		(QUADRU-PLICITIES)
♌ LEO	♂ MARS	MIDHEAVEN — MC	
♍ VIRGO	♃ JUPITER	RETROGRADE PLANET — ℞	THE ELEMENTS
♎ LIBRA	♄ SATURN		FIRE
♏ SCORPIO	♅ URANUS		EARTH
♐ SAGITTARIUS	♆ NEPTUNE		AIR
♑ CAPRICORN	♇ PLUTO		WATER (TRIPLICITIES)
♒ AQUARIUS			
♓ PISCES			

THE NODES

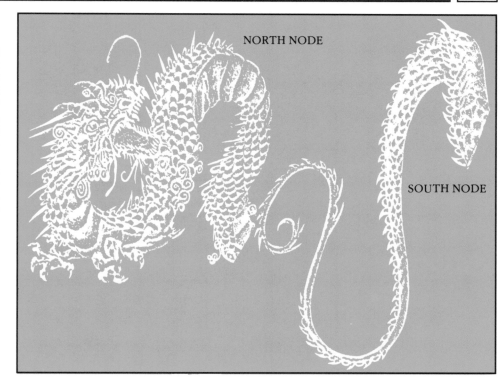

NORTH NODE

SOUTH NODE

Astrologers consider the Nodes of the Moon to be meaningful and will enter their position on a chart in the same way as the planets. The Nodes are imaginary points in space where the orbit of any heavenly body intersects the ecliptic. The North Node, which may also be called the Dragon's Head, represents the Moon's ascension North; while the South Node, or Dragon's Tail, denotes its point of intersection to the South. These Nodes are always exactly opposite each other and, because of this, need to be studied in terms of sign and house polarity.

The Dragon's Head is said to bring the most harmony into our lives and may show an area of benefit through little apparent effort. But, as these points have karmic connotations, this is not always so; any gains may come from very long ago. The Dragon's Tail is thought to show old habit patterns that may inhibit progress. Sometimes this point can indicate a need to break free of past restrictions in order to move forward, or it may show an area of required self-sacrifice.

Planets that fall very close to either of these points may either reinforce or counteract the Node's message; aspects to the Nodes may be important too. When the Nodes fall across the Ascendant/Descendant axis of a chart it is supposed to indicate that there may be something remarkable about the subject's height or appearance. Should the Nodes fall across the Midheaven/Immum Coeli axis, it emphasises the subject's career.

plete tables of Houses for London and for Houses of Liverpool.

You will also need *Raphael's Tables of Houses for Great Britain* and *Raphael's Table of Houses for Northern Latitudes,* as well as a good atlas with a fairly extensive gazetteer. To complete your requirements, blank chart forms, an ordinary pocket calculator, three coloured pens, a ruler, pencil or pen and scrap paper are necessary.

You are now almost ready to construct your own horoscope, but before you do this you must learn to recognise astrological symbols. Each planet and sign is represented by its own glyph and these should be learned from the table opposite before proceeding any further.

Left: The glyphs (symbols) for the planets, signs and aspects and the abbreviations commonly used on chart forms and in astrological tables.

Right: A typical blank chart form. The wheel is used for marking in the planetary positions at birth, the aspects made between these planets are entered on the grid in the bottom left-hand corner and the right-hand section is where calculations are shown. The text on the following pages will explain how to complete such a form, step by step.

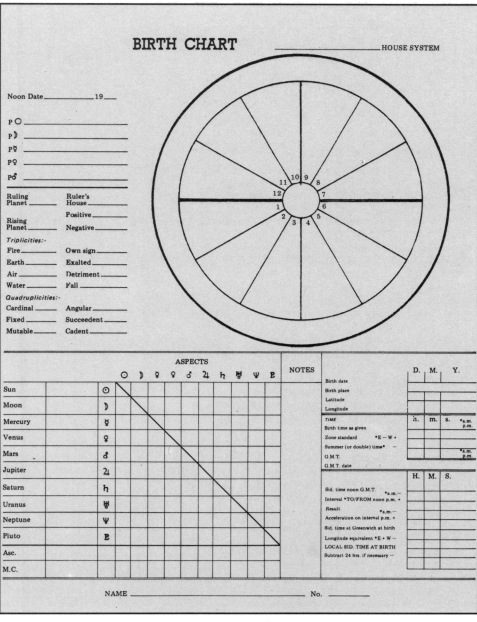

BIRTH CHART

_____ HOUSE SYSTEM

Noon Date_____ 19____

P ☉ _____
P ☽ _____
P ☿ _____
P ♀ _____
P ♂ _____

Ruling Planet _____	Ruler's House _____
Rising Planet _____	Positive _____
	Negative _____

Triplicities:-
Fire _____   Own sign _____
Earth _____   Exalted _____
Air _____   Detriment _____
Water _____   Fall _____

Quadruplicities:-
Cardinal _____   Angular _____
Fixed _____   Succeedent _____
Mutable _____   Cadent _____

	ASPECTS											NOTES		D.	M.	Y.
		☉	☽	☿	♀	♂	♃	♄	♅	♆	♇		Birth date			
Sun	☉												Birth place			
Moon	☽												Latitude			
Mercury	☿												Longitude			
Venus	♀												TIME	h.	m.	s.
Mars	♂												Birth time as given			
Jupiter	♃												Zone standard *E − W +			
Saturn	♄												Summer (or double) time*			
Uranus	♅												G.M.T.			
Neptune	♆												G.M.T. date			
Pluto	♇													H.	M.	S.
Asc.													Sid. time noon G.M.T. *a.m.			
M.C.													Interval *TO/FROM noon p.m. +			

Sid. time noon G.M.T. *a.m.
Interval *TO/FROM noon p.m. +
Result *a.m.
Acceleration on interval p.m. +
Sid. time at Greenwich at birth
Longitude equivalent *E + W −
LOCAL SID. TIME AT BIRTH
Subtract 24 hrs. if necessary −

NAME _____ No. _____

CACULATING A CHART

1. Enter date of birth.

2. Enter place (latitude and longitude) of birth.

3. Enter time of birth.

4.Zone Standard is only used for someone born abroad.

5. If applicable, subtract 1 or 2 hours for British Summer Time/Daylight Saving Time in order to arrive at GMT at birth (this can result in the Birth Date having to be put back or forward to the day before or after the actual birthdate).

6. Enter GMT date (see previous note).

7. Enter Sidereal Time for Noon GMT.

8. Enter interval TO/FROM Noon.
for *a.m.* birth, *subtract* interval from ST at Noon; for *p.m.* birth, *add* interval to ST at Noon.

9. Enter result.

10. Calculate acceleration on interval at the rate of 10 secs per hour. *Add* this to the previous 'result' shown in step 9 for a *p.m.* birth; *subtract* this from the 'result' for an *a.m.* birth.

11. Enter result as Sidereal Time at Greenwich at birth.

12. Adjust Sidereal Time at Greenwich at birth by referring to longitude of birth place. Longitude is expressed in minutes and seconds and, if necessary, can be expressed as hours, minutes and seconds once the calculations are completed.

To convert longitude to time simply calculate the longitude in seconds, multiply by 4 and convert this figure to hours, minutes and seconds. Enter result.

13. *Add* this result to running total if the birth place was *East* of Greenwich; *subtract* this amount if the birth place was *West* of Greenwich. This gives you the *LOCAL SIDEREAL TIME AT BIRTH.*

14. If this total is more than 24, subtract 24 hours and enter result in the following method: *LOCAL ST at BIRTH.*

BIRTH CHART

	D.	M.	Y.	
Birth date	19	10	1963	
Birth place	PERIVALE			
Latitude	51	30	N	
Longitude	0	20	W	
TIME	h.	m.	s.	*~~a.m.~~* p.m.
Birth time as given	2	45	00	
Zone standard *E — W +				
Summer ~~(or double)~~ time* —	1	00	00	
G.M.T.	1	45	00	~~*a.m.~~ p.m.
G.M.T. date 19 : 10 : 63				
	H.	M.	S.	
Sid. time noon G.M.T. ~~*a.m.~~	13	48	58	
Interval ~~*TO~~/FROM noon p.m. +	01	45	00	
Result ~~*a.m.~~	15	33	58	
Acceleration on interval p.m. +	00	00	18	
Sid. time at Greenwich at birth	15	34	16	
Longitude equivalent *~~E~~ + W —	00	01	20	
LOCAL SID. TIME AT BIRTH	15	32	56	
Subtract 24 hrs. if necessary —				
	15	32	56	

New Moon—October 17, 0*h*. 43*m*. *p.m.*

20 **OCTOBER, 1963** [*RAPHAEL'S*

D M	Neptune Lat.	Neptune Dec.	Herschel Lat.	Herschel Dec.	Saturn Lat.	Saturn Dec.	Jupiter Lat.	Jupiter Dec.	Mars Lat.	Mars Dec.	Mars Dec.
	° ′	° ′	° ′	° ′	° ′	° ′	° ′	° ′	° ′	° ′	° ′
1	1 N43	14 S 25	0 N44	9 N23	1 S 15	17 S 0	1 S 38	4 N33	0 S 21	16 S 4	16 S 17
3	1 43	14 26	0 44	9 20	1 15	17 1	1 38	4 27	0 22	16 30	16 43
5	1 43	14 27	0 44	9 18	1 15	17 2	1 38	4 21	0 24	16 56	17 8
7	1 43	14 28	0 44	9 15	1 15	17 3	1 38	4 14	0 25	17 21	17 33
9	1 43	14 29	0 44	9 13	1 15	17 4	1 38	4 8	0 26	17 45	17 57
11	1 43	14 31	0 44	9 11	1 15	17 4	1 38	4 2	0 27	18 9	18 21
13	1 43	14 32	0 44	9 8	1 15	17 5	1 38	3 56	0 29	18 33	18 45
15	1 43	14 33	0 44	9 6	1 14	17 5	1 38	3 50	0 30	18 56	19 7
17	1 43	14 35	0 44	9 4	1 14	17 5	1 37	3 44	0 31	19 18	19 29
19	1 43	14 36	0 44	9 2	1 14	17 5	1 37	3 38	0 32	19 40	19 51
21	1 43	14 37	0 44	9 0	1 14	17 5	1 37	3 32	0 33	20 1	20 12
23	1 43	14 38	0 44	8 58	1 14	17 5	1 37	3 27	0 34	20 22	20 32
25	1 43	14 40	0 45	8 56	1 14	17 5	1 36	3 21	0 35	20 42	20 51
27	1 43	14 41	0 45	8 54	1 14	17 5	1 36	3 16	0 36	21 1	21 10
29	1 43	14 42	0 45	8 52	1 14	17 4	1 36	3 11	0 38	21 19	21 28
31	1 43	14 44	0 45	8 51	1 14	17 3	1 35	3 6	0 39	21 37	

D M	D W	Sidereal Time. H. M. S.	⊙ Long. ° ′ ″	⊙ Dec. ° ′	☽ Long. ° ′ ″	☽ Lat. ° ′	☽ Dec. ° ′	MIDNIGHT ☽ Long. ° ′ ″	MIDNIGHT ☽ Dec. ° ′
1	Tu	12 38 0	7♎35 11	3 S 1	14♓17 48	4 S 14	10 S 5	21♓32 42	7 S 31
2	W	12 41 56	8 34 10	3 24	28 53 13	4 46	4 49	6♈18 24	2 1
3	Th	12 45 53	9 33 12	3 47	13♈47 13	5 0	0N 50	21 18 26	3N 41
4	F	12 49 49	10 32 15	4 10	28 50 47	4 53	6 29	6♉23 1	9 12
5	S	12 53 46	11 31 21	4 34	13♉53 52	4 26	11 46	21 22 14	14 9
6	𝕾	12 57 43	12 30 29	4 57	28 47 8	3 42	16 17	6♊ 7 46	18 9
7	M	13 1 39	13 29 39	5 20	13♊23 31	2 43	19 43	20 33 59	20 57
8	Tu	13 5 36	14 28 51	5 43	27 38 55	1 35	21 50	4♋38 15	22 22
9	W	13 9 32	15 28 6	6 5	11♋32 2	0 23	22 33	18 20 27	22 24
10	Th	13 13 29	16 27 24	6 28	25 3 45	0N 48	21 55	1♌42 13	21 7
11	F	13 17 25	17 26 43	6 51	8♌16 14	1 55	20 3	14 46 7	18 44
12	S	13 21 22	18 26 5	7 14	21 12 13	2 54	17 11	27 34 53	15 27
13	𝕾	13 25 18	19 25 29	7 36	3♍54 25	3 44	13 33	10♍11 5	11 31
14	M	13 29 15	20 24 56	7 59	16 25 6	4 22	9 23	22 36 43	7 10
15	Tu	13 33 12	21 24 24	8 21	28 46 4	4 47	4 53	4♎53 18	2 34
16	W	13 37 8	22 23 55	8 43	10♎58 34	4 59	0 14	17 1 58	2 S 5
17	Th	13 41 5	23 23 28	9 5	23 3 36	4 57	4 S 22	29 3 37	6 36
18	F	13 45 1	24 23 2	9 27	5♏ 2 7	4 42	8 47	10♏59 17	10 51
19	S	13 48 58	25 22 39	9 49	16 55 18	4 14	12 50	22 50 23	14 41
20	𝕾	13 52 54	26 22 18	10 11	28 44 48	3 36	16 23	4♐38 54	17 55
21	M	13 56 51	27 21 58	10 32	10♐33 1	2 48	19 16	16 27 34	20 25
22	Tu	14 0 47	28 21 41	10 54	22 23 2	1 53	21 21	28 19 56	22 3
23	W	14 4 44	29 21 25	11 15	4♑18 49	0 52	22 30	10♑20 17	22 42
24	Th	14 8 41	0♏21 11	11 36	16 24 58	0 S 12	22 38	22 33 30	22 17
25	F	14 12 37	1 20 59	11 57	28 46 34	1 17	21 40	5♒ 4 48	20 46
26	S	14 16 34	2 20 48	12 17	11♒28 50	2 20	19 35	17 59 16	18 8
27	𝕾	14 20 30	3 20 39	12 38	24 36 34	3 18	16 25	1♓21 11	14 28
28	M	14 24 27	4 20 32	12 58	8♓13 21	4 6	12 17	15 13 12	9 55
29	Tu	14 28 23	5 20 26	13 18	22 20 38	4 42	7 21	29 35 21	4 39
30	W	14 32 20	6 20 22	13 38	6♈56 48	5 1	1 51	14♈24 13	1N 1
31	Th	14 36 16	7 20 20	13 58	21 56 36	5 0	3 N 55	29 32 45	6 46

First Quarter—October 25, 5*h*. 21*m*. *p.m.*

Full Moon—October 3, 4*h*. 44*m*. *a.m.*

EPHEMERIS] **OCTOBER, 1963** 21

D M	Venus Lat.	Venus Declin.	Venus Declin.	Mercury Lat.	Mercury Declin.	Mercury Declin.	☽ Node.
	° ′	° ′	° ′	° ′	° ′	° ′	° ′
1	1N 4	5 S 25	5 S 55	0N 29	4 N 2	4 N 5	16♋12
3	1 1	6 25	6 55	0 57	4 3	3 56	16 6
5	0 58	7 25	7 54	1 20	3 45	3 29	16 0
7	0 54	8 23	8 53	1 37	3 10	2 46	15 53
9	0 50	9 22	9 50	1 49	2 20	1 50	15 47
11	0 46	10 19	10 47	1 56	1 18	0 44	15 41
13	0 42	11 15	11 43	1 59	0 8	0 S 30	15 34
15	0 38	12 10	12 37	1 58	1 S 9	1 50	15 28
17	0 34	13 4	13 31	1 55	2 31	3 13	15 21
19	0 29	13 57	14 23	1 49	3 55	4 38	15 15
21	0 24	14 49	15 14	1 41	5 21	6 4	15 9
23	0 20	15 39	16 3	1 31	6 47	7 30	15 2
25	0 15	16 27	16 51	1 21	8 12	8 54	14 56
27	0 10	17 14	17 37	1 9	9 36	10 18	14 50
29	0 5	17 59	18 21	0 57	10 59	11 39	14 43
31	0 0	18 42		0 44	12 19		14 37

Mutual Aspects.

1. ☉⚺♅, ⊥Ψ. ♀△♄.
3. ♀⊥♇. ♂☌Ψ. [♂⚹♇
4. ☉P☿. ☿±♄. ♂∇♃.
5. ☉P♃.
6. ☉⚺♇. ♀∠♅. ♂□♄,
8. ☉☍♃, ⊥♅, ⚺Ψ. [P♄.
9. ♀P♅. ♃∇Ψ.
10. ☉△♄. ☿∠Ψ. ♀∠♇. ♃±♅.
11. ☿⚼♄. ♂±♃. ♂Q♅.
13. ☉⊥♇. 15. ☿∠♂. ♂P♇.
16. ☿⚺♅, ⊥Ψ.
17. ☉∠♅, P♅. ♃∇♇.
18. ☿☍♃, ⚺♇.
19. ☿P♃, ⊥♅, ⚺Ψ. ♀⚹♅.
20. ☉⚺♂. ☿△♄. [♂Q♇.
21. ♀PΨ. ♄Stat.
22. ☉∠♇. ☿⊥♇. ♀∇♃. ♂⚼♃.
23. ♀⚹♇. 24. ☿⊥♂. ♀☌Ψ.
25. ☿∠♅. ♀□♄.
26. ☿P♅. ♀±♃.
27. ☿∠♇. ♀P♄.
29. ♀Q♅. 31. ☿⚺♂. ♀P♇.

D M	Ψ Long.	♅ Long.	♄ Long.	♃ Long.	♂ Long.	♀ Long.	☿ Long.	⊙	♇	Ψ	♅	♄	♃	♂	♀	☿
	° ′	° ′	° ′	° ′	° ′	° ′	° ′									
1	14♏ 3	7♍40	16♒47	15♈22	12♏58	16♎19	20♍57		☍	△	☍	⚺	⚺	△		☍
2	14 5	7 43	16 ℞45	15 ℞14	13 39	17 34	21 24			⚼		∠		⚼		
3	14 7	7 46	16 43	15 6	14 21	18 48	22 0	☍				⚹	☌		☍	
4	14 9	7 50	16 42	14 58	15 2	20 3	22 45		⚼		⚼					
5	14 11	7 53	16 40	14 50	15 44	21 18	23 38		△	☍	△	□	⚺	☍		⚼
𝕾	14 13	7 56	16 38	14 42	16 26	22 33	24 39	⚼					∠			△
7	14 15	7 59	16 37	14 34	17 7	23 47	25 47	△	□		□	△	⚹		⚼	
8	14 17	8 3	16 36	14 26	17 49	25 2	27 1			⚼		⚼		⚼	△	□
9	14 19	8 6	16 34	14 18	18 31	26 17	28 20	□	⚹	△	⚹		□			
10	14 21	8 9	16 33	14 10	19 13	27 32	29 44		∠		∠			△	□	⚹
11	14 23	8 12	16 32	14 2	19 55	28 46	1♎11		⚺	□	⚺		△			
12	14 25	8 15	16 31	13 54	20 37	0♏ 1	2 42	⚹				☍		□		∠
𝕾	14 27	8 18	16 30	13 46	21 19	1 16	4 16	∠			☌		⚼		⚹	⚺
14	14 29	8 21	16 29	13 38	22 2	2 31	5 52	⚺	☌	⚹				⚹	∠	
15	14 31	8 24	16 29	13 30	22 44	3 46	7 29			∠		⚼			⚺	
16	14 33	8 27	16 28	13 22	23 26	5 0	9 8		⚺	⚺	⚺	△	☍	∠		☌
17	14 35	8 30	16 28	13 14	24 9	6 15	10 49	☌	∠		∠			⚺		
18	14 37	8 33	16 27	13 6	24 51	7 30	12 30				⚹				☌	
19	14 40	8 36	16 27	12 58	25 34	8 45	14 12		⚹	☌		□				⚺
𝕾	14 42	8 39	16 27	12 51	26 16	10 0	15 54	⚺					⚼	☌		∠
21	14 44	8 42	16 27	12 43	26 59	11 14	17 36	∠	□	⚺	□	⚹	△		⚺	
22	14 46	8 44	16 D27	12 36	27 42	12 29	19 18							⚺	∠	⚹
23	14 48	8 47	16 27	12 28	28 25	13 44	21 0	⚹		∠	△	∠				
24	14 50	8 50	16 27	12 21	29 8	14 59	22 42		△	⚹		⚺	□	∠	⚹	
25	14 53	8 52	16 28	12 14	29 51	16 14	24 24	□	⚼		⚼			⚹		□
26	14 55	8 55	16 28	12 7	0♐34	17 28	26 6			□		☌	⚹			
𝕾	14 57	8 58	16 29	12 0	1 17	18 43	27 47						∠		□	△
28	14 59	9 0	16 29	11 53	2 0	19 58	29 28	△	☍	△	☍		⚺	□		
29	15 1	9 3	16 30	11 46	2 43	21 13	1♏ 8	⚼				⚺			△	⚼
30	15 4	9 5	16 31	11 39	3 27	22 28	2 48			⚼		∠	☌	△	⚼	
31	15 6	9 8	16 32	11 33	4 10	23 42	4 27		⚼		⚼	⚹		⚼		

Last Quarter—October 9, 7*h*. 28*m*. *p.m.*

©W. Foulsham & Co. Ltd.

Astrologers calculate birth charts very precisely; but one can also glean much information from a chart that has the house cusps and planetary positions rounded up to the nearest whole degree. The pages that follow will enable you to learn to calculate by the latter approximate method. Should you wish to learn to calculate everything in a chart to the exact hour (degree), minute and second, specialist text-books will help you to do this; there are also many classes available. The simplest method is, of course, to obtain a chart calculated by computer. There are programmes available for home computers, or one can subscribe to a chart service.

Having arrived at the Sidereal Time at birth, we are now ready to construct the chart by entering the zodiacal signs and the planets on the birth chart 'wheel'. As mentioned earlier, for the sake of ease and simplicity, whole degrees only will be used at this moment. As an example we will use the birth data shown left which is for Sally, born in Perivale at 2.45 pm (BST) on October 19th, 1963.

In this instance, the nearest Sidereal Time is between 15° 30' 35'' — 15° 34' 41'', in the tables for the equivalent latitude. If you look under the column which is headed by the word 'Ascen' (abbreviation for Ascendant), you will see that the Ascendant must fall between 20° 32' and 21° 48' Capricorn. Therefore, the nearest whole degree will be 21 degrees Capricorn, so we will erect an Equal House chart for this.

There are several systems of house division known to astrologers; far too many to mention in a book such as the present one. The simplest of these systems is called Equal House, which shows 12 equal segments that each contain 30 degrees, which derive from the degree given to the Ascendant. For instance, in the chart illustrated you will find (starting at the 9 o'clock position) an Ascendant of 21 degrees Capricorn, followed by a 2nd House that equals 21 degrees Aquarius, and so on, until one arrives at a 12th House cusp of 21 degrees Sagittarius.

The Midheaven, (usually referred to as MC), can also be found by reference to the *Table of Houses*. This will be found under the column listed as '10' and is seen to fall between 25 and 26 degrees of Scorpio. As the figure 20° 32' is actually closer to our chosen figure of 21 degrees Capricorn, we will enter 25 degrees Scorpio as the Midheaven. This could be entered in red, in the form of an upward pointing arrow on the chart. The opposite point, termed the I.C. (*Immum Coeli*) is also entered in red.

You now have the information needed to fill in the bottom left-hand corner of the chart. In the space provided, write Capricorn against Asc. and Scorpio against M.C.

The next step is to enter the planets' positions on the birth-chart wheel. Again you will need to refer to the ephemeris for the given date.

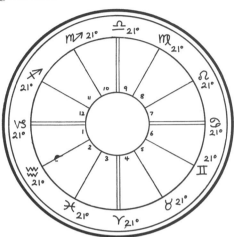

The Sun: Each page of the ephemeris is divided horizontally; look down the left-hand column below this line until you find the 19th, the date of birth. Then move across to the fourth column, headed by the Sun's symbol ☉ with the word long (longitude) beneath it and you will see the figure 25° 22' 39''. Now move your finger up this column until you come to the glyph for one of the signs of the zodiac. In this case you will find Libra ♎ at the top of the column.

Next, it is necessary to calculate the Sun's position at the time of birth, which occurred at a GMT time of 1 hour 45 minutes after noon. If you look at the figure below 25° 22' 39'' you will see that it reads 26° 22' 18'', which means that the Sun moved 0° 59' 39'' between noon on the 19th and noon on the 20th.

This final figure is the one used to find out how far the Sun has moved since noon on the 19th and the birth-time 1 hour 45 minutes later. First we will round this figure up to the nearest whole minute and express this figure as 60 minutes. This is then divided by 24 (the number of hours in a day) and multiplied by 1 hour 45 minutes (the birth-time). If using a calculator that does not have the facility for working in hours (degrees) and minutes, the birth-time should be expressed in decimals (1.75). The result is 0° 4' to the nearest minute.

Thus:

	degs.	mins.	secs.
At noon on the 19th the Sun was at	25	22	39
add 4 minutes for p.m. birth	00	04	00
	25	26	39

So, the Sun's position at the time of birth was 25° 26' 39'' Libra, or 25 Libra to the nearest whole degree.

Every other planet (apart from the Moon which will be demonstrated separately) is easily calculated by following the method given for calculating the Sun, with the exception of 'Retrogrades'.

If you look to the right-hand page of the ephemeris, in column 5, you will see that the position for Jupiter ♃ on the 19th is 12° 58' Aries but it is 12° 51' Aries on the 20th. The reason for this apparent contradiction is that, due to the motion of the Earth in relation to the planets, Jupiter appears to be moving backwards. The symbol ℞ is entered beside such a planet because some astrologers consider that when a planet is retrograde its effect is intensified in some way.

Calculations for such planets are, therefore, slightly different. It should be noted that retrograde motion can occur with planets from Mercury through to Saturn. The Sun and Moon can never appear in retrograde motion.

Jupiter's position at noon on 19th October	Aries 12°58' retrograde
Jupiter's position at noon on 20th October	Aries 12°51' retrograde
	= 00°07'

In 24 hours Jupiter has moved 7 minutes. We still divide this by 24 and multiply by 1 hour 45 minutes (decimal 1.75), but the result of only 31 seconds is *subtracted* from the position it held at noon on the 19th. In this instance, it makes no appreciable difference to the final figure which is rounded up to 13 degrees Aries.

The Moon: This is the fastest moving heavenly body, with an average daily motion of 13° 10', though it can be as high as 15° or as low as 11°. As a very rough guide, then, the Moon moves at the rate of about ½ degree an hour.

Returning again to the ephemeris, in the 6th column from the left, headed by the sym-

---

NEW MOON—October 17, 0h. 43m. p.m.

20   **OCTOBER, 1963**   [*RAPHAEL'S*

D M	Neptune. Lat.	Neptune. Dec.	Herschel. Lat.	Herschel. Dec.	Saturn. Lat.	Saturn. Dec.	Jupiter. Lat.	Jupiter. Dec.	Mars. Lat.	Mars. Dec.
1	1 N43	14 S 25	0 N 44	9 N 23	1 S 15	17 S 0	1 S 38	4 N 33	0 S 21	16 S 4
3	1 43	14 26	0 44	9 20	1 15	17 1	1 38	4 27	0 22	16 30
5	1 43	14 27	0 44	9 18	1 15	17 2	1 38	4 21	0 24	16 56
7	1 43	14 28	0 44	9 15	1 15	17 3	1 38	4 14	0 25	17 21
9	1 43	14 29	0 44	9 13	1 15	17 4	1 38	4 8	0 26	17 45
11	1 43	14 31	0 44	9 11	1 15	17 4	1 38	4 2	0 27	18 9
13	1 43	14 32	0 44	9 8	1 15	17 5	1 38	3 56	0 29	18 33
15	1 43	14 33	0 44	9 6	1 14	17 5	1 38	3 50	0 30	18 56
17	1 43	14 35	0 44	9 4	1 14	17 5	1 37	3 44	0 31	19 18
19	1 43	14 36	0 44	9 2	1 14	17 5	1 37	3 38	0 32	19 40
21	1 43	14 37	0 44	9 0	1 14	17 5	1 37	3 32	0 33	20 1
23	1 43	14 38	0 44	8 58	1 14	17 5	1 37	3 27	0 34	20 22
25	1 43	14 40	0 45	8 56	1 14	17 5	1 36	3 21	0 35	20 42
27	1 43	14 41	0 45	8 54	1 14	17 5	1 36	3 16	0 36	21 1
29	1 43	14 42	0 45	8 52	1 14	17 4	1 36	3 11	0 38	21 19
31	1 43	14 44	0 45	8 51	1 14	17 3	1 35	3 6	0 39	21 37

Mars Dec. (right margin): 16 S 17 / 16 43 / 17 8 / 17 33 / 17 57 / 18 21 / 18 45 / 19 7 / 19 29 / 19 51 / 20 12 / 20 32 / 20 51 / 21 10 / 21 28

D M	D W	Sidereal Time. H. M. S.	☉ Long.	☉ Dec.	☽ Long.	☽ Lat.	☽ Dec.	MIDNIGHT ☽ Long.	☽ Dec.
1	Tu	12 38 0	7♎35 11	3 S 1	14✶17 48	4 S 14	10 S 5	21✶32 42	7 S 31
2	W	12 41 56	8 34 10	3 24	28 53 13	4 46	4 49	6♈18 24	2 1
3	Th	12 45 53	9 33 12	3 47	13♈47 13	5 0	0 N 50	21 18 26	3 N 41
4	F	12 49 49	10 32 15	4 10	28 50 47	4 53	6 29	6♉23 1	9 12
5	S	12 53 46	11 31 21	4 34	13♉53 52	4 26	11 46	21 22 14	14 9
6	☉	12 57 43	12 30 29	4 57	28 47 8	3 42	16 17	6♊7 46	18 9
7	M	13 1 39	13 29 39	5 20	13♊23 31	2 43	19 43	20 33 59	20 57
8	Tu	13 5 36	14 28 51	5 43	27 38 55	1 35	21 50	4♋38 15	22 22
9	W	13 9 32	15 28 6	6 5	11♋32 2	0 23	22 33	18 20 27	22 24
10	Th	13 13 29	16 27 24	6 28	25 3 45	0 N 48	21 55	1♌42 13	21 7
11	F	13 17 25	17 26 43	6 51	8♌16 14	1 55	20 3	14 46 7	18 44
12	S	13 21 22	18 26 5	7 14	21 12 13	2 54	17 11	27 34 53	15 42
13	☉	13 25 18	19 25 29	7 36	3♍54 25	3 44	13 33	10♍11 5	11 31
14	M	13 29 15	20 24 56	7 59	16 25 6	4 22	9 23	22 36 43	7 10
15	Tu	13 33 12	21 24 24	8 21	28 46 4	4 47	4 53	4♎53 18	2 34
16	W	13 37 8	22 23 55	8 43	10♎58 34	4 59	0 14	17 1 58	2 S 5
17	Th	13 41 5	23 23 28	9 5	23 3 36	4 57	4 S 22	29 3 37	6 36
18	F	13 45 1	24 23 2	9 27	5♏2 7	4 42	8 47	10♏59 17	10 51
19	S	13 48 58	25 22 39	9 49	16 55 18	4 14	12 50	22 50 23	14 41
20	☉	13 52 54	26 22 18	10 11	28 44 48	3 36	16 23	4♐38 54	17 55
21	M	13 56 51	27 21 58	10 32	10♐33 1	2 48	19 16	16 27 34	20 25
22	Tu	14 0 47	28 21 41	10 54	22 23 1	1 53	21 21	28 19 56	22 3
23	W	14 4 44	29 21 25	11 15	4♑18 49	0 52	22 30	10♑20 17	22 42
24	Th	14 8 41	0♏21 11	11 36	16 24 58	0 S 12	22 38	22 33 30	22 17
25	F	14 12 37	1 20 59	11 57	28 46 34	1 17	21 40	5♒4 48	20 46
26	S	14 16 34	2 20 48	12 17	11♒28 50	2 20	19 35	17 59 16	18 8
27	☉	14 20 30	3 20 39	12 38	24 36 34	3 18	16 25	1✶21 11	14 28
28	M	14 24 27	4 20 32	12 58	8✶13 21	4 6	12 17	15 13 12	9 55
29	Tu	14 28 23	5 20 26	13 18	22 20 38	4 42	7 21	29 35 21	4 39
30	W	14 32 20	6 20 22	13 38	6♈56 48	5 1	1 51	14♈24 13	1 N 1
31	Th	14 36 16	7 20 20	13 58	21 56 36	5 0	3 N 55	29 32 45	6 46

FIRST QUARTER—October 25, 5h. 21m. p.m.

FULL MOON—October 3, 4*h*. 44*m*. *a.m.*

EPHEMERIS] **OCTOBER, 1963** 21

D M	Venus Lat. ° ′	Venus Declin. ° ′	Venus Declin. ° ′	Mercury Lat. ° ′	Mercury Declin. ° ′	Mercury Declin. ° ′	☽ Node. ° ′
1	1N 4	5 S 25	5 S 55	0N 29	4 N 2	4 N 5	16♋12
3	1 1	6 25	6 55	0 57	4 3	3 56	16 6
5	0 58	7 25	7 54	1 20	3 45	3 29	16 0
7	0 54	8 23	8 53	1 37	3 10	2 46	15 53
9	0 50	9 22	9 50	1 49	2 20	1 50	15 47
11	0 46	10 19	10 47	1 56	1 18	0 44	15 41
13	0 42	11 15	11 43	1 59	0 8	0 S 30	15 34
15	0 38	12 10	12 37	1 58	1 S 9	1 50	15 28
17	0 34	13 4	13 31	1 55	2 31	3 13	15 21
19	0 29	13 57	14 23	1 49	3 55	4 38	15 15
21	0 24	14 49	15 14	1 41	5 21	6 4	15 9
23	0 20	15 39	16 3	1 31	6 47	7 30	15 2
25	0 15	16 27	16 51	1 21	8 12	8 54	14 56
27	0 10	17 14	17 37	1 9	9 36	10 18	14 50
29	0 5	17 59	18 21	0 57	10 59	11 39	14 43
31	0 0	18 42		0 44	12 19		14 37

Mutual Aspects.

1. ⊙⚺♅, ⊥♆. ♀△♄.
3. ♀⊥♇. ♂☌♆. [♂⚹♇
4. ⊙P☿. ☿±♄. ♂▽♃.
5. ⊙P♃.
6. ⊙⚺♇. ♀∠♅. ♂□♄,
8. ⊙☍♃, ⊥♅, ⚺♆. [P♄.
9. ♀P♅. ♃▽♆.
10. ⊙△♄. ☿∠♆. ♀∠♇. ♃±♅.
11. ☿⚼♄. ♂±♃. ♂Q♅.
13. ⊙⊥♇. 15. ☿∠♂. ♂P♇.
16. ☿⚺♅, ⊥♆.
17. ⊙∠♅, P♅. ♃▽♇.
18. ☿☍♃, ⚺♇.
19. ☿P♃, ⊥♅, ⚺♆. ♀⚹♅.
20. ⊙⚺♂. ☿△♄. [♂Q♇.
21. ♀P♆. ♄Stat.
22. ⊙∠♇. ☿⊥♇. ♀▽♃. ♂⚼♃.
23. ♀⚹♇. 24. ☿⊥♂. ♀☌♆.
25. ☿∠♅. ♀□♄.
26. ☿P♅. ♀±♃.
27. ☿∠♇. ♀P♄.
29. ♀Q♅. 31. ☿⚺♂. ♀P♇.

D M	♆ Long. ° ′	♅ Long. ° ′	♄ Long. ° ′	♃ Long. ° ′	♂ Long. ° ′	♀ Long. ° ′	☿ Long. ° ′	⊙	♇	♆	♅	♄	♃	♂	♀	☿
1	14♏ 3	7♍40	16♒47	15♈22	12♏58	16♎19	20♍57		☍	△	☍	⚺	⚺	△		☍
2	14 5	7 43	16 ℞45	15 ℞14	13 39	17 34	21 24			⚼		∠		⚼		
3	14 7	7 46	16 43	15 6	14 21	18 48	22 0	☍				⚹	☌		☍	
4	14 9	7 50	16 42	14 58	15 2	20 3	22 45		⚼		⚼					
5	14 11	7 53	16 40	14 50	15 44	21 18	23 38		△	☍	△	□	⚺	☍		⚼
S	14 13	7 56	16 38	14 42	16 26	22 33	24 39	⚼					∠			△
7	14 15	7 59	16 37	14 34	17 7	23 47	25 47	△	□		□	△	⚹		⚼	
8	14 17	8 3	16 36	14 26	17 49	25 2	27 1			⚼		⚼		⚼	△	□
9	14 19	8 6	16 34	14 18	18 31	26 17	28 20	□	⚹	△	⚹		□			
10	14 21	8 9	16 33	14 10	19 13	27 32	29 44		∠		∠			△	□	⚹
11	14 23	8 12	16 32	14 2	19 55	28 46	1♎11		⚺	□	⚺		△			
12	14 25	8 15	16 31	13 54	20 37	0♏ 1	2 42	⚹				☍		□		∠
S	14 27	8 18	16 30	13 46	21 19	1 16	4 16	∠			☌		⚼		⚹	⚺
14	14 29	8 21	16 29	13 38	22 2	2 31	5 52	⚺	☌	⚹				⚹	∠	
15	14 31	8 24	16 29	13 30	22 44	3 46	7 29			∠		⚼			⚺	
16	14 33	8 27	16 28	13 22	23 26	5 0	9 8		⚺	⚺	⚺	△	☍	∠		☌
17	14 35	8 30	16 28	13 14	24 9	6 15	10 49	☌	∠		∠			⚺		
18	14 37	8 33	16 27	13 6	24 51	7 30	12 30				⚹				☌	
19	14 40	8 36	16 27	12 58	25 34	8 45	14 12		⚹	☌		□				⚺
S	14 42	8 39	16 27	12 51	26 16	10 0	15 54	⚺					⚼	☌		∠
21	14 44	8 42	16 27	12 43	26 59	11 14	17 36	∠	□	⚺	□	⚹	△		⚺	
22	14 46	8 44	16 D27	12 36	27 42	12 29	19 18							⚺	∠	⚹
23	14 48	8 47	16 27	12 28	28 25	13 44	21 0	⚹		∠	△	∠				
24	14 50	8 50	16 27	12 21	29 8	14 59	22 42		△	⚹		⚺	□	∠	⚹	
25	14 53	8 52	16 28	12 14	29 51	16 14	24 24	□	⚼		⚼			⚹		□
26	14 55	8 55	16 28	12 7	0♐34	17 28	26 6			□		☌	⚹			
S	14 57	8 58	16 29	12 0	1 17	18 43	27 47						∠		□	△
28	14 59	9 0	16 29	11 53	2 0	19 58	29 28	△	☍	△	☍		⚺	□		
29	15 1	9 3	16 30	11 46	2 43	21 13	1♏ 8	⚼				⚺			△	⚼
30	15 4	9 5	16 31	11 39	3 27	22 28	2 48			⚼		∠	☌	△	⚼	
31	15 6	9 8	16 32	11 33	4 10	23 42	4 27		⚼		⚼	⚹		⚼		

LAST QUARTER—October 9, 7*h*. 28*m*. *p.m.*

bol for the Moon with the abbreviation for longitude beneath, is the Moon's noon position. Column 9 gives the Moon's position for midnight, 12 hours later on the same day.

The noon position for October 19th is given as 16° 55' 18" Scorpio and the midnight position as 22° 50' 23" or, when reduced to whole degrees, 17° and 23° Scorpio respectively. Because we are using a 12-hour movement we only divide the daily motion of 6 degrees by 12, but we still multiply by the birth-time of 1 hour 45 minutes (1.75), the number of hours between noon and the birth-time. The result is 52 minutes and 30 seconds which we now add to the Moon's position at noon, arriving at a rounded up figure of 18 degrees Scorpio. As with every other position calculated, we enter the sign against the Moon's position in the bottom left-hand corner of the birth chart.

We also write the appropriate glyph and figure for this and every other planet on the chart-wheel.

BIRTH CHART   EQUAL _____ HOUSE SYSTEM

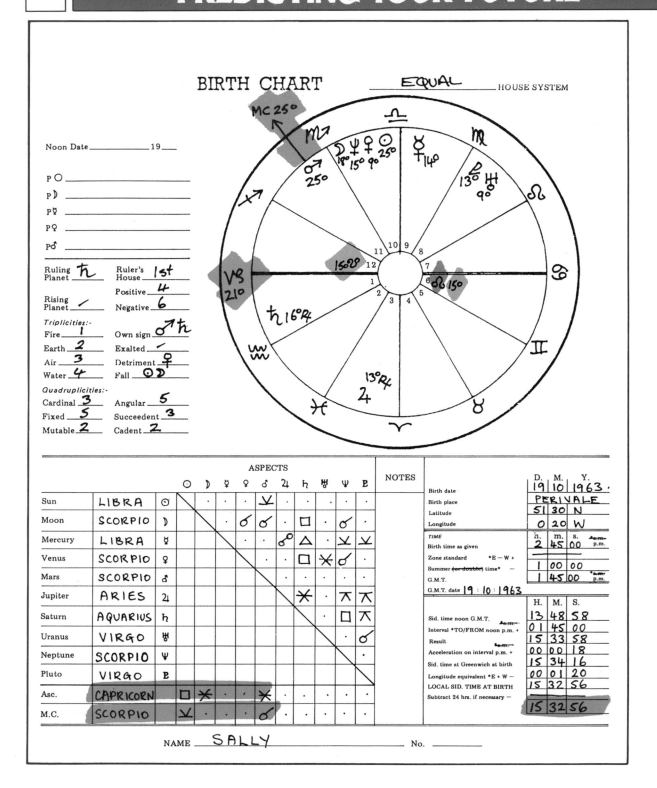

Noon Date _____ 19___

P ☉ _____
P ☽ _____
P ☿ _____
P ♀ _____
P ♂ _____

Ruling Planet ♄   Ruler's House 1st

Rising Planet ♐   Positive 4   Negative 6

Triplicities:-
Fire 1   Own sign ♂♄
Earth 2   Exalted ♐
Air 3   Detriment ♀
Water 4   Fall ☉☽

Quadruplicities:-
Cardinal 3   Angular 5
Fixed 5   Succeedent 3
Mutable 2   Cadent 2

ASPECTS

			☉	☽	☿	♀	♂	♃	♄	♅	♆	♇
Sun	LIBRA	☉		·	·	·	⊻	·	·	·	·	·
Moon	SCORPIO	☽			·	☌	☌	·	□	·	☌	·
Mercury	LIBRA	☿				·	·	☍	△	·	⊻	⊻
Venus	SCORPIO	♀					·	·	□	✳	☌	·
Mars	SCORPIO	♂						·	·	·	·	·
Jupiter	ARIES	♃							✳	·	⊼	⊼
Saturn	AQUARIUS	♄								·	□	⊼
Uranus	VIRGO	♅									·	☌
Neptune	SCORPIO	♆										·
Pluto	VIRGO	♇										
Asc.	CAPRICORN		□	✳	·	·	✳	·	·	·	·	·
M.C.	SCORPIO		⊻	·	·	·	☌	·	·	·	·	·

NOTES

	D.	M.	Y.
Birth date	19	10	1963
Birth place	PERIVALE		
Latitude	51	30 N	
Longitude	0	20 W	

TIME	h.	m.	s.	
Birth time as given	2	45	00	p.m.
Zone standard *E − W +	1	00	00	
Summer (or double) time* −				
G.M.T.	1	45	00	p.m.

G.M.T. date 19 : 10 : 1963

	H.	M.	S.
Sid. time noon G.M.T.	13	48	58
Interval *TO/FROM noon p.m. +	01	45	00
Result	15	33	58
Acceleration on interval p.m. +	00	00	18
Sid. time at Greenwich at birth	15	34	16
Longitude equivalent *E + W −	00	01	20
LOCAL SID. TIME AT BIRTH	15	32	56
Subtract 24 hrs. if necessary −	15	32	56

NAME SALLY   No. _____

The world is divided into time zones and adjustments have to be made for these, too, when calculating a chart. Any location East of the Greenwich meridian will be ahead of GMT and the time differential must therefore be subtracted at the zone standard; anywhere West of Greenwich will be behind GMT and must therefore be added at this stage of the calculations.

For example, Paris uses Central European Time (CET) which is one hour in advance of GMT; New York is five hours behind and is on Eastern Standard Time (EST); and New Zealand is twelve hours ahead of Britain. So it is essential to remember to make the necessary adjustments for any difference in 'clock time' each time you prepare a horoscope.

The dates when Summer Time was in force in Great Britain are included in this volume; but it should be remembered that a separate volume is needed when calculating charts for other parts of the world.

When calculating charts for the Southern Hemisphere, time is virtually reversed. So, if erecting such a chart, *add* 12 hours to the Sidereal Time before entering the Sidereal Time given for noon GMT. Then continue to follow the steps outlined until you come to the step that finds the Ascendant or rising degree. Simply 'reverse' this sign, enter it on the chart and continue filling in the rest of the chart in the normal way.

WORLD MAP OF TIME ZONES

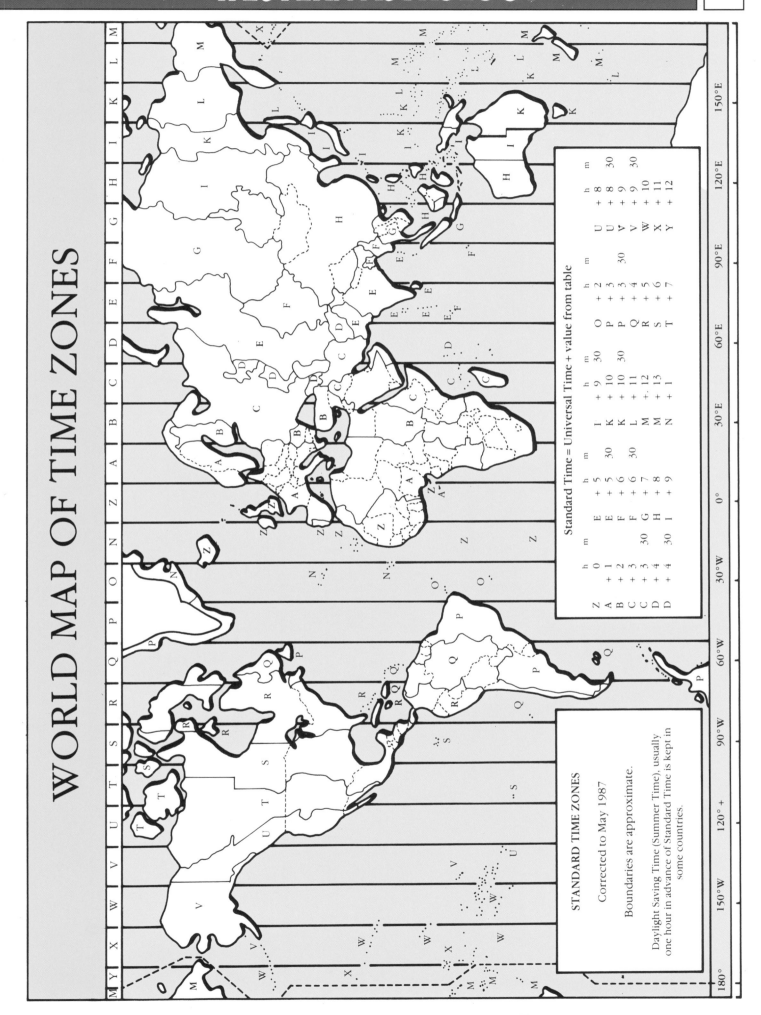

Standard Time = Universal Time + value from table

	h	m			h	m
Z	0		E	+5		I	+9	30	O	+2		U	+8	
A	+1		E	+5	30	K	+10		P	+3		U	+8	30
B	+2		F	+6		K	+10	30	P	+3	30	V	+9	
C	+3		F	+6	30	L	+11		Q	+4		V	+9	30
C	+3	30	G	+7		M	+12		R	+5		W	+10	
D	+4		H	+8		M	+13		S	+6		X	+11	
D	+4	30	I	+9		N	+1		T	+7		Y	+12	

STANDARD TIME ZONES

Corrected to May 1987

Boundaries are approximate.

Daylight Saving Time (Summer Time), usually one hour in advance of Standard Time is kept in some countries.

BRITISH SUMMER TIME

*Note: The change from GMT to BST (GMT + 1 hour) and the reversion occurs at 2 a.m. on the dates given except where marked ** . For a trial period of two years, 1981 and 1982, BST was in force from 1 a.m. on the dates given and reverted at 1 a.m.*

Year	Duration	Year	Duration
1916	May 21st — October 1st	1953	April 19th — October 4th
1917	April 8th — September 17th	1954	April 11th — October 3rd
1918	March 24th — September 30th	1955	April 17th — October 2nd
1919	March 30th — September 29th	1956	April 22nd — October 7th
1920	March 28th — October 25th	1957	April 14th — October 6th
1921	April 3rd — October 3rd	1958	April 20th — October 5th
1922	March 26th — October 8th	1959	April 19th — October 4th
1923	April 22nd — September 16th	1960	April 10th — October 2nd
1924	April 13th — September 21st	1961	March 26th — October 29th
1925	April 19th — October 4th	1962	March 25th — October 28th
1926	April 18th — October 3rd	1963	March 31st — October 27th
1927	April 10th — October 2nd	1964	March 22nd — October 25th
1928	April 22nd — October 7th	1965	March 21st — October 24th
1929	April 21st — October 6th	1966	March 20th — October 23rd
1930	April 13th — October 5th	1967	March 19th — October 29th
1931	April 19th — October 4th	1968	February 18th — (continues)
1932	April 17th — October 2nd	1969	All year
1933	April 9th — October 8th	1970	All year
1934	April 22nd — October 7th	1971	October 31st (ended)
1935	April 14th — October 6th	1972	March 19th — October 29th
1936	April 19th — October 4th	1973	March 18th — October 28th
1937	April 18th — October 3rd	1974	March 17th — October 27th
1938	April 10th — October 2nd	1975	March 16th — October 26th
1939	April 16th — November 19th	1976	March 21st — October 24th
1940	February 25th — (continues)	1977	March 20th — October 23rd
*1941	All year	1978	March 19th — October 29th
*1942	All year	1979	March 18th — October 28th
*1943	All year	1980	March 16th — October 26th
*1944	All year	1981	March 29th — October 25th**
*1945	January 1st — October 7th	1982	March 28th — October 24th**
1946	April 14th — October 6th	1983	March 27th — October 23rd
*1947	March 16th — November 2nd	1984	March 18th — October 28th
1948	March 14th — October 31st	1985	March 17th — October 27th
1949	April 3rd — October 30th	1986	March 30th — October 26th
1950	April 16th — October 22nd	1987	March 29th — October 25th
1951	April 15th — October 21st	1988	March 27th — October 23rd
1952	April 20th — October 26th	1989	March 26th — October 29th

* This indicates years when Double Summer Time/Daylight Saving Time (GMT plus 2 hours) was in force and special care should be taken when erecting a chart for anyone within this period.
As with BST, the change from BST to DST and the reversion occur at 2 a.m. on the dates given below.

British Standard Time, *also equal to GMT + 1 hour, was the name given to the time system in use between February 18, 1968 and October 31, 1971. As the effects were the same as British Summer Time, the same abbreviation (BST) has been used.*

Double Summer Time/Daylight Saving Time (UK)

Year	Duration of DST (GMT + 2 hours)	Year	Duration of DST (GMT + 2 hours)
1941	May 4th — August 10th	1945	April 2nd — July 15th
1942	April 5th — August 9th	1946	Not observed
1943	April 4th — August 15th	1947	April 13th — August 10th
1944	April 2nd — September 17th		

ELEMENTS AND QUALITIES

Before we consider the effects of planets by sign, house and aspect we should see whether they are in Positive or Negative signs, and note the Triplicities and Quadruplicities and mark these on the chart form.

In astrological terms six of the zodiacal signs (Aries, Gemini, Leo, Libra, Sagittarius and Aquarius) are regarded as positive/masculine and the other six as negative/feminine. The ten planets will fall in either a positive or negative sign. This has nothing to do with actual gender; it has more to do with self-assertion or passivity.

Despite their collective name, the triplicities refer to the four elements.

FIRE signs are eager and enthusiastic. Their energy is hard to suppress or contain.

EARTH signs are slower and more inclined to seek stability in the form of tangible security.

AIR signs are the thinkers of the zodiac, those who have an awareness of abstract concepts.

WATER is emotional, so these signs can be caring and compassionate or martyrish and moody.

The term quadruplicities refers to the qualities accredited to the 12 zodiacal signs which are reflected by the planets that occupy those signs.

CARDINAL signs are the instigators, those who may start things but not always finish them.

FIXED signs are the sustainers who preserve and carry matters through to their end.

MUTABLE signs ring in the changes and are renowned for their adaptability.

We should now turn our attention to the action of each planet by sign as this forms the basis of chart interpretation.

SIGN CLASSIFICATION

SIGN	SYMBOL	POLARITY	QUADRU-PLICITY	TRIPLICITY or ELEMENT
ARIES	♈	+	CARDINAL	FIRE
TAURUS	♉	−	FIXED	EARTH
GEMINI	♊	+	MUTABLE	AIR
CANCER	♋	−	CARDINAL	WATER
LEO	♌	+	FIXED	FIRE
VIRGO	♍	−	MUTABLE	EARTH
LIBRA	♎	+	CARDINAL	AIR
SCORPIO	♏	−	FIXED	WATER
SAGITTARIUS	♐	+	MUTABLE	FIRE
CAPRICORN	♑	−	CARDINAL	EARTH
AQUARIUS	♒	+	FIXED	AIR
PISCES	♓	−	MUTABLE	WATER

ARIES

☉ SUN

This enthusiastic leader of men often rushes in where angels fear to tread. Although impulsive and impatient, he or she is not lacking in courage. Often blunt and tactless, there is a need to learn to consider others more. Sometimes guilty of selfishness, they thrive on competition. Their almost child-like openness and honesty will often carry them through a difficult situation. They may tend to have minor accidents as they are always in a rush.

☽ MOON

High spirited and quick-tempered, this is a hotly emotional position. Although not inclined to listen to advice from others, they are often eager to give it out. Yet they react to any form of criticism in a highly personal manner. Anger often blinds them to understanding. Luckily, though, they are unlikely to hold grudges for long and are surprised when others do. They are prone to sudden whims which they rarely sustain.

♂ MARS

High on physical energy and self-assertion, these subjects need some sort of physical outlet for their restless energy. Little time is wasted in decision making, they are always eager to accept fresh challenges or tackle new enterprises. Natural leadership qualities combine with enthusiasm, making it easy for others to follow, yet they find it difficult to sustain their initial interest in projects for long periods of time.

♅ URANUS

There is a strong drive towards individual freedom and an uncanny knack of being able to understand the real truth of a problem. Often outspoken to the point of bluntness, these subjects are usually oblivious of the upsets caused by their remarks. Rarely afraid of taking chances, they will seek out change simply for the sake of it. Always able to produce new ideas and interests, they are rarely bored, but usually frantically busy.

☿ MERCURY

An extremely quick thinker who likes to be first with new ideas. Very outspoken, but often annoyingly right, they enjoy debate and argument. They tend to challenge others simply for the sake of it but, owing to their short attention span, a common Arien trait, are unlikely to remain provocative for long. Lacking patience, they will always try to take shortcuts, sometimes with disastrous results, but can laugh at their mistakes.

♃ JUPITER

Although often unwittingly self-centred, these subjects have high integrity and morality. Their biggest danger is smugness. Tremendous self-confidence arrives with maturity, usually accompanied by justifiable pride of achievement. Financially imprudent, they nevertheless tend to be lucky, help often arriving just when needed. Their broadminded tolerance and sense of humour make them very popular.

♆ NEPTUNE

Experts at getting their own way, these individuals easily use guile to advantage, frequently adding to the effect by shedding beautiful tears like pearldrops. A tendency towards being a martyr can sometimes make them their own worst enemy and they need to learn to step outside a situation. They are naturally drawn towards spiritual experiences and are often born with far knowledge, and may be very psychic.

♀ VENUS

Ardently romantic, feelings are easily aroused, although there may be a reluctance to settle down and be tied to one person. These individuals find it easy to verbalise their emotions and discuss these with candid honesty. Usually attractive and popular, they rarely try to cultivate this, being more concerned with their own feelings than those of other people. Money tends to slip through their fingers like water.

♄ SATURN

Carrying their independent attitude like a barrier wrapped around them, these characters tend to be lonely. Others are inclined to find them unapproachable yet they have a great need for companionship. Often very successful in the world of business, work may simply be a consolation. Not easily influenced by others, they are reluctant to take advice. Careful and over-cautious, they should learn to relax and let go.

♇ PLUTO

Strong will creates a formidable personality that has the spirit of the true pioneer; one totally convinced that barriers are made to be broken and frontiers made to be crossed, regardless of obstacles. This person has a great ability to sway others, so he or she should develop a sense of responsibility in this respect. Never afraid of hard work, there is a tendency to push beyond his or her natural limits simply for the sake of it.

 TAURUS

 SATURN

This position wants a life set on firm foundations in every department. Not afraid of hard work, these individuals will tackle even menial jobs if this adds to security. They tend to be rather selfish and inclined to lay down rules and regulations which other people are expected to follow regardless. Often stuck in a rut through a need for a regular routine and order, they may be a little miserly with money.

 SUN

Patient, pleasant and slow to anger, this apparently placid character often shocks people with his or her determination when feelings are aroused. Averse to change, he or she may obstinately refuse to move on. A great lover of comfort, with a tendency to over-indulge, there is often a weight problem. Good with finance, providing there is motivation, these people do well in business yet can also manage on a shoe-string if needs be.

 VENUS

Although often sensually beautiful, these subjects possess great loyalty in their affections and can sometimes be possessive over partners. Their sense of touch is very important to them and they enjoy the feel of rich fabrics as much as physical contact with other people. Money is a necessity, for they have luxurious tastes, and over-indulgence can be a very real problem. Music and art hold strong appeal.

 URANUS

Rarely do these people make deliberate attempts to pile up money, they know they can attract it if ever the need arises. They tend to be careless about possessions and will easily give everything away. They often find unusual methods of earning a living and are ready to learn new skills or techniques at any age. Some are ready to give up great personal security in order to gain a new experience.

MOON

Lovers of luxury, these people will go to any lengths to attain the comfort they desire and their homes are often showplaces. They, too, dislike change, preferring the reassuring presence of all that is familiar. Emotionally fixed, they tend to be loyal to the family and partner and will stubbornly persist in ignoring difficulties that should be dealt with. Security is their greatest need and they pursue this with dogged determination.

 MARS

Slow but sure, tremendous inner drive will force these characters to complete even the most onerous task. They rarely give up on a project even when the odds appear to be stacked against them. Being both practical and honest, they tend to be bluntly outspoken even if this is hurtful. Strongly sexed, they will seek a partner as a practical necessity. Although they may be very jealous, they can also be impulsively generous.

NEPTUNE

A person who firmly believes that man cannot live by bread alone, so will eagerly seek out spiritual experiences. If this planetary position is prominent in a chart, he or she would even give up material possessions in order to live as a recluse. Always idealistic and impractical, they truly love their fellow man. He could also be the financial backer for artistic projects as he has a keen appreciation of beauty.

 MERCURY

"Be prepared" is the motto here. Hating even pleasant surprises, these individuals often develop their intuition in order to avoid being taken unawares. Decisions are made seriously, slowly, and they react strongly against any attempt to rush them. Once their minds are made up, however, they will stubbornly refuse to change their opinions. Their concentration is good and they have a rich, earthy sense of humour.

JUPITER

Material possessions are important to these subjects as tangible proof of their success, yet they can be magnanimous as well. Their love of opulence makes them buy expensive clothing but their jewellery may be over ornate. They prefer dining out rather than the trouble of entertaining at home. Basically warm and friendly, they should beware of making others feel owned and smothered by their over-protective attitude.

 PLUTO

Never lacking in determination and will-power, when prominent this position could point to someone who builds up a financial empire. Even when a project proves to be a disaster, he or she is ready to come back and try again, usually successfully. Personal relationships may suffer though, for he or she tends to put people into categories; such people may be concerned with human rights, especially as regards the sharing of wealth.

GEMINI

 SUN

*A*daptable, versatile and chatty, this subject makes an interesting companion. Mentally alert and curious, he or she is a true seeker after knowledge, often for the sake of it. Easily bored, there is a need for continual change and stimulation; short journeys are preferred to long ones, unless on Concorde! A love of gadgets makes them an inventor's delight, he or she will buy anything for a few moment's interest.

 **MOON**

*C*hanging moods and restless emotions can make this an awkward position unless counteracted by stability elsewhere in the chart. These subjects find it impossible to keep a secret and must talk about their feelings. Although they have a love of learning, they may experience difficulty retaining information or maintaining interests. Worry is confined to small matters, while bigger things tend to be neglected.

 MARS

*R*estless nervous energy can cause these people to scatter their talents, perhaps never fully utilising them to best advantage. Impatience is a problem, as is intolerance of others' slowness, and they are always ready with a sarcastic comment. Given to provoke debate or argument, they are prepared to speak against their own beliefs in order to prolong one. Good ideas come easily and they are quick to spot short cuts.

 URANUS

*A*n unusual, inventive mind that is never afraid to consider new ideas is indicated here. These people are attracted to modern technology, especially in the field of communications. Lack of academic freedom could result in mental tension though, as they find it hard to learn in a structured environment. Freedom of speech is important to them, too, both for others and for themselves. Travel holds strong appeal.

 MERCURY

*T*his indicates a quick mind that needs constant stimulation but is usually intelligent enough to see that it gets it. A good conversationalist, this person may have writing ability and is an avid reader. Constantly seeking new people, new places and new experiences, he or she has the ability to do more than one thing at a time. There may be a tendency to gossip, though, as there is often a strong need to relay information.

 JUPITER

A potentially good mind may be wasted with this position due to a reluctance to undertake hard work. The subjects have a tendency towards pomposity and often boast about personal achievements whether this is true or not. They may have a talent for writing, which could prove lucrative. Their slightly superior attitude may cause them to play elaborate practical jokes on other people. They best utilize their talents in salesmanship.

 NEPTUNE

*M*ystical and idealistic, these individuals find abstract concepts more appealing than logic. Self-expression may present a problem as they find it difficult to put thoughts into words; but, if anyone else has a problem, they can probably resolve it successfully. Although impractical, they are usually kindly unless there are negative aspects in the chart, in which case a mantle of martyrdom can be donned.

 VENUS

*T*his charming, flirtatious individual is fully aware of the social graces and is probably popular. But, though not necessarily inclined towards unfaithfulness, may find it difficult to sustain interest in just one person. Often a need for mental stimulation will force him or her to outgrow their partner; Gemini can never be stirred by love alone. Unmaterialistic, he has a dry sense of humour and is very good company.

 SATURN

*T*his usually brings a clear, logical mind that is able to get straight to the point. Rarely deceived or taken in, this character naturally seems to know the truth about anyone or anything. Here is a strong need to work in a field that requires mental ability otherwise frustration could result. Disciplined and orderly, he or she may be wary of abstract concepts; ideas must have form and structure, and be based upon proven facts.

 PLUTO

*T*otally unafraid to speak his or her mind, this subject may challenge the beliefs of other people. In return he or she will respond well to challenges to their own beliefs by investigating alternative points of view. He or she has great concentration but can abandon mental pursuits with ease when necessary, even after expending considerable effort. Only if Pluto is adversely aspected will this subject be dictatorial.

SATURN

*L*ack of love in early childhood may have lasting effects in later life for this person. With a tendency to dwell on any such problems pessimistically, he or she will demand more proof of love from other people as compensation. Some subjects will, though, try to cut themselves off from domesticity in order to convince themselves they don't require it, instead of acknowledging their strong needs. They can be surprisingly adept at business.

SUN

*H*ighly sensitive and emotional, this person often tends to shut themself away from reality. Although basically kind and caring, he or she may become self-centred without noticing it because of the desire for total security. The home is always important: a protective castle to exclude the outside world. Having a very long memory, he or she tends to hold grudges and is in some circumstances likely to take offence very easily.

VENUS

*R*omantic and often very domesticated, these people were born for love and marriage. They need the support of a partner and family, for only then can they feel fulfilled. When they feel unloved, they can be jealous and possessive, holding on to outworn relationships with tenacity. Easily hurt, they need constant proof of being loved. Their home is a refuge from the outside world, and will usually be warm and comfortable.

URANUS

*C*onflicts may occur over family responsibility versus personal freedom, to be resolved only after chaos has reigned. These subjects often come from unstable backgrounds or break family ties early in life. Sometimes an unconventional attitude makes domestic bliss difficult to achieve; especially as they are inclined to fill their homes with useless clutter which they are loath to part with.

MOON

*T*his denotes strong family ties, often accompanied by a capacity for mothering, whatever sex the individual may be. However, there is a danger of collecting dependants in order to gain ascendancy over them. Openly affectionate, this subject needs reciprocal treatment from others and is never happier than when he or she has someone to look after. Sensitive and intuitive, there may be moodiness and feelings of inadequacy.

MARS

*T*hese subjects attack housework with exceptional vim and vigour, usually in an attempt to counteract negative moods. If their environment is fraught with problems, they will worry constantly yet their reluctance to bring anything out into the open can sometimes affect health adversely. Thoughtless remarks cut them to the quick and grudges are held forever, yet they will always defend their own.

NEPTUNE

*D*omesticity is the ultimate dream and these subjects find it hard to look beyond this. The outside world may be frightening to them; they may feel safe only in the family bosom. Often very intuitive, they make fine mediums for whom other-worldly visitations may seem perfectly normal. Always sensitive to the needs of other people, they are usually very caring individuals who will readily sacrifice their own desires.

MERCURY

*F*eelings are more important than facts for these people who find it difficult to view life objectively. Any criticism is taken at a deep personal level due to a lack of self-confidence. An almost photographic memory helps them through their schooldays and they can surprise others with their scholastic achievements. Highly perceptive, they are good at resolving problems; their sympathetic attitude usually makes them popular.

JUPITER

A strong community spirit combined with awareness of others' needs often leads this character to work for the underprivileged. Respect for the past can turn into a search for knowledge. Warmly hospitable, he or she is lavish with entertaining and can arrange a large formal occasion as easily as an intimate gathering. Although these people would prefer to be part of a family business, they can succeed anywhere.

PLUTO

*T*he need to be in control of their lives may make relationships rather difficult for these people who do not take kindly to outside interference although it may take them a long time to say no. They tend to be subjective and will seek solutions at a subconscious level; but when successful, their feelings will erupt like a volcano. Once their minds are made up they will never regret their decisions irrespective of the consequences.

LEO

 SUN

*G*rand Masters of the dramatic entrance, these subjects adore to be the centre of attention. Feeling they were born to rule, if they cannot have accolades from the public they will expect to be waited on hand and foot at home. Royal Leos rarely work in menial positions unless they intend marrying the boss and, whether genial and warm or arrogant and overbearing, will always stand out in any crowd, as is their right!

 **MOON**

*P*ride may be an issue here, mixed with voluble emotions. This subject needs to be sure that any praise received has been earned. Personal feelings are magnified and there may be some degree of self-deceit, which is fine if it only concerns a story that is being exaggerated for effect. But there is a danger that a desire for lazy indulgence will cause expectations of being able to achieve something for nothing.

MARS

*P*assionate and highly attractive, these subjects were born to be noticed. They use their personal charisma to good effect, have the courage of their convictions and can be highly persuasive. But they do not take kindly to being the butt of jokes for when their pride is hurt, so are they. Natural leaders, they usually succeed in their chosen career but are inclined to dominate their partners, who will probably let them.

URANUS

*C*reative individuals who often find more than one source of income, these characters are not afraid to try out new techniques or ideas. Adaptable, eager for change, their attitude to children is unusual; they expect early independence yet will grant them the same respect they would accord a friend. Romance may be erratic and involve issues of freedom, which may be from either side.

MERCURY

A talent is shown for organisation, but care is needed over other people's feelings as a self-centred streak could ignore these. This subject can be rather boastful, not at all reluctant to talk about his achievements, yet sometimes speaking with justifiable pride. Very opinionated and not easily influenced, they have the concentrated energy needed to complete projects. Their youthful charm and vigour will ensure their popularity.

JUPITER

*E*verything needs to be larger than life for these folk who crave attention. Their vanity extends from their perfect family to every purchase they ever make: theirs is always better than anyone else's. Good company and good humoured, their presence is eagerly sought. Adept at ignoring problems, they love luxury and glittering occasions, especially those attended by illustrious people with whom they feel an affinity.

NEPTUNE

*W*hen negatively aspected, there may be illusions of grandeur that cause the subject to live in a fantasy world. Often theatrical or artistic, but needing some prompting to make good use of talents, they will succeed if given encouragement. A child-like charm may make them appear helpless and appealing or they may be attracted by this trait in others and have a tendency to collect lame ducks around themselves.

VENUS

*T*his subject usually has an aura of glamour and revels in it. Yet a glorious sense of humour helps him or her see reality and laugh while enjoying attention. Extremely loyal to friends and family, they will defend themselves against criticism and are always ready to fight against any injustice. Kindnesses need profuse expressions of gratitude though, or they will feel unloved and unwanted.

SATURN

*T*hese subjects often tend to hold themselves exceptionally erect as if afraid to let go and become natural human beings. Often they will deliberately cut warmth from their lives, perhaps rejecting opportunities for satisfying relationships. Usually hard-working and responsible, they usually succeed in business where they quickly gain respect and recognition. But, unless other aspects counteract, they may be emotionally withdrawn.

PLUTO

A strong sense of self-worth may turn to arrogance and the desire to control other people's lives. It may be hard to force this subject to consider others' opinions as this may make them feel threatened in some way. They expect to be well treated and respected, whether they deserve this or not. Their love of nature is strong but they may involve their partners in power struggles; they will never compromise.

 SATURN

*P*ractical and efficient, these people may live for their work. Their sense of duty and responsibility make them well fitted for managerial positions yet they can be severe in their judgement of others and should cultivate tolerance. Any sort of personal failure hits them badly for they can be unforgiving even to themselves. Their seriousness and lack of humour could cause them to lose friends and lead to loneliness.

SUN

*M*eticulously neat, with an eye for detail, this person cannot bear anything to be out of place. He or she has high personal standards which they are likely to impose upon others, becoming nervously irritable when there is a refusal to comply. They enjoy helping others and appear to need to justify their existence by this; often perfecting some form of work in order to be of service. Highly critical of self and others.

 VENUS

*O*ften very attractive because of their attention to good grooming, these subjects may nevertheless criticize the appearance or failings of others. Contact with anything even mildly offensive or dirty can make them physically ill. They usually enjoy a good, friendly gossip, but avoid malicious chatter like the plague. Surprisingly passionate in romance, they are practical in money matters and may be hypochondriacs.

 URANUS

*T*hese are the innovators of the working world, who were born to discover new working methods. Finding it difficult to follow set routines, these people eternally look for short-cuts. Sometimes irrational and inconsistent, they may sometimes offend more senstive people. They may also follow the latest health fad or peculiar forms of diet. Often they are restless wanderers who roam from job to job.

 MOON

*V*ery creative in a practical sense, these people are usually clever with their hands. They tend to be rather fussy and may even be inclined to nag, mostly to prevent nervous energy building up inside them. Often interested in health and hygiene, they may pay particular attention to diet. Neat, tidy and methodical, they have good business sense. Emotionally inhibited; others may mistake shyness for coldness.

 MARS

*T*hese characters are frantically concerned with business; every moment has to be usefully employed. They find it hard to relax and probably feel guilty when they do. Always perfectionists, nothing ever meets their high standards, so there is a definite need to learn to let things go. Their ability to work in intricate detail often attracts them to crafts. They are, though, short on self-assertion and may feel obliged to please others.

 NEPTUNE

*E*asily taken advantage of, these people have a servile mentality; their ethics demand they serve others, even the undeserving. Some may need to take stock of themselves and contemplate equality and justice or an irrational urge to be good and kind could easily spoil their lives. Confusion may arise over working methods; they may be workaholics or feel inadequate about their own standards of efficiency.

 MERCURY

*H*ighly intelligent, with the patience to learn intricate techniques, this person always needs a mental outlet. There may be a tendency to criticize but often this is constructive rather than destructive. With his or her capacity to put things into categories they would enjoy any type of work that involves classification or research. A satirical sense of humour stems from an ability to see weaknesses in others.

 JUPITER

*T*hese people have a strong sense of duty but should try to avoid smugness. Very concerned about the world and other people, they often question traditional religious doctrines but will work hard at finding their own solutions. They need to learn to enjoy leisure without the need to combine this with some form of work. Usually they will have great faith in their personal ability and are prepared to put effort into any task.

 PLUTO

*O*bsession about working methods or concerned with reforming society are characteristics of these people. They have a talent for finding out information and will pay attention to every tiny detail, quite prepared to use this for good or ill. They are rather prone to physical exhaustion through overwork and may take an interest in alternative medicine or become addicted to following cranky forms of diet.

LIBRA

 ## SUN

*F*unctioning best in a partnership, this sign often lacks motivation without one. Objective and impartial, Librans are capable of stepping outside a situation even when closely involved. Although they can be diplomatic and tactful if they choose, they can also be disarmingly honest, usually to another's disadvantage. Good at negotiation and manipulation, they are oddly reluctant to speak up for themselves.

 ## MOON

*H*ighly sociable, these people can be very good company. Their appearance is important to them and they are aware of the social graces. Often indecisive, preferring other people to help them. Peace and harmony are vital to their well-being. There is a love of music and movement or they may be very artistic. They have a great deal of charm which they use to their advantage. Yet they may be quixotic in personal relationships.

 ## MARS

*T*hese subjects do their best work in the company of others when they will assume the role of leader. They may enjoy competition but are bad losers. Always ready to speak out against injustice, they make worthy champions. Decision-making may cause them to become moody because they can always see both sides of any question, yet they are reluctant to take another's advice. In matters of love, they tend to play the field.

 ## URANUS

*T*his position bestows an inventive mind that is often close to genius. These folk are sparkling companions who are eagerly sought after. Never lost for words, they may tend to dominate conversation. There may be some hesitancy over total commitment in personal relationships and those that are formed may be unusual in some way. Feeling the world is an exciting place to live in, they expect everyone to share their view.

 ## MERCURY

*G*ood at compromise, there is a tendency to veer towards moderation in all things. Not prone to take chances, every decision is weighed up very carefully. Although they can be sociable if need be, they do need some solitude. Often very creative, they may have a flair for design. Diplomatic, they can speak well on behalf of others but, if wanting something for themselves, will manipulate in a very subtle manner.

JUPITER

*F*eeling they are on a spiritual path that involves other people, every relationship is full of meaning to these people. Great appreciation of beauty, art or music is often very important to them and they may have actual talent. Highly moral, with a strong sense of justice, they can be very persuasive and make others feel good in their company. They are often very clever at organising very large functions.

 ## NEPTUNE

A tendency towards escapism is often prevalent with this position and this character has a tendency to put a partner on a pedestal or may expect to be placed upon one themselves. Idealistic, he or she may be drawn towards groups, often those without any real purpose. Lacking will-power, this person probably finds it difficult to make decisions. Glamorous professions will likely attract such a personality.

 ## VENUS

*T*hese folk may be coolly elegant or lighthearted social butterflies. Charming and attractive, they are usually an asset to any social gathering. They may marry for money or position, love alone rarely sways them, and greatly appreciate the things that money can buy. Often very talented, they lean towards artistic professions. Their aversion to commitment causes them to retreat from arguments.

 ## SATURN

*A*n unusually strong sense of truth and honour makes these people perfect partners, romantic or otherwise. They can be extremely faithful and loyal, even where there are difficulties, but they may take time forming personal relationships as everything must be exactly right. They are good at negotiation and work well before the public, especially if this involves organisation. They excel at any form of delegation.

 ## PLUTO

*T*hese people have a natural ability for counselling for they seem to understand the psychology of others. They are not afraid to speak their minds either, especially over any form of injustice. They can be very strong-willed and should be wary of manipulating others for the sake of personal power. When in a difficult relationship themselves, they would have no hesitation over ending it without remorse.

SCORPIO

SATURN

This is a dark position for this planet and deep, personal problems may be indicated. There is a reluctance for such a person to communicate his or her true feelings because of their tendency to try to conform to what is expected by society, even where this goes against their own nature; thus guilt feelings may arise. Material security is important to this person who is quite prepared to work to achieve this.

SUN

These magnetic personalities are very difficult to ignore: one always notices Scorpio. Intensely emotional, they often suppress their true feelings and when they do finally explode, their anger is terrifying. A strong sense of purpose makes them stick to their principles through thick and thin. They can be very jealous and possessive even in quite casual relationships yet their aura of mystery makes them very attractive.

VENUS

Extremely loyal, with intensely passionate feelings, these people are inclined to lose those they love because they allow them too little freedom. They are very possessive, both about people and things, and may well become obsessive, too, if not careful. They rarely form casual relationships, although they seldom lack the opportunity, because they feel every relationship has to be full of deep meaning and purpose.

URANUS

Erratic moods may be a problem which makes these folk appear unreliable and inconsistent. They hate to be controlled or pinned down, and will rebel if anyone tries. They rarely feel neutral about anything or anyone and have very marked likes and dislikes, often for no apparent reason. Everything is below a surface they don't really understand themselves, occasionally this may erupt as terrifying rage.

MOON

Strong feelings may dominate the lives of these subjects who, when they want something, become obsessive; they rarely feel neutral about anything. Usually, though, they get their own way in an almost magical manner. Attracted towards anything mysterious, they may study the occult. Being naturally secretive, they find it hard to discuss their true feelings and may often appear uncaring when this is not the case.

MARS

Although these people make extremely bad enemies they are also very loyal friends. They care deeply about everything and can be very persistent in getting their own way. They work on a very subtle level, firm in the belief that tenacity will win through in the end; but tend to waste their resources. Strongly sexual relationships are important to them and there is a danger that their intense feelings may lead to jealousy.

NEPTUNE

The occult, music and dance may well attract these people who understand the world of fantasy more than the mundane. Apparently very secretive, other people may find them difficult to understand. They sometimes find it hard to express their feelings verbally but may be able to do so on an artistic level. Money may be made by dubious means for they follow their own code of honesty, which is not necessarily conventional.

MERCURY

This denotes the eternal questioner who cannot bear to be denied answers to anything, though he or she can keep secrets. They are unlikely to forgive anyone who slights them as he or she takes everything very personally and can be very harsh with words when upset. Adept at getting to the roots of any problem, this person can be helpful to others but is apt to hide their own troubles. There may be an interest in metaphysical studies.

JUPITER

Once something captures the interest of these characters they will probe to the very depths. They may be drawn towards religion or the occult but are motivated by their desire for power. Often very successful in the world of business, they can attract money like a magnet if they choose but are usually reluctant to share it with others. Being acquisitive, they may equate status with the accumulation of possessions.

PLUTO

Trying to change or transform everything in sight, these people wield enormous power. They can be the dictators or saviours, depending on how the mood takes them, and others are easily attracted to them because of their exceptionally strong charisma. Matters of life and death interest them, as does the occult, so they may be drawn towards medicine or metaphysical studies. They show dogged persistence in the face of adversity.

SAGITTARIUS

☉ SUN

*T*hese people are cheerful, highly energetic, often athletic, lovers of freedom and liberty. Inclined to travel, it is very hard to tie them down to one place or person. In their search for wider knowledge they may ignore important details; they feel that the whole world is their oyster and plan to make the most of it. Honest and outspoken, their puppy-dog appeal rarely offends anyone and they attract a wide circle of friends.

☽ MOON

*B*eing reluctant to pay attention to detail, these people sometimes overstep themselves and make mistakes. They dream dreams and try to put them into action with tremendous bursts of energy. Usually very open and honest, they may be let down by other people with lower standards. A great curiosity about the world may make them travellers and they are always interested in people from different cultures.

♂ MARS

*W*ith tremendous energy and zeal at their disposal, these are avid workers. But they do have to believe in what they are doing and will never work for money alone. Often attracted to sport, an area where they excel, or perhaps to social causes. Easily bored with routine, they rarely take menial jobs. They tend to be here today and gone tomorrow in romantic liaisons as well as in more casual relationships.

♅ URANUS

*O*ften hyperactive, they may find it difficult to settle down. They rarely stay in one place for long and always have their sights on the golden horizon. Being attracted to all that is new or different, technological careers suit them. If spiritually inclined, they should avoid dubious sects. They invariably understand serendipity as they tend to find things by accident and usually rely on luck to get them out of tricky situations.

☿ MERCURY

*T*his denotes a curious mind that requires answers to its many questions, but one that is prepared to study. Such a person may, though, have trouble retaining information because of his or her eagerness to get on with yet another project. Honest and open, always ready to speak their mind, if something does offend them they will certainly say so. Speech may issue forth in such a rush in fact that he will stutter or muddle his words.

♃ JUPITER

*D*rawn towards pomp and ceremony, these people may be interested in religion, the law or foreign affairs. If involved in sports or athletics, they will aim to represent their country. Highly ethical and moral, they should be careful not to become too self-righteous. And, even though they expect personal freedom, they may be inclined to lay down rules for other people to follow. But they have exuberant good humour.

♆ NEPTUNE

A rather primitive attitude may make this individual yearn for the simple life; he or she is quite likely to relinquish worldly goods in order to go in search of his dreams. Intuitive, kindly and understanding, but rarely practical, they are always ready to help others with their own special brand of sympathy and understanding. This person may have a flair for graceful movement and could make a very good gymnast.

♀ VENUS

*T*hese subjects rarely tell people that they like or love them, they expect them to know. There is a reluctance to be totally committed, even when in a permanent relationship, and they always want to keep a certain amount of freedom for themselves; they may even insist upon separate holidays from their partners. Financially, they may demand separate bank accounts, too, in order to preserve personal liberty

♄ SATURN

*T*hese people have the stamina to sustain working towards a dream over very long periods and usually reach their objectives. Having the capacity to see further ahead than most, they are often in tune with the times. Self-discipline comes easily to them, making it possible to build up their resources. Others admire them for their tenacity and enthusiasm but they should beware of becoming over-zealous.

♇ PLUTO

*B*eing obsessed by discovery, these people are likely to dedicate their entire lives to research projects. They would be the ideal travellers in space as they are able to stay alone for long periods and can devote all their energies to a quest. Concerned with social equality, they could become avid workers in third world countries. Being persuasive, they easily convince others to carry out social reforms.

CAPRICORN

 ## SATURN

*A*lthough early life may be difficult, these individuals will rise above it. Their inborn sense of responsibility makes them inclined to put duty before pleasure, so they are somewhat intolerant of laziness in other people. Practical and efficient, they usually make their mark on the world but, being realists, rarely waste time on impossible dreams. They will, though, make the best of what talents and resources they possess.

 ## SUN

*P*ractical workers who aim to reach the top; these people are just as likely to be self-made as to be born to high position and status. Sometimes rather coldly calculating in relationships, they may marry for position but have a love-nest in the background. However, they rarely leave their partners as they like to protect their public image. Oddly, they can always laugh at themselves and have a delightfully dry sense of humour.

 ## VENUS

*R*arely displaying emotion, these people often lead lonely lives. They usually prefer the company of older people and may marry where there is a considerable age gap. Sometimes marriage is linked with status, and rarely with love alone, yet they will remain faithful. Being able to control desire, they can put love out of their life altogether for long periods. Usually careful with money, they may spend to impress.

 ## URANUS

*R*adical reformers in the world of business, these folk disregard conventions. But, as their ideas are usually sound, these will ultimately be accepted. When in positions of power, they are friendly to those beneath them and never forget the importance of team-work and combined effort. Sheer inspiration usually enables them to see an easier way of performing practical tasks as they are mentally inventive.

 ## MOON

*T*his often indicates deprivation in childhood that leads to a strong desire for emotional security. But, because these people find it hard to love themselves, they often find it difficult to form successful relationships. They will sometimes over-compensate by accumulating material possessions, working hard to obtain these. Others often, mistakenly, see them as cold, unapproachable, and difficult to know.

 ## MARS

*N*ever afraid of hard work or getting their hands dirty, these people will tackle any job with industry and enthusiasm. They have penetrating minds and are often quite ambitious. A strong sense of responsibility sometimes leads them to managerial positions. Being rather conventional, they may be a little hesitant about forming casual relationships and quite frequently marry rather late in life.

 ## NEPTUNE

*A*lthough these people may succeed in the artistic world, they are not very good in positions of power. They are apt to confuse issues or conceal their true motives; although they may have good intentions they can't always see the wood for the trees. When this planet is well aspected, they can have an uncanny knack for playing the Stock Market; but if the aspects are bad, they are usually hopeless with money.

 ## MERCURY

*N*eeding time to absorb information, these people often think and act very slowly. But once they have learned something they retain that knowledge. They tend to over-explain, or speak in long, drawn-out sentences. Very ambitious, they are prepared to work hard to achieve success. Tending to be realists, they may lack imagination. Their humour may be so dry that others fail to see the point of their jokes.

 ## JUPITER

*I*mpressed by status, these people tend to cultivate important people and enjoy grandiose occasions. They are determined to make their mark on the world and are prepared to work hard to do this; they will not settle for a menial job for they must have status. Mentally, they mature early although they may be emotionally naive. Concerned with right and justice, they will argue over principles and have strong morals.

 ## PLUTO

*W*anting power and control at all costs, these people are inclined to bend the rules to attain their objective, sometimes to the detriment of others. Often this is unintentional, they blindly see their goal and go all out to achieve it. They enjoy changing conditions and, because of this, may have a talent for healing. When well aspected, this planetary position could denote the healer that performs miracles.

AQUARIUS

☉ SUN

*P*eople not without their problems as they are highly independent yet need to share with other people. Not everyone understands this tendency to blow hot and cold in relationships, however. They often function best in group situations as this satisfies their need to keep something of themselves apart. Despite their rebellious natures, they like to control others' behaviour and may lay down stringent rules.

☽ MOON

*C*ool and detached, these individuals may appear totally devoid of feeling and may refuse to acknowledge emotion even to themselves. Sometimes this trait manifests on a physical level as a dislike of being touched. Usually intellligent, they are attracted to mental pursuits and their humanitarian instincts allow them to find practical solutions to other people's problems. They are, though, loath to admit their problems to others.

♂ MARS

*I*nventive and original, these are people who may have a perverse desire to do something different for the sake of it. They enjoy experimentation and are often attracted to scientific careers. Unconventional, they are rarely faithful to their numerous partners mainly due to their instinctual fear of being trapped. They constantly agitate for improved social conditions and become involved in action groups.

♅ URANUS

*L*ively and imaginative, this subject needs constant stimulation; when bored he or she will experience severe nervous tension. Usually having few close friends but many acquaintances, he or she may be quite knowledgeable on a variety of subjects. They have the mind of an inventor and often have flashes of genius. In personal relationships they are inclined to be attracted to someone who they feel they can reform.

☿ MERCURY

*T*his is one of the best positions for this planet because when well aspected it can indicate a clear, uncluttered mind. When badly aspected, though, the mental faculties may be blocked so that the subject displays a stubborn reluctance to investigate new ideas. Sometimes very opinionated, he or she tends to speak at length on a pet subject, much to others' dismay! Often unconventional, their off-beat ideas may create chaos.

♃ JUPITER

*A*lthough good fun in a crowd, these people tend to be bossy in their private lives. They like to entertain, have a good sense of humour and enjoy being the centre of attention; they often dress flamboyantly. They usually have a social conscience and can be good fund-raisers, willingly sacrificing time and effort for the less privileged. If involved in creative professions, their work will be highly original and eagerly sought after.

♆ NEPTUNE

*T*hese individuals are easily influenced by their friends and should be wary of being drawn into dubious pursuits through them. They should resist any inclination to experiment with drugs on a group level and redirect their curiosity to studying alternative medicine. Mystical subjects attract, but they may have somewhat odd ideas in connection with these. Their creative imaginations are ideally suited to film-making.

♀ VENUS

*U*nusually romantic souls, these folk may have many relationships; they are inclined to believe in fairy-tales but will refuse to spoil their dreams by attempting to make them real. Usually friendly and charming, often with a highly original dress-sense, they usually attract a large circle of friends. They may take an ambivalent attitude to financial matters and, therefore, suffer frequent changes of fortune.

♄ SATURN

*T*his is one of the best positions for this planet because it bestows keen, impartial judgement. These individuals usually see the truth of any situation although they may keep their knowledge to themselves. Drawn towards mental pursuits, they are always ready to investigate new ideas and, if found acceptable, will put these into practice. But they rarely accept another's opinion without first proving it.

♇ PLUTO

A person who probably has a scientific mind that is not deterred by the most complicated puzzle; he or she is the true researcher. Believing in equality and freedom, they will work hard to break down restrictive barriers. A staunch friend, he or she makes a vindictive enemy. Perhaps finding it hard to relate on a personal level, he or she may lay down rules for their partner which they would not apply to themselves.

PISCES

 **SATURN**

*T*hese people are inclined to brood over their problems and may lack energy and self-assertion. To others they may seem overly concerned with practicalities, yet this is not really so; they simply try harder than most because they are frightened of losing control. Although they may dream in private, they rarely get such ideas off the ground because their natural pessimism makes them afraid to try out anything new.

 SUN

*T*hese people are often easily persuaded and will accept anything for a quiet life. They will tolerate much ill-treatment from partners as they are always ready to make allowances and excuses for others. Sometimes they are so intent on pleasing others that they will promise the same thing to several people, thus creating the very confusion and upset they are trying to avoid. But they do have an ethereal charm.

 **VENUS**

*A*lways romantic, usually sensitive and understanding, these people tend to be popular. Often artistic, they may follow a creative career. Sometimes others will take advantage of their good natures for they rarely refuse to help anyone who asks. Although these characters enjoy the good things of life and can be very generous, their lack of financial acumen may be an inhibiting factor unless they have strong partners.

 **URANUS**

*S*ometimes artistically creative, often visionaries, these people seem able to tap into mystical realms. Inspiration often comes out of the blue, with little effort; they may rely on luck, yet this seldom lets them down. Problems are more likely to occur in practical matters than with abstract concepts which they handle with ease. Reluctant to conform, they may have difficulty deciding who they want to be.

 **MOON**

*R*eceptive and impressionable, this subject is likely to pick up feelings from other people and he or she may need to learn to distinguish between their own opinion and that of others. Usually very psychic, he or she may have difficulty in channeling this energy. Often reality is ignored in favour of a fantasy world. Easily hurt, but with an uncanny knack for understanding others' problems, they must learn to stand up for themselves.

 **MARS**

*T*hese subjects will rarely take the direct approach, they will always try to enter by the backdoor. Although inclined to be secretive themselves, they detest information being witheld from them. Usually highly observant, they will take note of even miniscule changes. Energy tends to fluctuate and they normally avoid too many late nights, knowing this causes irritability. They tend to be rather shy. They follow their own code of honesty.

 **NEPTUNE**

*T*hese subjects are usually drawn towards escapism in one form or other. They could become a religious recluse, which they find appealing, a drug-addict, artist or actor. Often they will refuse to accept the real world yet are unlikely to do anything to change it — they will always find a way to opt out. However, they may have pronounced psychic ability that could be put to practical use for the benefit of others.

 MERCURY

*T*hese people have fertile imaginations and make good entertainers; often they are fabulous story-tellers. They like to socialise and are willing hosts who can produce gourmet meals with apparently little effort. They do tend to take slights at a deeply personal level but are ultimately forgiving. Their natural facility for putting ideas across with simple clarity may sometimes manifest as writing talent.

 **JUPITER**

*E*xtremely kind and caring, these folk enjoy looking after people and often do well in professions such as nursing. They have the happy knack of making even strangers feel loved and comfortable. Negatively, there may be an excessive enjoyment of food and drink. Sometimes their dreams are shattered by mundane reality for these compassionate souls really do believe in an ideal world full of perfect people.

 **PLUTO**

*D*eeply psychological energies drive these people forward; they rarely recognise what motivates them themselves. Luckily, as they have such magnetically attractive personalities, they usually work for the good of others. Whether scientists or not, these are the natural seekers after truth who feel that they have their own private guardian angels which protect them from harm, and they are therefore willing to take risks.

THE HOUSES

As I have mentioned, there are many forms of House division but the method chosen for this book has been that of Equal House. But, whatever the chosen method of division, it should be remembered that each house has a particular meaning and these traditional meanings are retained within every system of house division.

But, before we come to study these meanings, it should be noted that the terms ANGULAR, SUCCEDENT and CADENT also refer to qualities allotted to the houses. The 1st, 4th, 7th and 10th Houses are regarded as Angular and any planets that tenant these Houses are said to be strengthened by position. Planets that reside in the 2nd, 5th, 8th and 11th Houses are termed Succedent and these are said to have staying power; while those termed Cadent, the 3rd, 6th, 9th and 12th House, frequently diversify and may not amount to much unless extremely strong or well-aspected.

Below: This chart shows the 'natural' rulership of the houses, starting with Aries at the 9 o'clock position, House I, Taurus rules the 2nd House, Gemini the 3rd, and so on. Each house, therefore, possesses the same qualities as does its natural ruler and, like the sign that holds sway over it, is associated with a certain planetary influence.

ANGULAR

SUCCEDENT

CADENT

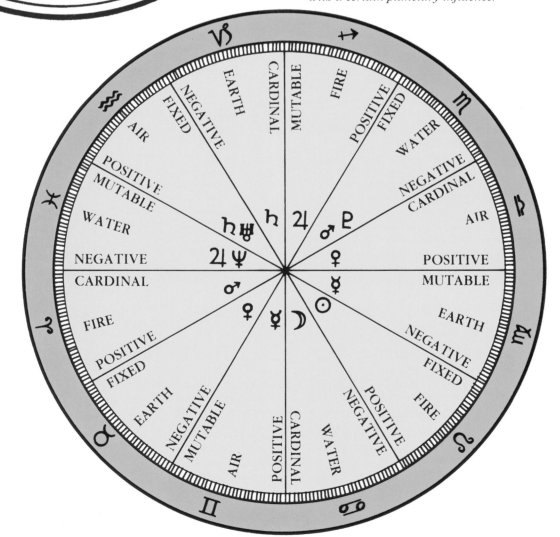

1st House

This house denotes the individual's personality, the image that is presented to the world. It may give some indication of physical appearance and often has bearing upon health.

Any planet in this house, together with the sign ruler, may therefore have strong influence on character, perhaps modifying or accentuating other factors, such as the Sun sign or the sign on the Ascendant. It has affinity with Aries.

2nd House

This house represents the subject's values and resources; it therefore has some bearing on the acquisition of money and possessions and the attitude towards these. It also refers to feelings and emotions and the value that these qualities hold for the subject.

The nature of any planets that occupy this house, together with the sign on the cusp and its ruler, will indicate the subject's manner of meeting obligations. It has affinity with Taurus.

3rd House

This house is concerned with the subject's mental attitude, all forms of communication and learning; the written and spoken word and short journeys — especially by road and rail. It also indicates normal day-to-day environment and contacts, such as brothers and sisters or neighbours.

Any planets that tenant this house, together with the sign on the cusp and its ruler, should be taken into consideration in connection with the above-mentioned areas. It has an affinity with Gemini.

4th House

This house signifies the foundations of the life, background, home, roots and heritage. It may also show the subject's personal private life, both as a child and as an adult. It also relates to property, real estate and inheritance.

Planets that fall in this house, together with the sign on the cusp and its ruler, will indicate the individual's attitude to the past or tradition, as well as the beginning or ending of life. It has affinity with Cancer.

5th House

This is the house of creativity, self-expression, procreation, pleasure and amusement, romantic love, gambling and speculation. It may also relate to enterprises and new undertakings, all that is done in a spontaneous fashion.

Any planet occupying this house, together with the sign on the cusp and condition of the planet that rules this, will therefore point to the subject's likely mode of expressing his creative instincts. It has affinity with Leo.

6th House

Here we find the house that rules work, health and service to others. It may show mundane employment and attitude to subordinates, superiors and those in authority. It may also show the subject's attitude to small animals.

If planets occupy this house it may denote that work is of prime importance. Alternatively, such a planetary emphasis, or the condition of the planet that rules the sign on the cusp, could indicate great concern with health, hygiene and related matters. This house has affinity with Virgo.

7th House

This is the house of partnerships, which may be personal or of a business nature. It relates to love, marriage, partner and close relationships — friends rather than relatives. Traditionally, it is also the house of open enemies and may refer to litigation, law suits, contracts and the like.

The sign on the cusp, the sign's ruler or any planets that are in the house will indicate the subject's attitude to his peers or his dealings with associates or rivals. It has affinity with Libra.

8th House

Traditionally, this house signifies death, wills, legacies and other people's money. It relates to the individual's financial ability and the partner's estate as well as to big business such as banking and insurance.

It is also the house of transformation and spiritual regeneration and therefore concerns birth, death, rebirth and the occult. The subject's attitude to such matters can be ascertained from the sign on the cusp, its ruler and any planets in the house. It has affinity with Scorpio.

9th House

This house denotes long-distance travel, sporting ability, the higher mind, religion and philosphy and the law. It relates to further education, foreign people and places, morals, conscience, visions and dreams.

The sign on the cusp, its ruler and planetary emphasis within the house will indicate the subject's attitude to wider concepts. His acceptance or otherwise of limitations — both geographically and metaphysically — will depend upon the planets or signs involved. It has affinity with Sagittarius.

10th House

This house is concerned with the external aspects of life, plus aims or aspirations. It may denote career, status or ambition. It relates to the subject's reputation, social and public standing, professional ambitions and achievements, responsibilities and so on.

The individual's attitude to these matters and the people who have authority over him — such as bosses, employers, parents, officials — will be reflected in the nature of the sign on the cusp, this sign's ruler or any planets within the house. It has affinity with Capricorn.

11th House

This is the house of friends, acquaintances, clubs and societies. It relates to group activity and, by tradition, hopes and wishes. Intellectual rather than physical pleasures also come under the auspices of this house.

An abundance of planets here would emphasise social relationships and, depending on the sign on the cusp and its ruler, indicate the subject's likely aspirations. It has affinity with Aquarius.

12th House

Traditionally known as the house of one's self-undoing, there is a correspondence to the inner, more secretive aspects of life such as fantasy, daydreams, conspiracy, intrigue and secret enemies.

It also relates to all places of seclusion or restraint such as hospitals, prisons, asylums, orphanages and so on. The nature of any inhibiting elements or karmic responsibilities in the subject's life will be indicated by the sign of the cusp, its ruler and any planets that reside within it. It has affinity with Pisces.

ASPECTS (PLANETARY RELATIONSHIPS)

Before we can begin to consider chart interpretation there is one final lesson in calculation — this involves aspects.

In astrology, the term aspect refers to the angular distance between two points as measured along the ecliptic. The ecliptic, or path of the Sun, is equal to 360 degrees — the measurement of a circle, which is what a birth chart represents. At any time, two or more planets may form recognised aspects to each other or to parts of the chart that are considered important: the Ascendant, Midheaven or the house cusps.

Astrologers use a variety of aspects but, for the purpose of this basic introduction to the subject of astrology, we will confine ourselves to those that are based upon multiples of 30 degrees. Four of these are termed major: conjunction, opposition, trine and square. The rest are termed minor: sextile, semi-sextile and inconjunct (or quincunx).

Conjunction ☌

When two planets occupy the same space or degree, or when they are approaching or separating from each other within a reasonably close orb, this is called a conjunction. Although different astrologers allow different degrees of orb for a conjunction, the distance between the two relevant planets must be small in order for them to be regarded as conjunct.

For example, if the Sun is at 5° Aries and Mars is also at 5° Aries, this is an exact conjunction. However, if the Sun were at 5° Aries and Mars at 10° Aries, they would still be in a conjunct position. Similarly, if the Sun were 5° Aries and Mars at 28° Pisces, this would also be considered as a conjunction. Some astrologers allow an orb of up to 15 degrees for the luminaries — the Sun and the Moon — and as little as 5 degrees for the other planets.

For simplicity, therefore, an orb allowance of 7 degrees is recommended for a conjunction as a general rule. However, a little commonsense and judgement are required. Do not always follow rules: experiment, learn to make judgements based upon personal experience.

The conjunction places a focus of concentrated energy in one particular area of a chart. The action of this aspect is often unconscious. If several planets are together at one point of a chart there will be great intensity in the house(s) and sign(s) involved. This is called a stellium and it may be effective even if the distance covered spans more than 7 degrees.

If you will refer to the example chart for Sally, you will see a conjunction of 4 planets in Scorpio — Moon, Neptune, Venus and Mars (which also conjuncts the MC). When involved together these planets appear as a glamorous combination, while the sign shows drama and passion. The houses and chart area covered relates to career. It would seem reasonable to assume that Sally is very concerned with career matters and that she is likely to be drawn towards glamorous professions. *This is true. Having first worked as a model, she now works in a television studio and has considerable interest in her career.*

Below: This chart wheel is marked off in degrees to show the exact planetary positions and angles of the chart for Sally; below is the completed aspect grid.

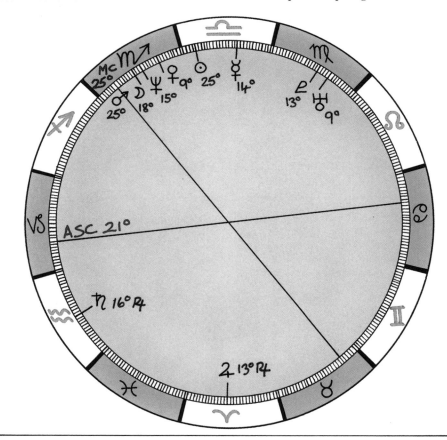

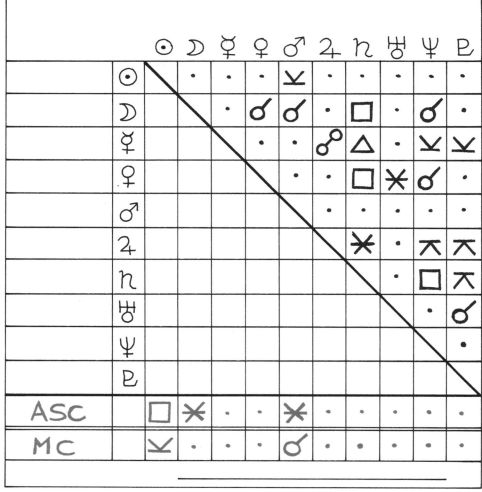

	☉	☽	☿	♀	♂	♃	♄	♅	♆	♇
☉		•	•	•	⊼	•	•	•	•	•
☽			•	☌	☌	•	□	•	☌	•
☿				•	•	☍	△	•	⊼	⊼
♀					•	•	□	✳	☌	•
♂							•	•	•	•
♃							✳	•	⊼	⊼
♄								•	□	⊼
♅									•	☌
♆										•
♇										
ASC		□	✳	•	•	✳	•	•	•	•
MC		⊼	•	•	•	☌	•	•	•	•

The Opposition ☌

An opposition occurs when two or more planets literally oppose one another in the chart. A planet at 15°, Cancer for instance, will be in opposition to another at 15°, Capricorn. Again, an allowance of 7 degrees is recommended. This aspect may indicate conflict and tension, or it might even show attraction. Oppositions invariably bring things out into the open, often through inter-action with other people. Any conflict indicated by such an aspect has every chance of being resolved.

If we return to the chart for Sally, you will see that Mercury and Jupiter oppose each other in her chart. These two planets in any aspect may indicate a supreme optimist who tends to rely upon chance. Fortunately, here this trait is modified by the Ascendant, Capricorn, a sign which has never yet been known to trust in luck alone. Even so, the aspect has effect and Sally has often displayed a happy knack for being in the right place at the right time.

She enjoys entering competitions and may occasionally have a modest gamble. But, so far, she has only been 'lucky' in respect of the latter when concerned in a joint venture with a friend. As well as showing that she is an avid reader on a variety of subjects (3rd-9th Houses), this aspect also requires a physical outlet. Sally is a student of Spirit Combat and is keen on horse-riding; she has also worked in the building trade.

The Square ☐

A square aspect occurs when two or more planets are 90 degrees apart. Using the same rule as before — allowing an orb of 7 degrees — this means that a planet at 1° Aries will be in square aspect to another planet at 1° Cancer or 1° Capricorn. This aspect is strongly challenging and will often indicate an area of limitation. But it should be remembered that we can turn challenging aspects to our advantage if we apply determination and effort to the required area.

SALLY'S COMPUTER CHART

Radix		MC	25	34	Sco					
——Sally		ASC	21	23	Cap					
			Equal——			Sun	25	27	Lib	10	10
DATE:	19 10 1963	11.	21	23	Sco	Moon	17	47	Sco	10
GMT:	13 45 0	12.	21	23	Sco	Mercury	14	19	Lib	9
LAT:	51 31 N	2.	21	23	Aqr	Venus	8	51	Sco	10
LONG:	-0 20 W	3.	21	23	Psc	Mars	25	37	Sco	11
						Jupiter	12	58	Ari R	3
						Saturn	16	27	Aqr R	1
		Node	15	15	Cnc 6	Uranus	8	37	Vir	8
		Part ft	13	44	Aqr 1	Neptune	14	40	Sco	10
						Pluto	13	22	Vir	8

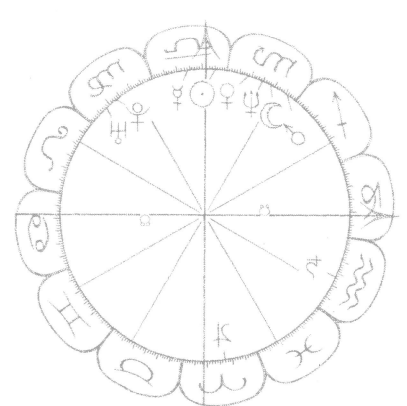

Many professional astrologers have used computers for calculating birth charts for the past decade or so. Now, with the increasing popularity of astrology, several companies supply software especially for home computer users. Some programs simply list the planetary positions, aspects and other astrological data while others will also display a chart wheel complete with house cusps, exact planetary positions and glyphs like that reproduced here which, again, is for Sally, born 19th October 1963, at 2.45 pm, in Perivale.

One square that is present in Sally's chart refers to her early life and background as well as to home and family: Moon square Saturn. Here it might be worth mentioning that she had a difficult start in life, being a 7-month baby who spent her first weeks of life in a premature baby unit — cut off from her home and family, as the aspect describes. The Moon in the 10th often describes something about the parents; this, too, is accurate. Her parents separated and divorced when she was only 5. But, so far, she is responding well to the challenge of the aspect and is making a success of her own life as an adult, perhaps being driven on by her early deprivations.

The Trine △

A trine aspect occurs where the planets are 120 degrees apart. Again, the same rules apply and the recommended orb is 7 degrees. So a planet at 7° Aries will be in trine aspect to another planet at 7° Leo or 7° Sagittarius. This aspect is said to provide comfort and ease and to be strongly helpful; but there is also a warning against laziness and lack of effort, as we may tend to take our trines for granted.

Sally has one trine in her chart: Mercury, ruler of 6th House (health and work) is very closely trine Saturn, Ascendant ruler, which tenants the 1st House (personality). This aspect may have aided her survival as a delicate baby and it also gives her a talent for organisation, which she has demonstrated in her work. She has often had total responsibility for the organisation of systems that control the routine work for new television programmes.

The Sextile ✳

The sextile is 60 degrees, or two signs apart. The suggested orb is 3 degrees. This is an actively helpful aspect which often reveals itself in the realm of the mind and ideas. One mostly uses sextiles to good effect.

Sally has a very close sextile between Venus and Uranus. Venus is not only in the 10th House (career) but also rules it; while Uranus (which is often concerned with TV) rules the 2nd House and is in the 8th (money). This is a very good astrological example of how she earns her living. When these two planets are in 'good' aspect, it is said they can create 'lucky-breaks'. This, too, is applicable. Sally was 'resting' as a model and took temporary work through an agency; when sent to a TV studio, she was asked to stay on a permanent basis.

Semi-sextile ⊻

The semi-sextile occurs when two or more planets are 30 degrees, or one sign apart. The suggested orb of influence is 2 degrees and it is recommended that anything greater than this should be discounted. Traditionally, this aspect is said to be mildly helpful but modern thought suggests that it might also create tension. Particular note should be taken of the signs and houses involved.

In Sally's chart there is a very close semi-sextile from the Sun in the 10th House to Mars, which is exactly on the MC in the 11th House. As has been demonstrated earlier, she is very career orientated and works in current affairs, which seems very appropriate for a 10th/11th House emphasis. But, initially, she experienced great difficulty in selecting a profession that she enjoyed.

The Inconjunct (or Quincunx) ⚹

The inconjunct, or quincunx, aspect is 150 degrees, or five signs apart. In the last few years or so this aspect has become widely used by astrologers. Not more than 3 degrees should be allowed for the orb. This aspect appears to force us to deal with reality in a manner that requires considerable effort and endeavour; it often has bearings upon health or work.

Sally has an extremely close inconjunct from Jupiter in Aries (3rd House) to Pluto in Virgo (8th House). At the age of 10 she was seriously ill with meningitis but was lucky enough to recover with no ill effects. The fact that she would recover in this way is shown by Jupiter's good aspect to Saturn, the Ascendant ruler.

PLANETARY EMPHASIS

The last thing we will consider in this brief introduction to the art of astrology is the distribution of planets in the hemispheres.

If the majority of planets in a chart fall above the horizon (Houses 7-12) the more extrovert aspects of the personality are highlighted. Self-expression is marked and the subject is likely to enter public service, politics or any career that deals directly with and depends on the approbation of others. Advancement is usually achieved through the good offices of those in authority, often without the necessity of soliciting such help.

When the majority of planets are below the horizon (Houses 1-6) the whole character is much more introspective. Such people are not easy to get to know and may be even more difficult to understand. They can be cautious, reserved and shy; in order to succeed they must work by their own efforts because they rarely receive assistance from those with influence.

If the planetary emphasis falls in the Eastern hemisphere — Houses 10, 11, 12, 1, 2 and 3 — it highlights initiative. Individualism is stressed and the subject is likely to be a self-starter, someone who will initiate ideas and actions. Leadership qualities will be apparent. The subject's underlying motives may be selfish and egotistic, however; there may, in fact, be a tendency to use others for his or her own ends.

A planetary emphasis in the Western hemisphere (Houses 4-9) accentuates the subject's concern with those matters that are outside the self. It focuses attention on emotions, relationships and the subject's attitudes towards others, his environment and career. Social awareness and humanitarian tendencies are likely to dominate such an individual's personality.

PREDICTIVE ASTROLOGY: TRANSITS

There are several methods that astrologers use to predict the future but lack of space prevents us from discussing more than one

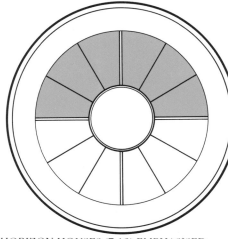

HORIZON HOUSES (7-12) EMPHASISED

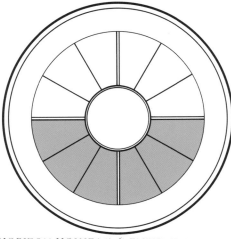

HORIZON HOUSES (1-6) EMPHASISED

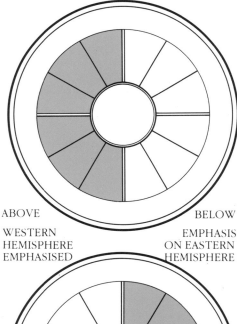

ABOVE   BELOW
WESTERN   EMPHASIS
HEMISPHERE   ON EASTERN
EMPHASISED   HEMISPHERE

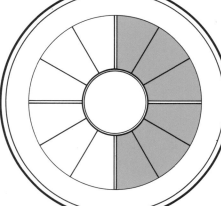

here. I have therefore chosen to explain one of the most popular, transits: this entails looking up the planetary positions for the date in question and comparing these to the natal chart to see whether any aspects are made to the planets in the birth chart.

Astrologers rarely consider the *Moon* in transit work because this planet moves so rapidly. But it is sometimes worthy of consideration, especially when a Lunation (New or Full Moon) aspects a chart strongly. As the Moon tends to reflect our emotions, it should be studied in this context.

The *Sun* moves at a fairly regular rate each year but, even so, has an effect. The reader may be able to identify with statements such as 'changes always occur in November' or 'February is always rather flat.' Learn to understand your own yearly Solar pattern in order to initiate activites or to know when best to take a well-earned vacation.

Any aspect from the Sun will add vitality and warmth. It might be worth noting here that even though a square from the Sun to Saturn may be challenging, the Sun will still liven up Saturn to a certain extent. But when the reverse happens, Saturn squares the Sun, the effect is colder and more inhibiting.

Mercury also moves very rapidly but, when aspecting our charts by transit, will tell us about movement or communication. When this planet is passing through the natal 12th House you may find that you are uncommonly quiet and retiring but, soon after, when it contacts the Ascendant, there may be a sudden urge to communicate or travel.

Venus is often involved with romance or finance; or it may simply make life a little easier or brighter when in any aspect to the natal chart. Venus-Mars contacts often signify a new partnership; whereas a Venus-Neptune transit warns that judgement may well be faulty at this time.

Mars may be an indicator of one's sex-life; or may simply indicate one's level of self-assertion. When Mars passes through (transits) the 7th House we might meet with aggression from other people; but when it occupies the 1st House, we may become uncharacteristically demanding ourselves.

Jupiter is given more consideration by astrologers than the so-called 'minor' planets mentioned previously because it remains in the same area of a birth chart for longer periods of time. This planet expands all that it touches, so will magnify difficulties as readily as it will bring luck.

Every 12 years we experience a Jupiter Return: that is, this planet returns to the same position that it held in our nativity. This is supposed to indicate a time of expansive opportunity but this will depend to some extent on what natal aspects Jupiter makes.

Saturn will test us in any aspect, particularly when transiting its own natal position. The Saturn Return occurs twice in an average lifetime; firstly around the 28-30 year mark and secondly between 58-60 years old. The first return is usually a time of adult maturity and often points to a period when important life decisions are made. If the chart is well-aspected, or the current attitude has been taken earlier, this period may involve professional advancement or may

refer to decisions regarding marriage or children.

Saturn always demands responsibility. When this planet appears in a negative light there may be losses in the area of finance or relationships; yet one always gains wisdom through such experiences. The second Saturn return occurs at another major age-point and may be a vital factor in decisions concerning retirement.

Uranus stays in the same area by transit for a period of seven years. People often refer to 7-year cycles and these can invariably be traced to Uranian activity. This planet always instigates change, which may be exciting or otherwise depending on relative position or aspect.

Neptune usually represents an attitude of unreality which may guide us positively or, more often, negatively. One should therefore be extra careful under very close Nep-

tune transits as one's judgement is not likely to be clear or reliable at such moments. What may seem to be 'a good idea' at the time so often proves sadly misplaced when viewed with hindsight later on.

Pluto can transform or destroy and will take from us as readily as he will give. We need to clear something from our lives under his auspices, whether this means an actual accumulation of rubbish or relinquishing something we treasure.

Now you will have learned the basics of chart interpretation and, provided you have acquired the basic equipment listed on pages 18-19, will be well on the way to understanding your own chart. But if you want to become proficient in the subject you will need to make full use of the many excellent specialist books available or should attend astrology classes.

For the moment, though, if you have an

ephemeris for any year later than your birth year, you might try your hand at predicting by transit. It might be better still to examine in retrospect an event that you know actually happened on a particular date. For this exercise you can use the planetary keywords already given together with the meanings of the houses; remember, too, that the section on planets by sign can be read futuristically as well as natally.

However, it should be realised that astrology can be a life-long study and even so-called experts should be wary of predicting doom and disaster, either for themselves or others. It is important to remember that even the most difficult aspect can be overcome by taking remedial action; we can even ignore great potential through inertia. It may be true to say that the stars impel us forth in specific directions but they rarely, if ever, compel!

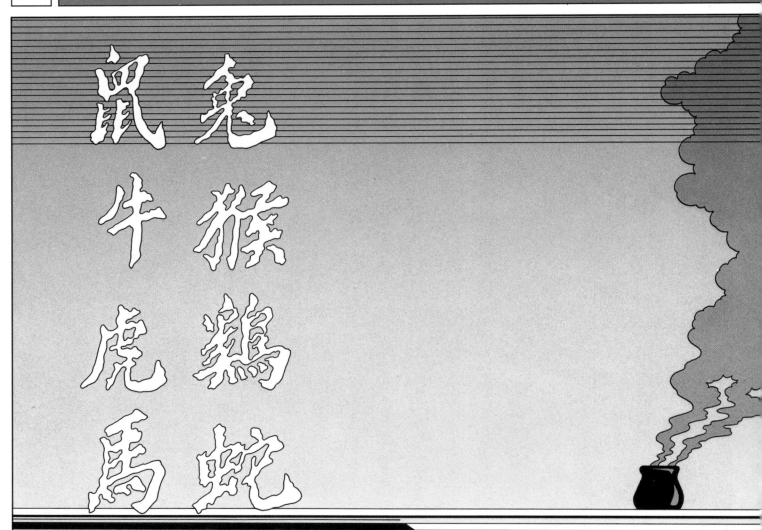

ORIENTAL ASTROLOGY

Astrology is a very ancient form of divination. Cicero said that the Chaldeans had records of the stars for 370,000 years and that the Babylonians kept the nativities of all births for hundreds of thousands of years. Obviously, over such a vast period, astrology took on many diverse forms. We have already looked at the way in which this ancient art has been handed down to us in the Western world in the previous chapter.

The Hindus claim to have the oldest astrology, though this is frequently disputed elsewhere! They use constellations instead of signs but the planets and houses are comparable to our own. The Hindus use a very precise and complicated astrological system which aims to chart a whole lifetime rather than the moment of birth and is too intricate to detail here, but it will be fun to look at the most popular form of Oriental astrology.

Apart from the numerous publications on the subject, there is usually considerable media coverage nowadays of that colourful event, the Chinese New Year, and the animal that 'rules' each year. It should though be pointed out that many other nations use a similar system to the Chinese, notably Tibetans, Japanese, Vietnamese and Koreans; but for the purposes of this book we will look at the basics of astrology as practised by the Chinese.

THE CHINESE CALENDAR

There are tremendous differences between the Western system and the Chinese; the latter is based upon duality, that is the principle of Yang and Yin (see the chapter on I Ching). The constellations used are different too, not only in name but in the way in which the stars are seen to be grouped; they are also of varying lengths. In fact, the Chinese do not use the zodiac as we do but base their calculations on the Pole Star.

Instead of using 12 houses, they use 28 Lunar mansions, all of which have very definite meanings, though lack of space prevents full discussion of these here. However, in some ways the Chinese system of animal rulers replaces our Sun signs although these do not equate exactly.

The Chinese calendar is based on Lunar months and their New Year will therefore begin on a different date each year; similarly, the Lunar months do not coincide exactly with our 'fixed' calendrical system. However, the following table of rough approximations may suffice to help you begin to understand the Chinese system.

Each year has its own ruler and, although the dates must be noted very precisely if one is born in January or February, at the moment the following table will be sufficient as a guide. (The exact date changes for each year will be found listed under the appropriate animal heading later in this chapter.)

1st month approximately equals FEBRUARY and is ruled by the TIGER.

2nd month approximately equals MARCH and is ruled by the HARE.

3rd month approximately equals APRIL and is ruled by the DRAGON.

4th month approximately equals MAY and is ruled by the SNAKE.

5th month approximately equals JUNE and is ruled by the HORSE.

6th month approximately equals JULY and is ruled by the SHEEP.

7th month approximately equals AUGUST and is ruled by the MONKEY.

8th month approximately equals SEPTEMBER and is ruled by the ROOSTER.

9th month approximately equals OCTOBER and is ruled by the DOG.

10th month approximately equals NOVEMBER and is ruled by the PIG.

11th month approximately equals DECEMBER and is ruled by the RAT.

12th month approximately equals JANUARY and is ruled by the OX.

RAT	1900	1912	1924	1936
	1948	1960	1972	1984
	1996			
OX	1901	1913	1925	1937
	1949	1961	1973	1985
	1997			
TIGER	1902	1914	1926	1938
	1950	1962	1974	1986
	1998			
HARE	1903	1915	1927	1939
	1951	1963	1975	1987
	1999			
DRAGON	1904	1916	1928	1940
	1952	1964	1976	1988
	2000			
SNAKE	1905	1917	1929	1941
	1953	1965	1977	1989
HORSE	1906	1918	1930	1942
	1954	1966	1978	1990
SHEEP	1907	1919	1931	1943
	1955	1967	1979	1991
MONKEY	1908	1920	1932	1944
	1956	1968	1980	1992
ROOSTER	1909	1921	1933	1945
	1957	1969	1981	1993
DOG	1910	1922	1934	1946
	1958	1970	1982	1994
PIG	1911	1923	1935	1947
	1959	1971	1983	1995

These 12 animals also have rulership over certain periods in the day. As mentioned earlier, Chinese astrology is based on the principle of duality and this is reflected in the way in which the 24-hour day is divided into 2-hour periods, or double-hours, each of which is 'ruled' by one of the animals.

Thus it can be seen that any astrologer in the Orient will request the time, month and year of birth in exactly the same way as would a Western astrologer. There is though one other factor that has prime importance in Chinese astrology but has no direct parallel in the Western system; the five elements.

These five elements, which are said to rule over every sphere of human existence, are: Wood, Fire, Earth, Metal and Water. Again maintaining the principle of duality, each element has its positive (Yang) and negative (Yin) side.

And, in much the same way as each animal has rulership over a double-hour, comprising one Yang hour and one Yin hour, each element is attributed to two consecutive years, one Yang the other Yin, in sequence.

```
DOUBLE-HOUR OF THE RAT
11pm-1am
DOUBLE-HOUR OF THE OX
1am-3am
DOUBLE-HOUR OF THE TIGER
3am-5am
DOUBLE-HOUR OF THE HARE
5am-7am
DOUBLE-HOUR OF THE DRAGON
7am-9am
DOUBLE-HOUR OF THE SNAKE
9am-11am
DOUBLE-HOUR OF THE HORSE
11am-1pm
DOUBLE-HOUR OF THE SHEEP
1pm-3pm
DOUBLE-HOUR OF THE MONKEY
3pm-5pm
DOUBLE-HOUR OF THE ROOSTER
5pm-7pm
DOUBLE-HOUR OF THE DOG
7pm-9pm
DOUBLE-HOUR OF THE PIG
9pm-11pm
```

The five elements

The five elements are the equivalent of the five seasons used by the Chinese. *Wood* is the beginning, the season of creation, and equates with the planet Jupiter; *Fire* relates to heat and Mars; *Earth* is the mid-point of the year and is comparable to Saturn; *Metal* is the harvest and Venus; finally, *Water* feeds the growth that will come from Wood and has affinity with Mercury.

Thus it can be seen that as well as recognising five elements, the Chinese use five of the planets used in Western astrology. The Sun and the Moon have special significance in their charts too, for these represent Yang and Yin respectively.

It is fascinating to learn that astrology is also incorporated into big business. Each concern, including major banks whose names are household words in the West, will not even erect a building without paying a vast sum of money to an astrologer in order to ensure that all the doors, windows and walls are aligned to the correct pattern for success; one bank opened its new branch on 8/8/88 as this was considered to be a very auspicious date.

Obviously, Chinese astrology is much more comprehensive than can be outlined in such a brief introduction to a vast subject. However, if you consult the following pages you may glean some idea of what it means to be born in a particular animal year; this meaning can be blended with that of your hour of birth and, possibly, the month too.

You will learn which other animal personalities you are most likely to be compatible with but must use your own knowledge and intuition too in this respect. Keep it in mind that, as with any other form of divination, there is always very much more to be learned and understood.

TABLE OF ELEMENTAL RULERSHIPS

YEAR	ELEMENT	POLARITY	YEAR	ELEMENT	POLARITY	YEAR	ELEMENT	POLARITY	YEAR	ELEMENT	POLARITY	YEAR	ELEMENT	POLARITY	YEAR	ELEMENT	POLARITY
1900	METAL	+	1920	METAL	+	1940	METAL	+	1960	METAL	+	1980	METAL	+
1901	METAL	−	1921	METAL	−	1941	METAL	−	1961	METAL	−	1981	METAL	−
1902	WATER	+	1922	WATER	+	1942	WATER	+	1962	WATER	+	1982	WATER	+
1903	WATER	−	1923	WATER	−	1943	WATER	−	1963	WATER	−	1983	WATER	−
1904	WOOD	+	1924	WOOD	+	1944	WOOD	+	1964	WOOD	+	1984	WOOD	+
1905	WOOD	−	1925	WOOD	−	1945	WOOD	−	1965	WOOD	−	1985	WOOD	−
1906	FIRE	+	1926	FIRE	+	1946	FIRE	+	1966	FIRE	+	1986	FIRE	+
1907	FIRE	−	1927	FIRE	−	1947	FIRE	−	1967	FIRE	−	1987	FIRE	−
1908	EARTH	+	1928	EARTH	+	1948	EARTH	+	1968	EARTH	+	1988	EARTH	+
1909	EARTH	−	1929	EARTH	−	1949	EARTH	−	1969	EARTH	−	1989	EARTH	−
1910	METAL	+	1930	METAL	+	1950	METAL	+	1970	METAL	+	1990	METAL	+
1911	METAL	−	1931	METAL	−	1951	METAL	−	1971	METAL	−	1991	METAL	−
1912	WATER	+	1932	WATER	+	1952	WATER	+	1972	WATER	+	1992	WATER	+
1913	WATER	−	1933	WATER	−	1953	WATER	−	1973	WATER	−	1993	WATER	−
1914	WOOD	+	1934	WOOD	+	1954	WOOD	+	1974	WOOD	+	1994	WOOD	+
1915	WOOD	−	1935	WOOD	−	1955	WOOD	−	1975	WOOD	−	1995	WOOD	−
1916	FIRE	+	1936	FIRE	+	1956	FIRE	+	1976	FIRE	+	1906	FIRE	+
1917	FIRE	−	1937	FIRE	−	1957	FIRE	−	1977	FIRE	−	1997	FIRE	−
1918	EARTH	+	1938	EARTH	+	1958	EARTH	+	1978	EARTH	+	1998	EARTH	+
1919	EARTH	−	1939	EARTH	−	1959	EARTH	−	1979	EARTH	−	1999	EARTH	−

RAT

January 31st 1900 — February 18th 1901
February 18th 1912 — February 5th 1913
February 5th 1924 — January 24th 1925
January 24th 1936 — February 10th 1937
February 10th 1948 — January 28th 1949
January 28th 1960 — February 14th 1961
January 16th 1972 — February 2nd 1973
February 2nd 1984 — February 19th 1985
February 19th 1996 — February 6th 1997

OX

February 19th 1901 — February 7th 1902
February 6th 1913 — January 25th 1914
January 25th 1925 — February 12th 1926
February 11th 1937 — January 30th 1938
January 29th 1949 — February 16th 1950
February 15th 1961 — February 4th 1962
February 3rd 1973 — January 22nd 1974
February 20th 1985 — February 8th 1986
February 7th 1997 — January 27th 1998

Contrary to general opinion in the Western world, the Rat is considered to be a charmer in the East. Intelligent and witty, Rat personalities like to socialise and will usually have a wide circle of friends and acquaintances. They may, however, gravitate towards those who have success or status for they invariably seek opportunities for advancement. This latter trait helps them to spot consumer bargains and they make worthy companions when out shopping!

When negatively expressed, the opportunist may become a penny-pinching miser who continually worries about loss of security. Even at their best, these characters are likely to be hoarders who are always afraid of the advent of a rainy day. But, although inclined to be acquisitive, Rats will usually share their bounty with any cause or individual who is genuinely deserving.

Most Rats can be very persuasive and are usually good at presenting ideas to other people; they are often successful in the world of business and can revive an enterprise that is fading. They work best when in partnership as they need to discuss ideas and methods in detail constantly; similarly in their personal lives, where their most pressing need is communication.

The Rat lifestyle may be frantic for these folk tend to get involved in numerous activities; they may have interest in the community, hold down demanding jobs or play host to lavish entertainment. Often, they appear to be afraid of missing something important if they are idle for any length of time.

Rat personalities like to be in control of their own environment and will mostly be attracted to weaker partners; but the danger is that they will eventually grow to despise such weakness in others and may ultimately drop them for someone more attractive.

These characters are stable and have the tenacity to face the most daunting situations; they make reliable friends and allies, even when they bemoan lack of prudence in others. They are the survivors who usually conserve their resources, erring on the side of caution rather than frivolity. Once an Ox decides on a chosen course of action there is little that will deter him or her; he or she tends to be the steady plodder who invariably attains their chosen goal.

Sometimes these people appear to lack humour yet their reliability wins them friends. The Ox is the pal you can depend on in a crisis or the willing person who makes up a fourth at Bridge. Usually a good listener, he or she may be the sympathetic soul to whom you bare your troubles; their advice is usually sound, constructive and well worth heeding.

Being selective in close contacts, their confidence must be earned on merit but, as it is rare for an Ox to take the initiative, it may take a considerable time to get to know these characters. It is a mistake to take these apparently placid individuals for granted, though, for they have their own personal code of ethics that they strictly adhere to; if you cross their invisible line of tolerance and offend them, they make unforgiving enemies who will hold grudges for ever.

They make splendid parents and loyal lovers who usually enjoy domesticity. Ox men are nearly always good providers and the women often agree that their rightful place is in the home! Some have a large number of children or care for elderly parents; often an Ox person's home will be a place of refuge for outsiders in need of solace and comfort.

Although perhaps not the most outwardly demonstrative of creatures, they have a great capacity for love deep inside them.

TIGER

February 8th 1902 — January 28th 1903
January 26th 1914 — February 13th 1915
February 13th 1926 — February 1st 1927
January 31st 1938 — February 18th 1939
February 17th 1950 — February 5th 1951
February 5th 1962 — January 24th 1963
January 23rd 1974 — February 10th 1975
February 9th 1986 — January 28th 1987
January 28th 1998 — February 15th 1999

HARE

January 29th 1903 — February 15th 1904
February 14th 1915 — February 2nd 1916
February 2nd 1927 — January 22nd 1928
January 19th 1939 — February 7th 1940
February 6th 1951 — January 26th 1952
January 25th 1963 — February 12th 1964
February 11th 1975 — January 30th 1976
January 29th 1987 — February 16th 1988
February 16th 1999 — February 4th 2000

*T*he Tiger lives up to his reputation in the animal kingdom by being appropriately brave and daring. Often unconventional, these people like to make their own rules and have others follow them. They usually have inventive, original minds and may thrive on competition; but their natural tendency towards aggression can easily become foolhardy rashness.

Born leaders, Tigers may acquire honour and status; but when they do so, should take care to remain aware of the needs of those beneath them. Common faults are a reluctance to compromise or a stubborn refusal to study what is best for the majority; there is also an element of rebelliousness in their nature.

Tigers may sometimes lack stability or be prone to sudden whims that instigate ill-considered changes; perhaps restlessly shifting from one job to another. This attitude may extend towards finance too, and they may either be absurdly generous or liable to trust to luck alone. A few Tigers may tend to be accident-prone and all could benefit from learning patience.

Tiger people rarely work in menial positions and will be happiest in occupations that contain variety or continual challenge. They enjoy the process of learning and can easily become bored once they have mastered a subject.

This wild creature is usually very attractive even when not really beautiful or handsome by conventional standards; he or she has presence, flair and originality: traits that make this character interestingly ``different'' from others. Usually eagerly sought after as partners but, unfortunately, not so easy to tame: Tigers may make unwilling captives. Even when their claws are firmly engaged, Tigers will still insist on a certain amount of freedom and independence. Keep him or her on a really long leash.

*T*he Hare likes to be with people and may yearn for the security of a partnership; yet their natural reserve often makes congenial company hard to find. These people are sensitive and intuitive and have the virtue of absolute discretion; once other people notice them, they are almost perfect friends.

These characters know when to sit back and listen or when active involvement is required; they have tact and diplomacy and respect privacy, both for themselves and others. Lovers of peace and harmony, they will mostly employ evasive tactics: Hares will always withdraw when trouble is brewing and, even when let down by others, rarely bother with revenge or recrimination.

Sometimes the Hare personality may appear to be enclosed in a world where feelings are not allowed to touch them. Often very psychic, it may simply be that he or she knows that the world is a difficult place in which to live and is determined to protect their own interests. Shrewd judges of character, Hares are rarely taken in although they don't always loudly voice their opinions on their observations.

Many Hares are creative, though their creations tend to be conventional; if artistically inclined, they will usually paint literal representations and seldom take chances on depicting abstract concepts. Caution and security are their watchwords; they like to have a solid home-base. Many will actually avoid travel if they can and most are inclined to collect possessions that tie them down.

Hare personalities rarely enjoy large families for they resent the disorder that children can create. They are happiest living in perfect surroundings with a carefully chosen partner who will not totally disrupt their carefully insulated comfort, for they are cautious and uncompromising.

DRAGON

February 16th 1904 — February 3rd 1905
February 3rd 1916 — January 22nd 1917
January 23rd 1928 — February 9th 1929
February 8th 1940 — January 26th 1941
January 27th 1952 — February 13th 1953
February 13th 1964 — February 1st 1965
January 31st 1976 — February 17th 1977
February 17th 1988 — February 5th 1989

SNAKE

February 4th 1905 — January 24th 1906
January 23rd 1917 — February 10th 1918
February 10th 1929 — January 29th 1930
January 27th 1941 — February 14th 1942
February 14th 1953 — February 2nd 1954
February 22nd 1965 — January 20th 1966
February 18th 1977 — February 6th 1978
February 6th 1989 — January 26th 1990

It seems fitting that Dragons always attract attention as this is their historical legacy; appropriately, the attention they command may not always be flattering yet one will always notice a Dragon in one's midst. Dramatic, selfish and strong-willed, these people rarely consider others; nevertheless, their personal magnetism always draws others to them. Whether you love them or hate them, you will never be able to ignore them and will usually allow them to persuade you to their every bidding.

Dragons can be unfaithful or unreliable yet are nearly always given a second chance, more often three or four. Their own sense of personal worth and superiority is infectious and effective, making others feel honoured to know them.

These folk will persuade you to play when you should be working, or vice versa if it suits their desires; you will overeat when you are meant to be dieting or jog around the park when you long to relax by the fire. Everything depends upon the Dragon's current mood of the moment, never your own!

Dragons have tremendous drive and energy and tend to be lucky in terms of finance; so, as long as others are prepared to stay in the background without asking too many questions, they make marvellous partners. You will certainly be proud to be seen with one. They are the entrepreneurs and top models, pop stars or film goddesses, or flamboyant artists. When they have an interest in the occult they can be powerful magicians; and if drawn towards politics, will become a force to be reckoned with.

It is probably significant that the Dragon is the only mythological character in Chinese astrology, the rest are fairly mundane, ordinary creatures. With this in mind, a dragon personality has to be larger than life.

The Snake complements the Dragon to a certain extent but will get his or her own way with more firmness; objectives are achieved through a subtle form of insinuation that makes others think it was their idea in the first place. Snake personalities are adept at making a good impression and can easily cause other people to believe that they are experts in any field. Not that they lie, of course; only by implication!

These subjects are mostly attractive and have a perfect sense of occasion; they dress tastefully and appropriately but manage to add those extra little touches that cause them to be noticed. All Snakes seem to be born with a sixth sense that they utilise to its full extent; they can always lay their hands on something useful, any time, anywhere. This talent for observation and adaptation can lead to successful careers in research or, for the more artistically creative, a facility for producing perfect miniature reproductions.

Never try to be evasive with a Snake personality for they can spot a half-lie instantly. Because of this trait, which often causes them to look for trouble where there is none, Snakes may become jealous and possessive lovers. Yet they can also be flatteringly romantic; their penchant for detail makes them notice every little change in their loved ones' moods or appearance. Be warned, though, that they will sulk if others forget to praise or notice them.

Snakes like to circulate and can be seen in the ''best'' places; indeed, those trend-setters who spot the right venues just that short time before the general public could easily be Snakes. Masters of understatement, they will casually mention where they have been in just the right tone of voice — and others will eagerly follow suit.

Snake characters often succeed in business as they have a talent for wheeling and dealing.

HORSE

January 25th 1906 — February 12th 1907
February 11th 1918 — January 31st 1919
January 30th 1930 — February 16th 1931
February 15th 1942 — February 4th 1943
February 3rd 1954 — January 23rd 1955
January 21st 1966 — February 8th 1967
February 7th 1978 — January 27th 1979
January 27th 1990 — February 14th 1991

SHEEP

February 13th 1907 — February 1st 1908
February 1st 1919 — February 19th 1920
February 17th 1931 — February 5th 1932
February 5th 1943 — January 24th 1944
January 24th 1955 — February 11th 1956
February 9th 1967 — January 29th 1968
January 28th 1979 — February 15th 1980
February 15th 1991 — February 3rd 1992

*H*orses come in many guises; there are a few who ploddingly pull the plough in an orderly fashion but there are also stupendous racers, outstanding jumpers, bucking broncos and those that trample all over you! Usually they are pleasantly sociable and prefer teamwork but, it is said every 60 years (1906 and 1966) when Fire Horses are born, the picture is different. The main desire of these fiery steeds is to change conditions through rebellion and revolution with little thought for the consequences. So it is worth remembering that every Horse has this latent potential.

The Horse character has great strength and endurance. He or she is prepared to work hard for his living although some may have problems through wanting to gallop ahead too soon while others dislike any form of control or intrusion into their private affairs. Thus these characters can sometimes appear rash or hot-headed.

These magnificent creatures need an outlet for their physical energy and many enjoy travel. They find conversation stimulating and like a good gossip with friends. In fact, the worst thing you can do to a Horse personality is to ignore him.

Although very honest, they are often lucky in finance and are also prepared to spend their gains. They like to be well dressed and many wear expensive clothes; but they will gladly pay someone else to do the housework as they may feel that such a mundane task is beneath their dignity. Horses often succeed in the world of hard business or in any career involving technical design.

Love is sometimes difficult because horses are very strong-willed and perhaps a little intolerant; luckily, though, they are usually gregarious too, so usually learn to compromise. If jilted, however, they tend to be self-pitying rather than admit the fault may be theirs. Happily, the majority always remain faithful.

*I*n China this is considered the perfect Yin sign but, of course, Orientals have a different idea of what comprises feminine virtue than do we in the West. However, perhaps males looking for the perfect mate should heed the Chinese dictum!

Sheep are said to be absolutely selfless characters and are therefore admirably suited to the caring professions. Many have artistic talent although, like their four-footed namesakes, they have a reputation for being followers rather than innovators so make better craftsmen than creators of original works of art. In practice, most Sheep personalities prefer to share decision-making rather than allow themselves to be led blindly by others though.

It can sometimes be difficult for the Sheep personality to make the best of themselves because he or she is so affable, perhaps a little complacent too, and therefore may lack motivation. So, in order to fulfil their potential, the Sheep needs the loving guidance, the encouragement, of family or partner. Sheep need strong, kindly partners, for it is easy to take advantage of their good natures.

They will avoid confrontation if at all possible and tend to retire when trouble is brewing. Yet their tact and diplomacy usually enable them to be the instigators of peace and harmony in touchy situations. Many, in fact, have a real talent for healing; others achieve similar results through their mere presence.

Sheep have a strong need for security and this may influence their choice in matters of the affections. When making romantic overtures they are generous but, when it comes to taking responsibility, they tend to be impractical; prone to forget appointments or even, perhaps, the weekly shopping. Impractical dreamers who often make mistakes in early life, they do however learn by experience; happily, most Sheep personalities blossom in maturity

MONKEY

February 2nd 1908 — January 21st 1909
February 20th 1920 — February 7th 1921
February 6th 1932 — January 25th 1933
January 25th 1944 — February 12th 1945
February 12th 1956 — January 30th 1957
January 30th 1968 — February 16th 1969
February 16th 1980 — February 4th 1981
February 4th 1992 — January 22nd 1993

These delightful creatures are exactly what one would expect: dextrous, agile, quick-witted and liable to bend rules when it suits them. Unfortunately, it is all too easy for their undoubted talents to pass others by as they are not often taken seriously; other people tend to regard Monkey folk as lighthearted companions and little more.

Monkeys are prone to meet with frustration when young because they lack stamina and endurance; if a good idea is not taken up quickly, it may be here today but gone tomorrow. Luckily, though, Monkeys are fast and avid learners so, when they do gain ultimate security, it is achieved through hard lessons and bitter experience.

Happily, Monkeys have an amazing sense of humour and can always laugh at themselves, so their company is eagerly sought although they may find it difficult to form lasting relationships of any kind. Though charming companions, they can be boastful, unreliable or two-timing on occasion; honesty is not a noted characteristic of Monkey folk, which can, of course, alienate others and make stable liaisons difficult to achieve.

Basically self-centred, these subjects need love and affection as much as everyone else. Perhaps their lesson in life is to try and stop demanding instant reaction and to concentrate more on earning the love and respect of others through endeavour. Highly emotional, Monkeys tend to have many relationships along the route to fulfilment. They need stimulating partners who, in some ways, make them feel a little inadequate for, when faced with sufficient challenge, Monkeys will work hard to attain success.

Great lovers of fantasy, most Monkeys are good story-tellers and some combine this trait with a talent for writing and make successful careers in publishing.

ROOSTER

January 22nd 1909 — February 9th 1910
February 8th 1921 — January 27th 1922
January 26th 1933 — February 13th 1934
February 13th 1945 — February 1st 1946
January 31st 1957 — February 17th 1958
February 17th 1969 — February 5th 1970
February 5th 1981 — January 24th 1982
January 23rd 1993 — February 9th 1994

These bluntly outspoken characters often offend others who find it hard to accept their frankness and honesty; Roosters rarely bother with tact or subtlety in any shape or form. Even when quiet, as they sometimes are, they possess a deep, inner confidence concerning their own ability; more extrovert types will virtually crow about their achievements in very down-to-earth manner.

Roosters have considerable interest in the world at large and many of them are inveterate travellers; those that stay at home will fulfil their interest by studying subjects that concern life itself. They are always confident that life has a definite purpose and will usually accept this without question. They tend to face each day as it arrives without hopes for the future or recriminations for past failures; they live in the moment.

These people are good workers who tend to gain something from every task undertaken, even the most mundane chores. Yet they prefer to work at their own pace and will rebel furiously against outside intervention; indeed, some Roosters resent the imposition of any rules or discipline.

Roosters usually have to strive hard to achieve their goals for little comes to them easily. Sometimes they take on too much work, which they try to accommodate, often to the detriment of personal relationships. Efficiency tends to assume god-like proportions and many a Rooster will nag his or her less able partner. Other signs frequently accuse Roosters of being bossy — and they probably are — but they are also efficient!

Although Roosters know how to flirt if this is deemed necessary, they are inclined to take their loved ones for granted. Ever practical, once they have declared their affections they expect others to realise that this means for ever and they are usually faithful.

DOG

February 10th 1910 — January 29th 1911
January 28th 1922 — February 15th 1923
February 14th 1934 — February 3rd 1935
February 2nd 1946 — January 21st 1947
February 18th 1958 — February 7th 1959
February 6th 1970 — January 26th 1971
January 25th 1982 — February 12th 1983
February 10th 1994 — January 30th 1995

PIG

January 30th 1911 — February 17th 1912
February 16th 1923 — February 4th 1924
February 4th 1935 — January 23rd 1936
January 22nd 1947 — February 9th 1948
February 8th 1959 — January 27th 1960
January 27th 1971 — January 15th 1972
February 13th 1983 — February 1st 1984
January 31st 1995 — February 18th 1996

These faithful friends are definitely dog-like in nature and are therefore well worth cultivating. The Dog will be your most reliable ally, the steadfast worker or the pillar of the community. Fidelity is the watchword of these people; indeed, they are somewhat averse to change and caution often thwarts their ambition. So perhaps Dog personalities need to learn to be more adaptable, especially the traditionalists of the pack who tend to think that everything should stay the way it used to be.

They do, however, learn rather slowly, so others will need to exercise patience in regard to their failings; but they respond well to training and can achieve much if they receive the necessary encouragement. Dogs can, though, be a little too gullible, tending to take what others say literally, without question.

Usually very sociable, these creatures need a physical outlet for their feelings. They are sympathetic and forgiving of other people's misdemeanours and will gladly provide a comfortable shoulder to cry on should this be needed. If a Dog likes you, he or she will stand by you, regardless of circumstances; but if they do not, they will be highly critical and refuse to acknowledge any merit in your nature.

These charming folk thrive on encouragement which they really need in order to make their best achievements but some, unfortunately, have a poor self-image due to a lack of security in early life. Often, they will allow others to dominate them yet, if this domination is combined with love, will still endeavour to go on to greater things; they are very dependent on outside influences and will respond to the amount of praise or otherwise that they receive.

Dogs make worthy marriage partners who cherish their homes, their spouses and their children; even if not devastatingly romantic, they will rarely let anyone down.

Pigs enjoy a better reputation in China than they do in the Western world for they are considered to be home-lovers whose prime concern is for the welfare of their families. Although they may, of course, have careers, their main interest lies in the long-term benefits that come at the end of life.

Pigs want to do everything properly and to succeed on merit, then to look back on a life of attainment which has probably been achieved through great endeavour. Most of this breed would, in fact, take enormous pleasure and pride from knowing that they could leave their descendants a good inheritance and will willingly struggle to obtain this.

Meticulously tidy and efficient, they are always interested in making improvements and many of them are excellent craftsmen or avid do-it-yourselfers. They enjoy making others feel comfortable and some Pigs are drawn to the caring professions, such as medicine or nursing, while others will happily make careers in catering.

They have absolute faith in the ultimate good nature of humanity and will continually wait for this to manifest itself. Their tolerance seems limitless and they will stick by their friends or partners despite any weakness in their natures — and Pigs often do attract those with problems such as drink, drugs, gambling or infidelity. Pigs should perhaps learn to say "No" sometimes, to issue ultimatums to those who push their tolerance to the limits.

Oddly though, when Pigs look back on their lives they will mostly find that their faith has proved justified; perhaps the other signs discover their own best natures when confronted by the lowly Pig personality for, at the end of the day, it is hard not to be influenced by this creature's shining example.

THE 12 ANIMAL YEARS

Obviously, Chinese astrology is much more intricate than the preceding pages suggest. A fully detailed, individual chart can be erected, as with any other form of astrology. As space limitations prohibit any further examination on a personal level, it might be interesting to ascertain how any of us are likely to fare in a particular Animal Year. The following will perhaps provide you with an idea for the best course of action to pursue in the future as well as demonstrating how well you handled previous years.

Year of the Rat:
1900
1912
1924
1936
1948
1960
1972
1984
1996

This is a time of initiation, for taking chances or beginning a new course of action; anything is possible in a Rat year. Although hopes may not be realised immediately, you should remember that you are laying down foundations for the future. Now is the time to utilise previously neglected potential, to make the most of your abilities and talents, in order to revitalise your life. Everything is just below the surface so whatever is done this year will have wider implications in the future.

Year of the Ox:
1901
1913
1925
1937
1949
1961
1973
1985
1997

Ox years represent the stability that has been gained as a result of previous ideas or actions. If you have not already set things in motion, you may have to follow other people; as you have sown, so shall you reap! Ox years can be periods of consolidation or completion, perhaps in areas such as already discussed or in contracts or marriages that follow engagements. Only previously thought out matters will succeed; if you have been negligent in this respect, keep plans in abeyance until a better time.

Year of the Tiger:
1902
1914
1926
1938
1950
1962
1974
1986
1998

The Tiger often heralds a turbulent year when everything appears to be in a state of flux and one can only blindly hope that one is following the right manoeuvres. Intuitive folk may fare better than most because they will instinctively act in their own best interests without even realising that they are doing so. Some may make stunning achievements therefore, almost by accident, while others may sustain unexpected losses. We have little control of our actions in Tiger years and are often led by sheer impulse alone.

Year of the Horse:
1906
1918
1930
1942
1954
1966
1978
1990

Horse years could be termed 'building and preserving' years as one should never instigate major changes but continue only with very definite plans that have already been set in motion. If not working towards a particular goal or project, wait until a more forward thinking phase. Honesty and integrity assume importance during such years as sins are apt to be revealed publicly. Health may improve at such times if the correct course of action is followed; neglect could rebound adversely however.

Year of the Sheep:
1907
1919
1931
1943
1955
1967
1979
1991

Sheep years tend to work in favour of the masses for those in authority often display a humane attitude; alternatively, new discoveries in medicine or space research could take place. It is easy to start a new fashion in a Sheep year as where one leads many others will follow: enterprising subjects could benefit from such trends. Love usually remains on an even keel during such times, so Sheep years are ideal for getting married and settling down although they are not so helpful for those wishing to end liaisons.

Year of the Monkey:
1908
1920
1932
1944
1956
1968
1980
1992

Monkey years tend to be unpredictable so it is no use making far-reaching plans that may be subject to sudden change or disappointment. Enterprising souls who are ever ready to spot opportunity may make a quick killing in the business world, though benefits are unlikely to last long. Romance, too, could prove erratic and should not be relied upon, though flirtatious types will enjoy themselves! Those working in research could win recognition because others are likely to be open to new or unusual ideas.

Year of the Hare:
1903
1915
1927
1939
1951
1963
1975
1987
1999

The Hare can mark a period of peace and harmony. For those not too eager to stride forward immediately, these years are usually a time of steady progress when past efforts are seen to be rewarded. Considering others is important and those who do this are likely to fare best because opportunities will most likely arise in situations where self-aggrandisement is not actively sought. Family bonds are usually strengthened or extended in Hare years which are good times for buying property that will increase in value.

Year of the Dragon:
1904
1916
1928
1940
1952
1964
1976
1988
2000

What seemed impossible may become reality in a Dragon year for these are always stunning in effect; it is a time for conquering adversity for anyone willing to take a calculated risk. It is quite common to take chances in Dragon years but those who expect something for nothing should beware; Dragons have karmic connotations and may only provide tantalising glimpses of "what might have been." But this can be a tremendous time of discovery, so take definite steps to be different in some way.

Year of the Snake:
1905
1917
1929
1941
1953
1965
1977
1989

Snake years allow revision of previous events or decisions although they may hold some strange undercurrents. There may be a highly critical tone to such years and some may wish to examine their motives or standards. If there is an area of life that could do with improvement, this may be the time to voice an opinion but use subtlety if you are seeking approval from others; it pays to be forthright on occasion but usually it is better to wait for the reactions of others. Oddly, the most unexpected liaisons can be formed this year.

Year of the Rooster:
1909
1921
1933
1945
1957
1969
1981
1993

Rooster years are generally helpful to those who wish to advance their careers as efforts made in them will definitely be rewarded. Order is likely to be restored in those areas where chaos once reigned and other people may suddenly be much more amenable to ideas they had rejected previously. Secure relationships may meet with squalls through one partner suddenly asserting his or her independence. This is a year for accepting challenges and thus attaining success which seemed out of reach before.

Year of the Dog:
1910
1922
1934
1946
1958
1970
1982
1994

Faithfulness and honesty may be the best policy in Dog years because these are times for cautiously defending what you already have. Money should be invested safely, without thought for stupendous gain, this is not a good time to take a gamble. Property values may rise significantly yet many will see the wisdom of retaining what they have for a while longer. Marriages that are made in Dog years are likely to last for a lifetime because they will be founded on mutual trust and deep admiration.

Year of the Pig:
1911
1923
1935
1947
1959
1971
1983
1995

The Year of the Pig is the last in the cycle so is a time for tying up loose ends. It may represent the reaping of karmic benefits for earlier good deeds or, for those who have acted unwisely in the past, it may mark a phase of remorse or regret. But, irrespective of events during the last 12 years, this will be a time for reflection. This could signify a period of glory or for deciding what would be best for the future; it may even be a time for simply resting on one's laurels and enjoying one's just reward.

CHAPTER THREE

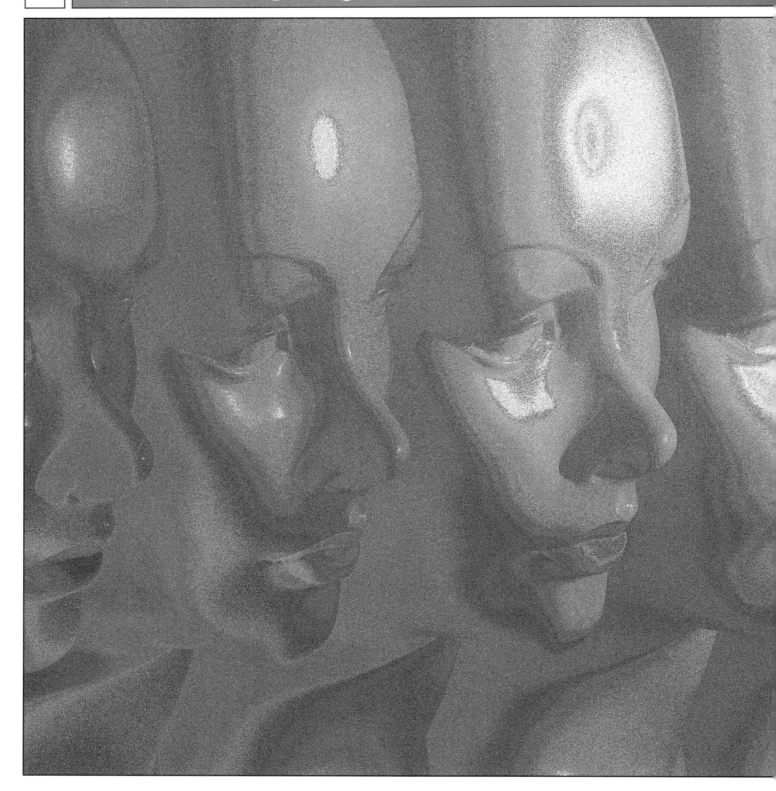

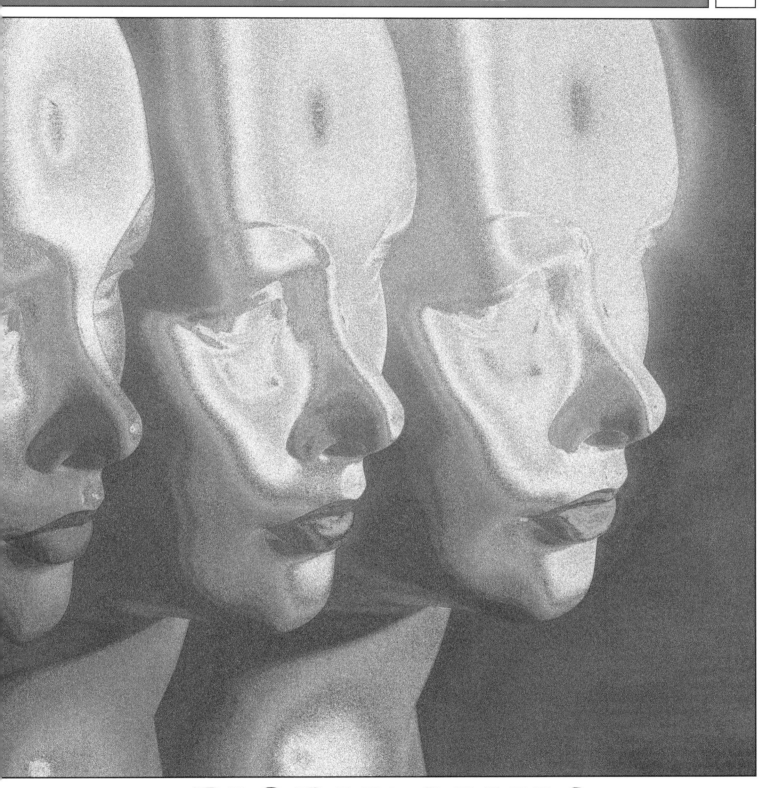

BIORHYTHMS

We all have good days and bad days. Some days are virtual disasters no matter what we do, feel or think, no matter how hard we try; then there are others when we emerge triumphant from everything we attempt.

None of us is exempt, we have all experienced these extremes over which we feel we have no, or very little, control. The question is why?

We must go back to the turn of the century, to Berlin, and in particular to Doctor Wilhelm Fliess, for the start of our explanation. A practising physician, he had noted these "on" and "off" days and decided to investigate. After much research and observation Fliess discovered that they occurred not only in rhythmic cycles but in definite, predictable patterns, nowadays known as physical and emotional cycles. Several years later, in the 1920s, an Austrian professor, Alfred Telscher, identified a third significant cycle, the intellectual, and biorhythms as we understand it today emerged as a separate field of study.

PSI — THE THREE CYCLES

Although the three biorhythm cycles are not the only ones we experience, they do influence our physical, emotional and intellectual well-being. It must be stressed at this point, however, that they have no direct cause and effect in themselves; each is subject to external factors happening around you in everyday life.

Fundamentally, biorhythms are a means of expressing continuous physiological changes which, when recognised and understood, can help you to plan your life more effectively. Each rhythm begins on the day you are born, follows its predetermined course throughout life and ceases only at death. Everyone has them and is subject to their influence although some people do not conform to the established patterns at all times.

As their names suggest, each rhythm affects your behaviour in a specific way:

The shortest of the three, the physical, has a duration of 23 days and controls strength, stamina, initiative, drive, confidence, energy, aggressiveness and courage.

The second cycle, the sensitivity or emotional, lasts for 28 days and determines moods, optimism, cheerfulness, social sense, creativity, well-being and, as its name implies, your emotional sensitivity.

The longest cycle, the intellectual, lasts 33 days and influences your powers of reason and perception, acuity, judgement, decision-making and common sense.

THE PHASES

Each rhythm has two stages or phases: the plus (positive or high phase) and the negative (minus or low).

When the physical cycle is in a plus phase you should be feeling in the pink; alert, perceptive and full of energy. A physical low denotes the reverse: lack of confidence, tiredness, little stamina and next to no drive.

A positive sensitivity rhythm suggests sociability, a good mood, a general sense of well-being in fact; whereas the low or negative stage implies a touchy, over-sensitive and moody phase.

An intellectual high means you should shine mentally; instinctively make the right decisions, display good common sense and above-average reasoning powers. When in its negative phase, though, you are more likely to make errors, lack co-ordination and be argumentative.

The day of transition from one phase to another is called a critical day. These change-over points are very important for it is then that you are most prone to accident, instability and error.

The biogram (right) shows that each rhythm has three critical days in its cycle, at the beginning, halfway through when it changes phase from positive to negative, and at the end of the cycle which is, of course, also the start of the next positive phase. It matters little which way the change-over occurs, whether from positive to negative or vice versa, either is a potentially hazardous period and you are advised to tread warily at these times.

During these periods of change-over, the critical days, we become vulnerable, temporarily off-balance and our normal reactions are slowed down; making us more prone to accident or error. The changeover period may extend up to 48 hours, so if you are aware of when these critical days are going to occur you can plan ahead effectively and, wherever necessary, make a simple adjustment.

CALCULATIONS

As all the cycles begin at the moment of birth, the first step is to calculate exactly how many days have elapsed since the day you were born to whatever date you wish to find out about. It is important to remember, though, to include your birthdate and the date in question in your calculations. This total is then divided by 23, 28 and 33 to establish what point has been reached in your physical, emotional and intellectual cycles, respectively.

In the sensitivity cycle the positive phase starts on day 1 and ends on day 14; the negative phase begins on day 15 and finishes on day 28; days 1 and 14/15 are therefore critical days. In the intellectual cycle, days 1 to 17 are in the plus stage; days 18 to 33 are in the minus phase; and the critical days are 1 and 17.

In the sensitivity cycle the positive phase starts on day 1 and ends on day 15; the negative phase begins on day 16 and finishes on day 28; days 1 and 15 are therefore critical days. In the intellectual cycle, days 1 to 17 are in the plus stage; days 18 to 33 are in the minus phase; and the critical days are 1 and 17.

If you don't have a pocket-calculator use the tables on pages 64 and 65 to work out the total number of days that have elapsed since your date of birth and the date for which you want to find out what is in store.

As an example, we will take someone born on September 8th 1965 and calculate the biorhythms for November 29th, 1989; for convenience, we will call our subject Jean.

On November 29th Jean would be 24 years old, plus some extra days. Therefore, using Table 1 we calculate:

$$20 \times 365 = 7300$$
$$+ 4 \times 365 = 1460$$
$$\text{DAYS } \underline{8760}$$

Turning to Table 2 we see that our subject will have lived through 6 Leap Years by the target date. This number must therefore be added to the running total in our sum:

$$8760 + 6$$
$$\text{DAYS } \underline{8766}$$

Table 3 shows us that November 29th is day number 333 and our subject's birthdate, September 8th, is day 251. Subtract one from the other and add the result to the running total, thus:

$$
\begin{array}{r}
333 \\
- 251 \\
\hline
82 \text{ DAYS} \\
82 \\
+ 8766 \\
\hline
= 8848 \text{ DAYS}
\end{array}
$$

So, we now know that by November 29th, 1989, 8848 days will have elapsed since Jean's birth. It only remains to add 1 day to this total to account for the target day itself (it is essential to remember always to do this) and we can calculate the exact position in each of the three biorhythms.

$$
\begin{array}{r}
1 \\
+ 8848 \\
\hline
\text{DAYS } 8849
\end{array}
$$

This final total can now be divided by 23 in order to determine the physical rhythm's phase on the target date. Thus:

$$
\begin{array}{r}
384 \text{ REMAINDER } 17 \\
23 \overline{| 8849}
\end{array}
$$

The whole figure represents the number of full cycles completed by November 29th and the remainder figure indicates the stage of the current cycle on that date. Jean's physical rhythm will, therefore, be in a negative phase on the target date.

Similarly, we divide 8849 by 28 to ascertain the state of the sensitivity cycle:

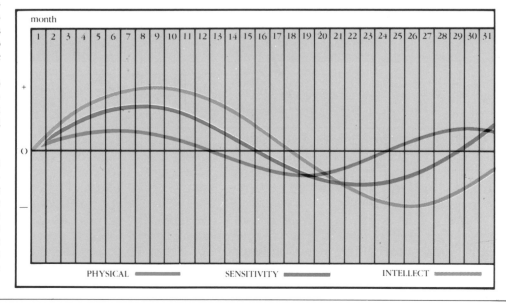

month
1 2 3 4 5 6 7 8 9 10 11 12 13 14 15 16 17 18 19 20 21 22 23 24 25 26 27 28 29 30 31

PHYSICAL ▬▬▬   SENSITIVITY ▬▬▬   INTELLECT ▬▬▬

$$\begin{array}{r} 316 \text{ REMAINDER } \mathbf{1} \\ \hline 28 \overline{)8849} \end{array}$$

Jean's sensitivity rhythm has, therefore, completed 316 full cycles and, as the remainder figure is 1, is in day 1 of a new positive phase; in fact it is a critical day.

Again, for the intellectual cycle, we divide 8849 by 33:

$$\begin{array}{r} 268 \text{ REMAINDER } \mathbf{5} \\ \hline 33 \overline{)8849} \end{array}$$

This shows that 268 full cycles have been completed and the intellectual rhythm is at day 5, a positive phase.

So, to sum up, on November 29th, 1989 our subject's full biorhythmic status would be: physical cycle day 17, negative mode; sensitivity cycle day 1, the start of a positive phase and a critical day; intellectual cycle day 5, again positive.

Having completed our calculations using simple arithmetic, we will do the same exercise using a pocket-calculator as this is very quick and easy to do and reduces the possibility of error. If we use the same birth and target dates as before it will eliminate the need to refer again to Tables 1, 2 and 3.

We have already calculated that 8849 days will have elapsed between our subject's birth date, September 8th, 1965 and the date for which we want to know her biorhythmic status, November 29th, 1989 (remember, this figure *includes* the target date itself). So, using your calculator, simply divide this grand total by 23, 28 and 33 to ascertain the physical, sensitivity and intellectual cycles:

$$8849 \div 23 = 384 \cdot 73913 \ (P)$$
$$8849 \div 28 = 316 \cdot 03571 \ (S)$$
$$8849 \div 33 = 268 \cdot 15151 \ (I)$$

Ignoring the whole numbers, which represent the numbers of full cycles completed, if the figures after the decimal point are multiplied by the number of days in each cycle we can establish the exact phase of all three rhythms:

$$73913 \times 23 = 16 \cdot 99999;$$
to the nearest whole number: **17**

$$03571 \times 28 = 0 \cdot 99988;$$
to the nearest whole number: **1**

$$15151 \times 33 = 4 \cdot 99983;$$
to the nearest whole number: **5**

So, the physical cycle is at day 17, in a negative phase; the sensitivity cycle on day 1, a critical day, is in a positive phase; the intellectual cycle on day 5 is also in a positive phase.

Now you know how to compute biorhythms for any day you choose, whether for yourself or others, you may wish to draw up your own biograms. However, whether you decide to devise your own graphs, print them out on a computer, purchase a biorhythmic calculator or whatever, the obvious next step is to make use of your biorhythms.

Planning ahead

Biorhythms provide an answer to why we have on or off days; they help us to understand why we feel as we do at certain times, they reveal our potential in specific areas of human behaviour. And if we know what to expect, on which days we are most likely to feel a sudden surge of energy, be particularly alert or experience a lessening of drive, it makes it that much easier to cope. We can plan our days more effectively and, wherever necessary, make minor adjustments in order to make the best of our potential.

As each of the three biorhythmic cycles may be in any of three stages — positive, negative or critical — on a given date, it follows that there are 27 different combinations or permutations that can be experienced at any one time. Research has shown that it is possible to predict what may be expected during any of these basic combinations, as the following brief assessments will demonstrate.

For quick and easy reference, each has been keyed:

H indicates a positive or plus phase

L indicates a negative or minus phase

X refers to a critical day, the change-over point

The three key letters always appear in the same order: the first refers to the physical cycle, the second to the sensitivity and the third to the intellectual.

Once you have calculated your biorhythms for a particular day, all you have to do, therefore, is to look for the key letters in the correct sequence and then read the accompanying text. If, for instance, the physical cycle is in a negative phase, the sensitivity cycle is positive and the intellectual critical, you would look for the key LHX.

So, go ahead, now is the time to make the most of your potential!

Right: Biogram for Jean, Born on Wed 8. Sep 1965

CURVE POSITION MEANINGS:
CRITICAL DAYS ON THE BASE-LINE

P = PHYSICAL STATE
E = EMOTIONAL BALANCE
M = INTELLECT PERCEPTION

Left: A complete biorhythm chart or biogram for a month. The red line is the physical cycle, the blue line the sensitivity or emotional cycle and the green line the intellectual cycle. Note the critical days in the sensitivity cycle on the 1st, 15th and 29th. The intellectual cycle shows critical days on the 4th and 20th; the physical critical days are the 11th and 23rd.

If you wish to draw up your biorhythms it is probably most convenient, though not strictly necessary, to do your calculations for the first day of any month and carefully note the day number and phase of each cycle on that date. Then mark in the critical days for each cycle in turn (it is easiest to deal with one rhythm at a time to avoid confusion), making sure to note whether these rhythms are changing from plus to minus or vice versa. Next, draw in the curves between these points using a protractor or any other regularly curved object.

If you choose three distinctly different coloured pens or pencils to draw up the graphs it will be much easier to distinguish the three cycles at a glance.

NOVEMBER 1989					LOW	BASE	HIGH
WED	1.NOV	1989	CRITICAL		I	EP	MI
THU	2.NOV	1989			I	P I E	MI
FRI	3.NOV	1989			I	P I E	M I
SAT	4.NOV	1989			I	P I	E M I
SUN	5.NOV	1989			I	P I	ME I
MON	6.NOV	1989			I P	I M	E I
TUE	7.NOV	1989			I P	I M	E I
WED	8.NOV	1989	CRITICAL		I P	IM	E I
THU	9.NOV	1989			I P	M I	E I
FRI	10.NOV	1989			I	P M I	E I
SAT	11.NOV	1989			I	M I	E I
SUN	12.NOV	1989			I	M P I	E I
MON	13.NOV	1989	CRITICAL		I	M P E	I
TUE	14.NOV	1989			I M	I E	I
WED	15.NOV	1989	CRITICAL		IM	E P	I
THU	16.NOV	1989			IM	E I	P I
FRI	17.NOV	1989	CRITICAL		IM	E I	P I
SAT	18.NOV	1989			IM	E I	P I
SUN	19.NOV	1989			I M E	I	P I
MON	20.NOV	1989			I	M I	P I
TUE	21.NOV	1989			I E M	I	P I
WED	22.NOV	1989			I E	M I	P I
THU	23.NOV	1989			I E	M I	P I
FRI	24.NOV	1989	CRITICAL		I E	M IP	I
SAT	25.NOV	1989	CRITICAL		I E	P M	I
SUN	26.NOV	1989			I	E P I M	I
MON	27.NOV	1989			I	PE I	M I
TUE	28.NOV	1989			I	P E I	M I
WED	29.NOV	1989	CRITICAL		I P	E	M I
THU	30.NOV	1989			I P	I E	M I

L L L With all three rhythms in the negative stage you won't feel much like doing anything at all. So don't push it; taking the initiative today simply won't pay off. Best just to relax and let the day pass as it will. You could perhaps tackle a few of those little jobs you are usually too busy to contemplate, such as sewing up the hem of a skirt or slacks, repot a favourite houseplant, tidy the desk drawers or whatever; but don't attempt anything that requires too much effort. You could, of course, simply watch television or read a book.

L H H Unfortuantely, the low phase of your physical rhythm means that you will not have the necessary stamina to support your emotional and intellectual highs: the mind may be willing but the flesh certainly won't! So resist the challenge of heavy physical activities and do not delude yourself that you can cope or you will be disappointed. Avoid frustration by concentrating your best efforts where they will be most effective; bring the office accounts up to date, plan your holidays, revise for an exam — mentally you're in fine fettle.

L L X This is an accident-prone day. Physically and emotionally at a low ebb, your thinking may not be entirely clear either and it would be only too easy to make a mistake in an unguarded moment. You are probably not feeling your best and may find yourself becoming upset too easily. Try to keep a low profile at home and at work, concentrate on recharging your batteries and avoid any potentially hazardous situations if you possibly can. For best results, don't initiate action; relax and just let things happen as they will.

H L L Physically you should feel fine, ready to tackle most things. Your emotional and mental rhythms are down, though, so don't trust your judgement, it may be faulty. Put off important decisions until another time if you can and think twice before committing yourself, especially to long-term arrangements. Try to curb impulsiveness too or you may regret it later. It would be best to find a suitable outlet for your physical energy — dig over the garden or saw some wood, perhaps; get some exercise playing with the kids or take the dog for a run.

L L H You will be better off on your own today. You will not be feeling very sociable and even less inclined to be physically active. Curl up in front of the television or read a good book; try to relax but keep your mind occupied. Above all, try to avoid confrontation of any kind because you are emotionally vulnerable today and therefore liable to come off worst in arguments. If you can't avoid company at home, perhaps you could go for a gentle stroll down by the river, find an amusing film to see or visit a museum.

L H X Although you will most likely feel out of sorts physically, you should be able to carry the day emotionally. Your intellectual cycle is in a critical stage, though, so don't make major decisions as your judgement could be clouded. Think carefully before taking action, exercise more caution than usual, especially if driving or using machinery, as this is another accident-prone day when there is an element of risk. Don't take on more than you can cope with comfortably, avoid stressful situations and seek the company of close friends.

H H L Emotionally and physically you are raring to go and will probably be feeling on top of the world. However, your judgement is likely to be poor today so, no matter how attractive propositions may seem, weigh them up carefully before taking action, particularly if big business or heavy expenditure is involved. Why not take advantage of how you feel and go out and enjoy yourself; take the family to the seaside, go for a country hike, play football with the boys, entertain a few friends to dinner or go out to a party or disco.

L H L You may not have too much energy to expend today and may find it difficult to concentrate for long periods, nonetheless you should be feeling quite sociable, probably affable too, and will be good company. Let others make the decisions and set the pace, just go along for the ride and enjoy whatever is on offer. If you are the creative type you could come into your own today; so why not get out that sketch-pad, decorate a cake, do some embroidery, or whatever else takes your fancy but requires little exertion.

H L X Another intellectually critical day when it may be difficult to think straight. You may find your reserves of energy are low too, making it a potentially hazardous time. Neither of these two factors combines well with an emotional rhythm that is in a negative phase as this implies irritability. So try to take things easy, exercise caution and avoid getting yourself into situations that may prove too demanding; you won't find it easy to cope. Best to confine your activities to well-known routines; this is no time to be adventurous.

H H H This is quite clearly your day: all three rhythms are in a positive phase so nothing should be beyond you. Make the most of your capabilities and grasp opportunities as they arise. Take the initiative, go all out to obtain your objectives because today's achievements should have long-term effects and could prove profitable. Decisive action will pay dividends now so it's an excellent time for important business meetings, taking examinations (even a driving test), attending a job interview, competing in sports, etc.

H L H You should excel at all physical and intellectual pursuits but may not feel inclined to be very sociable. As you will most probably find the company of others irritating, it would be advisable to avoid group encounters and take a lone wolf approach to activities. You are, though, in a decisive and energetic mood, so keep on the go if you can. This is a good time to sort out business problems or plan future strategy; or why not go for a long drive or sail a dinghy. Be adventurous and climb a mountain — you could today!

H H X Take extreme care today, you will be brimming over with confidence — too much, it really isn't justified. You will also be feeling quite energetic, ready for almost anything, but be warned, your mental powers may not be all you would like to believe because this is an intellectually critical day. Monitor your decisions carefully, you could make silly mistakes if you allow your enthusiasm to run away with you. And, whatever you do, don't take chances; this is most decidedly not a day on which to take a gamble of any sort.

L X L Yet another accident-prone day. Hasty decisions made now will cause greater problems later, so do try to think things through before taking action; better still, just lie low until you are better able to cope. Mentally and physically at a low ebb, you will only become irritable if or when things go wrong and this could lead to some very uncharacteristic behaviour on your part. This is not exactly a day when you are likely to win friends and influence people! Best to let others get on with it, don't try to interfere, let the world go by.

X L L A potentially hazardous day when you are likely to be feeling so down in the dumps that you may fail to recognise the dangers until it is too late. Exercise caution, think before you act, and don't be tempted to take on more than you can cope with at this time; much better to defer important matters till a later date if this is at all possible. But if you already have commitments that must be met, take things one step at a time, don't be rushed into making silly mistakes which will only have to be rectified later.

L X X Caution is today's watchword: this is a particularly accident-prone day. The unwary could meet problems head-on simply because they can't be bothered to think; so do check and double check for safety. This is definitely a time to lie low, you aren't likely to achieve anything worthwhile in any event, so it would be best by far just to relax and put your feet up. Even reading could prove too much of an effort, you are so below par all round, try listening to music instead; but don't allow yourself to wallow in self-pity.

L X H Over-confidence is the bugbear today. Although your intellectual rhythm is in a positive phase, your physical cycle is not, and it's an emotionally critical day. So you may be a bit too sensitive and could easily get into silly arguments where you say things you don't really mean. It would be for the best if you could avoid others today and seek the company of a good book instead. Or why not put some of that mental energy to practical use and devise a new stock-taking system or try your hand at computer programming?

X L H There is some danger of minor accidents if you are careless, especially as your reactions may not be as quick as usual. You could feel a bit tired or depressed and inclined to lose patience with others' stupidity, so best to keep yourself to yourself if possible. Take advantage of your mental high and do some serious studying or put time to use by making plans for the future; you may not feel like doing much today but at least you could prepare for tomorrow. If this sounds too much like hard work, settle down with a crossword.

H X X The biggest danger today is that you will not be aware of your own limitations. You'll have loads of energy, may even feel full of confidence and enthusiasm, yet your judgement will be impaired and you are liable to make gross errors if you are not careful. So do try to think — not once but twice — before rushing into action; if you heed this advice there is no reason why you shouldn't achieve at least some of your objectives. Try to be guided by others who may be thinking more clearly than you and you could enjoy yourself.

H X L Physically, you should be feeling great; mentally you won't be as alert as usual. It is an emotionally critical day so take care, a certain amount of instability is indicated. You may well find yourself at odds with those around you and are likely to make errors of judgement; so don't make decisions you will regret later. Taking physical exercise will burn off some of that surplus energy, but remember that it is a potentially accident-prone day, don't do anything that involves an element of risk.

X H H You will be feeling in the pink, full of confidence and energy, ready to face any challenge. The only danger lies in too much physical activity, you could overdo things and end up falling over your own two feet! Try to keep your enthusiasm within reasonable bounds and you could have a really enjoyable time. It's an ideal day for seeing the sights, going on a family outing or entertaining friends. Come to that, you'll really be on your mettle, so have a go at winning that business contract; or sell yourself — ask the boss for a raise.

X L X You may have a problem coping with your feelings today. You will not be at your best and could find it hard to deal with others who either can't or won't share your point of view. Don't allow irritation to lead to confrontation, try to realise that this is a passing phase and that everything will seem better tomorrow. Put off making major decisions and confine yourself to getting through the day without upsetting too many people — including yourself. Deal with routine matters that won't require too much attention to detail.

H X H You should be feeling very confident, able to achieve all your objectives with ease, and you'll have the energy needed to put plans into action. Your emotional cycle is in a critical phase, however, so you may be a bit too sensitive to atmosphere and to others. Don't overreact to criticism and fly off the handle without real reason and watch out for carelessness, it could lead to accidents. Set personal feelings aside and knuckle down to serious business; you could get a lot done today if you set your mind to it.

X H L Try not to rush in where angels fear to tread in your eagerness to please; rashness will only lead to mistakes that may be difficult to rectify afterwards. You will not be very clear-headed today and your body will be even less inclined to perform properly; so watch out for accidents, you are liable to be unusually clumsy. Best to stick to those activities that do not call for good co-ordination; skill and judgement are not on the agenda today. You should be feeling cheerful and sociable though, so spend some time with friends.

X H X A super abundance of confidence could mean that you will fail to spot the danger signals and rush headlong into disaster if you are not very careful. You may feel able to take on the whole world single-handed but your confidence belies your capabilities, for now anyway. Don't rely on your own judgement, it could be faulty, listen to those who may be able to see the way ahead more clearly and you should avoid the worst pitfalls. Stick to the tried and tested path today, this is not the time to attempt anything new; don't take risks.

X X H Above average high spirits coupled with an exaggerated sense of physical well-being could lead to accident or injury if not carefully controlled. The problem arises because you are unlikely to make due allowance for the possibility of error, so be warned. But if you can keep your enthusiasm within bounds you should be able to make the most of your potential. This is an excellent time for the enterprising business person to initiate schemes that require the support of others for you'll be at your most persuasive now.

X X L A difficult day when surplus energy and confidence combine poorly with mental lethargy; you may be so slow to recognise the potential dangers that you will not react quickly enough to avoid them all. You will feel off-balance and others will find your moodiness difficult to cope with, so curb your tongue and temper or you could become involved in disputes over trifles. Relieve the tensions of the day in whatever way you find most effective, whether this entails a vigorous work-out at the gym or a luxurious bubble-bath.

X X X Extreme caution is advised. You will most probably be very jumpy and on edge, inclined to fly off the handle at the slightest provocation — real or imagined; just stay as cool, calm and collected as you can. Don't be tempted to take risks, either in business dealings or more personal matters. This is an exceptionally hazardous day, fraught with pitfalls for the unwary, so take care in everything you do and opt out of any decision-making. There is one consolation, if could not happen every day of the week!

Below: This table will help you calculate the number of days that have elapsed since birth quickly. Where the exact number of years required is not listed, simply combine two figures to obtain the desired total.

1 × 365 = 365	10 × 365 = 3650
2 × 365 = 730	20 × 365 = 7300
3 × 365 = 1095	30 × 365 = 10950
4 × 365 = 1460	40 × 365 = 14600
5 × 365 = 1825	50 × 365 = 18250
6 × 365 = 2190	60 × 365 = 21900
7 × 365 = 2555	70 × 365 = 25550
8 × 365 = 2920	80 × 365 = 29200
9 × 365 = 3285	90 × 365 = 32850

Below: The Leap Years since 1756 when Great Britain adopted the Gregorian Calendar in favour of the Julian which was still in force up to September 2nd that year.

1756	1804	1852	1904	1952	2000
1760	1808	1856	1908	1956	2004
1764	1812	1860	1912	1960	2008
1768	1816	1864	1916	1964	2012
1772	1820	1868	1920	1968	2016
1776	1824	1872	1924	1972	2020
1780	1828	1876	1928	1976	2024
1784	1832	1880	1932	1980	2028
1788	1836	1884	1936	1984	2032
1792	1840	1888	1940	1988	2036
1796	1844	1892	1944	1992	2040
	1848	1896	1948	1996	

BIORHYTHMS

THE NUMBER OF EACH DAY THROUGHOUT THE YEAR, CALCULATED PROGRESSIVELY.

DAY	JANUARY	FEBRUARY	MARCH	APRIL	MAY	JUNE	JULY	AUGUST	SEPTEMBER	OCTOBER	NOVEMBER	DECEMBER
1	1	32	60	91	121	152	182	213	244	274	305	335
2	2	33	61	92	122	153	183	214	245	275	306	336
3	3	34	62	93	123	154	184	215	246	276	307	337
4	4	35	63	94	124	155	185	216	247	277	308	338
5	5	36	64	95	125	156	186	217	248	278	309	339
6	6	37	65	96	126	157	187	218	249	279	310	340
7	7	38	66	97	127	158	188	219	250	280	311	341
8	8	39	67	98	128	159	189	220	251	281	312	342
9	9	40	68	99	129	160	190	221	252	282	313	343
10	10	41	69	100	130	161	191	222	253	283	314	344
11	11	42	70	101	131	162	192	223	254	284	315	345
12	12	43	71	102	132	163	193	224	255	285	316	346
13	13	44	72	103	133	164	194	225	256	286	317	347
14	14	45	73	104	134	165	195	226	257	287	318	348
15	15	46	74	105	135	166	196	227	258	288	319	349
16	16	47	75	106	136	167	197	228	259	289	320	350
17	17	48	76	107	137	168	198	229	260	290	321	351
18	18	49	77	108	138	169	199	230	261	291	322	352
19	19	50	78	109	139	170	200	231	262	292	323	353
20	20	51	79	110	140	171	201	232	263	293	324	354
21	21	52	80	111	141	172	202	233	264	294	325	355
22	22	53	81	112	142	173	203	234	265	295	326	356
23	23	54	82	113	143	174	204	235	266	296	327	357
24	24	55	83	114	144	175	205	236	267	297	328	358
25	25	56	84	115	145	176	206	237	268	298	329	359
26	26	57	85	116	146	177	207	238	269	299	330	360
27	27	58	86	117	147	178	208	239	270	300	331	361
28	28	59	87	118	148	179	209	240	271	301	332	362
29	29		88	119	149	180	210	241	272	302	333	363
30	30		89	120	150	181	211	242	273	303	334	364
31	31		90		151		212	243		304		365

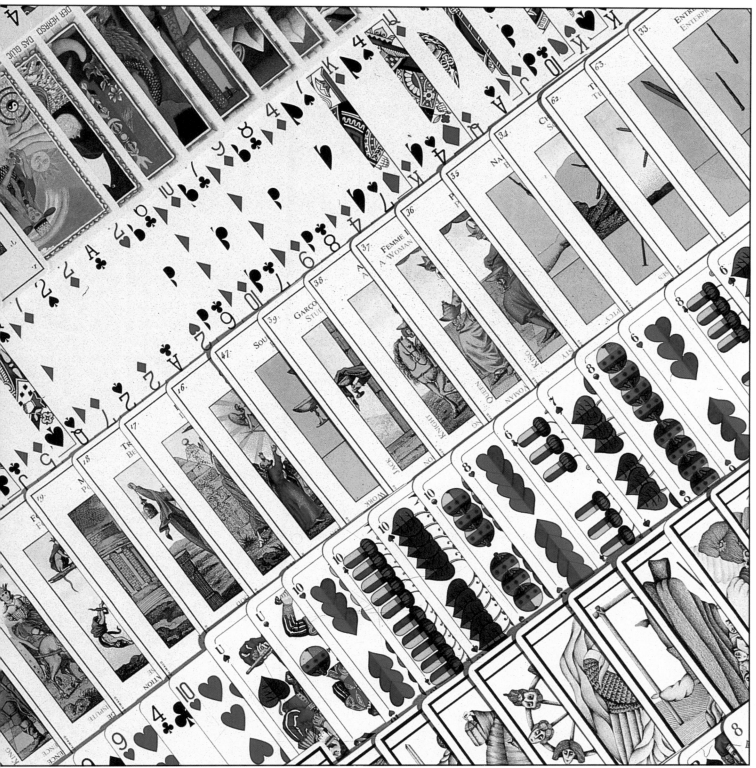

CARDS

Cartomancy is reading the future with cards, either Tarot, or what we now usually refer to as ordinary playing cards. No one knows for certain which came first or, indeed, when or where packs of cards originated. The earliest known references to cards of any kind date back to the late fourteenth century when card-playing was banned. In fact, cards seem to have had rather a chequered early history and were frequently the victim of State or Church decrees and edicts forbidding their use, along with other games of chance.

However, despite their controversial and hazy beginnings, records show that cards were not intended solely for amusement but were used for instructive purposes too, usually by children or those who could not read. Nowadays many people recognise their usefulness as an effective and easily accessible means of foretelling the future.

THESE REFER MAINLY TO PRACTICAL MATTERS OF ALL KINDS, INCLUDING BUSINESS AFFAIRS.

Success; either a financial gain of some kind or public recognition if the querent's position makes this probable. Whatever the case, expect good news concerning money, perhaps due to a legacy or gamble that has come off; or an improvement in personal status as a result of past efforts.

We know that cards have been used extensively as a means of divination for centuries and their basic symbolism has remained virtually unchanged for over 500 years in spite of the vagaries of fashion and the personal tastes of the artists and designers who have modified or embellished them during that time.

Tarot cards, with their colourful allegorical illustrations are perhaps more readily associated with arcane or occult knowledge than the less decorative images of playing cards and some people regard the former with a degree of suspicious awe. Yet playing cards, too, are inherently symbolic and in some ways it is possibly easier to recognise the basic correspondences than it is in a 78-card Tarot deck divided into Major and Minor Arcana.

There are, for instance, 52 cards in a modern pack of playing cards and this fact immediately puts one in mind of the number of weeks in a year; the deck's four suits relate to the four seasons and the four elements; each suit comprises 13 cards and there are the same number of Lunar months in a year; while the 12 court cards correspond to the Solar cycle of 12 months, 12 zodiacal signs, and so on. Even the two colours for the suits, red and black, reflect the quality of nature: the Yang and the Yin, masculine and femine, positive and negative, active and passive, day and night, etc.

Playing cards may be more familiar to most people than Tarot cards yet they contain as much hidden symbolism and can be used like any other divinatory tool to heighten one's awareness and thus help develop natural but perhaps latent resources of sensitivity and intuition.

READING THE CARDS

As should now be obvious, each suit is associated with a different aspect of life; the court cards generally refer to people or their thoughts and the pip cards signify actual events, situations, changes in circumstances, potentials and possibilities. Each card has a specific meaning which relates to its numerical or face value as well as the suit to which it belongs and once you are familiar with these you are ready to start reading the cards.

Sometimes a significator will be used to represent the enquirer or querent as this can

Business prospects look rosy, especially if you are offered the chance to become a partner in a going concern. Promotion — or at least a raise — is on the cards for employees. And the unemployed can expect a job offer in the near future. New friends could aid your success.

Minor worries or delays are likely if you allow someone of the opposite sex to interfere in your affairs. However, if you manage to avoid such an eventuality, the outlook is encouraging and success should be within your grasp. Take legal advice if necessary.

If considering a new business venture with friends or associates, this should prove profitable as long as no financial gambles are taken. If you are thinking about affairs of the heart, accept an invitation to a social occasion that you have been hesitant about as this could lead to love.

There is a danger that ignoring the wishes or feelings of others will result in loss of some kind. This could mean the end of a friendship or business partnership, so take care. If caution is exercised, though, the outlook is decidedly rosier and you could make new contacts.

THE SUIT OF DIAMONDS RELATES MOSTLY TO FINANCES, ALSO MATTERS OF PRESTIGE AND INFLUENCE.

Exciting and joyful news is forecast; perhaps an unexpected gift or small monetary windfall. This card may signify a marriage proposal for a female querent or a beneficial business proposition for a male. It can also refer to a successful examination result.

Although this may mark the end of a close personal relationship, it also holds out the prospect of a new romance or the healing of a rift between partners who have quarrelled recently. A gift from a loved one could aid reconciliation. If divorced, remarriage is a possibility.

Not a very auspicious card for it warns against taking risks of any kind, especially financial gambles. Guard against malicious gossip too, as this could mar business prospects. Best to avoid becoming involved in new projects until the outlook is rosier.

A happy augury, particularly for the very young or elderly. A business trip or holiday could result in a romantic meeting which proves enduring; or there is a possibility of a marriage with someone from abroad. Not a bad time for a little flutter either.

Opportunity is the watchword here. If money has been an inhibiting factor, preventing the implementation of long-term plans, you should soon have the wherewithal to turn the dream into reality. A change of job or residence is likely, perhaps both, or a new romance.

This signals a temporary setback that calls for a degree of caution. Do not rely too heavily on others for help as friendships may be under a bit of strain at this time. Resources look a little rocky too, so take care to budget wisely or it may prove impossible to meet unexpected bills.

A happy omen signifying a new and lasting relationship after a broken love affair. Or perhaps remarriage for someone who is divorced or widowed. At the very least, this card signifies a marriage proposal or the offer of a partnership that will prove very beneficial.

Misfortune or loss could result from another's deceit or trickery, so beware of false friends or shady deals. A time to be doubly cautious in business affairs and to read the small print in legal documents very carefully; if in doubt, seek professional advice even if this means delays.

A social gathering or chance meeting could lead to a happy union that will bring benefits to both parties. Often this card refers to a financially and emotionally rewarding marriage but can also signify a successful business partnership. In either case, it points to improvements.

A very happy omen signifying good fortune and improved circumstances. Even if other cards in the spread do not bode so well, this card's influence will act as a mitigating factor. It signals unexpected money coming your way or perhaps a profitable journey.

A kind and reliable friend of either sex who has your interests very much at heart. This person is willing and able to help the questioner and, in the case of a female, could be an admirer. This card also refers to trivial annoyances that can safely be ignored as they will soon fade.

A well-intentioned and warm-hearted woman of middle years who offers comfort as well as advice and support. If the questioner is male, this may refer to his wife or close confidante; for a female enquirer, it usually signifies her mother or a close friend.

A kind and helpful friend who plays a supportive role; probably a relative of a female enquirer or a work colleague if the questioner is male. Reliable and responsible, this is probably a professional man who can offer practical help as well as sound advice.

help focus the interpreter's faculties on the person concerned when considering the various aspects of a divinatory spread. One of the court cards is normally chosen for this purpose and the selection is based on the age, sex and physical characteristics or temperament of the querent.

AGE/GENDER

King
A mature man
Queen
A mature woman
Jack
A young person of either sex

CHARACTERISTICS

Clubs
People with rich brown or red hair, ruddy complexions and brown or hazel eyes; energetic, lively personalities.
Diamonds
Very fair people with blonde or white hair, pale skins and light blue or grey eyes; cool, confident, sophisticated types.
Hearts
Light brown or auburn-haired people with fair, pinkish complexions and blue, grey or hazel eyes; warm, friendly folk.
Spades
Sallow-complexioned people with dark brown or black hair and dark eyes; powerful, influential types with strong characters.

If the age or sex of the enquirer is unknown to the reader, as is possible when doing a postal reading for instance, the Ace may be used as a significator; the nature of the enquiry will dictate the suit selected: Hearts for emotional matters, Clubs for business affairs, etc.

Whether or not a significator is used, there is a traditional method of selecting and laying out the cards for a reading. This procedure is designed to put both interpreter and querent in a suitable frame of mind by focusing attention on the matter at hand. So, even if you eventually devise your own system, the following may well help you to get started.

First, as mentioned earlier, the interpreter should shuffle the deck to ensure that the cards are free of any previous associations before placing them on the table. If a significator is to be used, it should be selected at this point and placed to one side and the rest of the cards put, face down, in the centre of

A card of change; for good or ill depending on other cards in the spread. A possible new love affair may meet with disapproval from relatives or friends but will nonetheless bring happiness to the participants. Any potentially tricky situation that does arise can be handled with tact.

Friction is in the air, so relationships are likely to be under strain. Caution is therefore advised as a generally uncooperative attitude could lead to domestic disputes or severed business partnerships. Litigation is on the cards too, though this may ultimately be advantageous.

An encouraging card heralding improvements all round, especially if there has been a certain amount of stress recently. Current worries or difficulties should shortly fade away, leaving the way clear to further ambitions. Friends could prove unexpectedly helpful and supportive.

A fortunate omen signalling business success and marital happiness. New ventures are well favoured, whether on the business or domestic front, so be prepared to grasp opportunities as they arise; this is an ideal time to make long-term commitments. This card sometimes presages a birth.

A time to think carefully before you act as far as financial matters are concerned; if you do, the result should be profitable. An unexpected journey could lead to romance and eventual marriage. Future prospects are certainly very encouraging.

A warning against another's dishonesty; so don't believe everything you are told and beware of shady deals. News brought by a relative could prove a bit disappointing. However, none of this is very serious and if any difficulties do arise they will quickly fade away.

This card represents a challenge from a female known to the questioner and best advice is to avoid confrontation if possible. Men should not allow a woman to interfere in their business affairs as this could mar their prospects; women should beware jealousy.

This usually refers to a strong character, probably a professional man who is in a position to help or hinder. It may signify an unfaithful lover or husband for a female or an important business proposition for a male. In either case, ambitions may be thwarted.

THIS SUIT RELATES TO ALL EMOTIONAL MATTERS; LOVE, ROMANCE AND AFFECTION.

This signifies home and domestic affairs as well as highlighting emotional matters. Often, this card heralds news from a family member or friend who has been out of touch for some time. An end to family squabbles is indicated and a change of residence is highly likely.

the table. The enquirer is then invited to pick up the pile and shuffle them while concentrating on the matter that is uppermost in his/her mind at the time of the reading.

When he or she feels ready to do so, the querent should place the cards back on the table and cut them into three piles towards the interpreter with his or her left hand: literally and figuratively the one closest to the heart. The interpreter completes the cut by placing the first pile on top of the second and the third on top of that before spreading the cards face downwards across the table with their edges overlapping slightly. Once this is done, the querent is invited to select the required number of cards, one by one, with his or her left hand and give them to the reader who places them in a pile, still face down, in strict order. Any surplus cards can now be removed from the table.

If a significator is used it can be added to the selected cards by the querent at this stage; the easiest way is simply to fan the cards out carefully so as not to change their order and ask him or her to place the significator among them wherever they choose before replacing the pile on the table. The cards are now ready to be laid out but, remember, they should either be dealt from the bottom or the whole pile turned face up and dealt from the top if they are to retain the correct sequence.

The only thing left to do is to select a suitable spread for your reading. Which one you choose will depend largely on what sort of reading is required: do you want an overall picture or do you wish to focus on one particular situation, problem or 'question? Once this point is clear in your mind you will be able to select the spread that best fits your requirements and personal preferences. Most people will use fewer cards to answer a simple Yes/No question than for a full reading, but there are no hard and fast rules.

Some interpreters, for instance, use more than one spread during the course of a reading; others may use the same method of laying out the cards each time but ask the querent to shuffle, cut and select cards more than once or to choose further cards and add these to the original lay-out in order to clarify one particular aspect of the reading. Again, some may choose a spread that utilises the entire deck while others will use as few as

Beware of letting others take advantage of your generous nature or you may be out of pocket in more ways than one. On a more positive note, news concerning a youngster will bring pleasure or you could hear of a wedding as romance is on the cards.

Plans could fail to materialise due to the unreliability of others; beware of get-rich-quick schemes or shady business deals; keep your options open but be prepared for disappointment. Concentrate on domestic issues and spend some time enjoying familiar company.

Travel and romance seem to be linked, so even a business trip could have surprising results! Or perhaps a social invitation will lead to a romantic meeting which will develop into a long-term relationship. Heart matters are highlighted, and are coupled with good fortune.

Often referred to as the wish card, this is a very auspicious omen signifying that whatever is uppermost in the querent's mind will have a successful outcome. Even if matters have not been too rosy lately, they will certainly improve shortly, so take heed.

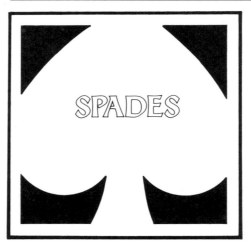

CHALLENGE IS THE KEYWORD. THIS MAY MEAN OBSTACLES OR PROBLEMS THAT MUST BE OVERCOME: BUT CAN EQUALLY REFER TO OPPORTUNITY.

A fresh start is in the offing as long as the querent is willing to face up to reality and discard that which is outworn in his/her life. A time to take stock, to resolve outstanding problems or to sort out past differences and begin anew. Once this is done, the future can be faced with confidence.

Expect delays and difficulties, especially on the business front. Don't be too discouraged though as this is only a temporary setback that can be overcome with perseverance. Effort will be rewarded in the long run, thus changing present apparent failure into success.

Misunderstandings are likely, so try to curb your tongue and temper until the situation is calmer. Also, put off major business decisions if at all possible as judgement maybe impaired at the moment. Don't allow imagination to make mountains out of molehills.

There is a danger that too much reliance on others could lead to disappointment as there is an aura of deceit around. So do check over any documentation carefully and make sure to read the small print before signing business contracts or agreements.

Not a very auspicious card this, for it warns of disappointment, even loss. Best to accept that some situations are simply beyond one's control, no matter how much we may wish otherwise. Face up to facts, come to terms with reality, and make plans for the future.

An auspicious omen indicative of success and happiness. Even if surrounded by less favourable cards, this merely indicates some slight delay due to minor obstacles. Benefits are likely to be greater than expected and a new friendship could develop into a long-lasting relationship or possibly marriage.

A need for caution; curb impulsive action and guard your tongue or disputes and mis-understandings could arise, much to later regret. If at all possible, put off making major decisions until you are more able to cope and think clearly. Instead, try to take a break from routine.

This card indicates a change in life-style, perhaps a new residence or change of occupation, even a move abroad in certain instances. Whatever the case, improvement in circumstances is indicated. Marriage or remarriage is possible, especially if such plans have been long-delayed.

An important decision needs to be made yet hasty action now may prove regrettable later; best to try and think things through slowly and carefully before making up your mind. Immediate family and friends may not be as helpful as hoped and tempers could become frayed.

Success and good fortune; perhaps a somewhat surprising stroke of luck or small windfall. Even if accompanied by inauspicious cards, this Ten will redress the balance and any problems that may arise will be quickly overcome. Family affairs are well starred.

Important and pleasing news concerning a young person well-known to a mature questioner; or, for a younger querent, a romantic encounter that could develop into a long-lasting relationship. This card can also signify an unexpected but welcome invitation.

If adversely placed, there is a warning of hidden rivalry. More usually, however, this card simply refers to the wife or lover of a male querent or a close female friend of a woman questioner. In either case, the person concerned is well-disposed towards the querent.

A mature man who is in a position to advise or guide the querent, most likely in a professional or official capacity. Alternatively, this card may refer to a loyal friend who will offer his support. If surrounded by adverse cards, minor financial problems could arise.

three cards or only one suit in order to answer a specific query; or the querent may be asked to cut or shuffle the cards in various ways depending on the interpreter's personal preferences.

The choices are numerous and the results very individualistic; as are those interpreting the cards. It really doesn't matter how the cards are cut or shuffled or what spread is chosen; what is important is the interpreter's knowledge of the cards' meanings and his or her ability to weigh up all the factors involved so that an accurate reading can be obtained.

Don't forget that each card in a spread must be interpreted according to the position in which it falls, the surrounding or opposing cards, the personal circumstances of the enquirer and the nature of the matter under consideration. It is therefore essential to familiarise yourself with the positive and negative aspects of each card as well as the significance of each position in a spread.

Probably the easiest method is to practise interpreting one particular lay-out using different cards each time until you build up confidence and then repeat the exercise using another spread, and so on. You may be surprised at how quickly you learn to know the cards and what they mean and will almost certainly find that your prefer one or two particular spreads rather than others. If so, stick to them, if they feel right they are right — for you. You never know, in time you may even devise your own spread but, meanwhile, the following pages may provide some ideas for those who are new to card-reading.

Take your pick, the choice is yours.

A change of life-style is indicated. Whether this means a new job, home or relationship (or any combination!) will be shown by adjacent cards. But, in any case, the future prospects are decidedly rosier than at present for this card marks the end of one cycle and the beginning of the next.

Partnerships are the focus of attention. Whether business or emotional, these are likely to be under great strain, mainly due to another's intervention. Best advice is to try and view the situation calmly, face facts and, if necessary, make contingency plans for going it alone.

A warning of upsets in both career and domestic affairs. Seek expert advice, especially where financial matters are concerned, rather than rely on colleagues who may be less than co-operative. Emotions could be running high, too, so try to keep a cool head and avoid confrontation.

Things may not seem to be going as well as hoped yet this may be due to unrealistic expectations. A more positive attitude will help clarify the situation and enable realistic plans to be made for the future. Discuss doubts with close friends and family, they may be surprisingly supportive.

This may signal a particularly difficult phase where everything seems to be going wrong. There is little point in making matters worse by worrying about it though, as all things pass in the end. At least this is only a temporary bad patch as you will soon realise.

An exciting and entertaining time with plenty of opportunity for widening your circle of acquaintances. Keep your plans flexible though as there is a possibility that a young friend will let you down suddenly, leaving your to cope single-handed.

A female acquaintance may not really be as friendly as she appears, so don't accept everything she says unquestionably. On a brighter note, romantic prospects are encouraging for the unattached and domestic harmony is on the cards for those who are married.

This card usually represents a man of prestige who has the power and inclination to help the querent. This may refer to the husband or father of a female querent or a professional colleague of male. On a less personal level, it warns of fierce business rivalry.

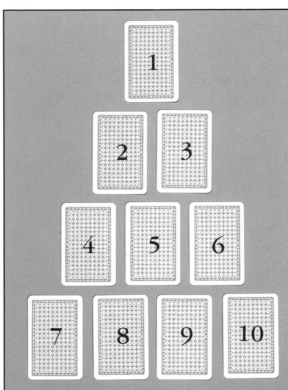

This spread is, perhaps, more suitable for considering a specific problem or question than for a general reading. Select 10 cards and deal them in the order shown; the cards are read in rows, starting at the apex of the pyramid:

1 represents the overriding aspect or current influence of the reading.

2, 3 indicate the options or alternatives open to the querent at this time.

4, 5, 6 denote the underlying forces at work that have given rise to the current situation.

7, 8, 9, 10 indicate the best way for the querent to handle the situation or resolve the problem.

MYSTICAL CROSS

A spread that calls for a significator which should have been selected by the querent as described previously and placed at random among the other 12 cards needed for the layout. The 13 cards are then laid out as shown in two rows to form an equal-armed cross.

The vertical row is read from top to bottom and refers to the enquirer's present situation; the horizontal row is read from left to right and relates to those influences that will affect current circumstances.

If the significator falls in the vertical row, it indicates that the enquirer is in the grip of circumstances beyond his/her control; if it falls in the horizontal row, it signifies that he has the matter in hand.

The fourth card laid, at the centre of the cross, represents the factor around which the whole situation revolves. This card will, therefore, provide the key to the matter under consideration.

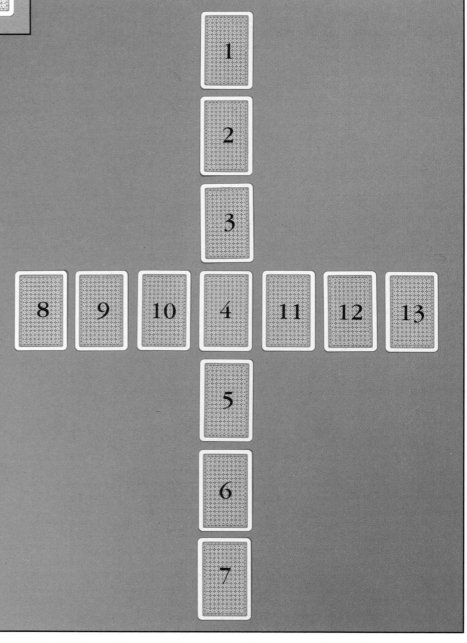

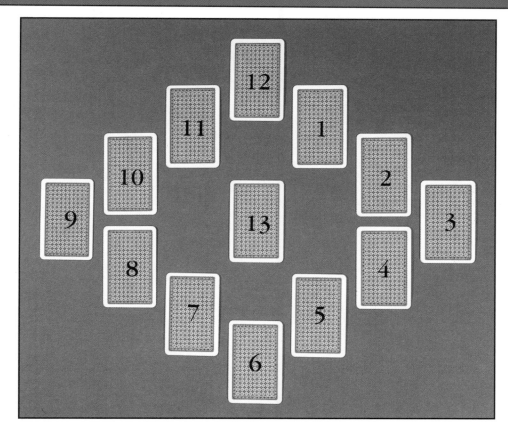

CELESTIAL CIRCLE

This is a nice simple spread for anyone wishing to have an indication of likely trends for the forthcoming 12 months. No significator is used, the querent selects 13 cards which are then laid out like a clock-face with the last card chosen being placed in the centre of the circle.

The last card laid, No 13, is read first as this will indicate the overriding influence for the' coming 12 months, according to its suit, whether Tarot or playing cards are being used. If, in a Tarot spread, this card happens to be a Major Arcana card it will still indicate the underlying influence for the year ahead.

The other 12 cards are then read in sequence, each representing one month. Card 1 relates to the month in which the reading takes place, irrespective of the date, and denotes the most dominant factor in the querent's life at that time. Card 2 refers to the calendar month following the reading, Card 3 the next, and so on.

21 CARD SPREAD

This simple spread is sometimes known as the Romany Spread and has been popular for centuries. Its accuracy does, though, depend greatly on the interpreter's knowledge of the individual card meanings and his or her ability to relate one to another.

The cards are laid in three rows of seven as shown and then read from left to right.

The top row refers to past influences and recent events that have contributed to the current situation.

The middle row signifies the querent's present circumstances, his or her feelings, hopes and wishes in the matter under consideration. It will also indicate possible alternatives, opposition and opportunities.

The bottom row denotes the likely future outcome of the current situation.

Each row is interpreted individually according to the cards that fall in it. The overall reading should provide a good indication of the events leading up to the querent's present circumstances, the choices that can be made and the probable outcome of these.

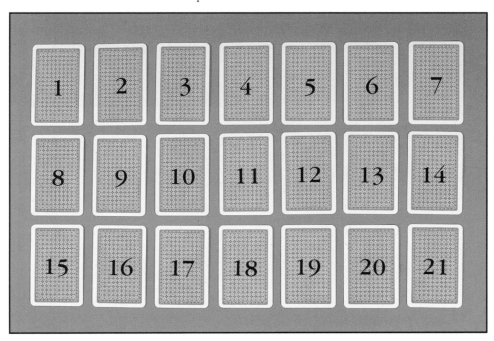

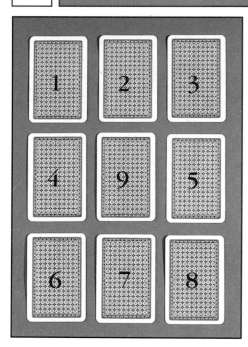

MAGIC SQUARE

A significator should be chosen and placed in the middle of the table before a further nine cards are selected and laid in three rows of three as shown; the last card dealt covers the significator. The cards are then interpreted according to their positions in the spread, as follows.

1 Individuality: personality and state of mind.
2 Outside influences and unexpected factors.
3 Environmental factors: friends, family, home, etc.
4 The querent's hopes and fears in the matter under review.
5 Alternatives: options, opportunities, challenges, etc.
6 The querent's aspirations and beliefs.
7 Negative, opposing or limiting factors.
8 Positive, constructive and helpful influences.

9 Potential: initiative, possibilities.

The rows are interpreted in two directions, first horizontally. The top row presents a general picture of the prevailing atmosphere; the basis of the querent's current situation and attitude are symbolised by the middle row. The bottom row, consequently, indicates future possibilities.

Reading the rows vertically, positions 1, 4 and 6 show three facets of the querent's nature; cards 2, 9 and 7 denote the major factors that must be considered before decisions are made; cards 3, 5 and 8 indicate opportunities and the favourable outcome of a correct choice.

The key position in the spread is the central square because this relates to every other and signifies the potential of the enquirer who, surrounded by possibilities, must make the moves.

BOHEMIAN SPREAD

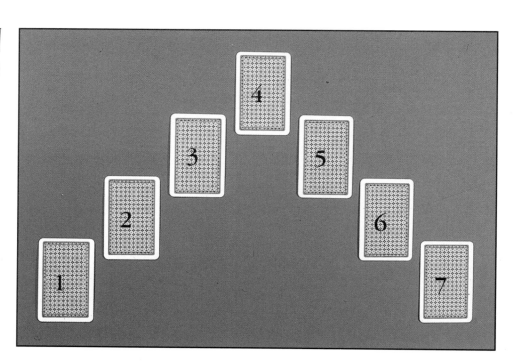

No significator is needed for this simple spread, just seven cards which should be laid out as shown and read individually according to their positions.

1 The querent's home environment and domestic issues: household goods, renovations, removals, structural alterations, etc.
2 Current influences: those factors that relate directly to the querent's present circumstances, such as hopes and wishes, worries or fears.
3 Relationships of all kinds: love, friendship, business or romantic partnerships or, of course, rivals, enemies, etc.
4 The querent's eventual wishes in the matter under enquiry: what he/she hopes or wants to achieve.
5 The unexpected: assistance or obstacles that are likely to help or hinder the aim signified by the preceding card.
6 Significant events: those things that are likely to effect the enquirer's immediate future; possibilities and probabilities.
7 Helpful influences: any opportunities or fortunate circumstances that the querent can use to his advantage; any chance of good fortune.

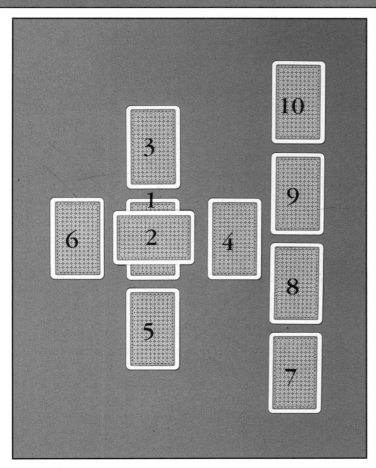

CELTIC CROSS

This is another spread where a significator is used and this should be selected first and placed face up on the table before the rest of the cards are shuffled, cut, etc. The first of the other 10 cards selected is placed on top of the significator, covering it entirely; the second card chosen is placed across these two and the remainder positioned as shown. As usual, each position has a specific meaning.

1   Present situation: the general atmosphere surrounding the matter under consideration and in which the other factors operate.

2   Immediate influences, especially contradictory forces: the nature of any obstacles in the matter.

3   Goal or destiny: hopes and wishes, the querent's aim or ideal in the matter; the best that can be achieved.

4   Distant past: the root of the question; the foundation or basis of the subject under consideration.

5   Recent past: events and influences that have a bearing on the situation and which have just passed or are now passing out of the querent's life.

6   Future influences: choices and alternatives; those factors or forces that are about to come into operation.

7   The question or questioner: the significator — whether person or object — and its position or attitude in the circumstances.

8   Environmental factors: assistance or hindrance; any trends that are likely to have an effect on the matter.

9   Inner emotions: the querent's innermost hopes and fears concerning the matter under review.

10 Final result or outcome: the likely culmination of all the influences shown by the other cards in the spread.

THE FAN

This traditional spread calls for a slightly different method of card selection than that outlined previously. First, a significator is selected but, unusually, this is not removed from the pack which should be shuffled and cut by the querent as already described. However, if this card is not among the first 13 chosen by the querent and handed to the interpreter the latter should, without changing their order, check whether the 7 of the same suit is present as this can be used as a substitute.

If neither card is present, the querent reshuffles, cuts and selects 13 cards as before and the interpreter again checks to see whether the chosen significator or the 7 is among them. If neither card appears in this second selection, the reading should be put off till another day as this is regarded as an indication that the cards are not ready to provide an answer.

However, assuming the time to be right, the selected cards are laid in a fan formation from left to right with their edges slightly overlapping as shown. The querent then selects a further five cards from the pack and hands these to the interpreter who will lay them as they are selected beneath the fanned cards.

The cards in the fan are read first and denote the underlying forces and current influences of the querent's situation at the time of the reading. Look for the significator or its substitute and, counting that card as number 1, interpret the fifth card to its right in the fan. Now, counting the interpreted card as number 1, read the fifth card to its right and repeat this process until all the cards in the fan, with the exception of the significator, have been interpreted.

This procedure sounds more complicated than it is but, just to make the sequence plain, we will assume that card number 3 in the lay-out shown is the significator. The card order for interpretation would then be: 7, 11, 2, 6, 10, 1, 5, 9, 13, 4, 8, 12.

The five cards below the fan formation are now interpreted in pairs, starting at either end of the row and working towards the middle; hence cards 14 and 18 are read as a pair, as are cards 15 and 17, leaving card 16 to be read on its own. These five cards denote the options and possibilities open to the querent and the likely outcome of the matter under consideration.

MYSTIC STAR

This is one of many spreads based on a stellar formation and is a very ancient card lay-out. 27 cards are needed in addition to a significator which should be selected as usual and placed in the centre of the table as shown.

Cards A, B and C are selected at the point where the querent makes his or her three cuts of the cards after shuffling them. Before completing the cut, the interpreter should turn the three piles over so that the bottom card is uppermost and then removes the top card from each heap and places them to one side of the table as indicated. The pack is then returned to the querent to shuffle and cut again in the usual manner so that a further 24 cards can be selected and laid as shown in the illustration.

The cards are interpreted in groups of three, first singly then in conjunction, starting with the three cards outside the star, A, B and C. These are known as the indicators and denote a key to the querent's current situation or problem; these cards therefore indicate the overriding influence at the time of the reading.

The cards immediately above the significator, cards 1, 9 and 17, are considered next and these are interpreted as a group before moving on around the circle in an anti-clockwise direction, reading each group in combination.

Finally, the spread as a whole should be considered and summarised within the context of the situation outlined or highlighted by the three indicators already mentioned.

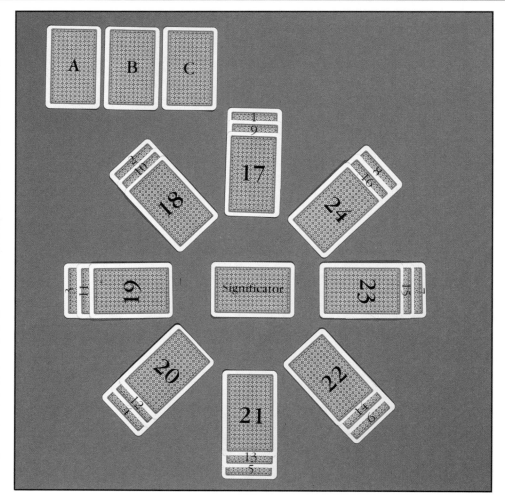

THE TAROT

The origins of the Tarot, from which playing cards probably derive, are shrouded in mystery and confusion. Many practitioners believe that the Tarot embodies remnants of ancient occult knowledge that has been lost to the world, others see it simply as colourful pieces of pasteboard embellished with symbolic images which conjure up subconscious faculties, or intuition, and there are countless alternative theories between these two extremes. Whatever the truth, the fact remains that Tarot divination has been practised for at leave five centuries, perhaps much longer, and continues to rank as one of the most popular forms of divination even now, on the threshold of the 21st century.

A full Tarot deck comprises 78 cards which are divided into two sections known as the Major and Minor Arcana. The latter is very similar to a deck of playing cards and consists of four suits which exactly parallel those of the more familiar pack: Wands equate to Clubs; Coins to

Diamonds; Cups to Hearts; Swords to Spades.

Like playing cards, each suit is made up of 10 pip or numbered cards plus court cards. It is in the latter that a slight discrepancy occurs because, instead of the usual three cards there are four; the extra card, the Page, slots between the Knight (Jack) and 10 of each suit. In all probability, it is likely that playing cards too once had four court cards and that at some point in their history the Knight and Page were replaced by a single card, the Jack.

Again like playing cards, each suit relates to a certain area or aspect of life; Cups to emotional matters, Coins to finances, and so on. Each is also linked to one of the seasons of the year and to the elements: Wands — Summer/Fire; Coins — Winter/Earth; Cups — Autumn/Water; Swords — Spring/Air.

There are, then, many similarities between playing cards and the four suits that make up the Minor Arcana of the Tarot. It is the remaining 22 cards which set the Tarot apart and give rise to much of the speculation concerning their origins. These cards are decorated with

symbolic pictures depicting allegorical figures and images which provoke a response in most people, making them ideal tools for meditation and psychic development as well as divination. However, it is the latter with which we are concerned here.

The Major Arcana cards, or Tarot trumps as they are sometimes called, signify the powerful influences and archetypal forces behind events. How these will manifest in the querent's life will be shown by the Minor Arcana cards, while the positions in which the cards fall in a divinatory spread will denote their area of influence.

The Major cards are, therefore, the underlying causes of a situation and often indicate important changes which are taking place or will do so shortly; they override the Minor cards and a spread dominated by trumps infers a significant change in the querent's life. Whether this refers to a change of attitude or outlook or to altered circumstances can usually be gleaned from other cards in the spread.

Tarot cards, like any other divinatory tools,

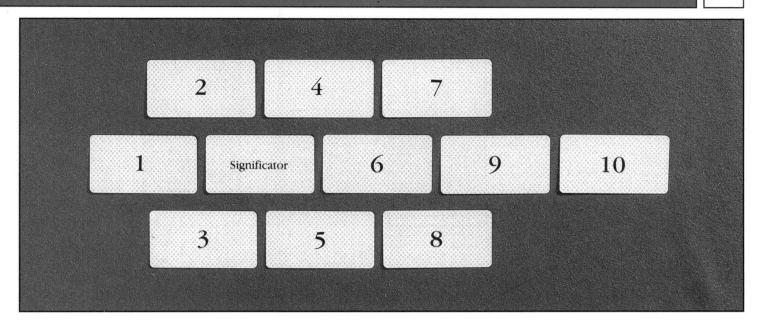

TREE OF LIFE

This is another spread calling for the selection of a significator which should be positioned as shown before the remaining 10 cards are laid out in the order indicated. Each card is then interpreted according to its position in the spread.

1 The aims or aspirations of the enquirer or the best that can be reasonably expected.

2 Non-physical resources such as wisdom, experience, initiative, etc, on which the querent can call.

3 The general nature of the obstacles, difficulties or limiting factors that must be overcome.

4 Current positive influences that have a direct bearing on the matter under consideration.

5 Current negative forces that can influence the situation.

6 The key factor; the foundation of the matter.

7 The querent's own conscious actions and reactions which can affect the situation directly.

8 Environmental or outside factors that are not directly under the enquirer's control.

9 The subconscious hopes and wishes of the enquirer or hidden influences that can affect the outcome.

10 The final result or outcome of the matter under review.

should be treated with respect and used solely for the purpose for which they are intended. It is therefore a good idea to keep them in their own container, wrapped in silk or otherwise set apart from everyday things until required. They can also be relatively expensive to buy compared to playing cards, so it is worth while giving some thought to the matter before making a selection from the numerous different packs that are available currently. Obviously, you should choose a deck whose design appeals to you but it is equally important that they 'feel' right; you should feel easy with them.

The Tarot can be one of the most satisfying methods of divination, but it isn't for everyone: it requires a certain amount of dedication, a 'feeling' for the cards. This is not to imply that it is not entirely feasible for a beginner to obtain a satisfactory reading — we are all novices in a sense — but it does require patience as well as experience to understand the Tarot to any great degree for each card is multi-faceted, it holds both esoteric and exoteric meanings.

However, we all have to start somewhere, so don't be put off by what might appear to be a complex subject, you may find that you have a natural affinity for the Tarot and are instinctively able to read the cards and understand their message. If so, count yourself fortunate and enjoy your gift. One word of warning, though: you have a responsibility to those for whom you read the cards and should never convey their message in such a way that it can cause harm or distress to the hearer. Always remember that any form of divination can only tell you what may happen if nothing is done to alter the situation described: it refers to possibilities not certainties.

The Tarot never lies but it can be misinterpreted, much depends on the knowledge of the interpreter and how he/she responds to the inspiration that the cards provoke. So always consider each card's position in a spread and its relationship to other cards when doing a reading; weigh up the possibilities and take into account the personal circumstances of the querent before making a pronouncement.

As with playing cards, a significator may be used on occasion, perhaps when interpreting a spread for a specific question or when the questioner is absent. If the former, the Ace of the appropriate suit will be used; if a personal card is needed, the King would represent a mature male; the Queen, a mature female; the Knight, a young male; the Page, a young female; the choice of suit would depend on the nature of the query rather than the physical characteristics of the enquirer.

The method of shuffling, cutting and selecting the cards for a reading will vary according to personal taste and inclination, but the methods detailed in this chapter will suffice. Also, any of the spreads shown is as suitable for the Tarot as for playing cards. So with these to guide you and the brief individual card meanings given on the following pages, you are ready to begin.

THE MAJOR ARCANA

There are 22 cards in the Major Arcana or Tarot trumps and each represents an archetypal image or underlying force. Some may refer to actual people known to the querent; more often, they signify principles. They are powerful images and always override the cards of the Minor Arcana in a divinatory spread: they are the causes, the suit cards in the pack are the effects.

Although the trumps are numbered, this can vary slightly in different packs so only their titles have been used in the following delineations. In most packs, The Fool's place is at the beginning, as No. 0, or at the end, No. 22; in some decks this card bears no number at all. Cards No. 8 and 11 are also transposed in some packs, just to lead to more confusion. And a few Tarots have completely different numbering systems to the norm; so it is as well to rely on the cards' titles and meanings rather than their order at this stage.

Remember, the Minor Arcana will indicate what is happening or is likely to happen in a querent's life whereas the Major cards will signify why, the underlying cause behind the effects.

There is one further point that should perhaps be made at this stage. Although some Tarot interpreters place emphasis on whether a card falls upright or reversed in a divinatory spread, others prefer to take a different approach.

Besides the fact that many of the cards do not have a 'top' and a 'bottom', none is 'good' or 'bad' in itself. Each has both a positive and a negative aspect, either of which may hold sway at any particular time.

For instance, depending on its position, it is possible for a card to represent prevailing conditions in the querent's life rather than his/her expectations. In which case, identifying the negative influences can often help the querent to combat them. Conversely, knowing the best that can be expected can give the enquirer renewed hope and something to aim for.

It is essential to recognise that the Tarot does not provide finite answers, it merely points to possibilities. The final choice must always lie with the querent who, like everyone else, has free will.

THE FOOL

Le Mat
The Fool

POSITIVE Unexpected, unplanned or challenging influences; an unlooked for opportunity. A questing attitude, eagerness; a willingness to experiment, to learn through experience. A fresh start or new direction. Childlike innocence; the self at the beginning of a journey; the questioner or querent, the person for whom the cards are being read. Idealism.

NEGATIVE Hidden problems; a warning of pitfalls ahead for the unwary. Foolhardiness; extravagance; eccentric or thoughtless behaviour. Fecklessness, indecision, indiscretion. A feeling of helplessness in the face of problems. A lack of commitment; reluctance to take responsibility for self or others. Illusion; a misguided course of action. Apathy.

THE MAGICIAN

Le Bateleur
The Magician

POSITIVE The ability to cause or influence events lies in the querent's hands. Strength of purpose; will-power; initiative; innovation. Creative opportunities and discoveries. Skill, subtlety, adaptability. Inspirational ideas; the power of thought. A seeker of spiritual truths. Potential; a choice to be made. The beginning of a new and important enterprise.

NEGATIVE A mind in turmoil, unable to see problems in their true perspective. Trickery and deception. Lack of forethought; loss of confidence, uncertainty, poor judgement; a lessening of control over one's destiny. A lack of perception. A sense of inferiority. Risky undertakings; misguided actions; use of power for destructive purposes. Impotence.

THE HIEROPHANT (POPE or HIGH PRIEST)

Le Pape
The Pope

POSITIVE A spiritual guide or supportive friend. Divine inspiration; revelation; enlightenment. Psychic awareness. Latent powers or energies; the key to inner strength; subconscious influences. Openness to new ideas or concepts. The accomplishment of practical schemes through intelligent imagination. Truth and justice.

NEGATIVE Bewilderment or confusion; an inability or reluctance to seek aid in resolving a dilemma. Turmoil. Anger and frustration. The dissipation of natural energies. Self-righteousness; craftiness and guile. Disorderly conduct. Inconsiderate actions; poor judgement. Incompetence; subservience; an ineffectual personality. Lack of motivation.

THE LOVERS

L'amoureux
The lover

POSITIVE A decisive point in the querent's life when an important choice must be made. An opportunity to revise fundamental beliefs. Balance; harmony; unity. A dramatic change of attitude or outlook leads to improved circumstances. Conquest; the defeat of enemies or business rivals. Reconciliation; co-operative effort; mutual attraction.

NEGATIVE An unsatisfactory situation or relationship. Uncertainty; jealousy, envy or spite. Conflict; antagonism; rivalry. Contradictory forces; the struggle between passions and conscience. An unhappy love affair; infatuation; unwelcome separation; emotional loss. A warning against making an unwise decision. A testing time; possible failure.

THE HIGH PRIESTESS

La Papesse
The High Priestess

THE EMPRESS

L'Impératrice
The Empress

THE EMPEROR

L'Empereur
The Emperor

POSITIVE Lunar power, symbolising the New Moon and feminine creative forces. Imagination, inspiration, spiritual awareness. Memory, the subconscious. Something hidden revealed. Presages dramatic changes; the beginning of a new cycle. An authoritative, persuasive female. Adeptship, one skilled in the mysteries; the Tarot interpreter.

NEGATIVE Unfortunate changes; unforeseen circumstances. A lack of proper control. Delusion; inconstancy; fickleness in relationships. Apparent improvements may prove illusionary or transient. Reluctance to heed advice causes problems. Conceit; superficiality; lack of understanding; hypocrisy; hostility. Needless secrecy; underhand dealings.

POSITIVE Venusian qualities; the feminine principle. Warmth, love and affection. A harmonising influence. Emotional security; happiness, pleasure; luxury, riches, material success. Celebration; public rejoicing. Fruitfulness, fertility, motherhood; the harvesting of past efforts. Action; movement; the implementation and fulfilment of plans. Wisdom.

NEGATIVE Inaction; sterility; deprivation; the dissipation of natural resources. Overindulgence; extravagance; waste. Domestic strife; maternal tyranny; possessiveness; jealousy; clandestine affairs. Sorrow and loneliness. Delay in accomplishing one's aims and aspirations. Vacillation; lack of concentration. Disagreement; disappointment.

POSITIVE Leadership; an authoritative figure, one who is in a position to help or advise the querent. Paternalism; protection and potency. Stability, status, respect; the establishment. Maturity; the successful completion of plans. A steadfast and loyal friend. Vigilence; courage; resourcefulness; wise counsel. Firmness; strength of character.

NEGATIVE Impotency; loss of wealth or position. Tyranny; selfishness; stubbornness; overweening pride; impatience; ill-temper. Disputes or misunderstandings. An inability to complete projects due to lack of enthusiasm or perseverance. Impracticality, indecision, weakness, inertia. Obstacles or temporary setbacks. Immaturity; intolerance.

THE CHARIOT

Le Chariot
The Chariot

JUSTICE

La Justice
Justice

THE HERMIT

L'hermite
The hermit

POSITIVE A hopeful omen heralding sudden change, probably of job or residence; perhaps both. Movement, travel, exploration. Unexpected good news. Conquest; the overcoming of obstacles. Renewed optimism, motivation. Progress; a new stage of development has been reached. Accomplishment; improvement; successful outcome. Self-reliance.

NEGATIVE An unexpected and perhaps unlooked for change of circumstances due to external factors. Temporary delays and hindrances to plans could cause discouragement. A reluctance to face reality and make concessions where necessary may lead to domestic disputes or resentment. Impatience, carelessness and loss of self control; confusion.

POSITIVE Helpful influences; sound advice. An advantageous business offer or favourable legal decision. The signing of contracts, agreements or treaties. Marriage or reunion; unity. Equilibrium; adjustment, balance, harmony. Successful negotiation and arbitration; reconciliation. The righting of a wrong. Truth, honesty, integrity. Absolute justice.

NEGATIVE Miscarriage of justice. Unfounded suspicion; false accusation; unjust condemnation. Inequality; an unfair decision. A test or ordeal. Legal disputes or court proceedings prove costly in more ways than one. Financial hardship; material or emotional loss. Retribution. Illegal activities; misplaced trust; illicit affairs. Remorse.

POSITIVE A teacher or wise counsellor who can help the querent's progress in unmaterialistic ways. Patience; discretion, circumspection. Necessary retreat from the world; a period of quiet contemplation; spiritual or occult studies. Wisdom sought and attained. Sagacity. Preparedness; protective influences. Long-term plans.

NEGATIVE Enforced retirement; isolation; loneliness. Self-induced fears and unreasonable suspicions. Immaturity; lack of prudence. A refusal to listen to those with more experience leads to unnecessary mistakes or foolish actions. Irritating delays or unexpected setbacks to plans. Unwanted revelations cause upset. Self-deception.

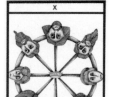

WHEEL OF
FORTUNE

La Roue de Fortune
The Wheel of Fortune

STRENGTH

La Force
Force

THE HANGED
MAN

Le pendu
The hanged man

POSITIVE *A reversal of fortunes brings improvement in whatever area of life has been troubling the querent. A lucky break; a golden opportunity. Transformation. An end to current difficulties; progress; the completion of plans. Promotion. Change; movement; action. The end of one cycle and the start of another. Success; satisfaction; abundance.*

NEGATIVE *Sudden misfortune; an unpleasant surprise. Loss. Unexpected delays or hindrances to plans. Inaction; stagnation. Past misdeeds come home to roost. Deprivation; poverty. Anxiety; despair. An unwanted separation or rejection. Unwelcome truths; a painful situation that must be faced. The imposition of another's will; helplessness.*

POSITIVE *Both moral and physical strength. Often refers to an improvement in health, either for the querent or a close relative. Courage, energy, vitality; youthfulness. Dogged persistence in the face of adversity; stamina, endurance, fortitude. Strength of purpose, the exercise of will; action. Deserved success and just rewards.*

NEGATIVE *A dangerous situation that must be handled with care. The abuse or misuse of power and influence. Oppression. Loss of reputation; disgrace. Obstinacy; a stubborn refusal to face reality. Lack of moral fibre; decadence. Weakness; ill-health. Reluctance to accept responsibility. Inability to sustain efforts to a successful conclusion.*

POSITIVE *The development of psychic abilities and awareness; intuition. Transformation. A conscious change of direction in the querent's life; a new perspective. Selfless devotion; willing sacrifice; service. Co-operation; tact and diplomacy. Self-knowledge and understanding. The attainment of inner peace and harmony; tranquillity.*

NEGATIVE *Escapism; a complete refusal to face up to reality or meet obligations. Self-deception, dishonesty, hypocrisy. Failure to achieve goals due to insufficient effort made or the useless dissipation of energies on worthless causes. A lack of discernment; pointless self-denial. Ineptitude. Pretentiousness; vanity. A warning of accident or loss. Defeat.*

THE LIGHTNING
STRUCK TOWER

La Maison Dieu
The Tower of Destruction

THE STAR

L'Etoile
The Star

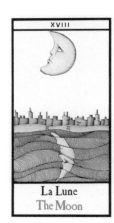

THE MOON

La Lune
The Moon

POSITIVE *Sudden reversal of fortunes when all seemed lost. Encouragement or help from unexpected quarters. Wisdom gained through experience. Determination; courage to face the future with renewed hope and vigour. Freedom to make a fresh start in life; realisation that the worst is past. Regeneration; a time of reparation and rejuvenation. Hope.*

NEGATIVE *Cataclysmic change portending great personal or material loss, perhaps both. A sudden or unseen calamity leads to complete failure of plans. Disaster, ruin or danger. Utter dejection; an inability to combat or recover from adversity. Insurmountable difficulty; an undesirable but unavoidable situation. Possible bereavement.*

POSITIVE *An omen of hope. Expectancy; encouraging possibilities. Fulfilment of dreams and ambitions, probably with the help of new friends or associates. Love and understanding. Intuitive insights aid the realisation of plans. Joyful news or unexpected good fortune. Protection; watchfulness. Co-operation. Potential; perhaps a birth.*

NEGATIVE *Temporary setbacks or disappointments. Short-lived success; minor theft or loss. Hopes frustrated through lack of foresight or misplaced trust. False friends. Bad luck; unfulfilled hopes or wishes. Self-deception; errors of judgement. Insufficient efforts are made to obtain objectives due to laziness or lack of incentive. Weakness.*

POSITIVE *Heralds an important change in attitude or outlook that will bring benefits in its wake. Illumination; inspiration. A pleasant surprise or revelation that brings joy to the recipient. An unexpected gift. Constructive imagination; creative endeavour. Conception, either in the literal or figurative sense. Emotional security; peace and contentment.*

NEGATIVE *Illusion, delusion or dissolution. A warning against any form of speculation. A too easy compliance with others' wishes leads to doubt or disappointment. Deception; bewilderment; confusion. Impractical schemes or impossible dreams. Hopes are dashed due to failure to face facts. Minor errors of judgement; trivial worries.*

DEATH

La Mort
Death

TEMPERANCE

Tempérance
Temperance

THE DEVIL

Le Diable
The Devil

POSITIVE Usually signifies that the matter on the querent's mind at the reading has already been resolved. Conclusion; completion of a project or end of current phase. Transformation. New beginnings; opportunity. Necessary change; the inevitable progression of events. Advancement; improvement. Recovery from illness. Liberation.

NEGATIVE Unexpected or unwanted change. The end of a relationship; loss of job or position. Deprivation; insecurity. A sudden or unwelcome shock. Failure of prospects. Lethargy; boredom; depression. An unresolved dilemma or unsatisfactory situation. Frustration and anger. The gradual diminution of resources; lack of momentum.

POSITIVE Moderation; a harmonising influence in the querent's life. Unification; a sound partnership. Economy; careful conservation of assets through wise management. A beneficial change; an improvement in status or replenishment of that which was lost. Good health; vitality. Reconciliation through mediation; the middle way. A strong ally.

NEGATIVE. Conflicting energies are at work, so an implicit warning against excess of any kind, whether of action or inaction. Stalemate; inertia, dissatisfaction, resentment. Lack of initiative; complacency. Wasted opportunities. Confrontation, discord, hostility; clash of interests. Self-indulgence. A careless frittering away of resources. Fickleness.

POSITIVE An important choice must be made. Opportunities abound; a chance for the querent to utilise his/her potential to the full. Self-control; strength of purpose. A beneficial business partnership or fortunate marriage. An unexpected stroke of good fortune. A flash of sheer genius allows ambitions to be realised. Material advancement; abundance.

NEGATIVE Uncontrollable forces. A strong temptation that stands little chance of being resisted. Oppression; destructive tendencies. Malicious slander; irresponsible actions. Animosity; hatred; fear; revenge; retribution. Rash and impulsive behaviour. Unforeseen hazards that will be difficult if not impossible to avoid. Lust; seduction; violence.

THE SUN

Le Soleil
The Sun

JUDGEMENT

Le Jugement
Judgement

THE WORLD

Le Monde
The World

POSITIVE Success; rewards for past efforts. The satisfactory culmination of plans; the fulfilment of long-held wishes. Often refers to marriage or remarriage. Maturity. Social status and respect. Material gains; the achievement of ambitions. Power and influence. Triumph; justifiable pride. Freedom to enjoy the fruits of one's labour.

NEGATIVE Partial or short-lived success. The misuse of power or money for selfish ends. Vanity; arrogance; domination; tyranny. Over-confidence leads to foolish mistakes or financial loss. Too much emphasis on material considerations may mar relationships and result in alienation or separation. Stagnation; lack of motivation or momentum.

POSITIVE Necessary change; a decisive point has been reached. A card of aspiration and attainment. The promise of rich rewards and great happiness; deserved success. An outstanding problem is finally resolved; the realisation of long-term plans. Personal satisfaction and recognition. Unsuspected blessings. Awakened consciousness; development

NEGATIVE A time of reckoning when past actions are called to account. Onerous duties that must be performed. Loss of status or material security. A warning against prejudging events. Incompetence; schemes fail to produce the desired effects due to unrealistic expectations. A lack of achievement; disappointment. Obstacles; missed opportunities.

POSITIVE A hopeful omen, signalling a favourable turn of events. Achievement of personal ambitions. Assured success, heralding public acclaim and material benefit. An enduring and happy partnership. Knowledge gained through experience. A broadening of horizons; travel and exploration. Renewed enthusiasm. Opportunity for advancement.

NEGATIVE Delayed or transient success. Achievements do not come up to expectations and efforts are ill-rewarded. Inaction; stagnation; lack of motivation. Fear of change or reluctance to make a decision means that opportunities are lost. A warning against lengthy and costly litigation. Self-indulgence. Opposition; stubbornness.

SUIT OF WANDS

**THE MINOR ARCANA
THE SUIT OF WANDS (or RODS, STAVES,
BATONS, SCEPTRES)**

TRADITIONALLY ASSOCIATED WITH THE
ELEMENT FIRE, THE WANDS SUIT
RELATES TO ENTERPRISE, GROWTH AND
CREATIVITY.

ACE

POSITIVE The start of an enterprise, business undertaking or relationship; sometimes literally a birth. Energy, drive and enthusiasm; creative efforts of all kinds, the germ of an idea or a new project.

NEGATIVE A tendency towards excess; an uncontrolled desire for change and variety for their own sake. False hopes bring disappointment. Rash or impulsive behaviour. Pointless pursuits or unfulfilled wishes.

TWO

POSITIVE Opportunities for personal advancement and improved status. Past efforts will be recognised and rewarded, perhaps unexpectedly. An important transaction or contract brings financial benefit.

NEGATIVE An unpleasant or unsatisfactory situation. The frustration of plans due to poor judgement and bad decisions or foolish speculation. Feelings of uncertainty or unnecessary anxiety.

THREE

POSITIVE An end to opposition means that a current worry will soon be resolved. A profitable partnership. The forging of new business links and successful negotiation; favourable collaboration.

NEGATIVE A warning that pride or arrogance could prevent one from recognising obvious impediments. The possibility of double-dealing or treachery. A lack of initiative results in lost opportunities.

FOUR

POSITIVE A satisfactory conclusion to a current project. Material success or personal achievement. A harmonious situation; pleasurable company; a cause for celebration or justifiable optimism.

NEGATIVE Ingratitude or dissatisfaction with present circumstances. The threat of loss. Unfulfilled hopes or promises cause regret. Plans suffer delays due to unsuspected obstacles. Complacency.

FIVE

POSITIVE An exciting challenge; a competitive situation. A good time to hold discussions, negotiate a deal and initiate plans for future expansion. A happy outcome to a contractural or legal dispute.

NEGATIVE Quarrels or misunderstandings disrupt progress or cause unnecessary complications despite gains. Uncertainty over the results of litigation or court proceedings cause worry. Deception.

SIX

POSITIVE The arrival of good news. A long-term project reaches a successful conclusion. Increased prosperity and a sense of achievement. Hopes realised after initial setbacks and uncertainty.

NEGATIVE Unsuspected difficulties arise to upset plans and cause delays. Friends or business associates prove unreliable and let you down at the last moment or perhaps cast doubts on your ability.

SEVEN

POSITIVE Useful discussion and successful bargaining. A creative venture will pay dividends and bring great personal satisfaction if perseverance is shown despite strong competition. Efforts are rewarded.

NEGATIVE Misgivings about the outcome of a project cause anxiety and confusion. An embarrassing situation or unwelcome encounter. Opportunities are lost due to indecisiveness and hesitation. Self-doubt.

EIGHT

POSITIVE The end of an unhelpful or unproductive phase. Good news from afar brings relief and raises expectations. Recent setbacks are overcome and rapid progress can now be made. Renewed energy or activity.

NEGATIVE Domestic disputes or lovers' tiffs. Professional jealousy could cause misunderstandings or difficulties at work. A proposed scheme fails due to impatience. Travel plans are disrupted.

NINE

POSITIVE A good time for long-term planning and preparing for an important project. Despite opposition, this is a time to stick to one's guns as a matter of principle may be involved; stand firm and win.

NEGATIVE Legal wrangles or proceedings against formidable odds. Delays and mishaps threaten future prospects. Unexpected or additional responsibilities hamper progress towards material goals.

TEN

POSITIVE A heightened sense of responsibility and willingness to help others, even at cost to oneself. Perseverance in resolving problems and overcoming hardship. Progress will be made despite restrictions.

NEGATIVE Oppressive work conditions or resentment of colleagues. Difficult ending to a love affair or disappointing result of a law suit. A warning that someone is out to cause mischief due to envy.

Valet de Baton
The Knave of Clubs

KNAVE

POSITIVE A young person or someone with a youthful outlook who proves helpful. Good news. A message from or about a loved one. A brilliant idea or scheme that leads to ultimate success. Inventiveness; inspiration.

NEGATIVE Childish pranks or concern over a child's well-being. Disappointing news or displeasure. Erratic behaviour or doubts concerning another's sincerity. Slander or misleading information.

Cavalier de Baton
The Knight of Clubs

KNIGHT

POSITIVE A friendly young man heralds a new beginning. Patience, rectitude and practicality in the face of disruptive influences. Journeys, a new home, change of job or direction; possible emigration.

NEGATIVE Professional rivalry or pettiness of work colleagues. Impulsive actions or unpredictable behaviour can result in unwanted partings. Disputes, misunderstandings and interruptions to progress.

Reyne de Baton
The Queen of Clubs

QUEEN

POSITIVE A charming, generous woman. Success in a business venture with a female partner. Sound investments favoured, especially if linked to property deals. Domestic stability and harmonious relationships.

NEGATIVE Hoped-for backing fails to materialise, thus inhibiting progress and temporarily frustrating ambitions. A business deal is marred by another's intervention. Marital infidelity — real or suspected.

Roy de Baton
The King of Clubs

KING

POSITIVE An honest, upright man offers moral or financial support in an enterprise. An inheritance or unexpected monetary windfall. Good advice from a professional person; a beneficial partnership.

NEGATIVE Failure to stick to the straight and narrow has disastrous consequences. A harsh but just decision. Restrictive business practices impose a heavy burden on available resources. Possible loss.

SUIT OF COINS

THE SUIT OF COINS (or PENTACLES, DISKS, DENIERS)

THIS SUIT IS ASSOCIATED WITH THE ELEMENT EARTH AND THEREFORE LINKS WITH MONEY, FINANCIAL STANDING AND MATERIAL STATUS.

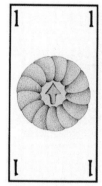

ACE

POSITIVE A period of prosperity and contentment. Bright prospects and successful business ventures. An unexpected gift or an inheritance. the start of a financially rewarding partnership.

NEGATIVE Misuse of wealth or power causes unhappiness. False economies or a gamble that doesn't quite come off. A lack of appreciation for what has been achieved causes dissatisfaction. Greed or avarice.

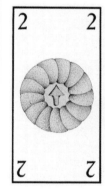

TWO

POSITIVE An improvement in circumstances. Harmonious and stable relationships; satisfactory working conditions. Important news and written messages. A time of recreation and pleasure; profitable hobbies.

NEGATIVE Conflicting interests cause problems and upset the status quo. An inability to keep pace with changing circumstances. A hasty decision that could meet with disapproval and lead to friction.

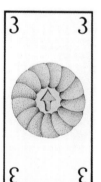

THREE

POSITIVE A deserved success; recognition for past efforts brings fame or fortune. Integrity in business dealings pays dividends. Good exam results or the attainment of professional qualifications.

NEGATIVE A lack of co-operation from others and a warning that petty-mindedness will place relationships under severe strain. Indifference leads to carelessness and could seriously mar career prospects.

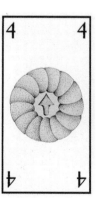

FOUR

POSITIVE The acquisition of power and influence. Financial gain as a result of inheritance or the skilled manipulation of resources. The consolidation of assets through wise and judicious investment.

NEGATIVE A reluctance to delegate authority causes resentment among colleagues. Financial loss or the reversal of fortunes. A tendency to be miserly with money or with affections. Possessiveness.

FIVE

POSITIVE A good time to lay the foundations for future security. Friends or partners offer support and encouragement. Coming to terms with misfortune or realising limitations and adapting to reality.

NEGATIVE Heavy losses indicate a practical need to find a solution to present difficulties. Disruptive influences are very much in evidence and cause worry and uncertainty. Discordant relationships.

SIX

POSITIVE Material success and fruitful business transactions. An unexpected gift from a loved one; past generosity is repaid by financial sponsorship. Opportunities for business expansion arise.

NEGATIVE Envy or jealousy causes material and emotional losses. Duplicity in business dealings. Heavy financial obligations frustrate ambitions. Material security is threatened by outstanding loans or debts.

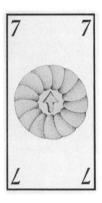

SEVEN

POSITIVE Surprising news and an exciting social invitation. A business proposal that offers an opportunity for steady expansion. The co-operation and collaboration of others proves profitable.

NEGATIVE Complicated financial arrangements cause unnecessary delays. Shady monetary deals or loans could give rise to litigation. Adverse criticism and gossip. Unfulfilled promise; unprofitable speculation.

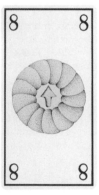

EIGHT

POSITIVE Financial gain though one's own skill and talents. Material benefits and improvements to current circumstances. A small windfall or unexpected gift. A new romantic attachment brings happiness.

NEGATIVE Outside influences or a lack of real ambition impede progress. A warning against lending or borrowing money as this could lead to a compromising situation. Duplicity is on the cards.

NINE

POSITIVE Assured success; accomplishment. The time is ripe to negotiate large-scale business contracts or to invest in the future. The prospects are encouraging for any form of expansion.

NEGATIVE Risky deals come to naught, probably due to deception. Loss of income or home, perhaps both. The frittering away of resources on ill-considered schemes. The frustration of plans.

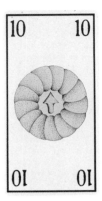

TEN

POSITIVE Affluence and established wealth. Important family affairs: wills, legacies, endowments. Beneficial domestic changes of all kinds. Successful property deals or home improvements.

NEGATIVE Loss of possessions, emotional security or reputation; a complete reversal of fortunes. Restrictive circumstances. Danger of slanderous gossip or underhand dealings. Shame or guilt.

Valet de Deniers
The Knave of Money

KNAVE

POSITIVE Good administration plus acumen reap benefits; prudence and diligence increase profitability. Favourable news concerning a new enterprise or an academic achievement. A birth in the family.

NEGATIVE Disappointing results or errors of judgement. Wastefulness; bad management results in poor return for initial outlay. Failure to seize an opportunity. Indulgence, laziness, complacency.

Cavalier de Deniers
The Knight of Money

KNIGHT

POSITIVE A responsible and hard-working young man or a trustworthy person who can help the questioner. Practical ideas or useful discoveries. An unemployed friend. Sound financial investments.

NEGATIVE A warning to watch out for trickery or petty interference. Discouraging news. A lack of foresight, indolence or negligence will inhibit progress. Economies will have to be made.

Reyne de Deniers
The Queen of Money

QUEEN

POSITIVE A warm, generous woman who has the querent's best interests at heart. Increase in earnings; monetary gifts from relatives; payments from insurance companies, etc. Sincere advice.

NEGATIVE A lack of self-reliance. Fear, mistrust or suspicion. A threat to security; a struggle to maintain that which has been achieved so far. Doubts and disappointments; loss of enthusiasm.

Roy de Deniers
The King of Money

KING

POSITIVE A man in authority or an influential friend. Legal matters, including legacies; official documents and the signing of important contracts. Sound financial advice; profitable business.

NEGATIVE A warning that financial problems or losses could arise, especially if linked to family affairs. Unsuccessful litigation. An elderly and spiteful man who can create trouble for the querent.

SUIT OF CUPS

THE SUIT OF CUPS (or CHALICES)

ASSOCIATED WITH THE ELEMENT WATER, THIS SUIT PERTAINS TO ALL EMOTIONAL MATTERS, CREATIVITY, FERTILITY AND INTUITION.

ACE

POSITIVE The essence of love, joy and contentment; spiritual tranquillity. Psychic protection; intuition, creative abilities. Emotional stability and domestic harmony. Fertility; nourishment.

NEGATIVE Unexpected and unwelcome changes; instability. Inconstancy or unrequited love. Illusion and disillusionment. Unfulfilled hopes and wishes; discouragement, disappointment and depression.

TWO

POSITIVE Unity, whether in business or personal relationships. A warm friendship, passionate love affair or marriage. Harmonious conditions; a partnership based on trust and respect. Reconciliation.

NEGATIVE All forms of opposition; friction and misunderstandings. A temporary parting from a loved one. Fickleness or infidelity. A warning not to be taken in by glib words and charm of manner.

THREE

POSITIVE The start of a bountiful and pleasurable phase. Fulfilment, happiness, a successful outcome. Mutual attraction: consolidation. Recuperation and recovery from illness; good health.

NEGATIVE The end of an affair or a business loss. Extravagance — either emotional or material. Self-indulgence; unbridled passions. The unwanted attentions of an admirer. False friendships.

FOUR

POSITIVE A time for contemplation and long-term planning. New directions and new relationships. Any problems will turn out to be far less serious than first supposed. Consolation; conciliation.

NEGATIVE Dissatisfaction and displeasure. Unrest and misunderstandings. Unexpected hitches add to the general air of unease. Disadvantageous alterations to living conditions or work environment.

FIVE

POSITIVE A happy reunion with a relative or friend following a long absence. A surprise gift or a small legacy. Coming to terms with a broken love affair. An unexpectedly beneficial alliance.

NEGATIVE Financial and emotional affairs fail to live up to expectations, thus causing bitterness or frustration. Plans that are not fully realised; disappointments or unpleasant shocks.

SIX

POSITIVE The beginning of a more helpful phase brings relief from past anxieties. Satisfaction and steady progress towards goals. Fulfilment following disappointment. Harmonious relationships.

NEGATIVE A tendency to cling too much to the past. Stagnation. An inability to adapt or adjust to changing circumstances. Uncertainty; a lack of direction inhibits personal development. Suspicion.

SEVEN

POSITIVE Imaginative schemes and creative projects. A search for knowledge and understanding, especially on the spiritual or philosophical level. The establishment of a firm plan for the future.

NEGATIVE A lack of realism; self-delusion and deception generally. Unfulfilled promises and unsubstantiated hopes. Internal conflict despite external display of confidence and success. Fantasies.

EIGHT

POSITIVE Domestic changes; deep satisfaction. A new emotional involvement; marriage. Agreement and material success. A change of environment brings about an improvement in health. Improved status.

NEGATIVE Disruptive influences, especially on the domestic front. Departure from the family home, probably due to changes within the family circle. The abandonment of material success. Disorder; dismay.

NINE

POSITIVE The satisfactory completion of a project or profitable conclusion of a business deal. Prosperity; financial and emotional security. Stability and contentment. The realisation of hopes and wishes.

NEGATIVE Serious errors of judgement; the failure of an enterprise. An unsatisfactory situation or relationship. Costly mistakes. Results fail to live up to expectations due to a lack of effort.

TEN

POSITIVE Complete emotional happiness and domestic harmony; marital bliss. Enduring friendship and respect within the community. Love of home, family and birthplace. Well-earned security; personal success.

NEGATIVE Sadness or great disappointment. Indignation or serious disputes; opposition or rivalry. An unexpected and unpleasant change of circumstances. Loss of status. A sudden departure.

Valet de Coupe
The Knave of Cups

KNAVE

POSITIVE A young and willing helper; a student. Children or their affairs bring joy and pleasure. Good news and important messages. A birth within the family. A change of direction; beginnings.

NEGATIVE Seduction or deception; a warning against falling for flattery. A lack of discretion. Obstacles of all kinds. Elusive elements; failure to seize opportunities. An unpleasant surprise.

Cavalier de Coupe
The Knight of Cups

KNIGHT

POSITIVE A business proposition or proposal of marriage. An unexpected visitor brings welcome news or a surprise gift. An idealistic, romantic interlude; a creative phase or flash of inspiration.

NEGATIVE A strong temptation to indulge in pleasure of the flesh has far-reaching but unpleasant consequences. Duplicity or fraud. An unsubstantiated rumour causes great distress. Rivalry in love.

Reyne de Coupe
The Queen of Cups

QUEEN

POSITIVE A mature woman, possibly the wife, mother or trusted friend of the querent. Honesty and feminine intuition; good, sound advice. A beneficial marriage or stable relationship. Wisdom and virtue.

NEGATIVE An unsatisfied longing for love, harmony and romance; an emotional sacrifice. A warning to watch out for deception or immorality. Smugness; a refusal to accept the help or advice of others.

Roy de Coupe
The King of Cups

KING

POSITIVE A professional man of some standing who is well disposed towards the querent. A benefactor or counsellor. Established relationships, material security. A judgement in favour of the querent.

NEGATIVE The danger of scandal; legal complications or disputes with those in authority. Hypocrisy, pretentiousness and unfairness. A ruthless business rival or the loss of an important contract.

SUIT OF SWORDS

THE SUIT OF SWORDS (OR ÉPÉES)

TRADITIONALLY ASSOCIATED WITH THE ELEMENT AIR, THIS SUIT RELATES TO CHALLENGE, OPPOSITION, AMBITION AND AUTHORITY.

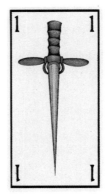

ACE

POSITIVE Will-power, determination and ambition. Triumph over opposition; conquest of all sorts. Courage, firmness and integrity; initiative and the start of an enterprise. Intellectual activity.

NEGATIVE Fierce rivalry, especially in business matters. A clash of wills, fury and conflict. Weakness in the face of difficulty; the dissipation of energies. Disruptive influence. Animosity.

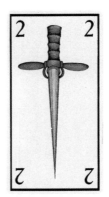

TWO

POSITIVE Stability; harmonious circumstances and inner security. Reconciliation or the cementing of friendship. A conformist personality. Accomplishment, improved status and the respect of colleagues.

NEGATIVE A tense relationship or false friends. Others' dishonesty could lead to material loss or tarnish one's reputation. Confrontations with authority could prove unfortunate for the querent,

THREE

POSITIVE A dramatic end to unpleasant associations brings relief from anxiety. A good time to sort out priorities and to make long-term plans. Decisiveness; dedication to ambition; progress.

NEGATIVE Retreat from emotional involvement; separation from loved ones. Traumatic events; deliberately disruptive influences. Confusion, complications and disappointments. Sadness; regret; alienation.

FOUR

POSITIVE Repose and recompense for past efforts. Recovery and recuperation from illness or emotional hurt. Solitude and meditation; a time for gathering one's inner resources; preparation.

NEGATIVE Isolation or an enforced retreat from society, perhaps imprisonment. Inhibition and restriction; the imposition of others' wills; a sense of helplessness; despair. Unpleasant circumstances.

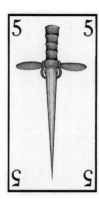

FIVE

POSITIVE A coming to terms with reality; realisation of one's own limitations and capabilities. Awakening awareness; an opportunity to make a fresh start, possibly in entirely new surroundings.

NEGATIVE Dishonour, degradation and loss; sorrow or mourning. A business defeat. The possibility of others' treachery or slanderous gossip. Afflictions, crises and difficulties. Theft.

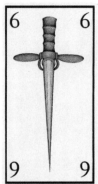

SIX

POSITIVE Travel on or over water, probably abroad. Relief following anxiety. Declarations of friendship or support; a marriage proposal. Freedom from recent restrictions and easing of difficulties.

NEGATIVE Impasse; an unresolved problem; an inability to find solutions. A feeling of powerlessness. Unfavourable judgement in a lawsuit. Poor health caused by worry, anxiety and stress.

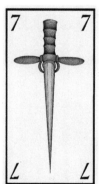

SEVEN

POSITIVE The renewal of hope or confidence in the future. Improvements to circumstances. Wise advice; practical schemes; competence. Prudence and perseverance. Ambition, effort and endeavour.

NEGATIVE Disappointment over the failure of plans. Annoyance or irritation. Delays and uncertainties. Clandestine activities, secret intrigues. Embarrassing or compromising revelations. Tricky problems.

EIGHT

POSITIVE The easing of problems or the end of a difficult phase. New direction and decisive actions. Retribution: a past injustice is righted. Relief from past tension; resolution and reconciliation.

NEGATIVE Disappointing news causes disquiet. Difficulties and setbacks. Opposition or rivalry. Unforeseen debts or accidents. Criticism and blame that are unfounded. Temporary misfortunes.

NINE

POSITIVE The resolution of inner conflict; the beginning of recovery from past traumas. Recuperation from emotional hurts. Renewed hope. A positive change of outlook and determination to start afresh.

NEGATIVE A miscarriage of justice; deception and suspicion. Shame and reasonable fear; anxiety and stress; disappointment or desolation. Failure of a project. Loss of possessions, reputation or freedom.

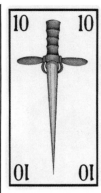

TEN

POSITIVE A temporary advantage; the defeat of opposition. An improvement in material circumstances. The realisation that the worst is now over and that the future can be faced with hope and courage.

NEGATIVE Sudden despair and desolation; abject misery and total sense of failure. Financial ruin or emotional loss; reason divorced from reality. An unavoidable end to a close relationship.

Valet d'Epée
The Knave of Swords

KNAVE

POSITIVE Vigilance, preparedness and acumen. The help of an active, younger person. Unexpected good news; a surprise gift or financial aid. A successful scheme or advantageous business deal. Promotion.

NEGATIVE An unscrupulous youngster; childish cruelty. Unforeseen problems or unexpected delays to plans. The interference of others; devious actions and slanderous tongues. Unfortunate incidents.

Cavalier d'Epée
The Knight of Swords

KNIGHT

POSITIVE Triumph over opposition; the end of adversity; the defeat of a rival. A practical solution to a problem or the successful implementation of a plan. The healing of emotional/psychological wounds.

NEGATIVE Erratic or unreasonable behaviour; unsuccessful speculation. A breach of confidence causes emnity. A stupid blunder or extravagance leads to failure. The possibility of an operation.

Reyne d'Epée
The Queen of Swords

QUEEN

POSITIVE A woman of great strength of character who can help or advise the querent; supportive influences. Confidence, ambitious schemes; business success. Discernment, ingenuity and independence.

NEGATIVE A subtle but deceitful character; underhand actions. Unreliability, disappointment and frustration of plans. Sorrow or bereavement; personal losses of other kinds, such as pets, lovers, friends.

Roy d'Epée
The King of Swords

KING

POSITIVE A mature, professional man; the help of those in authority; the respect of the community. Status and influence; promotional opportunities; business advancement. Beneficial contracts or agreements.

NEGATIVE Unfavourable legal proceedings or official decisions. A warning that the querent may fall foul of the heavy hand of authority. A ruthless enemy or business rival. Fierce opposition; bigotry.

CHAPTER FIVE

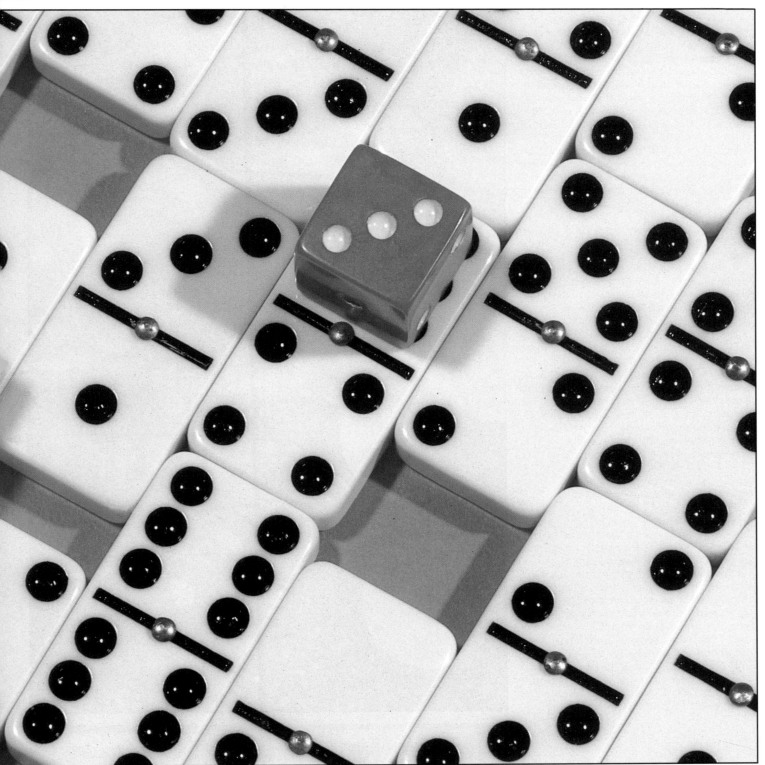

DICE & DOMINOES

Divination by dice is a very ancient form of predicting the future, probably dating from around 2000BC. The use of dice, which show specific numbers, probably derives from tossing of lots, coins for instance.

In the West the most commonly used dice have the one spot facing the six spot; therefore the two spot is opposite the five and three opposite the four. However, in other parts of the world different numberings are still in use. Predicting with a pair of dice is the norm, though sometimes three dice may be used.

The first record of dominoes is from China in the 12th century BC. Each tile is divided in half, and each half has spots indicating numbers from zero to six. Modern sets consist of 28 tiles — one tile for every combination from double-blank to double-six, and are readily available.

DICE

There are many superstitions connected with dice, one of which is that they should not only be thrown in silence, but that someone else should throw them for the answer to a personal question. Nowadays many practitioners of this art believe that you can only answer a question from dice once you have drawn a circle of approximately 12″ in diameter, using chalk, then throw the dice. If all the dice land outside the circle you should throw them again; if this happens twice in succession it should be assumed that you are not meant to have a reading at this particular time.

If any dice should land inside the circle, they are to be added together and an interpretation given according to their numerical value.

Traditionally any dice that fall outside the circle indicate quarrels or estrangements and, should the dice fall on top of each other, you must refuse a gift or opportunity that is known at the present time.

If a number recurs during a reading, it indicates that important news is likely to be coming your way shortly.

Prophecies by dice are said to occur within nine days of any reading and you should not try to obtain more than one consultation a week; it is also thought by some to be unlucky to try dice on Mondays and Wednesdays. My own feelings are that you should use your own judgement as long as you do not manipulate the process by asking various forms of the same question in order to obtain a favourable answer.

Casting the dice

The most widely used method of casting dice is to throw a pair to answer a specific question. Place both dice in a cup and shake them while concentrating on the question that is uppermost in your mind at the time of the reading. When you feel ready, tip the dice into the chalk circle while keeping your eyes closed. Should both dice fall within the circle, add together the number of dots shown on the uppermost face of each. If only one dice falls within the circle, note the numerical value of its upper face and ignore the other dice. If neither lands within the circle, cast the dice again.

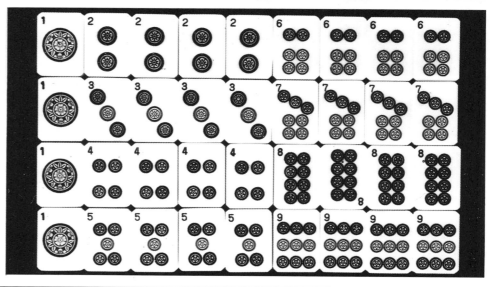

Right: An elegant set of traditional Mah Jongg tiles, the forerunners of both dice and dominoes. Such tiles were once used by the ancient Chinese not simply as a game, but also as a means of divination.

ONE spot only means an absolutely positive answer to any question; presumably because it is so unlikely that it will be obtained.

TWO spots mean the reverse, so invariably the answer is "No".

THREE spots indicate that all is not lost, but that care needs to be taken in the process of achieving your heart's desire.

FOUR spots suggest that achievement is possible but that you need to ascertain that the proposal is really practical.

FIVE spots suggest luck in any undertaking.

SIX spots say "Go ahead" even when the outcome is debatable.

SEVEN spots indicate reliance upon blind faith.

EIGHT spots say that patience is needed; perhaps there will be delays.

NINE spots are an absolute "Yes" however impossible the situation.

TEN spots suggest doubt but, presumably, you could overcome this with tenacity and perseverance.

ELEVEN spots mean that you are asking an irrevelant question.

TWELVE spots may mean that you are not asking the right question or that what seems to be of importance now may not be so in the immediate future.

Some people feel that they obtain the best results by the use of three dice; although this method is usually used when you want a general reading of the trends for the immediate future, without asking a specific question. In this instance, you still need to draw a circle in order to see whether the dice fall inside or outside. As though you were using two dice, the values of ONE and TWO spots remain the same, an undisputable "Yes" and "No" respectively. Below are the traditional answers — using three dice.

ONE spot only means an absolutely positive answer to any question; presumably because it is so unlikely that it will be obtained.

TWO spots mean the reverse, so invariably the answer is "No".

THREE spots indicate a pleasant surprise or that good news is on the way.

FOUR spots may mean the reverse.

FIVE spots indicate happiness, even if this is not expected.

SIX spots may be unfortunate, especially in business or finance. You should also take extra care of possessions if this combination is thrown.

SEVEN spots suggest caution in all matters, especially in connection with privacy; you should never discuss plans under such a combination.

EIGHT spots say that the past will catch up on you in some way and can suggest retribution, unless you have been previously blameless.

NINE spots show luck in love, either for you or for someone dear to you. This combination can suggest marriage or reconciliation.

TEN spots suggest beginnings, whether this is in the area of friendship or business; it may also suggest achievement or promotion.

ELEVEN spots show changes, perhaps partings.

TWELVE spots are always indicators of good news, which may be received through the post. Any job offers should be viewed with suspicion; the advice of others should always be consulted.

THIRTEEN spots are regarded as unlucky and may suggest that current plans are of little value.

FOURTEEN spots suggest luck through friends, perhaps via an introduction; or they may mean that admiration or applause comes your way.

FIFTEEN spots are warnings of danger and indicate that you should take care to act within legal boundaries.

SIXTEEN spots show journeys that are lucrative or profitable in some way.

SEVENTEEN spots indicate changes, perhaps involving someone from a distance; but this combination may indicate profit in the world of business.

EIGHTEEN spots show the best possible combination and signify prosperity, wealth, happiness and success in any enterprise.

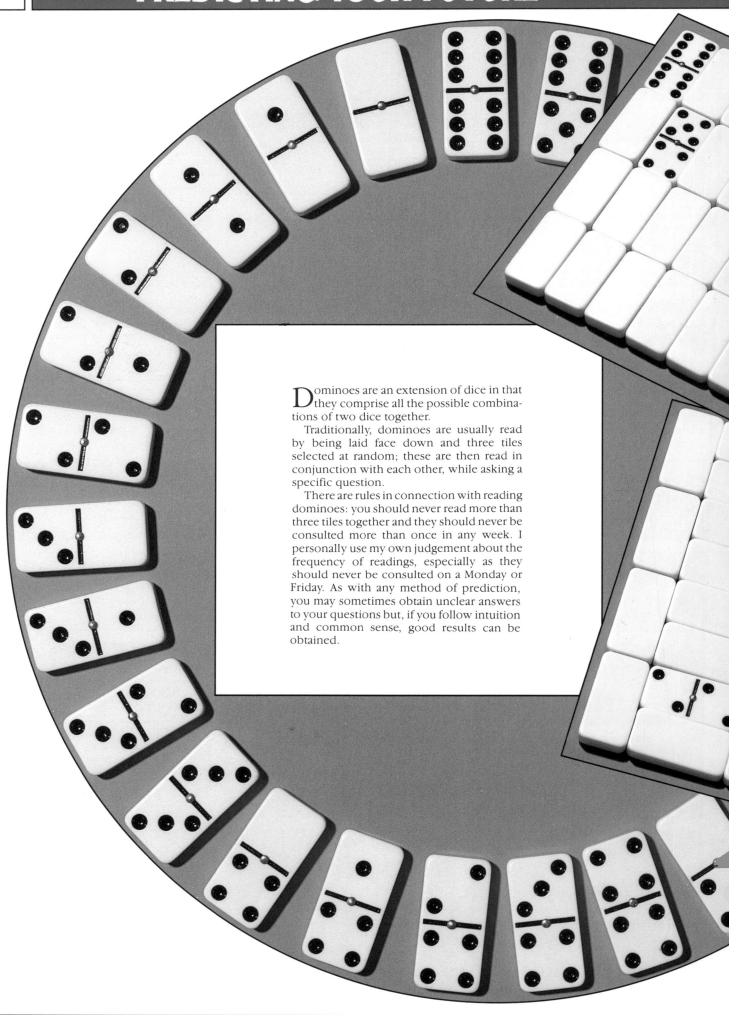

Dominoes are an extension of dice in that they comprise all the possible combinations of two dice together.

Traditionally, dominoes are usually read by being laid face down and three tiles selected at random; these are then read in conjunction with each other, while asking a specific question.

There are rules in connection with reading dominoes: you should never read more than three tiles together and they should never be consulted more than once in any week. I personally use my own judgement about the frequency of readings, especially as they should never be consulted on a Monday or Friday. As with any method of prediction, you may sometimes obtain unclear answers to your questions but, if you follow intuition and common sense, good results can be obtained.

THE INDIVIDUAL MEANINGS OF THE TILES

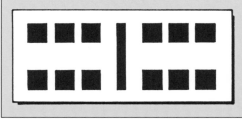

This is considered the best domino of all and is said to presage success, happiness and great joy. Tradition says that farmers drawing this tile may have to sell land to make ends meet, but that they conquer their difficulties by doing this. You should regard it as an omen of achievement and ultimate rejoicing, however much the odds seem stacked against you.

A combination which suggests that a previous kindness or unselfish act will reap benefits in the present, even though you were not seeking reward when performing the good deed. You may not even realise that you were receiving good karma at the time of benefit. Close friendship is around you and this will be helpful; although you must exercise patience when this domino appears, as luck is not immediate.

This tile speaks of partnerships — good and bad. Impersonal relationships seem to fare worst and there may be quarrels or even litigation in connection with acquaintances; this may or may not go in your favour. Personal relationships appear to be under better auspices and here you could find romance where it is least expected; such love may come through shared problems.

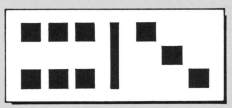

This tile indicates travel but you must call upon intuition to decide whether this be for pleasure or through business. There may be the holiday of your dreams on the horizon and this will be as good as expected, or you may be on the verge of a journey that will change your lifestyle. This could be through a business success overseas or even through emigration.

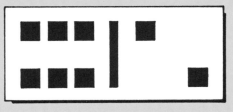

Good luck or a definite improvement of current adverse circumstances is indicated here. Apparently the most important issue at the moment is the honesty of the question; those who are scrupulously honest will receive the most benefits, whereas dishonest folk may get their just deserts. This tile brings recognition for previous effort or hard work, or even through thriftiness.

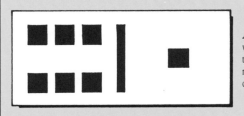

Another favourable tile this; it may even indicate a wedding. At the very least, it signifies the ending of current problems, especially where there has been a long period of adversity. Older folk drawing this tile may look forward to a happy retirement; whilst youngsters may settle down and have families. However, if adjacent tiles are dubious in nature, you may have to learn to let go of the past.

This tile is not especially pleasant but it does contain the possibility of being able to stave off any adverse effects. There is a warning to beware of gossip or false friends, so you should keep plans or ideas to yourself. There may also be such trivial chatter around you and if so you are well advised to stay clear of it. You should decide to be very self-contained when drawing this tile.

THE INDIVIDUAL MEANING OF THE TILES

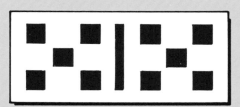

This tile speaks very strongly of change and will only work well when you are not resistant to this. This change may relate to job, home or relationships; but will nevertheless prove beneficial in the long run. Often this domino will appear when you are aware of impending change and this should be encouraged, especially where there is any reluctance to break out of a rut: the omens are favourable.

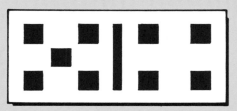

Always a sign of good fortune of the material kind. Yet it should be noted that this increase is never to be sought but always comes through orthodox means, such as tax rebates or bonuses that have been earned. There could also be an improvement of your position at work in the form of promotion or even the offer of a better job. Traditionally, females may have to support their partners yet will be in a position to do this.

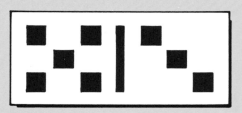

In any reading this is a pleasant tile to find because it suggests that life is running on an even keel. There should be a calm atmosphere around you both at home and at work. Other people are ready to co-operate and to further current plans and ideas. Good news may be on the way, perhaps through a visitor or from your boss. Financial security should be long-term.

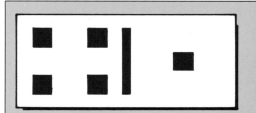

This tile is frequently an omen of birth, either for you or for someone close to you. In a general way it brings the message that tolerance or patience is needed and that you should take time to study what is of long-term benefit. Meditation is often recommended to those who draw this tile. Marriage is not considered favourable at the moment; you should reflect whether this is the best course of action.

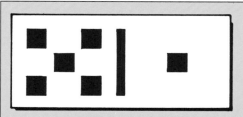

Many invitations are likely to come your way and these may produce useful contacts for the future. Financial dealings should be handled with care in order to avoid disappointment. If you are married, or in a permanent relationship, there may be an increase to the family — not necessarily a new baby. Widen your horizons when you draw this tile and look to future prospects.

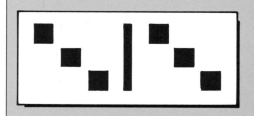

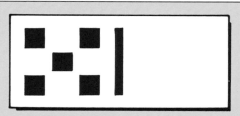

This tile indicates a need for caution and may even suggest that you should keep a careful eye upon expenditure: otherwise there may be trouble. There may also be a warning against selfishness or self-indulgence; this, too, could create problems. A friend may have a problem, and you may well be able to offer a solution, even if this is only because you can provide a friendly shoulder to cry on.

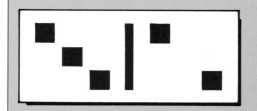

Work may be under good auspices if you draw this domino, especially if this is in a field that is creative or artistic. It is not so good for mental pursuits, though, and you should not expect life to follow a logical pattern at the moment. It may also indicate a light-hearted period that contains many celebrations and festivities. Perhaps you should just relax and have fun.

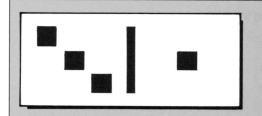

If you turn up this tile do not be too confident about your immediate future; luckily, your worst fears will not be realised. Life should be lively and comfortable, even if you do not expect this. Young people may marry or form a liaison that is successful against all odds. It would appear that this domino shows reason for hope where this has been lacking, however improbable this may seem.

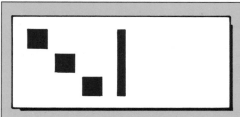

This appears to be a bad omen and may indicate quarrels and disagreements. If you are male, you should take care over choice of partner or you could end up with a very independent woman; a female querent may find her partner is rather foolish and inclined to get into unnecessary fights. Apparently negative trends can apply to anyone who is contacted and care should be taken when accepting social invitations.

A domino that indicates change of any sort, usually for the better. However, you should guard possessions carefully and take care to avoid deceptive people. It would seem to carry a warning of taking nothing for granted but not to ignore the possibility of beneficial change coming from an unexpected source. You may attract notice in career or take calculated risks with finance, but must always be self-reliant.

Business success is predicted by this domino, although this seems to indicate steady progress rather than vast riches. Some say that outsiders may be jealous of you but this is presumably because you have something to envy. Home life is said to be good, with faithful partners and children that add to happiness and fulfil their parents' dreams: this tile sounds quite idyllic!

Traditionally, this tile always heralds the appearance of financial problems and you should take care to pay-off debts before this occurs. It seems to suggest that following a straight and narrow path is the correct route and that you should not deviate and take chances. Marriage may be under good auspices, yet this will be for love instead of money, and there will probably be many children.

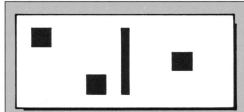

Tradition has it that marriage will include financial benefit and that early widowhood could occur. Presumably you inherit the money and are then able to please yourself! It is also said that if you are male you will suffer financial losses — perhaps through all those females who wish to marry you for your money! Luckily, this tile is also considered to indicate a good life and may suggest reunion with friends.

Disappointments, quarrels even, are indicated here; in some instances there may be delays before plans can be completed. It also contains the warning of keeping confidences or personal secrets otherwise there may be trouble. Tradition has it that if you are pregnant, you can expect a multiple birth and that you should be careful about disclosing this — or you may immediately go into labour — so don't say you haven't been warned!

Apparently this is a good omen for travel and you may even meet someone who will become important en route. It may also indicate worries of a trivial nature that could be solved by contemplating a change of scene. Perhaps the implication is that you are bored, and stuck in a rut and could benefit from well-considered changes.

This is a very fortunate tile for finance — the money just keeps on rolling in — and it may come from more than one source. But it is not so good on the emotional level and you may be subject to jealousy — perhaps because financial luck is currently in your favour! Perhaps the true message from this tile is to concentrate on the material side of life and leave love for later on.

Harmony is signified by this tile which will act beneficially whatever the problem. It appears to indicate a worry that is without foundation, one that will be resolved without any need for effort. It would also seem to suggest that if a definite decision is called for, you should be self-reliant and take immediate action. There may be happiness in all aspects of life.

Apparently this is a good domino unless you are pregnant, in which case you should consult expert advice. However, as it also contains the message of happiness in love and marriage, I doubt if there is any real cause to worry. Apparently travel and finance are also under good auspices and even careful investment is favoured. I imagine that dire results only happen to those who take chances, so act accordingly.

Tradition suggests that this tile always means an important visitor who will bring interesting news, possibly concerning finance. However, one should never take anything on trust without checking facts to the fullest extent. Presumably this means that life is interesting and lively at present but matters may only hold temporary importance, which should be judged by the surrounding tiles.

If you draw this tile you should be extremely wary of outside involvements, especially any that have the potential of leading to lawsuits. There is a warning about listening to rumour or gossiping, but any harm that is indicated can be avoided with cautious action. Some say that if a specific question has been asked the answer is "No" but my advice is to pay attention to the surrounding tiles.

Every source seems to suggest that this is the blackest tile you can have but, conversely, if you are involved in fraudulent activities you will receive benefit! As predicting by dominoes is very ancient I feel this must refer to karma, so perhaps you should take a slightly fatalistic attitude when drawing this tile and consider the result to be left in the hands of the gods.

CHAPTER SIX

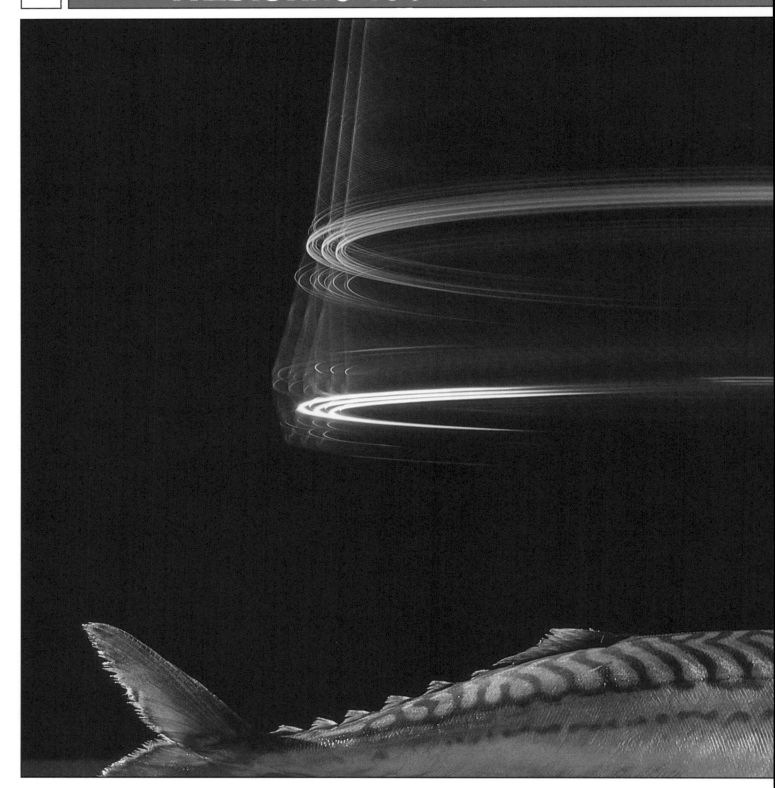

DOWSING

Dowsing, or radiesthesia, is a very simple method of divination which allows the dowser to obtain a "Yes" or "No" answer to a specific question. It is a very old art, practised in one form or another for centuries.

In fact dowsing is a much more common feature of everyday life than most people think. Some mineworkers, for example, still use the traditional method of divining to find the exact location of underground springs or specific mineral deposits as was done throughout Europe in the 17th century. These prospectors perform exactly the same exercise as does a modern metal-detector. Another form of dowsing with a 20th century application is medical dowsing or radionics, which among other things is used to detect the sex of an unborn child. Now trained operators use specially-designed equipment, but in the past the simple practice of suspending a pendulum over specific points in the human body enabled a diagnosis to be made.

TOOLS OF THE TRADE

Dowsing has numerous applications and it can be practised by anyone with very little cost. What implement is chosen for the purpose will, of course, depend on personal circumstances and individual preference but any of the following can be used.

Angle-rods

These are well worth making yourself although it is possible to purchase manufactured ones quite cheaply. All that is needed are two metal coat-hangers which should be cut as illustrated and, for safety's sake, have their shorter ends bound with tape.

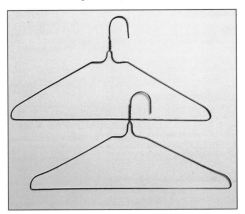

Two wire coat-hangers, such as those used by dry-cleaners, make ideal angle-rods for dowsing. Simply cut through the wire at the points shown below.

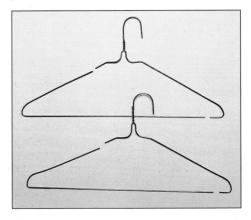

Holding the long side firmly — use a flat surface or bench vice — gently bend the angled, shorter arm until it forms a right-angle. For safety and comfort, bind the 'handles'.

If you wish to add a further refinement, two ball-point pen holders or some plastic tubing will act as handles if slipped over the shorter ends. This would make the rods more comfortable to hold and still allow them to move quite freely.

To use, simply hold the rods (one in each hand) with the shorter ends grasped loosely in your fists. Relax your shoulders and, keeping your elbows tucked firmly in to the side of your body, make sure that your forearms are held parallel to the ground in front of your body and that the long arms of the rods, too, are parallel. They should act as "extensions" to your own arms.

If dowsing outdoors, you may find that you need to place your thumbs lightly on the point where the rods bend in order to inhibit any excessive movements caused by a high wind or the unevenness of the ground. Make sure that you feel comfortable, not too tense, and that the rods are held loosely enough to enable them to swing from side to side but not so loosely that their tips droop down. They must remain parallel to the ground.

You should know immediately that whatever you are seeking has been located by the action of the rods; as you walk forward they will swing gently from side to side but may suddenly both swing inwards to meet, then cross when your objective has been found. Confirmation can be had by slowly circling the designated spot to see whether or not the rods return to their original position. In this way it is sometimes possible to trace the course of an underground stream, water pipe, electricity cable, seam of ore, or whatever else it is you are looking for.

Forked twig

Most people will probably immediately associate dowsing, particularly water-divining, with the use of a forked twig. Traditionally, a hazel branch was used and the cutting and preparation of this was carried out with due ceremony to ensure that the omens were fortuitous. The Moon had to be in the correct phase, the appropriate incantations recited, and so on. However, it is highly unlikely that anyone goes to such extremes nowadays.

Below: The traditional dowser's tool: a y-shaped hazel branch with the minor twigs removed. Newly-cut wood is best as a degree of springiness is needed. Trim the single length to 18-24ins and pare away any rough bark from the forked, 'handle' end.

Ideally, you need a Y-shaped branch with a long "V" somewhere between 18 and 24 inches in length and no more than an inch in diameter with its open end no wider than your body. As with the angle-rods, the two ends act as handles and the single arm is held in front of you, like a pointer, parallel to the ground. But here, of course, the similarity ends as there are not two separate rods, only one, and it does require a certain amount of expertise to get a positive response from a "live" rod.

Beginners may find it a little difficult at first to master the art of holding the rod properly although with practice this can be overcome. Try to place the rod under slight tension by gently pulling the two ends apart so that the whole branch acts as a kind of spring. It may take a little while to get this quite right but, once you have, you should be able to tell: the rod will seem to "come alive" in your hands.

Again, the method of use is identical to that of the angle-rods, the difference lies in the dowsing tool's reaction. On approaching the object sought, the rod will usually seem to twist and turn, sometimes quite dramatically, to finally come to rest pointing firmly down towards the site of whatever it is that you are seeking. Because you are here dealing with a tool that must have a certain degree of flexibility in order to operate, you may have to replace the divining-rod from time to time when the wood becomes too brittle and snaps under tension; newly-cut wood works best.

Pendulum

This very simple divining tool is probably more convenient for detailed work than for trampling about over muddy fields searching for conduits and the like! Basically, any small objects that can be suspended by a thread held between the fingers can be used, though it is possible to buy quite cheap turned wood, brass, glass or ceramic pendulums.

Ideally, the suspended object should be pointed, like a crystal drop from a chandelier or a plumber's bob, but a wedding ring, key or small stone with a hole through which the thread can pass will suffice. If you make up your own pendulum, ensure that the thread (nylon, cotton, twine or whatever is to hand) is firmly knotted and cannot come undone; the length of thread needed will vary from person to person but should be long enough so that it can be wound once or twice round you index or middle finger, to prevent slipping, and still almost touch the table top when your hand is held out at about shoulder height.

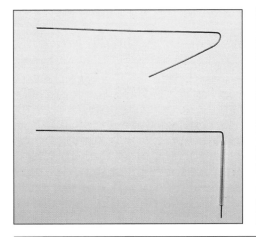

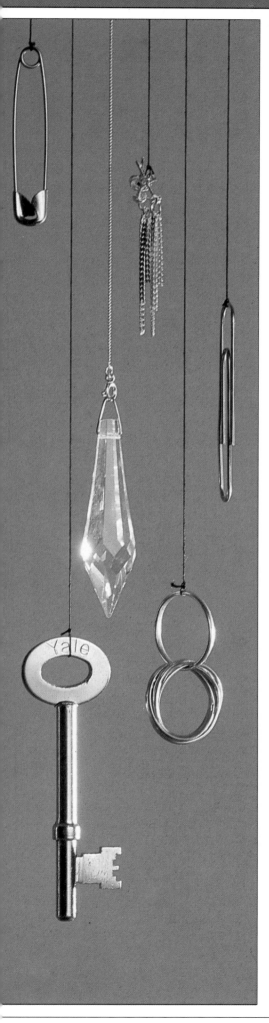

HOW TO DOWSE

Whether you use an angle-rod, a forked twig or pendulum, it is acting merely as a bridge between the subconscious and conscious worlds, so that what is sensed with your natural abilities can be translated into a visible signal (the twitch of the rod, the swing of the pendulum) which is recognised and understood by the diviner. In other words, dowsing is only one method of developing and using your psychic abilities, intuition, clairvoyance, call it what you will.

That said, it remains a simple and convenient method of obtaining information which can be used in a variety of ways. As I have already mentioned, it is possible to dowse in the field in order to locate water, minerals or ores, perhaps even buried treasure! If a large area has to be covered, this will usually be marked out into smaller sections, perhaps by means of pegs driven into the ground and cordoned off with lengths of string, which will then be systematically surveyed by the prospector until a positive response is evoked.

It is also possible to dowse for missing articles, perhaps actually in the general area where the item was lost. More probably, though, it may not be practicable to search the area because it is too vast or too far away, in which case the use of a pendulum will provide the solution.

Pendulums are often used this way for "absent" or "distant" dowsing, sometimes in conjunction with a map of the area. The underlying principle remains the same: the map will be scanned section by section until the pendulum gives a positive response. This will help to locate a specific site which can be be more thoroughly investigated on the ground or perhaps re-dowsed using larger scale maps until a more conveniently-sized area to search has been pinpointed.

On a much smaller scale, it is possible to sketch a rough floor-plan of a house or flat, say, where a precious object has been mislaid in order to discover its exact location. This is a very useful method which you can try out for yourself.

You also may be able to answer questions relating to all manner of things, whether you are trying to locate a missing article, lost animal, archaeological site or, of course, trying to identify an illness or discover what is wrong with the car, determine an auspicious date for an event, or decide whether to do something.

Always remember that dowsing can only give a "Yes" or "No" response; it cannot offer opinions. Whether you pose a mental question, make out a list or use something pertaining to the question (perhaps a lost dog's ball, a photo, an object belonging to an absent person for whom you are dowsing), the principle remains the same. The question posed must be very clear and allow only for a straight "yes" or "no" answer.

The success of your dowsing depends entirely upon the clarity with which you ask your question, not on any outside factors. Dowsing is a simple and versatile method of tapping into the subconscious (or collective unconscious, if you prefer) in order to obtain the available information. You could be pleasantly surprised at the results if you take the time mastering the technique of dowsing.

Above: A typical, turned wood pendulum; this one is made of beech. The weight is carefully calculated to hold the thread taut but not cause the operator's hand to shake with prolonged effort. Also popular are small brass pendulums or plumbers' bobs.

Left: In an emergency almost any small item that can be suspended on a length of cotton, thread, twine or cord will suffice as a substitute pendulum, as can be seen from this collection.

DREAMS

It is a sobering thought to realise that if we do not understand our own dreams, we do not understand ourselves. And since we created them, only we can truly explain and unravel them. "Know thyself" is a quest we are all on and few complete the course in one lifetime. Since dreams reflect our inner fears, hopes, phobias and potentials, what better source of information can we possibly tap than these!

What is a dream? Is what we remember simply a fragment from a continuous performance that goes on 24 hours a day or is it a specific item related to some mystery, fear or desire? The answer seems to be both but who can really say for sure?

What we do know is that dreams contain personal and sometimes secret messages from the dreamer to the dreamer. We also know that it is often difficult to extract these messages. Obviously, since we created them, the best people to interpret them are ourselves by following the interpretations on the following pages and applying them to our personal circumstances.

Tonight, in every home, most of us will go to bed and, as Shakespeare said, "Sleep — perchance to dream." After a hectic day, the best moment is when we climb into a nice warm bed, place our head on the pillow and close our eyes. With luck, it is only a matter of minutes before we are whisked away on that blissful nocturnal journey which lasts, on average, 7 hours 20 minutes.

During sleep our muscles relax into a state of complete rest. Our minds, on the other hand, do no such thing; in fact, our brain activity actually increases as the events of the day are replayed and filed away in our memories.

At regular intervals this process of reassessment is interrupted by sessions of dreaming which may or may not be associated with what happened that day. From psychological tests it has been discovered that we all dream each night, even though some of us do not remember. This may well be so, but it does not explain the reason for dreaming.

Without doubt the purpose of dreaming is to draw attention to particular situations which have escaped recognition when we were awake and, in so doing, increase our insight so that we unconsciously change our opinions or even constructively alter our way of life. This is why problems which seem insoluble the night before appear to be much less formidable the next morning. Fresh information, added during the night, has clarified and simplified matters so that we are able to adopt an entirely different attitude.

The importance of dreams is fast becoming acknowledged as an unrivalled source of enlightenment. Personal messages, reminders and warnings are offered, to be heeded literally or metaphorically, depending on the circumstances and secret knowledge of the dreamer concerned.

INTERPRETING YOUR DREAMS

Messages are meant to be acted upon so unless we take some form of action our dreaming has been in vain. Action, of course, always brings change — but not neccessarily physical change, at least not initially. The majority of dream messages are urging an emotional change of viewpoint which, in turn, produces a change in attitude and appreciation. Many dreams in fact implore us to take up a new viewpoint.

DREAM MEANINGS

ABBEY A wedding invitation.
ABYSS A warning of loss of reputation; if, however, you land at the bottom without hurt, your honour will be restored.
ACCIDENT Take care while travelling.
ALIEN You need greater security.
AMBULANCE Possible news of a friend's or relative's illness.
ANCHOR A change of job is likely.
ANGEL An improvement in health; creative ideas.
ANVIL Possible marital disputes; hard work will result in success.
APPLES Prosperity.
ARROW You are the object of envy.
ATTIC A fear of being tied down.
AUCTION Beware of shady deals.
AXE You will receive unexpected help.

BABY An ending followed by a new start.
BALCONY You will gain respect and admiration.
BALL An opportunity is coming your way.
BALLET A desire for freedom.
BALLOON Promotion at work.
BANDAGE A domestic dispute is settled.
BANKS News regarding business or finance.
BANNER Fame and great honours.
BANQUET Good news regarding friends.
BAR Great activity in your social life.
BARLEY A time of great physical well-being.
BARN Prosperity.
BASEMENT A trifling worry.
BASKET A welcome invitation.
BATH Great happiness.
BATS Harsh words with a rival.
BATTLE Your plans will be upset.
BEAR A serious disagreement with a friend.

BEARD Advice from friends proves profitable.
BED A change of residence.
BEES A period of prosperity.
BEER Disappointments.
BELLS Unexpected good news.
BELT Friends are very supportive.
BIKE Success will come soon.
BISCUIT Happy reunion with a long absent friend.
BLADE Beware of deception.
BLOOD Risk of an accident.
BOAT News from afar.
BOOKS A need to study.
BOTTLE Your wishes will shortly be realised.
BREAD An unexpected stroke of good fortune.
BRIDGE A feeling of loneliness.
BURGLAR You need to keep a secret.
BUTTERFLY A period of fluctuation.
BUTTON A harmonious domestic situation.

CAGE A lack of freedom.
CAMP You will shortly take a holiday.
CANDLE A stroke of good fortune.
CAR An unexpected journey.
CARDS Financial problems.
CARPET A change of residence.
CASTLE An unexpected happening.
CATS Fame and fortune.
CAVE A need to keep silent.
CEMETERY News of a birth.
CHAINS Sudden difficulties.
CHAIR An unexpected invitation.
CHEESE A possible financial gain.
CHILDREN Health and happiness.
CHOIR Your life will improve within a few weeks.
CHURCH Peace after struggle.
CIRCLES You are discontented.
CLOAK A friend will be helpful.
CLOCK An important transaction.

CLOUDS Family matters cause problems.
COFFEE Disappointment.
COLLEGE Rejoicing.
CONFETTI Confusing.
COTTAGE Your life will improve.
CRADLE News of an unexpected pregnancy.
CROSS You are proved right.
CROSSROADS An important decision.
CROWD Annoying trifles.
CROWN Honour and glory.
CRUTCHES Your hopes will be dashed.
CURTAINS The end of a friendship.

DAGGER A warning to take care.
DANCE Unexpected pleasure.
DAUGHTER Disharmony in the family.
DAWN A new way of life.
DEATH A sign of good health.
DESERT Your hopes will not be fulfilled.
DEVIL The beginning of an exciting period.
DIAMONDS Harsh words with a loved one.
DICE A material loss.
DITCH Success will follow efforts.
DOCTOR A friend will ask for help.
DOG A loyal friend.
DOVE Affection and love.
DRAGON Great success.
DRUM Act on news you receive.
DRUNK A small but unexpected gain.
DUNGEON A need to rid yourself of deep-rooted prejudices.
DUST Minor irritations.

E

EAGLE Public success.
EARRINGS A sign of good news.
EARTHQUAKE A need to take special care of loved ones.
EGGS Financial increase; physical well-being.
ELEPHANT If trunk is up, problems; if down, a lucky break.

Every dream is unique and, like finger-prints, no two are identical. Nevertheless, there are basic themes upon which many dream structures are built and by far the most common are dreams about houses or buildings.

Dream houses invariably represent a symbolic image of the dreamer in relation to a problem, fear or regret.

If we think of dream houses as mansions of the soul, then the whole idea of their symbolic masquerade does not seem so unusual. It is, however, in the secret rooms, hidden stairways, locked cellars and dusty attics that we find the real surprises. Relating what we find in these places to the ambitions, talents and submerged fears of the dreamer, it is possible with thought and time to create an accurate picture of character.

Left: The ancients of Greece and the shamans of so-called "primitive societies" understood the prophetic value of dreams. Our Western, rational culture chose to ignore them. A major breakthrough occurred in 1900 when Freud published his book "On Interpretation of Dreams", pushing their importance back into focus.

ELVES   A rumour is unfounded.
EMERALD   A new romance.
ENGINE   Business or financial problems.
ENVELOPE   News is on its way.
EXAMINATION   A decisive period.
EYES   A joyful period ahead.

F

FACTORY   Your efforts will be rewarded.
FAIRY   An omen of joy.
FATHER   An advantageous change.
FEAST   Your plans prove satisfactory.
FEATHER   Financial problems will ease.
FENCE   You have a business rival.
FIELD   Prosperity and good fortune.
FIRE   Hasty news.
FISH   Unexpected good news.
FLAG   An important change.
FLOWERS   Pleasure and harmony.
FLYING   Marital problems.
FOG   An argument with the boss.
FOOTBALL   You will have the last laugh.
FOREST   A friend will ask for help.
FOX   A warning against deception.
FROG   Guard your health.
FRUIT   Problems with earning your livelihood.
FUNERAL   You will shortly be married.
FURNITURE   You need more order in all areas of your life.

G

GARDEN   Temporary financial difficulties.
GAS   Heed your own advice.
GATES   The start of something new.
GEM   News of an engagement.
GIANT   Obstacles to overcome.
GLASS   (Broken): Unexpected good fortune.
GLOVES   Self-doubt.
GOLD   Success in a new venture.
GOSSIP   Family problems.
GRASS   A need to be practical.

GUITAR   An invitation to a party.
GUN   Disappointing news.
GYPSY   A change of residence or partner.

H

HAIR   A sign of vanity; an expensive gift.
HAMMER   Do not overplay your hand.
HAND   A new and profitable friendship.
HARE   Guard against feelings of insecurity.
HAT   Disappointing changes at work.
HEARTH   Good family relationships; constant mutual love.
HEAVEN   A need for realism.
HELL   A stormy love affair.
HENS   A chance to improve your living standards.
HERD OF ANIMALS   Great wealth and prosperity.
HERMIT   A need to avoid society.
HILL   You want to escape from your mundane life.
HOLIDAY   A current problem will be favourably resolved.
HOLLY   Honesty is the best policy.
HONEY   An increase in earnings.
HORSE   A happy relationship.
HORSESHOE   A change of residence.
HOSPITAL   Greater optimism is needed.
HOTEL   Unexpected visitors.
HOUSE   It represents your subconscious.
HUNTER   A man with experience.
HUT   A loved one is going away.

I

ICE   Others are out to trick you.
ICE CREAM   Financial gains are on the way.
IDOLS   Current plans prove impractical.
ILLNESS   Unnecessary worry.
INJURY   Beware of thoughtless words.
INN   Pleasure with a person of the opposite sex is a likely prospect.
INVITATION   A disappointment.
ISLAND   A fear of isolation.

J

JAM   You are likely to quarrel with your friends.
JAR   Success if full; failure if empty.
JELLY   Insecurity in your business life.
JESTER   You have been taken for a ride.
JEWELLERY   Your finances will prosper.
JOCKEY   Don't be tempted to gamble.
JOURNEY   An important change in personal relationships.
JUDGE   News of a court case.
JUNGLE   You yearn for a more exciting life to fulfil you.

K

KANGAROO   Try to be more organised.
KETTLE   Pay attention to your diet.
KEY   A new opening; a golden opportunity.
KING   You expect too much from others.
KISS   Reconciliation.
KITCHEN   Life is boring, change it.
KITE   Wealth later in life.
KITTEN   Greater happiness.
KNIVES   Quarrels and misunderstandings are likely.
KNOT   Business complications.

L

LACE   Future pleasure and enjoyment.
LADDER   Patience will ensure success.
LAKE   Temporary illness.
LAMB   Be prepared to take a gamble.
LAMP   Heed a friend's advice.
LAUGHING   Sad circumstances.
LAUREL   Peaceful times ahead.
LEGS   You are running away from reality.
LETTER   Unexpected news.
LIGHTNING   An upset followed by reconciliation.
LOCK   A likelihood of theft.
LOG   Possibilities open up for you.
LUGGAGE   Loss of something important.

But psychological character analysis is by no means the only aspect; interwoven throughout most dreams runs a prophetic thread as well. How often have you picked up the morning paper and read something that reminded you of last night's dream? Or perhaps you have dreamed of someone whom you have not seen or thought of for several years, then, with the very next post, you receive a letter from them. When these things happen, we inevitably say 'That's broken my dream.' Incidents like this are common enough and the tendency is to dismiss them as mere coincidences. Unfortunately, only when they herald really dramatic events is their true precognitive worth acknowledged.

In ancient times dreams were believed to be direct messages from the gods, foretelling the future. The Bible has many illustrations of this and all kings and leaders once had their personal dream interpreters. Today, however, dreams are given no credence in this respect. Yet, if we look back in time, we find dream power has moulded not only the lives of individuals, but dramatically altered the entire course of history.

Quite apart from their religious influence, national heritages are, in this century, still reverberating from the interpretation placed on dreams thousands of years ago. If Joseph had not correctly deduced the meaning of the Pharaoh's dream of seven fat and seven lean kine, then his 11 brothers, the fathers of the Tribes of Israel, would not have gone down into Egypt to buy corn. It is not overstating the case to say that from that episode can be traced the story of the present day conflict between Jews and Arabs.

More recently, it can be claimed that a German soldier's prophetic dream, 60 years ago, resulted in World War II. In 1917, Corporal Adolf Hitler was fighting the Allies on the Somme. One night he dreamed he was entrenched in molten metal and falling earth and immediately awoke and rushed outside. Seconds later a shell demolished the bunker from which he had just fled, killing every sleeping occupant.

Hitler looked upon this dream as a little short of miraculous. He took his amazing escape to be a sign indicating his predestined future as founder of the Third Reich. From his subsequent rise and fall we can see that the power of dreams cannot be underestimated.

Apart from substituting our innermost feelings with outer, man-made creations, our dreaming minds also have the ability to operate beyond the accepted laws of space and time. With a code of its own, the language of dreams is quite different from logical thought. The difficulty with dreams, however, lies not so much in interpreting their symbolic messages but in accepting and acting upon their unbiased and sometimes blatantly outspoken advice.

But, whether merely trivial or profoundly mystical, our dreams remain personal documentaries about ourselves and our relationship to others. This, of course, makes dreaming the greatest ego trip of all. Where else can we be the star performer, producer, manager and audience, all rolled into one, other than in those nightly dramas that unfold behind our sleeping eyelids?

Right: A major milestone in dream interpretation occurred in 1945 when filmmaker Alfred Hitchcock and artist Salvador Dali combined talents to create the film "Spellbound". Dreams were once more in the picture, as the hero, played by Gregory Peck, undergoes Freudian dream analysis.

M

MACHINERY Subconscious fears.
MAGPIE Do not listen to gossip.
MAKE-UP Beware of deception.
MANURE Family riches.
MAP Changes in your home life; a long journey.
MARRIAGE Brief intense joy.
MASK Dishonesty.
MATCH Your motives will be misinterpreted.
MEADOW A happy reunion.
MEAT Great prosperity.
METEOR Disorder.
MICE Domestic troubles.
MILK Good health for the family.
MILL An important aim.
MINE A sudden gain.
MIRROR An important crossroads in your life.
MISTLETOE A new romance.
MONEY A loss is likely.
MOON Happy news regarding the home.
MOTH Watch your investments.
MOTHER You can rely on the support of friends.
MOUNTAIN A hard task lies ahead.
MUSHROOMS Mental and physical well-being.
MUSIC Pleasant news.

N

NAILS Hard work and difficulties.
NAKEDNESS You are ready for love.
NECKLACE A celebration.
NEEDLE Do not give others cause to gossip.
NEIGHBOUR Seek the company of others.
NEST A new home or unexpected windfall.
NET Watch your words.
NEWSPAPER Keep your own counsel.
NIGHT You will soon feel happier.
NUN Friends prove willing to help.
NURSE A visit to a doctor or hospital.
NUTS A happy solution to your problems.

O

OAK Security.
OFFICE A new responsibility is likely to come you way soon.
OIL A captivating enthusiasm.
ONIONS The backing of an influential person.
OPALS Happy love affair.
OPERA An enjoyable invitation.
ORANGES Attend to your health even though you feel in fine fettle today.
ORCHESTRA Unsatisfactory romance.
OVEN Your plans can now be put into operation.
OWL Do not allow others to distract you from your goal.

P

PACKAGE Pleasant surprise.
PAIL A new friendship.
PALACE Your financial status will improve if you are patient.
PALM TREE Good news from abroad.
PANTHER Someone is being unfaithful; and you may be completely surprised that this occurs.
PARK A widening of interests.
PARROT A friend betrays your trust when you least expect this to happen.
PARTY An invitation leads to an exciting friendship.
PATH You surmount your obstacles.
PEACOCK An exciting experience you didn't expect.
PEAR News of a windfall.
PEARLS A project will fail.
PEBBLES A keen rival at work.
PEN An important document to be signed — read the small print.
PHOTOGRAPH An unexpected meeting.
PIANO A joyful occasion.
PIG A future of plenty.
PINS A quarrel.
PIPE Guard against ill-considered words and acts.

PIRATE A danger of theft.
PIT Insecurity.
PLAIN A longing to move or change job.
PLANE Easy victory.
PLATE A debt which will soon be paid.
PLOUGH Fertility in the family.
POISON Do not trust too easily.
POLICE A court hearing.
POND Stagnation.
POT Unforeseen expenditure.
PREGNANCY Good news is on the way.
PRISON Much will be demanded of you.
PURSE If full, a slight loss; if empty, money from an unexpected quarter.

Q

QUARREL Beware unwise actions.
QUAY A travel opportunity — think twice.
QUEEN News regarding your mother.
QUICK-SAND Trifling problems.
QUILT A yearning for comfortable surroundings.

R

RABBIT News of a pregnancy.
RAFFLE Future good luck.
RAILWAY A change in your circumstances.
RAIN A major change is imminent.
RAINBOW A brighter future.
RAT A friend deceives you.
RAZOR Disagreement with a close friend.
RICE Dissatisfaction.
RIDING A joyful turn to events.
RING A new and successful enterprise.
ROCKET An unexpected wage increase.
ROCKS You need to make an effort to change things.
ROPE Complications.
ROSE Great social success.
RUINS Difficulties, possibly a broken relationship.

S

SAFE Unnecessary worry.

SAILING Family happiness.
SAILOR A flirtation.
SALESMAN Take care of your property.
SAND Business is bad.
SAPPHIRE A surprising but fortunate gain.
SALT Advancement.
SCAFFOLD Disappointment regarding property.
SCALES Possible litigation.
SCHOOL Don't underestimate your abilities.
SCISSORS Cutting a friendship.
SCORPION Don't allow yourself to be bullied.
SEA Chaotic circumstances, if choppy; tranquility, if calm.
SEAT Bad news.
SHAMPOO You seek admiration.
SHARK Conflict with an enemy.
SHEEP Improved prospects.
SHELLS You are too extravagant.
SHIP Your troubles are coming to an end.
SHOES Domestic arguments over possessions.
SHOP You will soon have a chance to buy a bargain.
SHOWER Physical well-being.
SIGNPOST An end to indecision.
SILVER Knowledge brings advancement.
SKATING Your job is in danger.
SKY Your wishes will be fulfilled.
SMOKE A shady deal.
SNAIL Gradual achievements.
SNAKE A decisive change in life.
SNOW The triumphant realisation of your wishes.
SOAP An unpleasant duty.
SOLDIER You will receive respect and honour.
SPADE Harsh words.
SPIDER Imminent good luck.
SPOON A welcome visitor.
STAIRS Important changes, probably for the better.
STALLION Prosperity.
STAR Excellent prospects.
STATUE A lack of energy.

STEEPLE Ambitions.
STOCKINGS Caution is indicated.
STRANGER An argument.
STRAWBERRIES A joyful love.
SUN Great benefits.
SWAN A new lease of life.
SWEETS Guard against flattery.
SWIMMING Arguments.
SWING A stroke of luck.
SWORD High public reward.

T

TABLE Material well-being; a happy reunion.
TANGLE Don't get involved in other people's arguments.
TARGET An admirer.
TATTOO A fear of reality.
TEA You yearn for a better social life.
TEARS Denotes happiness.
TEETH Trivial problems.
TELEPHONE Getting in touch with an ex-lover.
TELESCOPE Journeys.
TENT A change of situation; possible move.
THEATRE A change.
THIRST Your expectations are high.
THUNDER Extra responsibility.
TIGER Irritating travel delays.
TOBACCO Your plans will go up in smoke.
TORTOISE Avoid hasty decisions.
TOY Indecision.
TRAIN A hasty journey.
TRAMP Someone asks for a loan.
TRAVEL Disenchantment or fear of present circumstances.
TREASURE Your hopes will be dashed.
TREES Prosperity and new doors open.
TRUMPET A decisive conflict.
TUNNEL Great effort is required.

U

UMBRELLA When open, helpful friends; when closed, business prosperity.

UNICORN A need to face reality.

V

VASE A pleasant surprise from an admirer.
VEGETABLES Unexpected events.
VEIL Insincerity.
VELVET Prosperity.
VIOLIN A happy love affair.
VOLCANO Great activity.
VULTURE Guard against scheming colleagues.

W

WAGON Unhappy marriage.
WAITER An enjoyable date with a charming companion.
WALL Caution is needed.
WASP Watch out for envy.
WATER If clear, plenty; if muddy, watch the pennies.
WATERFALL Legal problems.
WAVES Big changes are imminent.
WEB You need to be more forceful.
WEDDING Misfortune.
WEEPING A joyful forthcoming event.
WELL A wish will come true.
WHALE A struggle, but you will overcome.
WHEEL Great change.
WIND A stroke of good fortune.
WINDMILL Fruitless endeavours.
WINDOW Open, a quick solution; shut, escape from an unsuspected danger.
WOLF Secure your home.
WOOD Complications.
WOOL Prosperity.

Y

YACHT Sudden change of fortunes.

Z

ZEBRA Avoid procrastination.

CHAPTER EIGHT

GEOMANCY

The method of divination by geomancy has changed over the ages; originally it literally included the life of earth or sand. By believing the earth was alive and thus able to answer questions, the diviner would mark out a circle on the ground and either throw pebbles within this or make random marks or shapes that could be "read". Although practised continuously in certain areas, notably North Africa, geomancy's popularity as a means of divination has fluctuated considerably over the centuries.

Strangely, Napolean Bonaparte was responsible for a revival of interest in the subject in Europe. His "Oraculum", or Mystic Oracle, provides answers to specific questions by means of a complicated process involving a master chart with key numbers, letters and geomantic figures. The latter are formed by making random pencil strokes on paper.

PAPER GEOMANCY

Nowadays, although a few sand-readers still exist, the most common form of geomancy is to make a series of random dashes on a piece of paper which will ultimately produce a geomantic figure. Because the earth is said to have four corners, this number is deemed important, so the number of figures that can be produced by this method is 4 x 4 = 16. Each of the 16 figures will have a different pattern of dots and these are often assigned an astrological sign but it should be noted that the sources that have been handed down to us rarely agree on what these should be. However, there is agreement on the Latin name that each possess.

In order to arrive at any of these figures take a clean sheet of paper and write the question posed very clearly at the top. The question must be thought out very carefully as it is all too easy to ask one that should actually be two: "Should I take this job or marry Sandy?" must obviously be altered into two separate questions or the answer will cause unnecessary confusion, but it is easy to ask such questions and seek positive advice on a much more subtle level too.

Once the question has been clarified and written down make a series of dashes in a single line across the page. Be very careful that you do not even inadvertently count these dashes during the process. Repeat this until there are at least four lines of dashes, the minimum required to produce any single geomantic figure. If the number of dashes in any single line is odd, this will correspond to one dot in the resultant geomantic figure; if the number is even there will be two dots.

For example, the four lines of random dashes (below) will produce the geomantic figure shown to the right of the diagram.

Once you have a single geomantic figure, consult the list of meanings for a simple answer. Sometimes eight lines of dashes are made in the first instance which means that two figures must be consulted and their meanings combined; it is said to be very lucky if the two figures are identical.

Another initial choice might be 12 lines of dashes which will produce three figures; in this instance, the central geomantic figure will contain the principal answer, although the other two figures will have some bearing upon the question.

If you are patient it is possible to use a general layout such as shown under astrological houses or any layout as displayed in the section devoted to cards.

FIGVRA.	NOMEN.	ELEMENTVM.	PLANETA.	SIGNVM.
* * * *	Via Iter	Aqua	☾	♌
* * * * * * * *	Populus Congregatio	Aqua	☾	♑
* * * * * *	Coniunctio Coadunatio	Aër	☿	♍
* * * * * *	Carcer Constrictus	Terra	♄	♓
* * * * * *	Fortuna maior Auxilium maius Tutela intrans	Terra	☉	♒
* * * * * *	Fortuna minor Auxilium minus Tutela exiens	Ignis	☉	♉
* * * * * *	Acquisitio Comprehensum intus	Aër	♃	♈
* * * * * *	Amissio Comprehensum extra	Ignis	♀	♎
* * * * * * *	Laetitia Ridens Sanus Barbatus	Aër	♃	♉
* * * * * * *	Tristitia Damnatus Transversus	Terra	♄	♏
* * * * *	Puella Mundus facie	Aqua	♀	♎
* * * * *	Puer Flavus Imberbis	Ignis.	♂	♈
* * * * * * *	Albus Candidus	Aqua	☿	♋
* * * * * * *	Rubeus Ruffus	Ignis	♂	♊
* * * * *	Caput Limen intrans Limen superius	Terra	☊	♍
* * * * *	Cauda Limen exiens Limen inferius	Ignis	☋	♐

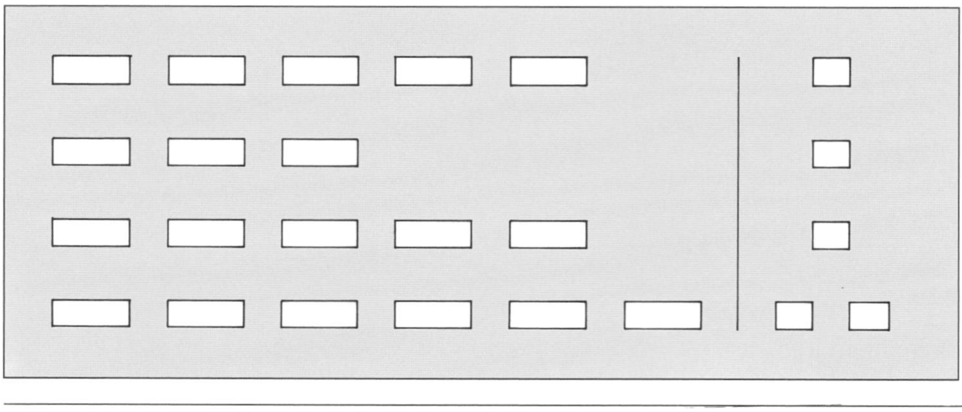

Above: A table of Geomantic Correspondence from Henry Cornelius Agrippa's 'De Occulta Philosophia', published in 1532. The five columns show the geomantic figure, its name or time, the element, the planetary symbol, and the corresponding zodiac-sign.

Left: A stylised version of four rows of pencil-marks, showing 'CAUDA' as the derived geomantic figure. This signifies that no apparent reward will be forthcoming, and that some kind of sacrifice is likely to be required.

VIA

Via is the Latin word for street or way, therefore it is not surprising to learn that this figure often indicates actual travel. But where such a meaning is inappropriate it may show a journey along the hard road of trouble.

In Roman times roads were very straight in their course and led directly from one place to another; any obstacles along the way were literally demolished. So, this figure can also denote method, a straight course of action that disregards any form of deviation. You must only keep the ultimate goal within your sight and assume that any problems encountered on the way can be dealt with.

As Via is said to be injurious to all the other figures, it tends to be rather selfish; therefore it is not a good answer to receive when asking questions about relationships. You might fare better when travelling alone.

 CONJUNCTIO

The Latin translates as "uniting or joining together" so this figure very obviously indicates marriage or close partnerships. It is therefore an excellent figure to obtain when asking about love matters as it is a sure sign of alliance and success.

Even where the question bears no resemblance to a query about relationships, it may contain the omen that you are due to meet the man or woman of your dreams! Should your question concern any sort of consultation, either to ask advice or even a favour, the answer will be a very definite "yes".

A Conjunctio's meaning also contains the precept that "like attracts like", it could herald a period of meaningful coincidences that lead to happy outcomes or even those of the type that provide the feeling that you are following the right path in life. This figure relates to harmony and balance and shows that, even if you are unaware of it, your life is in order.

 FORTUNA MAJOR

As the name implies, this figure of course means "chance, fate, fortune or luck" and usually has a very positive outcome. It can show long-term success, especially when asking about a commercial enterprise, and will usually be a tangible indicator of success in the form of monetary rewards.

This is a good figure to draw when one is at the beginning of any enterprise as you are then assured of eventual success. It may also indicate the beginning of a long run of luck, as protected by a benign providence.

The querent can also be sure of a favourable outcome when asking questions about property, possessions or illustrious positions; this figure appears to incline towards status and worldly success. Perhaps this figure results when asking a more aesthetic question, it becomes a sign that one should look after worldly concerns first, before entering into questions that pertain to the spirit.

 POPULUS

As the title for this figure quite literally means "the people", the interpretation for this figure will relate to a crowd or a gathering. It might indicate an important social occasion, such as a party or a wedding, but it could also apply to group effort or endeavour, possibly through business.

The message that this figure contains is that you should undertake any ventures at group level in order to ensure greatest success. Being the true opposite of Via it must include the warning that, in this instance, it does not pay to enter into anything alone.

Although Populus inclines towards sharing interests, these are usually fairly impersonal; it would only bring a happy answer to a love question where both parties share similar goals or ideals. This figure is essentially humanitarian and must embrace such concepts.

 CARCER

Whereas Conjunctio related to the unexpected and expansion, this one is narrow and constricting. The actual title carries the meaning of "prison, jail or cell". This restriction of freedom need not, of course, come from an outside influence, it may simply derive from your own attitude or life-style and might be totally self-imposed.

There may be actual obstacles, delays or difficulties to any project implied by the question. But the appearance of this figure may also indicate that the questioner is not making the best of personal ability or potential, or even ignoring opportunity that is around them. Only the intuition of the diviner will provide the answer.

The only time this figure is said to be lucky is if the question pertains to an actual birth, when it becomes necessary to slow down a little in order to create new life; but the "new life" could as easily be an idea in its initial, formative stages.

 FORTUNA MINOR

Although the literal translation of this figure is "the lesser fortune", it appears to place more reliance upon blind faith, luck and chance. Perhaps the message is that it is, in truth, better to be self-reliant than to depend on the benefaction of the gods, but, if needs must, "they" are there.

This figure appears to indicate divine intervention, whether this be from illness, legislation or any other problem, and there is little else to do but "hope and pray". It may also show luck that was not expected or even strived for, perhaps because the Fates decide that you deserves a break.

Traditionally it is said to be a better omen if you are looking for a successful outcome to any venture that has already been embarked upon; but not so good if you are at the stage of beginning. Consider a question that will be relevant over a long period of time as it is not good for new ideas or sudden whims.

ACQUISITIO

This means acquisition or addition, which mostly relates to finance or possessions. It can also indicate fame, honour or achievement in worldly pursuits. At the lowest level, you are due to receive your heart's desire in connection with the question.

Although the implications are usually financial, you can also obtain recognition or success in your chosen field. The better the position it holds in the spread of your choice, the greater the success. Even if you are "merely" a seeker after knowledge, this will be forthcoming, but monetary rewards will also surely follow.

Most sources seem to attribute this figure to Jupiter, that harbinger of luck and expansion; it would appear to be hard to fail when you draw this figure and you may also find public acclaim in the process. The message seems to be that you should persist in the current sphere of activity, as prestige is sure to follow.

LATITIA

The name for this figure translates as "joy, happiness or delight", so you can be optimistic for the outcome of the question. It always suggests a happy person so, if the questioner is currently downcast, he or she can be assured that the future looks uncommonly bright.

Should anyone's health have been a problem, there will be a recovery that lightens the way ahead; legal matters will work in your favour or there may be an unexpected stroke of good fortune.

When you receive this figure it might be good to change your appearance or surroundings in some way. A new hairstyle or new clothes could create benefit, or even a brightening up of your environment may produce good fortune or a feeling of well-being. There is an implied need that spreading happiness to others will also improve the querent's fortune. Perhaps part of the message of this figure is that you should live for the day rather than for the long-term future.

PUELLA

As Puella means "girl or maiden" it relates to the feminine principle, if not to an actual female. It therefore indicates harmony and co-operation, cessation of strife and resolution of any argument. It does tend to avoid any form of confrontation and is adverse to causing upset or disagreement.

Where the questioner is unable to relate to an actual innocent, young female, it might be wise to suggest that he or she assumes an attitude of peacefulness and innocence rather than set out to conquer or demand what they feel is their due.

This figure may indicate a need to show compassion to others; or it can also show a new beginning in love. Where there has been previous disagreement, it may allow a totally new start without dwelling on past grievances. Unconditional love is demanded from this figure, together with forgiveness and understanding. However, if you are a female and draw it, perhaps you can depend upon your feminine wiles to get you through!

AMISSIO

Unfortunately, Amissio translates as "lost", so this is not a good figure to obtain. Luckily, this is only bad when you are seeking financial reward, so it might be good for love. But then you should bear in mind that you must definitely take the object of desire "for richer, for poorer" and decide if it is, in fact, possible to live on love alone!

Tradition has it that one should also check the phraseology of the question that provoked such an answer, as mistakes are possible under Amissio. Care is needed in business when drawing this figure because mistakes, trickery or deception are highly possible. One may also be the victim of theft or even lose or mislay a treasured object.

Perhaps the message here is that, as long as love alone is most important, this figure can herald absolute success. But if you are looking for material rewards alone, perhaps you should examine your motives.

TRISTITIA

Tristitia in Latin means "sadness or sorrow" and will work in this way unless you are prepared to put in considerable effort, with little thought of immediate reward. Usually this figure is drawn by someone who is currently unhappy or who has the feeling that life is against them. Perhaps there has been a recent bereavement or a fall from grace in some way. He or she may have been made redundant after a long period of self-sacrificing service. Whatever, the querent will feel that the future appears bleak at the present moment.

More patience is needed, and no immediate remedial action should be taken. Wait until a later period when the portents might fall more favourably.

Perhaps donning a false mantle of cheerfulness might help to give a more appealing face to other people. Often those who draw this figure are so obviously depressed that others fail to see their attributes.

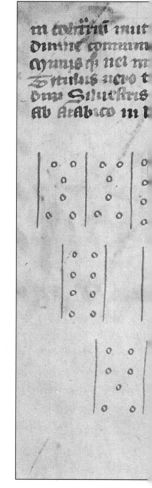

Right: An example of geomantic figures, taken from a 14th Century Ms, translated from the Arabic by Bernardus Silvestris. These would appear to be a series of answers, as "Populus" appears four times. It may be surmised that Bernardus did not work on the translation alone!

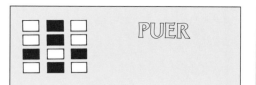

PUER

As this word means "boy" in Latin, it also takes on the masculine attribute of fearlessness, rashness and, sometimes, selfishness. Usually the questioner who draws this will be ready to take action in the matter in question, regardless of any consequences. Perhaps the first advice from the diviner in such cases should be to urge consideration of what is truly wise.

It may be that the situation under consideration demands a positive, courageous approach; in such cases, proceed and demand what you feel is your due.

This figure can also indicate fairly immediate success in any form of competition, however much the odds appear to be stacked against you. If you are hesitant about taking the initiative in a new love involvement, you should take the plunge as the other party desires this. Much depends upon your ability as a diviner when this figure is drawn, as you must decide whether the chosen course of action is reckless or otherwise.

ALBUS

The Latin translates as "white, dead white", a concept which can include wisdom or sagacity. Rather than be associated with purity, its meaning seems more to suggest a clean slate or a new beginning. The astrological attributes all appear to include Mercury, which suggests the use of logic and the mind.

Drawing this figure may indicate a new job, new home, or even the opportunity to travel to a new area. Freedom from any old debts or obligations and the ability to begin anew is signified. Where there has been a quarrel there is compromise or resolution and any blot on the reputation is forgiven, enabling the questioner to start with a clean sheet.

As an omen, it portends success as long as one is venturing into a new and different area; but if you are guilty of clinging to the past in any way, perhaps you should be urged to relinquish such an attitude as this may be what is holding back progress.

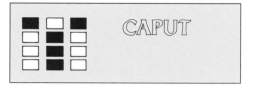

CAPUT

Universally associated with the Dragon's Head or North Node, this figure has karmic implications. Traditionally that which is signified by Caput comes to us as a well-deserved right. Of course, if we have not put in the correct previous effort the chosen goal may appear to be within sight yet escape us: the choice is up to each and every individual.

Some say that drawing this figure indicates news, progress or an event in connection with the question eight days ahead. This, you must test for yourself. On the whole it is a favourable omen and indicates success, especially in worldly terms. With this, you may obtain the exact amount of money to achieve an ambition, or even take that dream trip overseas which is the promised reward for a life-time of effort.

It can indicate supreme luck (which has really been earned) or extreme depression from that which only just escapes our reach (and is deserved if we acknowledge this).

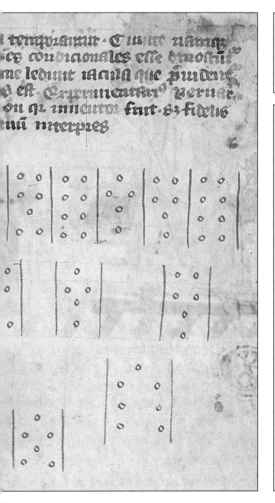

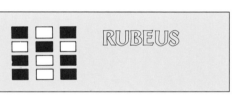

RUBEUS

Rubeus means "red" and thus has associations with blind passion or bad temper. If you draw this figure you should examine your motives very carefully, otherwise you may be guilty of sublime selfishness.

This figure can signify a very passionate love affair which may, perhaps, hurt another person. There may be a favourable outcome to this but you should stop and consider the best interests of all concerned. It always contains the possibility of severe damage to your reputation, so consider your priorities.

Where the questioner is the object of another's desire, he or she should be warned that a relationship might be difficult to escape from; some might even be best advised to take proper legal advice for their situation. If the questioner's desire is for money or for worldly possessions he or she should be advised that there might be a heavy price to pay on a karmic level if they are guilty of dishonesty or greed.

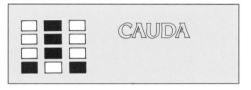

CAUDA

This means the Dragon's Tail or South Node, and it often signifies an area where sacrifice is required. But, instead of dwelling upon the message of "abandon hope all Ye who enter here", perhaps one should remember that this figure may also carry the benefit of past wisdom, of things that have been experienced before, even in a past life. So, all may not be lost as long as you remember previous lessons.

Some say that this figure is helpful in matters of the heart, perhaps when we make no specific demands other than the amount of love that the recipient of our affection is able to give or the type of loyalty he or she can accommodate. If you draw this figure you must be prepared to persist without obvious signs of reward; you need to carry on loving regardless or to keep trying in any project you believe in, even when everything appears to be against you.

Even where there are no obvious benefits to be obtained in worldly terms, who is to say that they will not receive their accolade later?

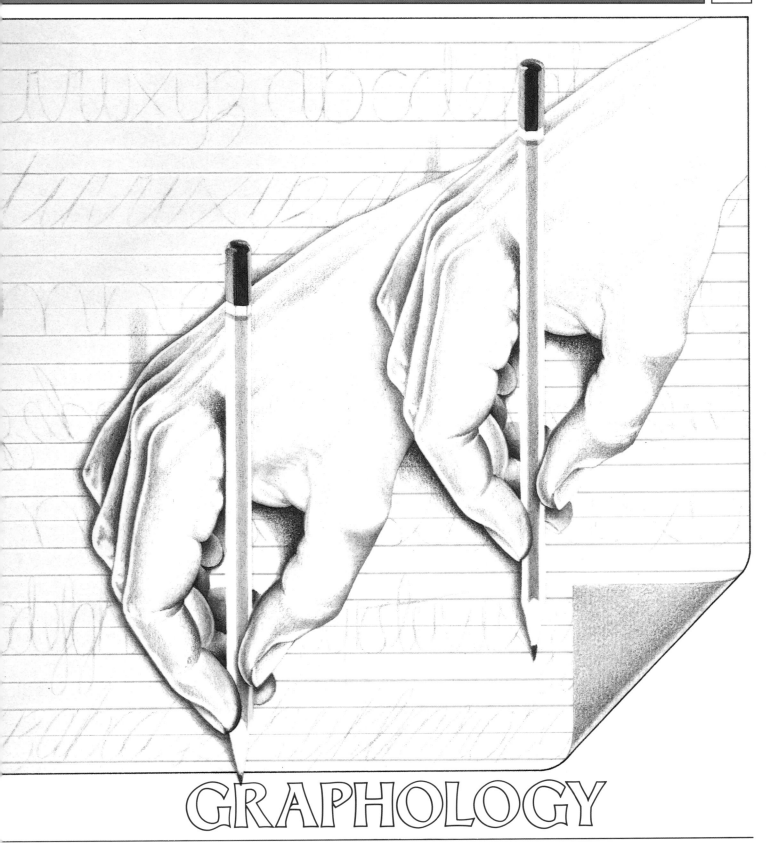

GRAPHOLOGY

Graphology is the art of assessing character and personality from a person's handwriting. It is possible to tell much about a writer's potential, abilities and limitations, behavioural patterns and interactions with others from studying a handwritten script. The Romans are thought to be the first to study character in handwriting, followed by monks in the Middle Ages. French and German graphologists have developed the science during the last two hundred years and their methods of analysis are very much relevant today. The psychologist Carl Jung believed handwriting to be an important indicator of a person's character and personality. Graphology is a psychological tool which can be used to great advantage to advise or guide the writer on the best ways to achieve his or her potential. It has many modern applications, the most obvious of which is as an aid to personnel selection.

A graphologist will study the minutest details of a script, right down to the i-dots, t-bars and individual strokes and flourishes of each separate letter against the background of the writing as a whole and the way in which it is presented on a page. Although it is obviously not practicable to go into such fine detail here, it is possible to gain a good general picture of a person's character and personality make-up from the type of writing someone produces if you have a basic knowledge of graphology. To this end a list of pointers to look for and what these imply is given below. It must, though, be understood that the information thus gained is indicative rather than definitive.

INCLINATION

Note the level of the lines of the handwriting; are they horizontal, do they rise at the right-hand end or the left, or are they irregular?

Horizontal This indicates a normal, calm, well-balanced individual. Someone who is logical and keeps his or her impulses in check.

Rise at right-hand end Denotes a person full of ambition, of an excitable and energetic nature. He or she will get things done and is ever active.

Rise at left-hand end A morose, pessimistic nature is indicated. Such a person will be easily discouraged or disappointed and may lack the energy and enthusiasm to achieve his or her potential.

Irregular This marks moodiness; life will be a series of ups and downs to such a person. This tendency to be happy one moment and depressed the next can affect personal relationships.

SLANT OF WRITING

The angle at which the writing slopes from the upright will reveal a great deal about the writer's basic personality. Usually, people will adhere to one of the following slants each of which has a specific meaning and will reveal useful insight into a person's personality.

Extreme backward sloping
The head dominates the heart. This cautious individual is undemonstrative and inclined to be over-critical; too restrained by far.

Backward sloping
A measure of timidity is indicated here. This person may not face up to facts as he or she should and is inclined to evade issues.

Upright
This indicates a somewhat cold nature, someone who is not influenced by sentiment. Rather reserved, he or she will nonetheless be mentally acute and dependable.

Average
This is the most common angle of handwriting and implies a well-balanced, moderate personality.

45 degrees
A vital, energetic and strong character is implied. This person will have plenty of willpower and determination.

60 degrees
Extreme sensitivity is indicated. The writer may be rather gullible, inclined towards too much sentimentality and rather lacking in will.

Acute angle
A person of extremes, given to excesses of behaviour. Over-sensitive, he or she lacks the confidence to make the best of themself and acts impulsively, often to their later regret.

SIZE

This is basically indicative of a person's powers of concentration and appreciation of details.

Small
A lover of details. This writer can concentrate without much difficulty upon his or her problems and is generally rather cautious by nature.

Average
Another indicator of a well-balanced, moderate personality.

Large
This is a sign of great ambition and desire for publicity and popularity. Although gregarious and generous, this person may lack attention to details.

Irregular
A restless, sensitive nature is indicated. A hard-worker, this individual cares little for relaxation or socialising.

ANGULARITY

Whether writing is basically angular or well-rounded will furnish clues to the writer's general disposition and attitude towards others.

Roundness
This marks a genial, lovable personality, someone who is very friendly and warm-hearted. Very demonstrative, such an individual will never want for companionship for he or she is inherently co-operative.

Angularity
This strong-willed character is energetic and super-efficient. Although he or she may be emotional, they will rarely show their feelings; independence means everything to such a person.

Mixed
Many people mix roundness with angularity in their script thus showing that they have developed their stronger mental qualities without losing the kindliness indicated by the rounded parts of their writing.

SPACING

The spacing left between letters, words and lines of writing will, to a large extent, indicate the ease or difficulty which a writer feels in relating to other people.

LETTERS

Narrowness
A script where all the letters of a word appear to be cramped up together may refer to meanness or secrecy. Certainly, it shows a degree of inhibition in the writer's nature.

Width
Widely-formed letters mark a generous, outgoing personality, someone who is very aware of those around him and considerate of their needs.

WORDS

Close
A person who leaves little space between words is normally over-cautious and rather reserved. Cool-headed, he or she knows where his or her ambitions lie and will not deviate from aims.

Average
Well-adjusted, this writer strikes a happy medium between extravagance and miserliness. Even-tempered, he or she will plan ahead carefully but always allow for unforeseen circumstances and be able to adjust their behaviour accordingly.

Wide
When words are separated by larger than average spaces, this indicates someone who thinks quickly and clearly but is inclined to disregard the thoughts and feelings of others.

LINE

Wide
Wide spacing between lines of script denotes an openness of mind; one who is willing to explore every avenue in order to learn something new. Generous and warm-hearted, he or she is inclined to be extravagant and rather too impulsive on occasions.

Narrow
Economy of mind and emotions is denoted by narrow gaps between lines of writing. Narrowness of vision inhibits this introspective character from winning friends that he or she subconsciously needs, thus he or she can become isolated from those around them.

CONNECTIVENESS

Whether or not words and letters are joined together relates directly to how the writer's thought processes work.

Joined
When a writer tends to join words together this shows that he or she thinks very fast and that their ideas are well connected. The ideas flow regularly, as does their writing. Logical and essentially practical, such a person has no difficulty in putting his or her thoughts into action.

Broken
Breaks in words and between words reflect the writer's action in lifting his or her pen from the paper as their mind "jumps". Although such a

person may have good mental abilities he or she will tend to leap to conclusions rather than thinking things through.

MARGINS

Take careful note of the margins. These, together with the spacing, indicate the writer's imagination.

When the margins are wide, especially the one on the left, you can be sure that the writer has a sense of beauty and is a person of good taste. Such margins may indicate extravagance or at least the tendency to sometimes spend lavishly without thought.

If the right-hand margin is wider than the one on the left, it shows a writer who is afraid of extravagance and one who is continually

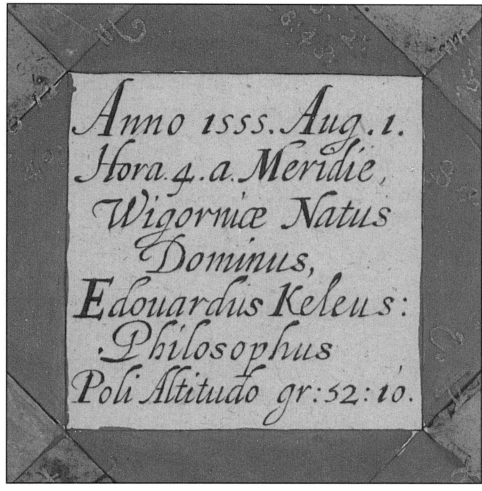

trying to be more thrifty.

If the right-hand margin is narrow, but the left is very wide, you can be certain that this is a person who is miserly over trifles but who will spend lavishly on other matters.

A left-hand margin that narrows towards the bottom of the page indicates an innate sense of thrift. The handwriting of an extremely generous person will often show a left-hand margin that gradually widens as it nears the bottom of the page.

Very narrow margins, or their total lack, show bad taste and a false sense of economy.

PRESSURE

Writing pressure will give further clues to the writer's character.

Light
Indicative of a love for details, critical ability, strong imagination and extreme sensitivity to everyday life. Idealistic and perhaps romantically inclined, such a person will be very aware of his or her interrelationships with others.

Heavy
Good physical vitality, great vigour and a strongly materialistic outlook are shown. Down-to-earth and practical, this person is realistic rather than idealistic.

Below: This ornate inscription decorates the title page of a coloured horoscope of one Edward Kelly, which was cast for him during the 16th century by Dr John Dee.

Uneven
This is the sign of a person who does everything by fits and starts. He or she lacks concentration, quickly loses interest in what they are doing and is constantly on the lookout for something new through every stage of their life.

Average
This marks that the writer has achieved a good equilibrium between the great physical vitality of the heavy writer and the mental alertness of those who use light pressure in their script.

THICKNESS

In general, people who make thick writing know how to enjoy themselves and are

prepared to work hard in order to obtain the good things in life. They can, though, be rather over-possessive under certain circumstances, which can lead to problems.

THINNESS

Fine writing tends to indicate the intellectual type. Such a person has his or her own views and is reluctant to listen to the opinions of others.

END-STROKES

When the last letter of a word ends in an upward curving stroke, a social nature is indicated. This person will have a good sense of humour.

When the final stroke is long and horizontal, especially if the capitals are large and the handwriting angular, you may presume a courageous nature, forceful, active, often too bold.

If the last letter ends abruptly in a blunt downward stroke, you may be sure of a domineering temperament. But if the short downward stroke is thin, sensitivity is indicated.

If the final stroke is knotted or shows any peculiarity, presume an eccentric, unconventional nature.

LOOPS

The way in which a writer forms the looped letters in his or her script will, to some extent, show their sensitivity and emotional responses, especially the lower loops of letters such as "g", "y", and "j".

Wide
The wider the loops the more emotional the writer is likely to be. He or she will have plenty of vitality and much prefer physical activities to sitting around reading or studying. However, if a lower loop is widely drawn, it can point to pronounced creative ability.

Narrow
In general, this refers to a rather inhibited personality; someone who has difficulty in expressing his or her feelings. Small lower loops, in particular, may indicate a lack of vitality although the writer may be mentally alert.

Absence
Ascenders and descenders that are made without any elaboration whatsoever normally denote the person whose head tends to rule their heart. Such a person will be more concerned with intellectual pursuits than those who ornament their script.

CAPITALS

The most important point to note is whether the capital letters in a script seem to be in proportion to or dominate the lower-case letters. If the latter, it implies a certain amount of pride and conscious self-awareness.

CHARACTERISTICS

As it is impractical to go into further details here, the following list will prove helpful if you wish to check what features of a person's script will give the best clues to a particular character trait.

Ability Well-formed writing on the small side; letters not too rounded; capitals well-formed.

Activity Regular handwriting with medium-to-moderately-thick letters standing upright. The words tend to rise just above the base-line.

Affectionate nature Gently sloping or upright writing; letters rounded and rather heavy.

Ambition Lines of writing that ascend from left to right; signature rather large and imposing.

Amiability The letters are well-rounded, with flowing curves and gentle slopes.

Argumentative Words that closely connect; writing small.

Boastful Long dashing bar on the "t's"; writing large; capitals larger than normal.

Calmness The letters are clear and uniform, open and well-rounded; the handwriting runs evenly in a straight line; the capitals are well-formed but on the small side.

Candour Closed letters like "o's" and "a's" open at the top; capitals are clear and rounded. Letters are plain and have no curves and frills.

Carelessness Untidy writing; letters ill-formed; few punctuation marks; the "i's" are not always dotted.

Caution The writing is precise and neat; the punctuation careful; the letters are close to one another and upright.

Changeability Letters that vary in form; eccentric capitals; spacing variable.

Conscientious All details carefully attended to. Punctuation is clear and accurate.

Right: A detail taken from an English 17th century treatise concerned with alchemy, Theatrum Chemicum Britannicum, *by Elias Ashmole. The portion of the manuscript seen here is from a section entitled "An Aenigma of authorship/fosterhood (by E.A.) and of Everyman's journeyhood in the Holy Art by extension of the promised Gift".*

Courage The lines of handwriting rise upward towards the right-hand side of the page. The letters are large, bold and well-defined.

Economy Each letter carefully formed and, sometimes, marked economy in making each letter. Only enough pressure is used. The writing is angular with no flowing words or spreading letters. Letters are short to avoid waste of paper and pen.

Enthusiasm There is dash and fire in the writing and the line rises from the page and flows along again.

Energy Lines ascending from left to right; "t's" crossed high up; downstrokes short.

Exaggeration Signature very showy with a large flourish underneath; capitals very large and out of proportion.

Extravagance Writing large; ascenders and descenders well looped and large; margins wide.

Frivolity Lines of writing irregular; varying forms of letters; writing light and sometimes uneven.

Generosity The final marks of each word are turned up and rounded. The final "y" is given a broad curve. Capitals are large and generous.

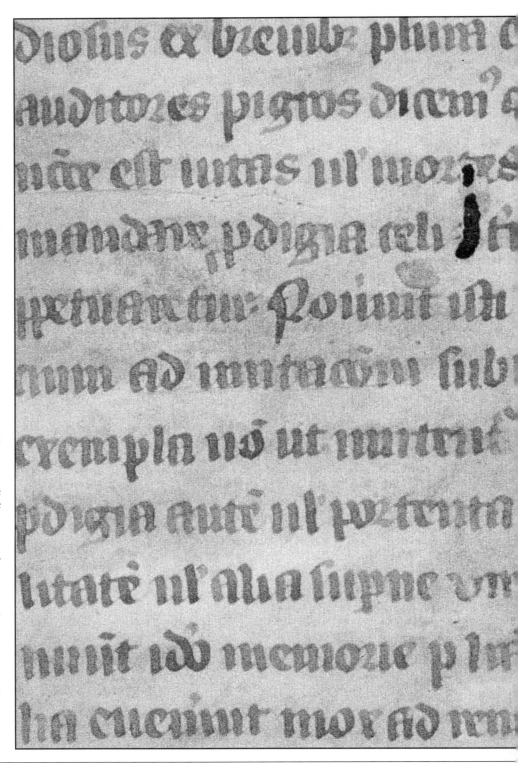

Honesty Clear handwriting that is neat and regular; very even alignment.

Humility Small writing free from any flourish or heavy lines.

Imagination Large and original capitals but the handwriting may be difficult to read, irregular and angular.

Impetuosity Large, long, well-marked commas and semi-colons.

Indolence The letters are rounded and consist of many curves which have no real connection with the word. Often letters are only half-formed and toward the end of a word the writer almost drops into a scrawl. The writer gives the impression that he or she is too lazy to form letters accurately or to finish a word.

Insincerity Thin letters, endings of words indistinct; handwriting rising above the usual level.

Intuition Letters separate from one another; letters in the signature are disjointed and in general the writing is angular.

Judgement Here words may be joined in a complete sequence. There are many flourishes and curls which have no meaning but stand out on a page.

Meanness Cramped handwriting; letters and lines compressed.

Melancholy The words run down below the base-line. Letters are rounded but they appear careless. Words may not finish and letters may not be closed.

Obstinacy Handwriting small; heavy crossing of the "t's"; letters angular and sloping to the right.

Originality Form of letters not conforming to the usual shapes, especially the capitals.

Perseverance The handwriting is angular and runs straight across the page, neither rising nor falling; the formation of the capitals is conventional and they are well-formed. There is a definiteness about the writing.

Pride Letters are large and the capitals emphasize the largeness. Often a flourish under the signature.

Selfishness Terminations of letters turning to the left and often looping in on themselves.

Sensitivity The handwriting is flexible, curving and sloping without any sign of stiffness; there is no angularity.

Sensuousness The writing, especially the signature, is heavy and coarse; the letters are not too well-formed.

Tact The handwriting is small and fine; the letters are upright; the loops of the lower-case letters well-formed.

Vanity Margins are wide; capitals large; writing shows many flourishes.

Versatility The letters are of different shapes and sizes and tend to have spear-shaped loops. The letters are well-rounded and each is completely formed.

Willpower There is a strength in the writing; the "t's" are crossed with heavy strokes and there will be a definite under-score below the signature. The downstrokes of the letters are firm and well-formed and there is angularity in the writing in general.

CHAPTER TEN

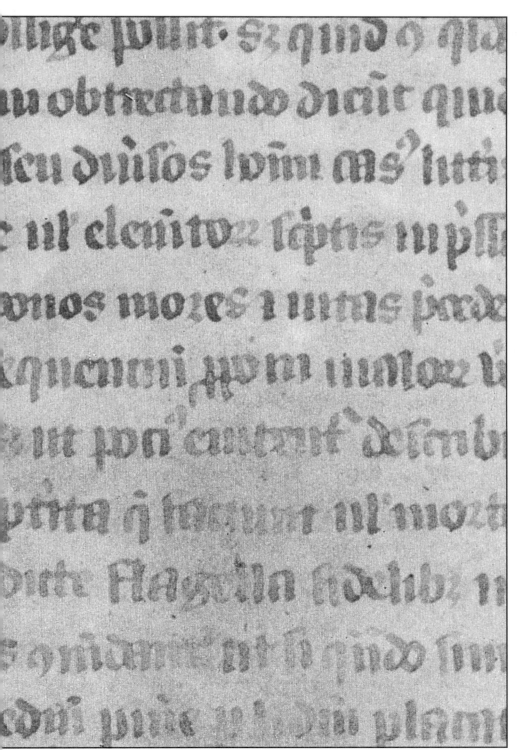

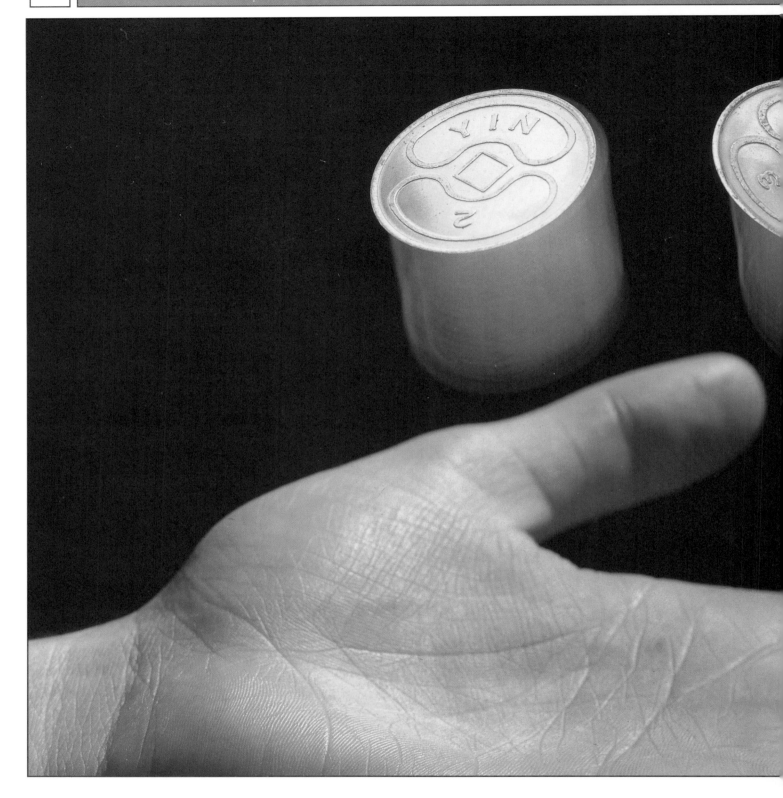

I-CHING

The Chinese believed that anyone who was able to understand the I Ching could answer all questions, solve all problems and heal all ills. He or she would also have the key to the riddle of the Universe. The I Ching, or Book of Changes, was first written down between 1000 BC and 500 BC, although it was known to have been used at least a thousand years before that. The actual author is not known but, in the years since then, additional com- mentaries were added by sages such as Confucius. In modern times, many Westerners have found the "Changes" useful not only for divination but for philosophical contemplation. The I Ching exemplifies what the eminent psychologist Jung termed synchronicity — that is, meaningful or significant coincidence — and he advocated its study to lovers of self-knowledge, of wisdom, in their search for universal truth.

The principle of polarity lies at the heart of the I Ching. In the West, polarity is thought of as two opposites. The Chinese, however, understand apparently opposing energies to be complementary. One cannot exist without the other or, more properly, the one is inherent in the other. This is clearly expressed in the ancient T'ai Chi symbol.

It will be apparent that the ancient Chinese would not have considered the existence of light without the complementary dark, or the day without the night. They believed it is impossible to understand the concept of light if darkness has not been experienced.

List of complementaries:

YANG	YIN
DAY	NIGHT
SUN	MOON
MALE	FEMALE
ACTIVE	PASSIVE
POSITIVE	NEGATIVE
HEAVEN	EARTH
HOT	COLD

From the polar energies is generated everything that exists in the Universe. Springing from the observation of these interrelationships, comes the idea of change. Just as the Greek philosopher, Heraclitus, said "All is flux," the Chinese saw that the Universe and everything in it is in constant motion. This observation is particularly impressive in the light of modern discoveries in particle physics. As the Sun reaches its highest point in the sky at noon, it continues its movement towards the horizon and sunset. In the night-sky the Moon waxes, achieves its fullness, then begins to wane. Observing the sea, it wil be realised that when the tide is at its lowest, the flow imperceptibly changes direction, moving towards high-tide. All these things follow regular cycles, which occur in time. Thus, it was reasoned, there is a pattern to existence, and this can be discerned by those who seek it.

At a point lost in time, someone decided to represent *Yang* by a straight line:

Yin was represented by a line of the same length, but broken:

The on-off states symbolised by these two lines can be compared with what actually happens with the computers of today. The information processed by them is in the form of electrical impulses. First though, this information is turned into binary code. This simply means that instead of having numbers 0-9 as we are used to, every number consists of a zero or a one. Thus any number can be shown as a zero/one series of impulses. Just think of a switch which has two positions, "on" and "off", where "one" is equivalent to "on" and "zero" is equivalent to "off". A series of on/off/on/off commands is registered as information by the computer.

TRIGRAMS

For the Chinese, it was probably a natural step to visualise a cycle of change as REST-MOVEMENT-REST and then draw this:

or MOVEMENT-REST-MOVEMENT, drawn like this:

These 3-line figures are called trigrams. There are eight possible combinations of these unbroken-broken lines which form a set of relationships representing the family, the seasons, or types of energy, for example.

Ch'ien (The creative)

K'un (The receptive)

Ken (Keeping still)

Sun (The gentle)

Chen (The arousing)

K'an (The abysmal)

Li (The clinging)

Tui (The joyous)

Left: Early morning sun on the face of the mountain, the foreground in darkness. By late afternoon, the situation will be reversed. This clearly shows the principle of Yin-Yang, light to darkness, darkness to light as an ever-changing process.

HEXAGRAMS

One trigram can be placed above the other to symbolise the sky or the heavens above the earth, illustrating the maxim, "as above, so below". A six-line figure is thus formed, and this is known as a hexagram. The computer analogy above would allow us to see a row of six switches which can be on or off. There are only 64 possible arrangements of these lines, which is the number of hexagrams in the I Ching. They were thought to signify the total number of situations that naturally occur in the ever-changing pattern of existence. Some say that the pattern was first seen in the shapes on a tortoise-shell.

Whatever the origins, it is only a short step from perceiving a pattern to the desire to apply it, in an attempt to understand the human condition. We can imagine a person standing on the earth (Yin), gazing up at the sky (Yang) and asking the question "How do I fit into the scheme of things?" By using a suitable method of selection, a nexagram helps to answer that question.

USING COINS

There are many time-honoured methods in use in order to arrive at a hexagram which will enable the intuitive person to answer a question or find the solution to a problem. The traditional methods of counting out yarrow-stalks, pebbles or grains of rice may be used. They ensure that the correct reflective state of mind is achieved, as any of these can take some time to master. In the West, the most popular method in use is to take three coins, and toss them six times; the resultant combinations give rise to an appropriate hexagram.

First, sit comfortably and quietly for a few minutes in order to define the wording of the question. Write it on a slip of paper and place it in front of you. If the question is vague, allow some time to let your mind wander until the appropriate words pop into your mind, then write them down. Avoid asking a question with an either/or choice, as the answer you will receive will be ambivalent. The exact wording will enable the answer to be precise and definite.

If you have only vague thoughts of a question, then it is permissible to write down that you want guidance on that particular subject; you could write "job" or "house", for example. The resulting hexagram will not always be obvious in its meaning but if you reflect on it, you will always be quite surprised by its suitability. The question in this example is "Should I accept the offer of this new project?"

Next take the three coins and shake them in your hands until you feel the moment is right, then cast them, and note the total. It is important to remember that the first line of the hexagram is the lowest; always draw the hexagram from the bottom upwards.

Now the hexagram has been thrown; in order to identify it, it must be split into its component trigrams, the upper and the lower, and its identification can be made from the table.

Upper Trigram — Chen or Thunder

Lower Trigram — Ch'ien or Heaven

This combination gives the hexagram number 34, which is "The Power of the Great," which suggests that it would be right to accept the project but that mere strength of purpose alone is not enough. The task must be persevered with and be performed with the right attitude. Corresponding skills must be employed in order that the project may be successful. In other words, if the project will employ the talents one has to the full and if there is the time available to persist with it, then it would be good to go ahead and accept it.

If the answering hexagram had been number 33, "Retreat", for example, then it would be better to turn the project down until more details were found out about it, or suggest that a later time would be better.

This is all that there is to the consultation of the I Ching. Practicing the art of asking questions over a period of time will give the feeling that the ancient Chinese oracle has a life and a personality of its own; it will succeed in clarifying your purpose and direction with uncanny accuracy, and often a dash of humour, just like a wise and valued friend.

THROWING THE COINS

Take three I-Ching coins or coins of the same denomination. Give one face, heads, the value 3. The other face, tails, has the value 2. Therefore, totals will be 6, 7, 8, or 9.

If the total is 6, draw a Yin line
If the total is 7, draw a Yang line
If the total is 8, draw a Yin line
If the total is 9, draw a Yang line
If six throws are made, a six-line hexagram will form a title to answer your question.

Sixth throw: Heads/Heads/Tails
3 + 3 + 2 = 8 (Yin line)
Fifth throw: Heads/Heads/Tails
3 + 3 + 2 = 8 (Yin line)
Fourth throw: Heads/Tails/Tails
3 + 2 + 2 = 7 (Yang line)

Third throw: Heads/Heads/Heads
3 + 3 + 3 = 9 (Yang line)
Second throw: Heads/Heads/Heads
3 + 3 + 3 = 9 (Yang line)
First throw: Heads/Heads/Heads
3 + 3 + 3 = 9 (Yang line)

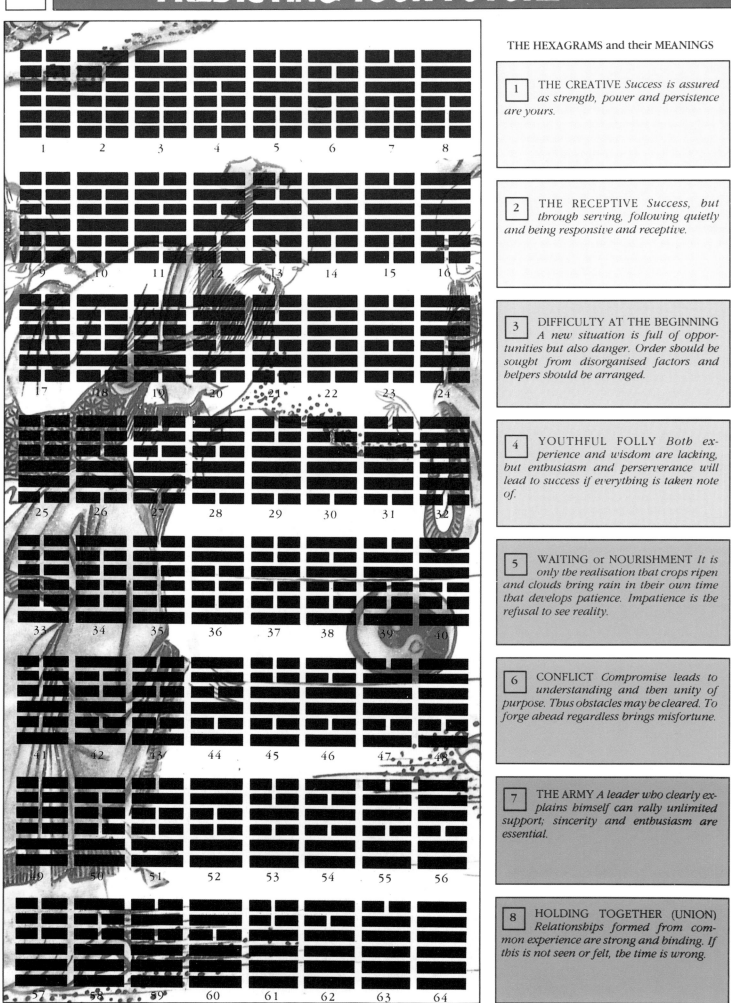

THE HEXAGRAMS and their MEANINGS

1 THE CREATIVE *Success is assured as strength, power and persistence are yours.*

2 THE RECEPTIVE *Success, but through serving, following quietly and being responsive and receptive.*

3 DIFFICULTY AT THE BEGINNING *A new situation is full of opportunities but also danger. Order should be sought from disorganised factors and helpers should be arranged.*

4 YOUTHFUL FOLLY *Both experience and wisdom are lacking, but enthusiasm and perserverance will lead to success if everything is taken note of.*

5 WAITING or NOURISHMENT *It is only the realisation that crops ripen and clouds bring rain in their own time that develops patience. Impatience is the refusal to see reality.*

6 CONFLICT *Compromise leads to understanding and then unity of purpose. Thus obstacles may be cleared. To forge ahead regardless brings misfortune.*

7 THE ARMY *A leader who clearly explains himself can rally unlimited support; sincerity and enthusiasm are essential.*

8 HOLDING TOGETHER (UNION) *Relationships formed from common experience are strong and binding. If this is not seen or felt, the time is wrong.*

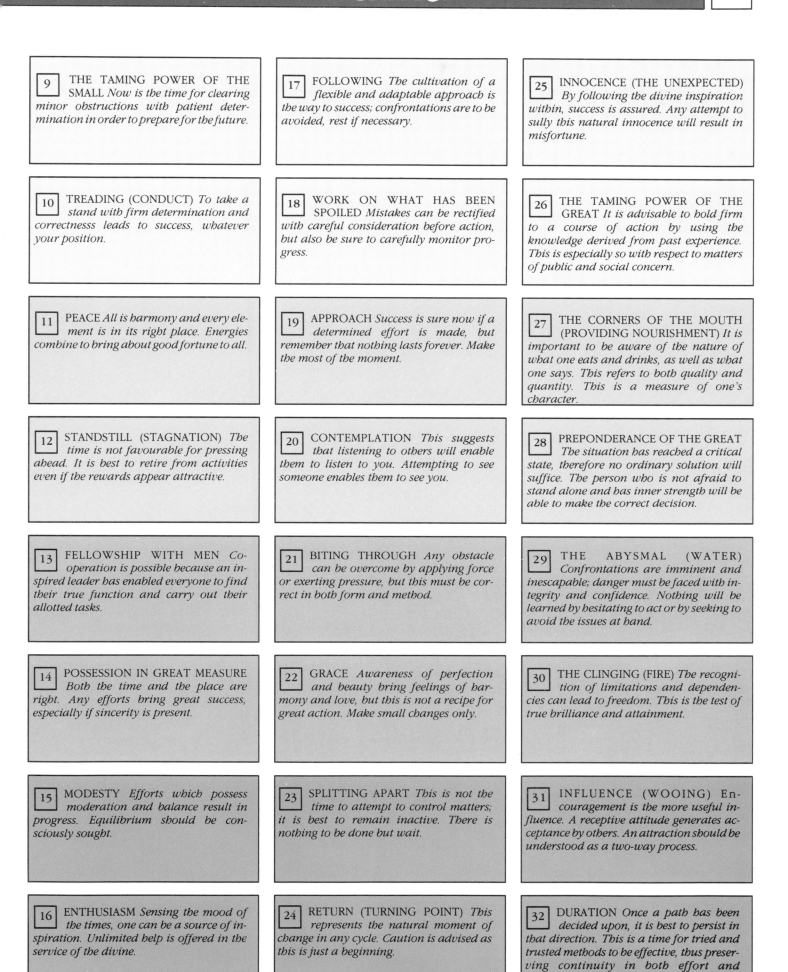

9 THE TAMING POWER OF THE SMALL *Now is the time for clearing minor obstructions with patient determination in order to prepare for the future.*

10 TREADING (CONDUCT) *To take a stand with firm determination and correctness leads to success, whatever your position.*

11 PEACE *All is harmony and every element is in its right place. Energies combine to bring about good fortune to all.*

12 STANDSTILL (STAGNATION) *The time is not favourable for pressing ahead. It is best to retire from activities even if the rewards appear attractive.*

13 FELLOWSHIP WITH MEN *Co-operation is possible because an inspired leader has enabled everyone to find their true function and carry out their allotted tasks.*

14 POSSESSION IN GREAT MEASURE *Both the time and the place are right. Any efforts bring great success, especially if sincerity is present.*

15 MODESTY *Efforts which possess moderation and balance result in progress. Equilibrium should be consciously sought.*

16 ENTHUSIASM *Sensing the mood of the times, one can be a source of inspiration. Unlimited help is offered in the service of the divine.*

17 FOLLOWING *The cultivation of a flexible and adaptable approach is the way to success; confrontations are to be avoided, rest if necessary.*

18 WORK ON WHAT HAS BEEN SPOILED *Mistakes can be rectified with careful consideration before action, but also be sure to carefully monitor progress.*

19 APPROACH *Success is sure now if a determined effort is made, but remember that nothing lasts forever. Make the most of the moment.*

20 CONTEMPLATION *This suggests that listening to others will enable them to listen to you. Attempting to see someone enables them to see you.*

21 BITING THROUGH *Any obstacle can be overcome by applying force or exerting pressure, but this must be correct in both form and method.*

22 GRACE *Awareness of perfection and beauty bring feelings of harmony and love, but this is not a recipe for great action. Make small changes only.*

23 SPLITTING APART *This is not the time to attempt to control matters; it is best to remain inactive. There is nothing to be done but wait.*

24 RETURN (TURNING POINT) *This represents the natural moment of change in any cycle. Caution is advised as this is just a beginning.*

25 INNOCENCE (THE UNEXPECTED) *By following the divine inspiration within, success is assured. Any attempt to sully this natural innocence will result in misfortune.*

26 THE TAMING POWER OF THE GREAT *It is advisable to hold firm to a course of action by using the knowledge derived from past experience. This is especially so with respect to matters of public and social concern.*

27 THE CORNERS OF THE MOUTH (PROVIDING NOURISHMENT) *It is important to be aware of the nature of what one eats and drinks, as well as what one says. This refers to both quality and quantity. This is a measure of one's character.*

28 PREPONDERANCE OF THE GREAT *The situation has reached a critical state, therefore no ordinary solution will suffice. The person who is not afraid to stand alone and has inner strength will be able to make the correct decision.*

29 THE ABYSMAL (WATER) *Confrontations are imminent and inescapable; danger must be faced with integrity and confidence. Nothing will be learned by hesitating to act or by seeking to avoid the issues at hand.*

30 THE CLINGING (FIRE) *The recognition of limitations and dependencies can lead to freedom. This is the test of true brilliance and attainment.*

31 INFLUENCE (WOOING) *Encouragement is the more useful influence. A receptive attitude generates acceptance by others. An attraction should be understood as a two-way process.*

32 DURATION *Once a path has been decided upon, it is best to persist in that direction. This is a time for tried and trusted methods to be effective, thus preserving continuity in both effort and character.*

33 RETREAT *It is a sign of strength to withdraw from a situation at the right moment; too soon implies a giving-up, too late implies a hasty flight. A sensible withdrawal allows small measures to be taken, plans to be made.*

34 THE POWER OF THE GREAT *Perseverance and persistence, when allied with correct behaviour, bring progress. Your influence is strong as a result.*

35 PROGRESS *The influence that a person has is due to the twin attributes of skilled leadership and the willingness to serve for the benefit of all. Thus intelligent suggestions are greeted favourably and honours are bestowed.*

36 DARKENING OF THE LIGHT *It is impossible to have any direct influence, so it is wiser to keep quiet and remain in the background. Keep to your aims and principles within, while appearing outwardly yielding.*

37 THE FAMILY *All matters should be considered in the light of the relationships between the members of a family. This implies love, respect and responsibility. Words must find substance in conduct and action.*

38 OPPOSITION *If this situation is thought of as containing purely contradictory opposites, then little can be achieved. If these opposites can be thought of as complementary, then small matters may be successful.*

39 OBSTRUCTION *Whichever action is chosen, difficulty will ensure. Therefore a pause and a period of introspection will enable much to be learned. It is also useful to seek advice or help.*

40 DELIVERANCE *Obstacles that are blocking progress can now be overcome and tensions can be relieved. It is important to act clearly and decisively. Do not dwell on mistakes and be forgiving, just be pleased that progress can begin again.*

41 DECREASE *A loss in one area can result in a gain in another; it is wise to think in terms of sacrifice now in order to receive benefits later. Simplicity, self-restraint and moderation can teach valuable lessons.*

42 INCREASE *Great enterprises should be undertaken now as these conditions will not last for long. It is also best to work for the benefit of all and to imitate good behaviour where it is seen.*

43 BREAKTHROUGH (RESOLUTE-NESS) *Contentious issues must be raised in a place of influence. In order to succeed, force should not be used, but rather a firm resolution to do the best that is possible. Allies should be informed.*

44 COMING TO MEET *A seemingly harmless person or opportunity appears. If a contract or liaison is accepted, it will prove to be damaging. Uphold your principles and standards, and you will come to no harm.*

45 GATHERING TOGETHER *A shared purpose is furthered by an enlightened leader. It is important to foster unity by an open and sincere attitude; and a sacrifice may be called for, which results in good fortune.*

46 PUSHING UPWARD *Efforts are rewarded now by advancement. The times are right for all obstacles to disappear, especially if persons in authority are consulted.*

47 OPPRESSION (EXHAUSTION) *In times of adversity, a positive attitude prevents loss or failure. Even if actions seem to have no effect, accept that this is your fate and remain true to yourself. Spare your words.*

48 THE WELL *There is an inexhaustible souce of nourishment, which remains stable and fixed, even though all around it may change. A superficial attitude invites disaster, therefore an intuitive seeking will penetrate to the truth, which is universal.*

49 REVOLUTION *Change can be brought about by taking note of the right time and recognising a genuine need. Change should be neither arbitrary, nor for purely selfish motives, but the fulfillment of a natural cycle.*

50 THE CAULDRON *An exceptionally fortunate time when both material and spiritual affairs are in harmony. It is a flowering, a culmination of previous efforts. This also suggests further progress.*

51 THE AROUSING (SHOCK) *Whatever it is that may be shocking or surprising, its real effect is to show the great powers with which we are surrounded and which are also inherent in us. Fear should be followed by joy.*

52 KEEPING STILL (MOUNTAIN) *All unnecessary movement should be halted. Deal with the situation at hand. This is also a suggestion for meditation.*

53 DEVELOPMENT (GRADUAL PRO-GRESS) *Events move at the speed at which the correct procedures allow. Everything must be attended to in the right order and in the right time. This calls for cultivation and gentle perseverance.*

54 THE MARRYING MAIDEN *Taking a subordinate position is useful as any attempt to control or dominate will lead to misfortune and misunderstandings. Keep the eventual goal in mind, though.*

55 ABUNDANCE (FULLNESS) *Like the Sun at midday, a peak is reached. It is the height of power, thus goals are fulfilled, potential is reached. Therefore a decline follows, but this should not be dwelt on, rather use the time at hand well.*

56 THE WANDERER *A traveller does not stay in one place for long; therefore choose your situations well. Only short-term goals can be achieved and problems should be passed over, or avoided altogether. Keep moving.*

57 THE GENTLE *The influence and effect here are produced by gentle but persistent effort. There is steadfastness of purpose and a clearly-defined goal. Be inconspicuous.*

58 THE JOYOUS (LAKE) *Joining with friends encourages the heart-felt joy that comes from purity of feeling. The exchanges that take place are real learning-experiences. Co-operation is the key to success.*

59 DISPERSION (DISSOLUTION) *The time for separations is past. A re-union is suggested, based on a common spiritual need. There may be a celebration or ceremony that enables barriers to be broken down.*

60 LIMITATION *This is a double-edged admonition. Limitations and restrictions are necessary in order to curb excesses, but they should not be used as an excuse to limit progress and self-development.*

61 INNER TRUTH *Achievements may be made as even the most intractable of people respond to you. The secret is finding the right way of approach and this is based on a will to communicate. To succeed in this fashion, all your prejudices have fallen away.*

62 PREPONDERANCE OF THE SMALL *It is of no use to strive to accomplish great things now; only small matters may be concluded. However, maintain a conscientious outlook and do not gloss over details.*

63 AFTER COMPLETION *At the end of a cycle, the natural inclination is to relax. It is well, however, to take note of minor items as these could turn into major setbacks if not attended to straightaway.*

64 BEFORE COMPLETION *The stage prior to transition is indicative of a great task, with great responsibility at stake. Therefore it is best to be cautious at the beginning, until all aspects of the matter are understood.*

CHAPTER ELEVEN

NUMEROLOGY

Numerology is a controversial subject as everyone seems to have their own ideas about its origins and the method to use.

People have studied numbers and have used them as a form of divination for many thousands of years; man is said to have learned some form of counting system in the prehistoric era. The Babylonians and the ancient Egyptians also had their numerical theories and considered that numbers had occult sig-

nificance. Many people still feel this to be true, especially those interested in the Kabbala.

But, of course, the man that everyone first thinks of when considering numerology is Pythagoras, a Greek philosopher, mathematician and astrologer who was born about 580 BC. He formed the notion that everything can be expressed as a numerical value and that this would allow man to understand the structure of the universe a little easier.

Pythagoreans believed that each number had its own personality and that certain figures are stronger than others. Odd numbers are considered to be more powerful and, therefore, masculine; even numbers are thought to be less strong and, therefore, feminine.

The following table will allow you to see the Pythagorean method of converting the letters of our Western alphabet to numbers:

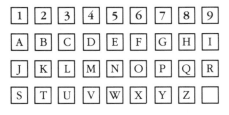

1	2	3	4	5	6	7	8	9
A	B	C	D	E	F	G	H	I
J	K	L	M	N	O	P	Q	R
S	T	U	V	W	X	Y	Z	

As I explained earlier, there are numerous methods of prediction based on numbers, and it is as well to mention the Kabbalistic system, which many people prefer to the Pythagorean one.

However, as the 22 letters of the Hebrew alphabet on which the Kabbalistic system is based do not correspond exactly to our alphabet, the latter must be transcribed. For those who would like to try both methods, here is a table of letter and number conversions that you can use.

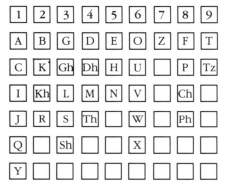

1	2	3	4	5	6	7	8	9
A	B	G	D	E	O	Z	F	T
C	K	Gh	Dh	H	U		P	Tz
I	Kh	L	M	N	V		Ch	
J	R	S	Th		W		Ph	
Q		Sh			X			
Y								

LIFE NUMBERS

This is the first number to be considered. It comes from adding up the figures of your birth date to produce a number that will remain dominant throughout your lifetime, and it indicates the lesson that you have to learn.

As an example, if you were born on 19th October 1964 add up your birth date like this:

$$1 + 9 + 1 + 0 + 1 + 9 + 6 + 4 = 31 = (3 + 1) = 4.$$

Your birth number is 4. The single numbers arrived at by this process are then interpreted according to the qualities and characteristics that have been assigned to them down through the ages.

Once you have calculated your own Life Number make a note of it and refer to the section on Life Numbers for a short analysis.

If the figures come to 11 or 22 these are not reduced any further as these represent *Master Numbers* and have special significance.

The following birth date will serve as an illustration of this: 11th October 1972 is expressed as:

$$1 + 1 + 1 + 0 + 1 + 9 + 7 + 2 = 22$$

This is not reduced to 4 as was the figure in the first example, but is left as 22.

WHAT YOUR NAMES REVEAL

Now you have calculated your Life Number the next stage is to discover what further insight into personality and potential can be gleaned from your names. Names are divided into consonants, which will give you your *Expression Number,* and vowels, which will reveal your *Desire* or *Heart Number.* Both these numbers should be noted separately and then added together to provide a third number which relates to *Destiny.*

The calculations for this are quite simple and you can, of course, choose either the Kabbalistic or Pythagorean numbering system. In the following examples the Pythagorean method has been used.

4	3 8	3	4	4	4	5	99	1
M I C H A E L	D A V I D	N O R R I S
9	1 5	1	9		6	9		

First add together the value of the consonants and reduce this to a single digit, unless they add up to a Master Number, which is 11 or 22:

Consonants:
$$4 + 3 + 8 + 3 + 4 + 4 + 4 + 5 + 9 + 9 + 1 = 54 = 9$$

This gives us Michael's Expression number, which is 9. Now add together the vowels:

Vowels: $9 + 1 + 5 + 1 + 9 + 6 + 9 = 40 = 4$

Michael's Heart number is therefore 4. To calculate his Destiny number, we must add the Expression and Heart numbers together;

$$9 + 4 = 13 = 4$$

Before you calculate your own numbers to discover how these will act in your life and how they colour your personality, there is one more number to calculate. This is called the Fadic Number and you arrive at its numerical value by adding together the Life number and the Destiny number.

Our example, Michael, was born on July 1st 1955, therefore his Life number is:

$$1 + 7 + 1 + 9 + 5 + 5 = 28 = 10 = 1.$$

This is added to his Destiny number:

$$1 + 4 = 5.$$

His Fadic number is therefore 5. It might be convenient to list all this information in order to read meaning of each number under the appropriate heading, thus:

Michael David Norris, born 1-7-1955
Life number = 1
Expression number = 9
Heart number = 4
Destiny number = 4
Fadic number = 5

The most difficult part of calculating numbers from your name is deciding which names or how many of them to use. My advice is to use the version you feel most comfortable with; or you could perhaps experiment with them all and then see which numbers seem to "fit" your personality and life pattern most accurately. When interpreting the numbers it is important that you remember that no single characteristic will represent "you" as a complete being. Also, if you don't like the result, always remember that not only can you change your name or alter its spelling, you can also change your life-style as well!

The Expression number indicates how others first see you.

The Desire and Heart number will reveal how you feel inside.

The Destiny number shows how you handle your affairs.

The Fadic number indicates your life purpose, or karma.

Associated with the Sun, the symbol of life. Number 1 people therefore are or aspire to be born leaders. Often they will succeed through their sheer force of personality but, even if confronted with obstacles, they have sufficient willpower and determination to succeed. Decisive, confident and courageous, these people are also very creative and excel in those occupations where their full potential can be realised. They do, however, lack tolerance and their life lesson is to learn how to earn the respect of others without needing to dominate them.

Number 2 is connected with the Moon, a balancing force. These people are concerned with the home and family life. They are reactive rather than active so need the company of others in order to feel fulfilled. Number 2 people make good deputies, providing behind-the-scenes support for partners or colleagues. Persuasive rather than forceful, they are as considerate of others' feelings as they are of their own. Although functioning well as part of a team, both at home and at work, they do need to learn to control their emotions as their inconsistent behaviour can lead to misunderstandings.

Because this number is associated with Jupiter, the planet of expansion, Number 3s seek constantly to broaden their horizons, both geographically and metaphorically. Inclined to view everything on a grand scale, they are gregarious, good company and magnanimous. However, their goals may not always be realistic and they should guard against extravagance. They do, though, often achieve positions of authority and are best suited to careers that allow them to travel. They desire personal freedom but, sadly, are not always willing to respect that of others.

Closely associated with Venus, planet of love, the number 6 person is concerned with harmony and balance. This can lead to a degree of dissatisfaction in a negative personality but, more usually, results in comfort, contentment and understanding. Material ease is important to this individual and he or she has the mental capacity to obtain it. Successful businessmen and women, especially if working in partnership, these subjects often make their careers in the arts or luxury trades. Self-indulgence is their probable weakness and they need to learn to curb their possessiveness.

Mars, the planet of action, ensures that these dynamic folk attack life with vim and vigour. Energetic, restless and aggressive, their supreme enthusiasm enables them to achieve their goals through others' efforts. Good at initiating schemes, they lack the patience needed to sustain their interests for long. Their competitive spirits may lead them into making rash decisions at times yet they enjoy challenging situations and are adroit enough to win through more often than not. Their greatest fault is their lack of consideration and they need to learn greater control.

These folk are the salt of the earth; solid, dependable and hard-working. They stand for security and solid foundations and are often attracted to careers in well-established organisations. Number 4 people are able to combat difficulties with dedication and persistence and have the facility to learn by their mistakes. They are thorough in their approach to all aspects of life and if you win their affections will make loyal and devoted partners. But as they may be narrow-visioned and reluctant to take chances, they must learn to unbend a little or they can become too complacent.

Long considered a mystic number, 7 is a symbol of completion and has strong associations with the Moon. Its subjects are often noted for their psychic abilities or, at the very least, sensitivity and idealism. Kind, considerate and compassionate, these people may be found in the caring professions or could be drawn towards occupations that require a vocation. They are also strongly imaginative and are well suited to creative careers in films and television. The danger lies in their losing touch with reality to such an extent that they seek unorthodox methods of escapism.

One of the master numbers, 11 is associated with true strength, of spirit as well as of physical stamina. These powerful personalities can, therefore, achieve virtually anything they set out to do but should beware of using their influence for selfish ends. Determined, courageous and energetic, they easily earn the respect and admiration of others and are natural leaders. Good at expressing their feelings, these people should not lack love or affection. Well equipped to be an inspiration to others, they are best suited to teach through example.

First of the intellectual numbers, and is associated with Mercury. Alert, lively and enterprising, these subjects are fascinated by anything new or untried for they have insatiable curiosities. Witty, their impish sense of humour may sometimes upset others, yet their child-like charm will usually get them out of tight corners. Best in jobs which provide opportunities for exchanging ideas and dealing with the public, Number 5s are often attracted to teaching, publishing, selling, tourism or any form of communication. However, they should beware of being jacks-of-all-trades and masters of none.

Because Saturn is the planet which stands for endurance, these subjects are very status conscious. Ambitious, career-minded and determined, they often succeed through sheer persistence and hard work. Self-assured and totally in control of their emotions, they may pursue their goals with relentless tenacity to the detriment of personal relationships. This can lead to a sense of loneliness or isolation once material ambitions have been fulfilled. These subjects must, therefore, learn to share with other people or they may be faced with an unintentional emotional void at the centre of their lives.

Regarded as the number of perfection, 22 is associated with solar power and the fulfilment of earthly ambitions. People born under this master number are likely to achieve perfect balance in all aspects of life. Their potential is limitless and their deep knowledge and understanding allows them to help and guide others on the path to enlightenment. The only danger lies in a tendency to rest on their laurels, to believe that because they have knowledge and wisdom there is nothing more to learn. Once they understand that the material plane is but one of many, these subjects will realise their full potential.

EXPRESSION NUMBERS

Number 1 people present a boldly confident exterior to the world, however different their innermost feelings may be. Usually loyal and trustworthy, they attract a large circle of friends and can be very supportive in a crisis. They have a natural air of authority and gravitate towards leadership in any situation but should beware of appearing arrogant or pushy to avoid unintentionally alienating those they care for.

People who like to live in peace and harmony with other people; unfortunately they often make it difficult for others to reciprocate their feelings. Their desire for absolute perfection in relationships may make them appear over-critical and continually carping about how perfect life "could" be. They need to learn how to control their emotions and must sometimes place greater trust in others.

Apparently cheerful, confident folk they may be the life and soul of the party yet quite often be very lonely in their private lives. Wanting to be the centre of attraction, they may be somewhat flashy in the way they dress and they usually have a good supply of "after dinner" stories. Often appearing boastful, their main desire is to feel needed yet they rarely allow others to get close enough to them for this sentiment to be understood.

Sometimes accused of being stuck in a rut, these are people who make reliable friends and co-workers. Being great defenders of tradition may make them reluctant to accept new ideas. Once someone wins their respect they will stand by that person forever. If, however, an individual lacks moral fibre, they will be ignored. Cautious with money, they are sometimes accused of meanness yet will always buy a round of drinks!

An inquisitive character out to learn everything; interest can be captured by any subject and this person is usually a veritable mine of information. Some may see them as a garrulous gossip, while others may respect their knowledge; but they always attract attention. Number 5s can be found in all walks of life and on any rung of the social ladder. Make the most of their company when you meet them, they rarely stay in one place for long.

These charismatic personalities are usually very popular and enjoy eager competition for their company. Attracted to the good things of life, they like to frequent cinemas, theatres and 5-star restaurants, preferably with equally charming companions. Desirous of peace and harmony, they rarely provoke argument and, though basically self-centred, this seldom causes problems. They usually tread an easy path through life.

Outsiders may wrongly assume that Number 7s are reserved and off-hand, but this is not really so; once others take the trouble to get to know them they discover that they are really warm and friendly. Often interested in philosophy or the occult, these folk will avidly study such subjects; they sometimes appear to have been born with deeper knowledge than other people. Cultivate them, they may have something to teach you.

People who desire popularity but should learn to be less high-handed and demanding; they sometimes push others away from them by the superior attitude. They have tremendous drive and energy and often become powerful figures in the world of business; piling up plenty of money may be their greatest goal. However, they are more successful as employers, an area where they realise the importance of teamwork.

Lively characters who can be devastatingly attractive even when not endowed with physical beauty, because they possess a magnetic quality that draws others to them. As they enjoy personal liberty and freedom it is often hard to pin them down, and they may not be too reliable about keeping appointments. They are usually honest and truthful, perhaps even bluntly outspoken — so don't expect flattery from Number 9s.

Idealists who are always ready to fight over principles. If you support their causes, you will worship them; but if you don't, you may be afraid of them for they make formidable enemies. It is difficult to get close to Number 11s and others often feel intimidated by their presence. But once someone wins their love and affection, the Number 11 person will remain a faithful and loyal friend for the duration of life.

Anyone with this Master Number may have an aura of innocence that makes them very attractive and appealing. Others may mistakenly imagine that this individual is in need of their protection yet the Number 22 is actually a very shrewd judge of any situation and possesses the ability to make fair assessments of character. Someone invariably eagerly sought after as a companion who enjoys a happy life.

DESIRE/HEART NUMBERS

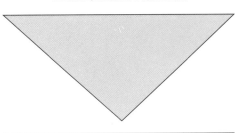

People who possess strong inner confidence, even when this is hidden behind a passive exterior. Having tremendous stamina, they will pursue chosen objectives determinedly and seldom give up on any task. But they may be a little inflexible and will rarely listen to advice from other people. In romance they may be complacent, tending to take love for granted: they should try to be more demonstrative.

No matter how outwardly confident these individuals may appear they are highly sensitive and very vulnerable deep down inside. Above all else, they long for security in relationships and are prepared to make every effort for these to work. Kind, caring and considerate, many Number 2s are natural healers; even when this trait is undeveloped, their presence can have a soothing effect on others who find them sympathetic.

The eternal optimist who continually lives in hope of a better future is indicated by this number. It is difficult to ruffle this person's inborn equanimity, then "know" that life has purpose and meaning and that effort will eventually be rewarded. This individual has a good sense of humour and usually has a cheering effect on others. He or she will encourage their partner and offspring to achieve, and makes a desirable friend.

Nervous of being noticed, these people prefer seclusion. They are happiest when in secure family units where life can follow set routines and order. Inclined towards domesticity, their homes are normally comfortable and attractive: females are perfect housewives; the husbands are keen do-it-yourselfers. Although not unfriendly, shyness inhibits sociability, thus these sensitive souls often play the role of observer throughout life.

Students who will study many diverse subjects; yet they do not take too kindly to discipline and thus may prefer to learn in private. Although perhaps inconstant in their love lives, they usually have many friends and acquaintances and their homes are often meeting places for groups of like-minded people. As long as they are constantly exchanging ideas and opinions with others they are likely to be content.

Although Number 6s may need a great deal of praise and appreciation showered upon them they usually go out of their way to ensure that it is deserved. They are concerned with the welfare of others, make splendid parents and marriage partners, but may also include those outside the family in their kind actions. Many of these folk have artistic talent and some may, perhaps, undertake creative work from their homes.

This is often the number of the mystic who hides away from society, preferring to perform the eternal quest for enlightenment alone. Number 7 may be regarded as an odd-ball by some yet they are happy and contented simply to seek answers to the riddle of the meaning of life; books and music may be a passion, too. This individual rarely cultivates romance but, when they do, it invariably fails, unfortunately.

When they are successful and wealthy these people have immense inner satisfaction; but if the odds have been stacked against them, they become complainers. They like to be head of their household, whether male or female, yet make extremely loyal partners in any situation. These subjects need to learn how to relax more and take pleasure occasionally or there is a danger that resentment could occur later in life.

Dextrous folk who usually have penetrating minds and great curiosity about how mechanical objects work. They enjoy taking things apart, often skilfully, and are useful friends to call upon in an emergency. Their personal lives can present certain problems as they tend to over-analyse relationships, mostly to the detriment of their partners. They have an inner restlessness that they find hard to control.

Number 11s live by their principles even if this mars their private existence. Having an inner conviction that their mission in life is to put the world in good order, they will inevitably find a cause to champion. Forced on by inner stirrings they don't always understand themselves, they would even abandon home and family if this was necessary. They do, though, have complete faith in their own abilities.

These individuals are born with the conviction that they are special in some way and their ultimate achievements will usually prove this view to be correct. They like to live in peace and harmony and their pleasant personalities make this a reality. Their biggest danger is to dream in private, without acknowledging the need for effort. This member has more potential than any other, yet these people are also those likeliest to waste it.

DESTINY NUMBERS

Leaders rather than followers, these characters need to feel in control of their environment. They avoid working as subordinates and will at least become head of their department. Often creative or artistic, Number 1s thrive in such professions. At home they tend to rule the roost and may have large families because they feel happiest when there are lots of willing slaves to obey their every command.

Outwardly cool, calm and collected, these subjects work well in any field that requires arbitration. When attempts are made to thwart them, they retreat into their shells and refuse to comment, often winning the day through sheer tenacity. In private life they will act in similar fashion but should guard against becoming over protective towards their loved ones. They may also tend to hold on too long to outworn relationships.

Someone who may be likened to the clown who readily hides disappointment and heartbreak behind laughter, or the cock who really does have something to crow about. Always desirous of achievement, Number 3s often have remarkable success. Drawn towards careers in the public eye they are able to spread happiness on an impersonal level yet, in private life, may be afraid of being trapped or tied down to domesticity.

If you want to get your office functioning well, employ a number 4. Quietly efficient and expert at setting up systems, these people like to be usefully employed and rarely waste time on idle chatter. There is a caring side to their nature too, though they are sometimes reluctant to form close relationships. Some may prefer pets to people as these are less likely to disturb their rigid routines yet provide companionship.

Versatile and adaptable, people who can turn their hands to most things. They make good workers as long as their jobs entail variety, and function best through involvement with the public or in the field of communications. They may, though, prefer to remain free of serious entanglement in their personal lives. Some are inveterate travellers and many finally settle down and live in a land far from their birthplace.

Professions such as nursing, catering, hairdressing or the theatre often have many Number 6s for they often earn their living by pleasing others in some way. Good at handling finance, they have the potential to make money and, when in business for themselves, are usually very successful. Oddly intolerant in their private lives, they will abandon without a qualm any relationship that is not working satisfactorily.

Not only do these people dream of a better world for all, they are quite prepared to put in considerable effort to create it. They also believe that people should learn to help themselves and thus make excellent teachers; if they work for the underprivileged or disabled, they will take a surprisingly forthright and practical approach. As long as partners don't encroach on their personal space too much, relationships succeed.

This denotes the executive, the organiser of big business, or the high-powered politician, even a local government worker. People who need to be in control of their environment and are prepared to work hard to stay at the top; they may, however, neglect family relationships in the process. They need to learn to be more tolerant of others' failings otherwise there is a danger of loneliness and alienation later in life.

Number 9s have a talent for organisation; they can usually see the quickest solution to any problem that may arise. Impatient of other's slowness, they tend to be highly critical in their comments. They enjoy change and variety, wanting to experience all that life has to offer, but once their love and affection has been won, they will stand by their loved ones through the most daunting trials and tribulations.

Influential and creative people; many turn their talents towards working in the media. They usually feel they have messages they wish to pass on to mankind and may find they can do this best by working in fashion, films, TV or publishing. As they have the ability to sway the masses, Number 11s must learn to use this power wisely for, whatever they do, others will listen; what they choose to preach is therefore important.

This powerful Master number is born to be noticed; Number 22s will stand out in any crowd. They tend to attract the attention of superiors and, even if they start at the bottom, will rise rapidly to the top. They must, however, learn to avoid complacency or they will lose their not inconsiderable achievements. The biggest danger that faces any Number 22 is that he or she has the potential to revert to an ordinary Number 4.

FADIC NUMBERS

These numbers have to be treated rather differently because the life purpose — or karmic lesson — will depend on what specific combination of numbers have made up this final total. For this reason I feel it is best to follow the formulae of keywords so that you can use your own judgement to decide which seem most appropriate.

For instance, one of the major lessons facing Number 1 subjects would be issues of dominance. If the final addition had included a 2 or 4 (perhaps both), you might need to learn how to take more control of your own environment but, if the final total included 11, you may need to curb a tendency to dominate people.

So do try and bear in mind what numbers have contributed to the total which, when reduced, reveal your Fadic number when reading the following.

Qualities ☐ dominance ☐ power ☐ control ☐ self-assertion ☐ initiation ☐ tyranny ☐ arrogance ☐ awareness ☐ hostility ☐ independence ☐ frustration ☐ authority ☐ optimism ☐ pessimism ☐ tolerance ☐ confidence ☐ self-respect ☐ creativity ☐ flexibility ☐ warmth ☐ drama ☐ glory ☐ self-aggrandisement.

Qualities ☐ expansion ☐ joviality ☐ extravagance ☐ superiority ☐ boastfulness ☐ praise ☐ knowledge ☐ counsel ☐ conceit ☐ wastefulness ☐ hypocrisy ☐ intolerance ☐ greed ☐ enthusiasm ☐ equanimity ☐ achievement ☐ personality ☐ envy ☐ zeal ☐ zest ☐ audacity ☐ jurisprudence ☐ realism ☐ eloquence ☐ luck.

Qualities ☐ emotions ☐ nurturing ☐ clannishness ☐ passivity ☐ moods ☐ feelings ☐ sensitivity ☐ responses ☐ fears ☐ shyness ☐ delusions ☐ paranoia ☐ kindness ☐ constancy ☐ vascillation ☐ carefulness ☐ compromise ☐ tranquility ☐ martyrdom ☐ adaptability ☐ co-operation ☐ balance ☐ persuasion ☐ consideration.

Qualities ☐ perseverance ☐ organisation ☐ dedication ☐ loyalty ☐ trust ☐ complacency ☐ duty ☐ endurance ☐ substance ☐ inflexibility ☐ suppression ☐ tradition ☐ routine ☐ respectability ☐ caution ☐ domesticity ☐ efficiency ☐ security ☐ devotion ☐ stability ☐ rigidity ☐ tenacity ☐ moralising ☐ economy ☐ work.

pitagoras

Left: A 14th century portrait of Pythagoras, the Greek philosopher and mathematician who lived in the 6th Century BC. The theorem for which he is best remembered from our schooldays is of minor importance when it is realised that we owe to him most of the occult symbolism of numbers, as well as the doctrines of the transmigration of souls and "the harmony of the spheres". He was also said to be a great healer and miracle-worker.

Right: Europe in the Middle Ages saw a great revival of interest in matters of classical learning, such as philosophy and mathematics. One of the chief reasons was the contact with the Arab world, which had spread westwards as far as Spain. They possessed many translations of Greek works of antiquity: European scholars were eager to exchange knowledge and ideas with them. This is a table of numerological meanings from a 14 century manuscript.

Qualities □ curiosity □ communication □ wit □ salesmanship □ intelligence □ movement □ inconsistency □ inconstancy □ sloppiness □ versatility □ variety □ humour □ thought □ teaching □ sincerity □ honesty □ citicism □ geniality □ eloquence □ restlessness □ fluency □ ingenuity □ adroitness □ adaptability □ dexterity.

Qualities □ mysticism □ completion □ idealism □ sensitivity □ illusion □ delusion □ imagination □ allurement □ escapism □ confusion □ deception □ seclusion □ aloofness □ unreality □ metaphysics □ seeking □ creativity □ vision □ compassion □ tranquility □ mission □ privacy □ repentance □ self-abnegation.

Qualities □ action □ vim □ vigour □ vitality □ energy □ restlessness □ aggression □ enthusiasm □ initiation □ competition □ rashness □ boldness □ challenging □ forcefulness □ attraction □ magnetism □ unreliability □ honesty □ bluntness □ analysis □ enterprise □ originality □ constructive □ resourcefulness.

Qualities □ harmony □ balance □ charm □ contentment □ understanding □ selfishness □ laziness □ materialism □ indulgence □ possessiveness □ greed □ cynicism □ carelessness □ appreciation □ art □ welfare □ fairness □ compassion □ self-righteousness □ beauty □ valuation □ satisfaction □ popularity

Qualities □ ambition □ effort □ determination □ endurance □ persistence □ isolation □ loneliness □ covetousness □ materialism □ practicality □ leadership □ direction □ bias □ control □ detail □ responsibility □ success □ power □ demanding □ envy □ drive □ teamwork □ resentment □ neglect □ conventionality.

Qualities □ power □ strength □ stamina □ courage □ expression □ inspiration □ determination □ admiration □ respect □ intimidation □ idealism □ principles □ loyalty □ influence □ creativity □ persuasion □ conviction □ faith □ support □ fanaticism □ superiority □ pragmatism □ comprehension □ reform.

Qualities □ perfection □ complacency □ fulfilment □ knowledge □ understanding □ enlightenment □ laziness □ innocence □ wisdom □ achievement □ realisation □ awareness □ mastery □ imagination □ humanitarianism □ concentration □ dreams □ indifference □ diplomacy □ purpose □ balance □ imbalance □

LOOKING TO THE FUTURE

Numbers can be projected on to the future, as with any other form of divination. To discover what any particular year is likely to hold for you, the numerologist will simply add the day and the month of birth to the figures in the year under consideration.

To return to our previous example, Michael who was born on 1/7/1955, if we wished to examine his major trends for the year 1973, we would calculate the numerical value for 1/7/1973 in the usual manner:
$1 + 7 + 1 + 9 + 7 + 3 = 28 = 1$. 1973 would obviously be important for Michael as it echoes the year number for his birth; and it was, for this was the year in which Michael came into some money and got married.

This method of calculation can be used for any year past, present or future. Likely events can be assessed from the interpretations given for the numbers on previous pages; special attention should be paid to any year that becomes a Master number or which reflects a number that was dominant at the time of birth.

Although this type of forward-looking calculation is derived from one's birth-date, years that total any number arising from one's name will also have importance. These can be assessed on an individual level and through the creation of a new annual Fadic number. In the example above, for instance, Michael's year number for 1972 would have been 9, a number associated with charisma.

It was in fact in 1972 that he met his future partner and 9, of course is Michael's Expression number at birth.

CHAPTER TWELVE

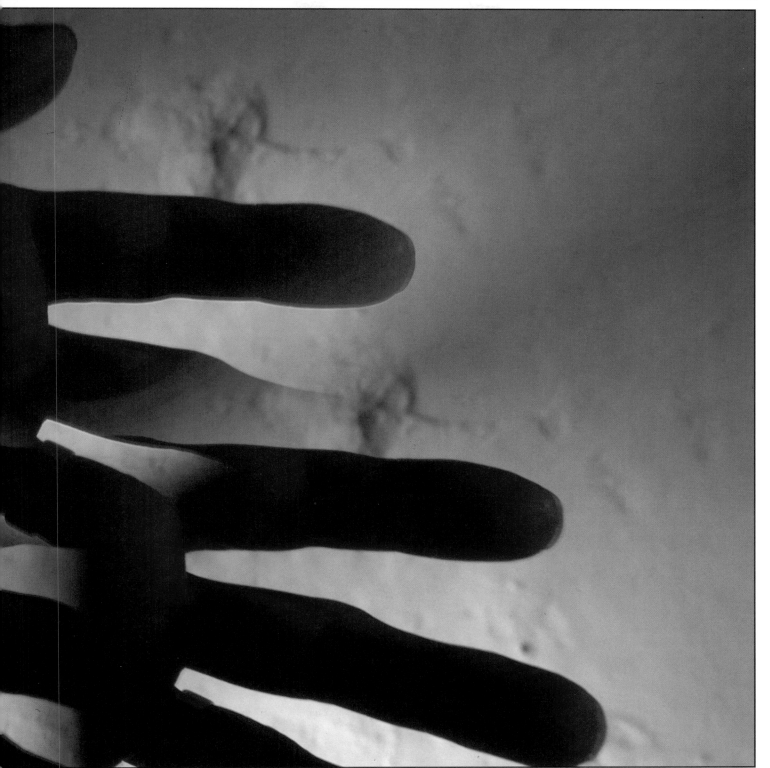

PALMISTRY

Palmistry is an age old interpretative art by which we are able to infer character, define capability and talent, judge health, verify disposition and estimate potential.

Three quite separate branches make up the study of palmistry. Chirognomy is the study of the shape of the hand, chiromancy is the study of the lines and other features of the palm, and dermatoglyphics is the study of the skin patterns of the palms and fingers. One golden rule of palmistry is that no single feature, however strong it may appear, should ever be taken in isolation. Always check elsewhere in the hands before reaching conclusions. Both hands should be examined. The left hand usually indicates hereditary gifts, traits, leanings and implications; the right will show how far these aptitudes have been developed. It is therefore essential to compare one hand with the other.

HAND SHAPE

Generally speaking, there are two hand types referred to, the square and the conic, or round. To classify a hand for shape, view the palmar surface from the wrist to the base of the fingers noting the outer edge for a bulge or for straightness.

If it looks square then classify it as such. If it appears slightly round then it is a conic palm. It takes practice and study, but don't be afraid to practise on friends. Apply common sense, there are no hidden or occult rules.

Next, judge the length of the fingers in relation to the palm. If it is not immediately apparent they may be of equal length, give or take a centimetre or two. Often, the palm is longer than the fingers. Note the size of the thumb in relation to the hand. It should always look as though it belongs to the hand. A heavy thumb may offset a routine assessment as would a weak looking affair that seems stuck on the side of the hand as an afterthought. So, when assessing the shape of the hand, you should note the basic shape, the relative length of the fingers and whether the thumb 'belongs' to the hand.

The square hand

This hand type denotes convention, self-reliance and practicality. Its owner has a strong respect for law and order. There is a love of discipline, such people automatically fall into their place in the hierarchy of things. They are materialists and are prepared to accept the habits and customs of conformity, they 'know' their place.

There is an innate sense of responsibility; they are rarely at a loss for what to do, they have reason and capability. This type of hand is often referred to as the useful hand, for this is the hand of the doer. These are the folk who supply method and order for they know how to delegate and organise.

The conic hand

Conic-handed folk are at their best in company, for they quickly catch the mood of the moment. They have a ready wit and are inclined to be the life and soul of the party. Such people will provide ideas galore to restore a flagging situation. They will be instrumental in getting others to do things and get things and people going. These people have a strong sense of luxury and the better things of life but may be equally reluctant to knuckle down and work hard to achieve anything really constructive. Often, there is a lack of staying power and they are easily distracted when they do try to concentrate. Emotionally, they are fickle and inconsistent.

Relative finger and palm length

Where the fingers and the palm are of equal length and feel fairly firm to the touch, then there will be a firmness of approach in the overall attitude.

Such a person is likely to enjoy a greater success in life. Square-handed people will achieve good solid success in the practical matters of their choice. Conic hands imply success in the artistic fields, creative or interpretative.

When fingers are longer than the palm attention to detail is increased. Such a person will employ their talents to sway or influence others in a practical manner. When the palm is longer than the fingers, impulsive behaviour becomes more apparent.

On a hand soft to the touch there will be inconsistency in the overall character. There will also be materialism and self indulgence. On a firm hand it is usually the case that attention to detail is not so weak.

Backs of hands

When you meet someone for the first time have a quick glance at the back of their hands — there is no need to touch or obviously examine them. A small hand with short fingers imply the owner prefers short sharp answers to questions and will not be interested in long detailed explanations. The person with large hands will require more detailed information and will want to consider all the possibilities before making a decision. A large hand that is wide across the back of the palm belongs to those who will not stand any nonsense. A large broad hand indicates someone who enjoys the great outdoors and sporting activities. The firmer the hand the more competitive the spirit.

A small narrow hand implies a degree of selfishness; an opportunist who can move very quickly to secure an advantage. The long narrow hand denotes the thinker, one who may ponder for some time over most things. Should the fingers seem to be 'knotty' at the joints the owner will be quite a philosopher. Note the colour of the backs of the hands. Normal fleshy pink colouring reflects an average, well balanced personality. A very pale skin is an indication of selfishness and someone who drives a hard bargain. The dark or weatherbeaten hands show a nature committed to a love of the open air. A finely

textured skin, soft to the touch, will belong to the indoor type. A coarse textured skin, firm to the touch, belongs to those who prefer the great outdoors.

Well kept nails belong to those who have a certain amount of pride in their appearance, whereas bitten nails are found on the hands of those who have short tempers, and may be inclined to some inconsistency of approach and who may be unable to concentrate for long periods.

Long, wide and square nails imply that a person has a basically peaceful nature, whereas the short nail can incline to criticism, both of self and others.

The palm

Beneath the base of each finger there should be a certain amount of fleshiness — the mount. To test the development, or otherwise, touch it lightly with your fingertips so you can feel the sponginess and firmness of the mount. The mounts are said to represent a storehouse of power, of raw material in the sense of energy and feelings. The digital mounts, Jupiter, Saturn, Apollo and Mercury form the base from which the fingers grow. So, the fuller, firmer and healthier the area, the more the fingers should reflect this strength in their development. The Jupiter mount represents leadership; Saturn, stability; Apollo, creativity; Mercury, communication, and the mount of Venus, vitality.

Venus is not really a mount but the third phalange of the thumb. It is the seat of the libido, affections, emotions and physical energy. When full and well developed it shows the ability of the owner to live life to the full.

The palmar mounts, those not directly associated with the digits, have also been named after the traditional gods of old, and these are, in turn, associated with astrology.

The Luna mount is associated with imagination and the ability to communicate but in a different way to the Mercury mount. Where the mount of the Moon appears to push the mount of Venus over it indicates an intensely passionate nature. But if the mount of Venus encroaches upon the Lunar mount it indicates an excess of physical energy.

Below: When you meet someone look at the back of their hands for overall shape and proportion.

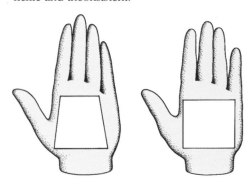

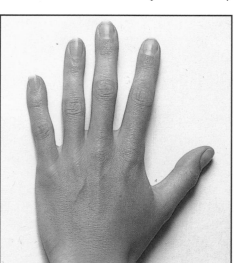

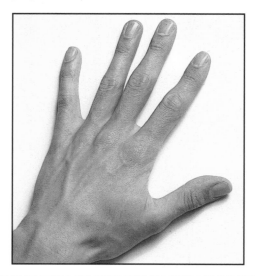

The mount of Neptune is a recent innovation and not of traditional origin. When developed, the personality is lively, full of life and gifted with the instinctive knowledge of how to act in any given set of circumstances. If under-developed, the nature tends to be indifferent to people, their problems and the world in general.

The zone of Mars consists of three traditional areas: the mount of Mars Positive; Mars Negative; and the Plain of Mars. I have always preferred to think of them as one area or zone which stretches across the centre of the palm. Always test this area by touch for firmness or a thin and bony feel to it.

A developed zone implies an interest in the world and its affairs, someone who is active and positive. Thin, or underdeveloped, suggests a nature with little or no interest in mundane affairs.

The creative curve at the side of the hand is not really a mount in the strictest sense. When developed at the top of the percussion there is mental creativity and energy, someone who has ideas but is not always able to make a product. If the bulge occurs lower down toward the bottom of the hand, it signifies physical creative energy: the type who can make a product. If the bulge is greatest in the middle of the percussion it signifies a person who is persistent in their creativeness. Someone who not only has creative ideas but is also able to follow these things through to completion. When the curve is under developed or non-existent, the subject will probably not have any creative gift.

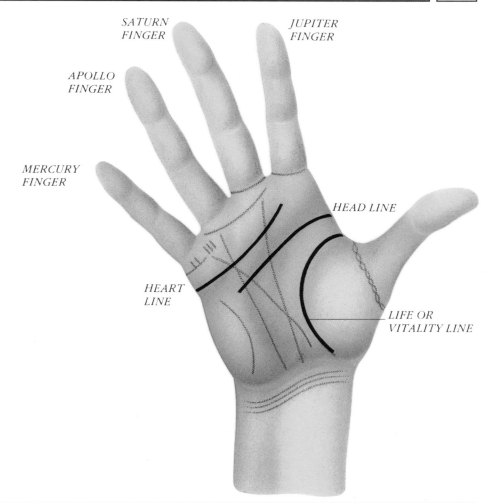

SATURN FINGER

JUPITER FINGER

APOLLO FINGER

MERCURY FINGER

HEAD LINE

HEART LINE

LIFE OR VITALITY LINE

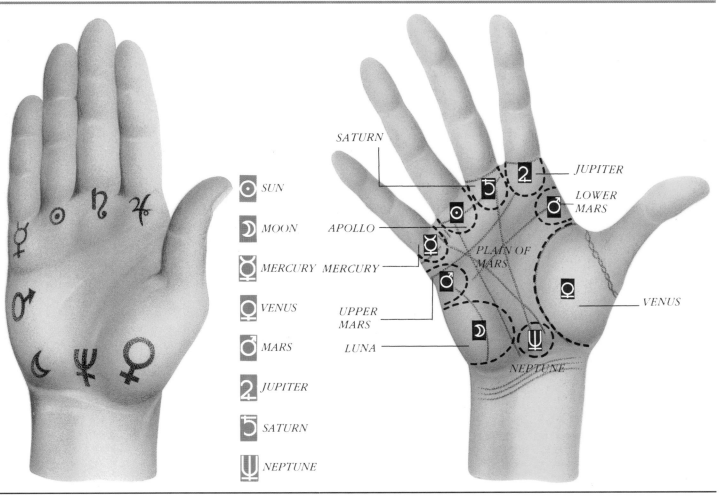

☉ SUN

☽ MOON

☿ MERCURY

♀ VENUS

♂ MARS

♃ JUPITER

♄ SATURN

♆ NEPTUNE

SATURN

JUPITER

APOLLO

LOWER MARS

MERCURY

PLAIN OF MARS

UPPER MARS

VENUS

LUNA

NEPTUNE

The thumb

The thumb is the signature of the hand, the key to personality. Always remember to compare thumbs. Is one stronger than the other? Does each individual thumb look right for the hand on which it is found? The thumb should come to about halfway up the basal phalange of the index finger when held close to it. When relaxed, the thumb should form an angle of between 45° and 90° to the forefinger. An angle of less than that reflects a tendency to be small-minded, selfish or prejudiced. The wider the angle, the more self reliant, sensible and outgoing the personality. Wider than 90° implies good leadership qualities but one who will take chances or attempt foolhardy actions. The hero, dead or alive.

A low-set, wide-angled thumb depicts an adventurer with a good sense of self-protection. A high-set thumb with a narrow angle shows a personality who will bend rather than break rules in order to protect himself at all times. Where the right hand seems to be the more positive and the thumb supports your findings you may expect the subject to have made great efforts to better himself and improve his lot. The reverse of this implies the subject may have suffered reversals from which he seems unable to recover and he may have opted for the easy way out. A drifter.

The basal phalange of the thumb, or mount of Venus, should be full and springy to the touch. The more developed the area the more energy there is to meet the challenge of life. When the phalange is under developed, there is less energy, less willingness to join in, the character may be weak and vacillating.

The middle phalange denotes reason. When overlong it suggests an argumentative type. If too short it implies a nature which lacks rational perceptions. A short and thick phalange denotes poor diplomatic powers, while a short and thin version shows the owner works best under direction — and then only on set routines. A waisted phalange, one that is noticeably thinner than the other two, has a refining influence on the personality. There is tact, diplomacy and an accommodating nature.

The first or top phalange is the indicator of purpose, decisiveness and energy. If longer than the middle phalange willpower is strong and well directed. If shorter, the subject's ability to lead is lessened. If short and very thin, the owner knows how to handle people. If thick and heavy, expect a temper and strong basic appetites.

If the thumb overall appears long and heavy in comparison to the rest of the hand it indicates dictatorial behaviour, obstinacy, and to a lesser degree, coarseness.

When short or weak looking it implies a weak and vacillating character. A stiff thumb suggests conventional behaviour. A flexible thumb, not just the tip, reflects a flexible and adaptable approach to life. Should the thumb oppose the fingers, or stand at right angles to them, the subject possesses strong self control, sometimes too much on occasions.

Do spend time on the thumb when examining hands — it is quite possible to misread, especially if one forgets to compare the right hand thumb with the left hand partner. With time and practise this will help you to understand the personality.

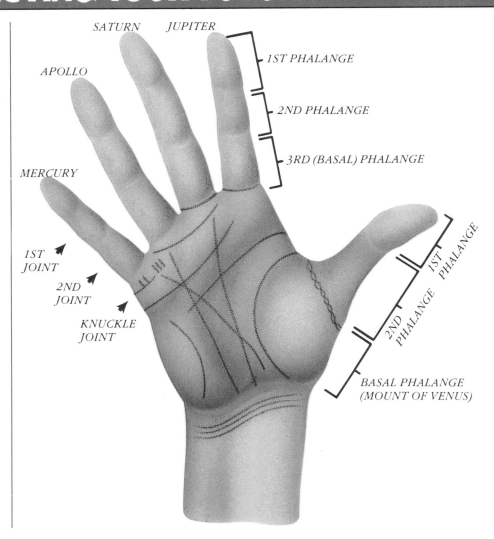

SATURN   JUPITER

APOLLO

1ST PHALANGE

2ND PHALANGE

3RD (BASAL) PHALANGE

MERCURY

1ST JOINT

2ND JOINT

KNUCKLE JOINT

1ST PHALANGE

2ND PHALANGE

BASAL PHALANGE (MOUNT OF VENUS)

The fingers

The four fingers are strong indicators of character because they supply the instinctive facet of personality, whereas the palm represents the practical aspect.

Their appearance, shape, position and development should be observed from both the front and back of the hand. Note the inclination of one finger to another. Finger length in relation to the palm as well as to each other is equally important.

Smooth fingers denote versatile, intuitive and adaptable personalities. If short, the owner will see the whole plan or scheme but may miss the detail needed to effectively carry it through.

Those with long fingers take time to assimilate detail but impulsiveness still remains. Fingers which are 'knotted' at the joints belong to those who stop and think before they act or pronounce their judgement. Knotting of the top joints only denotes a critical nature. These folk tend to be slow to respond and are often difficult to please. When the lower joints only are prominent the nature inclines to be tidy, methodical and rather pragmatic.

When both joints are prominent it denotes the true sceptic: cold, logical, calculating and precise. These people are best left alone to pursue their own interests.

Should the knuckles be prominent the subject will be neat and orderly. There may be concern with diet, appearance, fitness and personal disciplines. The Jupiter finger represents ego, pride and ambition. There are usually clear-cut beliefs and ideas if the finger is long and straight. If short, there may be an inability to concentrate for long periods at a time. When this finger stands away from the middle finger the owner is able to think for himself and prefers to work on his own. Should the index finger be shorter than the third the nature may be cold and hard. There will be a dislike of petty restrictions.

The Saturn finger represents balance, stability and self-control. Often, this finger is the longest, but when short, the owner will not take life too seriously: the happy-go-lucky type who is unreliable and promises more than he can produce. An overlong or stiff medius shows strength of character. Someone with a serious nature and who accepts responsibilities. Such a person will study hard either as a hobby or in the pursuit of career.

The Apollo finger is concerned mainly with the artistic pursuits of life. The longer the finger the better. There will be creativity and good, inward personal happiness. A short finger indicates a pessimistic nature and, unless the finger is very straight, there will be little creativeness even though the subject may show some artistic talent. A short, flexible Apollo finger is the sign of the gambler who may be inclined more to the 'easy' way of life.

The Mercury finger rules communications at all levels, so when it stands away from its neighbour a distinct individuality will be present. If it stays too close to the Apollo finger expect the traditionalist who prefers to stay with the tried and trusted ways of life.

THE MAJOR LINES

The colour of the lines should suit the palm. Reddish, deeply etched lines indicates an aggressive or strong personality. Pale lines almost always refer to a lack of vitality and a negative nature. Occasionally, you may find one or more of the major lines missing, or so faint as to be practically non-existent. In this event the line affected will be a focal point in the personality of the subject.

The life line missing or formed in such a manner points to a lack of enthusiasm for life; the head line, an inability to concentrate for long periods at a time; and on the heart line expect a poor emotional response or a potentially poor vascular system.

The head line

The ideal head line will start quite clearly, just touching or very near the life line and will sweep out into the palmar plain in a smooth but slightly bowing style ending approximately at a point below the middle of the Mercury finger.

The universally accepted measure of one's intellect, this line indicates the extent of our thoughts and how we apply them in a practical sense, also the general level of perception. The right hand will show the development, if any, of the characteristics indicated in the left hand. Obvious differences denote changes.

A strong line in the right hand shows the subject to be able to break away from restrictive elements in the earlier life by utilising the willpower to best advantage. A weak line in the right hand shows a less than positive willpower. When both lines are of equal formation the subject has accepted his lot and makes do.

Sometimes the head line has a very irregular appearance. It may start well then fade out for a while and reappear again at a later point in the hand. This shows the subject has had to struggle to keep his head above water. The time of your observations will show whether he is currently coping or has temporarily given up his efforts.

Lines that fork or branch show a diversification of interests. The wider the fork the more wide-ranging the interests have become. Fraying, the ultimate in the branching appearance, shows a dissipation of energies.

A short head line will show that the owner will approach problems in a practical manner, probably has a high level of concentration and a good memory. By contrast, the long, slightly bowing line is associated with those who have varied interests and difficulty in concentrating for long periods. It is quite possible for there to be two head lines on a hand but it is rare to find such a formation on both hands. It is usually found in the right hand only. The owner can exist quite comfortably in two worlds at once, perhaps holding down two entirely different careers at the same time. When a head line sweeps across the palm as though cutting it in two, expect to find someone whose mental strength will override all emotional considerations if he deems it necessary, irrespective of any other contradictory markings.

A chained line implies poor mental concentration. Influence lines that rise from the head line refer to efforts made to improve the life style. Dots signify worry, islands periods of weakened power of the line. A firm palm will strengthen the line; a soft palm weaken it.

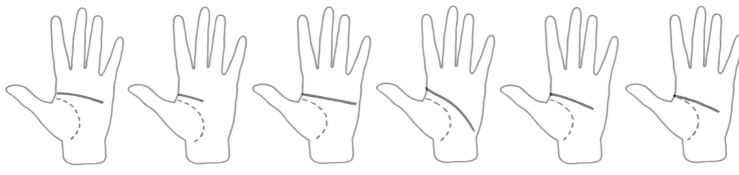

Long, gently curving, well-formed head line, starting just above the life line. This shows a strong intellect, a degree of independence and a realistic attitude.

Short, straight head line ending below the Saturn finger, denoting a very practical, down to earth manner, good concentration and retentive memory but little imagination.

A straight, deeply-etched line right across the palm, almost cutting it in two, implies very strong will-power; someone who will always place more value on intellect than emotion and be quite capable of sublimating his or her feelings to his or her will in order to achieve ambitions.

Long, sloping line ending well down the palm on the mount of Luna. This implies poor concentration but a good degree of self-expression and heightened imagination; probably a very creative personality.

Well-defined head line, unmarred by minor marks, ending at a point below the middle of the Mercury finger. Practical, methodical, confident and ambitious, this character will have a well-balanced outlook on life.

A head line tied to the line of life at its start implies a cautious, conservative nature; perhaps a degree of inhibition. The longer this tie, the more sensitive the owner will be to others' wishes and the harder it will be for him/her to make a bid for independence.

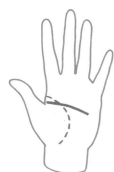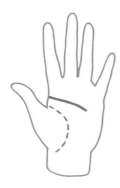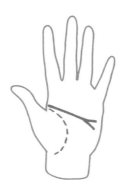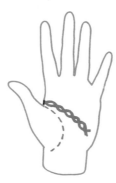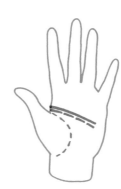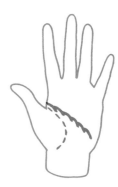

When the head line starts from inside the life line it indicates a very inhibited character whose lack of confidence and inability to express freely may cause him or her to act irrationally on occasion.

A high start to the head line, on the mount of Jupiter, implies a good intellect and memory, well-balanced reasoning powers, honesty and integrity. This formation signals leadership qualities, good organisational abilities and a quick intelligence

A well-marked head line that ends in a fork denotes a twofold talent. Creativity will be both mental and practical, thus the owner may either follow two careers or utilise his or her creative talents outside their usual occupation.

Chained and fuzzy, with numerous interference marks, this formation may refer to an inability to think clearly or logically, perhaps due to temporary ill-health, stress or worry. However, the head line will usually become stronger and better-defined once any such period of instability is past.

Although rare, especially in both hands, a double head line denotes that the owner lives in two worlds simultaneously. Perhaps he or she follows two distinct careers or has two quite separate homes and lifestyles due to the nature of his or her work. In any event, this formation marks an unusual talent.

Minor branch lines that drop down from the head line refer to incidents that have interrupted the owner's progress or ambitions; rising lines, however, indicate that efforts have been made to counteract any such setbacks and to improve circumstances in general.

The life line

The line of life should start anywhere in the region of the mount of Jupiter or Mars positive, or even be the dividing factor between them. It should move easily out into the palm with a firm gentle curve encircling the mount of Venus and may end in a number of different ways.

It may sweep further into the palm and end somewhere in the region of the lower part of the Lunar mount. It may fall straight towards the mount of Neptune or tuck itself in under the mount of Venus. It may fork once, twice or any amount of times. It may tassellate, end abruptly or simply fade away.

This line should be taken as the gauge of vitality and zest for living because it is a reliable factor in physical well-being and will show how robust or otherwise the constitution is.

A long life line does not signify a long life, nor does a short line imply a short life. People can and do exist with only token or very short lines; indeed, some actually exist with no line of life at all. Of the three main lines of the hand, the life, head and heart lines, some palmists consider the life line to be the most important because it shows the basic approach a person has to life itself.

Should this line appear to be the strongest of the three then it may be taken that physical matters will take precedence over everything. This type of formation is frequently found on the hands of those who thrive outdoors. Influence lines from the mount of Venus, inside the line of life, show interference from the family or very close friends. As the lines of head and life part look for influence lines running between them. The more there are, the greater the owner's need to look to others for leadership. The less there are, the more self reliant the subject.

A line of life that starts from the mount of Jupiter suggests an ambitious side to the nature. Between the mounts of Jupiter and Mars the owner is less self assured and a little reticent. Should the line start on the Mars mount the subject will almost certainly prefer to be a follower. The ideal line should sweep out into the palm indicating good vitality. Should the line start to restrict the mount of Venus the overall outlook of the subject will also be restricted.

A comparison of the two hands is essential. When the life line on the right hand swings further into the palm than it does on the left, it signifies that the owner has made a sustained, conscious effort to attain greater personal freedom. The converse implies that the subject has had to come to terms with reduced circumstances, has had to learn to make do, either materially or emotionally.

The line that sweeps out into the palm suggests an extrovert character. Conversely, the light straighter line indicates introversion. If the line begins to swing in, under the mount of Venus, it shows the subject likes to feel safe and secure. However, should the line continue onward and outward to the Luna mount it implies a love of travel to seek fresh experiences.

When the line forks it is a clear sign of restlessness, particularly if one of the forks ends on the mount of Luna.

When a break occurs on any part of the line of life look to the other principal lines for verification. If the other lines are free of any mark then this defect may refer to a period of poor health or possibly an accident; a temporary obstruction to the normal physical life style. Any mark, cut, dot, crossbar, pitting, discolouration, chaining, break or island is an indication of poor health: doubly so if it occurs on both hands.

The line of life indicates awareness of the reserves of vitality. The slightest interruption or imperfection, therefore, suggests an indication of trouble.

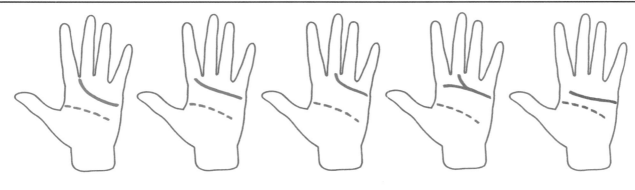

The "ideal" heart line begins between the Jupiter and Saturn fingers, sweeps in a smooth curve to end below the Mercury mount at the edge of the hand. This denotes a well adjusted emotional outlook, someone who is warm, outgoing, responsive to others yet realistic.

A heart line that rises on the Jupiter mount signifies a romantic, somewhat idealistic approach to emotional matters and, in particular, personal relationships.

Sensuality is denoted by a deeply curved heart line rising on or below the Saturn mount. Although demonstrably passionate, such a person may be rather self-centred and insensitive or inconsiderate of others' needs and thus lack tenderness in his/her relationships.

A heart line that forks, one branch going to the Jupiter mount and the other to Saturn, shows a better balance between sentiment and passion. Well adjusted emotionally, the owner of this configuration should find it easy to relate well to others.

There may be a conflict between emotions and intellect where the heart line runs very close to the head. The stronger of the two lines will indicate which of these two aspects of the subject's personality is most likely to dominate.

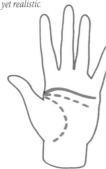

When the heart, head and life lines share a common source, this may point to an even greater conflict if all three major lines are equally well-developed. More often, though, such a formation denotes a remarkable ability to recover from any traumatic experience the owner may suffer.

A long, clear-cut heart line running right across the palm signifies a strong desire for affection, someone who is motivated mainly by his/her emotional needs and may, therefore, be inclined to romanticise situations that do not warrant it.

If very short, shallow or ill-defined, a lack of emotional warmth is indicated, especially if the line rises under the Apollo finger as this may point to an egocentric personality.

A chained heart line, or one that is marred by numerous small interference lines, points to inconstant affections. This is the mark of the flirt and may denote that the subject lacks self-confidence or mistrusts the intentions of others.

Shrewdness is indicated if the heart line forks on the Mercury mount. Sociable, charming and persuasive, such an individual will be able to express him/herself well in almost any situation.

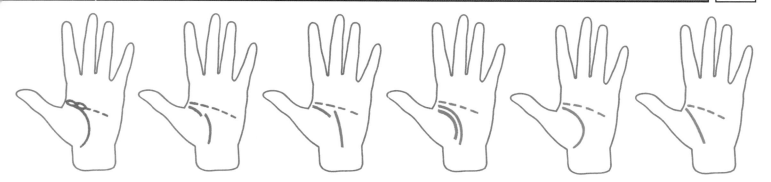

Often, the life line's start will be tied to that of the head and there may also be chaining. This indicates a degree of reticence or uncertainty, perhaps due to early restrictions brought about by parental domination, deprivation or childhood illnesses.

If the life line runs normally for a while, fades completely and then reappears a little further into the hand to continue its course down the palm, this usually denotes an interruption to the vitality and good health of the subject.

Sometimes the hand shows a very short life line, perhaps only an inch or so long, and a second, longer more vigorous-looking line further into the palm, probably starting from the head line. This indicates the subject's complete dissatisfaction with his/her home and environment and reflects his/her efforts to, quite literally, start a new life more to his/her liking and inclination.

A 'sister' line, a line that runs parallel to but inside the life line on the mount of Venus is often seen. Known as the inner life line or line of Mars, it plays a supportive role and lends strength and protection to the line of life, thus enhancing its qualities.

The 'ideal' life line is well-defined, sweeps out into the centre of the palm, forming a broad curve around the Venus mount, to end well down the hand, near the wrist. This shows a warm, spontaneous nature and a robust constitution; someone full of vitality who will always bounce back after any sort of setback.

A shallow curve that seems to cut into the Venus mount signifies a degree of inhibition, a lack of response to others or to life in general. The more this line restricts the Venus mount, the more such traits will prevail.

The heart line

The line of heart may start on the mount of Jupiter; between the first and second fingers; on the extreme edge of the hand under the index finger; or it may have a forked beginning. It may start on the mount of Saturn. This line may be short, long, thick or thin; it may appear chained or with islands; be clear of all influence lines except for those that are expected to cross it; or it may have many and varied little influence marks rising and falling all along its course.

The heart line is connected with all emotional matters in the personality, some health matters and the vascular system generally. When the line starts from the mount of Jupiter, curves smoothly and evenly under the fingers and runs to the percussion with little or no interference marks it shows that the subject's emotional approach to life is well balanced. The lower the line reaches into the palm, the more physically expressive the nature; the higher its path, the more the owner will express the mental side of the emotions. High-set, and with little or no curve, suggests a hard and cold basic emotional nature, especially if the head line is also high in the hand.

Should these two lines be low in the hand and close together it means you are dealing with a passionate and rather possessive personality. A forked start to the line of heart is an indication of adaptability. The stronger of the branches will indicate which side of the subject's nature dominates. A predominant Jupiter fork suggests an honourable and upright approach, while a more dominant Saturn fork implies practicality and straightforwardness. Traditionally, a three pronged fork, trident style beginning to the heart line is considered lucky, and good fortune is said to stay with the owner throughout the life.

If the lines of heart, head and life are connected at the beginning it should be taken as a strong warning sign because at some time in the life the owner will undergo a sudden, and perhaps traumatic shock from which it may take time to recover fully.

Note the comparative differences, if any, between the two heart lines. When there is a significant difference, look to see which way the subject now leans. If there is no apparent difference, it shows the owner to be content with his lot.

The heart line also has close links with health factors. It should be clear of all imperfections. An islanded or chained line, or one that is made up of a series of little broken lines refers to poor health. It is suggested that a physically or mentally ill person may also be emotionally disturbed, which could explain the importance of the heart line in health matters. An island at the beginning of the line under the Saturn mount is an indication of hearing and/or balance problems; under the Apollo mount, sight or eye troubles; and under the Mercury mount an island suggests anxiety, weight and blood pressure problems. One should not attempt to diagnose heart ailments or, indeed, any other kind of ill-health problems unless trained to do so. If there is an indication of potential trouble tactfully persuade the subject to seek medical attention, but do so with care.

Simian line

Basically, this is a fused line of head and heart that stretches across the palm effectively cutting the hand in two. Usually found on one hand only, it does sometimes appear on both. When it does exist, the emotional nature of the owner becomes very intense and the ability to love or hate with equal intensity is present. Such a person will be egocentric and capable of excluding anything and everything in order to concentrate with extreme ferocity.

Ruthless, emotionally unstable, often entirely without any compunction at all, shrewd and very clever, a person with this mark may come within an ace of the law without detection. A bully, immature when taken to task, such a person should never be fully trusted with the affairs of others. Do not expect this type to display such extremes of behaviour all the time. For the most part he or she will tend to behave quite normally and should be treated as though there is nothing unusual.

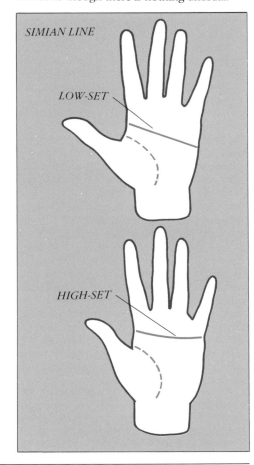

SIMIAN LINE

LOW-SET

HIGH-SET

THE MINOR LINES

There are a number of smaller, minor lines to be found in the hand. Few hands, if any, will have them all, but most will have some of these little influence marks in various forms.

The girdle of Venus

This may be a firm straight line between the first finger mount and the Mercury mount, or it may be broken or islanded, chained or frayed, tassellated or long or short. Whatever its appearance, it signifies sensitivity in the subject's emotional life. If found with sensitivity pads at the finger tips as well, expect hyper-sensitivity and aesthetic appreciation. These two combinations may also produce an intense fastidiousness in all or part of the subject's nature.

Via lasciva

This line will either appear as a small curved link between the base of the mount of Venus and the Luna mount, or it may run as a sister line to the health or Mercury line. Often, this mark is found when the Girdle of Venus is also present and when they are both present there will be an added intensification of the need for physical stimulation to relieve boredom. On its own, the owner may be inclined to a natural way of life, a vegetarian diet, or an avoidance of drugs in favour of natural remedies. It is sometimes referred to as an allergy line, for it will often point the way to cure a health defect by avoidance of certain foods because a person has an allergy to them.

The fate line

Only the line that goes from the wrist to the base of the finger of Saturn should be called the line of fate. All other forms are not strictly fate lines, but may be known variously as milieu, career, destiny, duty, awareness or environment lines or marks.

It is rare to find the fate line proper in both hands. Its presence can often be a restrictive factor. The line is said to govern ambitions. However, the aims of the individual become subject to certain limitations which are self imposed according to the degree of faith the owner has in his ability. The presence of the line implies that the subject shoulders responsibility as a mature adult should. The absence of the line suggests poor social adaptability, a lack of direction and responsibility and the overall personality may be unsettled.

If found on the left hand only, it usually refers to the dreams and desires of the owner, but little or no effort may be expended to achieve them. A fate line on the right hand only shows a character who has the determination to achieve but who requires a sustained effort for anything to come of it. A line that starts inside the line of life on the mount of Venus should be called a duty line. Until the line leaves the line of life the subject is probably following the wishes or traditions of the family. The higher the line starts, the later in life the owner will develop sufficient self determination and confidence to pursue an aim.

A line that starts from the Luna mount suggests an independent nature. The clearer the line the less the character will brook opposition. It often refers to a career that involves being in the public eye. A small line between the line of life and the larger version of the fate line is called a milieu line and is certain to cause problems as long as it lasts. Opposition from any source is likely. Once it stops, so do the restrictions and problems. Another line, or lines between this line and the fate line proper intensifies the troubles.

A forked beginning to the line of fate shows the subject is aware of family obligations as well as the pull of his own inner ambitions. The stronger looking of the two will inform which effect wins, but there may be a sense of looking back, of what might have been.

Should the fate line stop at the head line, poor judgment will mar the career and may cease this activity altogether. If the line should stop at the line of heart, emotional considerations will be the root cause.

A fork at the end of the line of fate may occur. Use traditional chronological principles to determine the outcome. For example, a fork to Apollo and one to Mercury suggests communication and artistic ability: an actor? Look to the rest of the hand for support.

A triple forking at the end of the line of fate is said to be very fortunate, especially if it occurs at the head or heart line and is free of all influence marks. A line that starts at the wrist may have an influence line of equal strength join it from the mount of Luna. This should be interpreted as the start of a partnership, not necessarily marriage, but a relationship based on sound mutual trust.

A fate line may begin at, or just above the heart line. This is an indication that a spare-time activity or hobby will eventually become the focal point of the career. Marks on the line nearly always refer to problems. However, a square on the line implies protection. A square between the fate line and the line of life suggests protection from danger; while between the fate line and the percussion shows protection from danger(s) while travelling. A line of fate that is made up of a series of lines up the palm shows that a number of exercises have been attempted but have come to nothing.

The line of the Sun

The line of Sun may begin from almost any point in the palm and should make a path to the centre of the mount of Apollo. This is sometimes why it is known as the Apollo line; other names are the line of success, fortune, brilliance, luck or fame.

When this line is present, whatever the formation, one can expect to find talent and the capacity for hard work. Such a person is only happy when stretching themselves to the full. The owners of this line earn the respect of those around them, people admire them for their ability and the way they carry themselves through life. A late start to this line indicates persistence, especially when the line starts from the plain of Mars. A forked start suggests more than one gift or the owner may hold down two entirely different careers. If this is not the case, two distinct interests are likely to fill the life, both of which may bring success.

A fork at the end of the line of Sun implies a similar meaning. Often, a fate line and Sun line appear together. Examine them closely to see which is the stronger. A stronger fate line represents a more serious, nature; a stronger line of Sun, a more instinctive personality.

The Mercury line

Also known as the liver line, health line, hepatica, business line, line of intuition or, in ancient writings, the line of stomach, it is better for this line not to be present in the hand. If not present, the subject will be largely unconcerned with health matters. Its presence implies that the owner is aware of his subconscious system in some way and may be concerned with health problems more than most.

When the line runs from the line of life direct to the centre of the mount of Mercury, the character will be actively interested in health affairs. It may be a dietary fad, fastidiousness, inclination to be prone to allergy problems or simply watchful of health. Basically, the owner will be interested in the natural way of life.

A high start to the line, from the plain of Mars, implies less interest in health and more in worldly affairs. There is often an instinctive flair for business interests of all kinds: sales, market trends, manufacturing levels or buying ability. A Mercury line that seems to start from the outer edge of the hand at the lower part of the Luna mount, bow inwards and upwards and end near the outer edge of the Mercury mount, is often referred to as the line of intuition. Rarely properly formed, often made up of bits and pieces, it implies a good level of latent prescience. The clearer the line, the greater the inner, sixth sense.

There are a number of minor, smaller influence marks or lines.

Ring of Solomon

This line curves around the base of the index finger on, or at the top of the mount. It is said to be the mark of the teacher. There is a marked ability or talent for learning and being able to pass that knowledge on in such a way that the owner becomes known for his style.

Ring of Saturn

This line curves around the base of the middle finger on, or at the top of the mount of Saturn. It is said to be largely unfortunate. The owner tends to be a lone wolf and, while not exactly shunning society, does not actively cultivate a social life.

Ring of Apollo

This line curves around the base of the third finger on, or at the top of the mount of Apollo. In a poorly developed hand it indicates poor judgement in everyday affairs. In a well developed hand it confers special gifts to do with entertainment and the arts.

The Rascettes

Also known as the bracelets, these are the lines that cross the wrist at the base of the palm. Eastern palmistry credits them as indications of longevity, two being the normal, three implying a long life and four suggesting not only a very long life, but a very lucky one as well. If the top line should rise into the base of the palm there may be lower stomach disorders. If the second line should also rise, this may become an aggravated condition.

Ring of Mercury

This line curves around the base of the little finger on, or at the top of the mount of Mercury. It is said to confer business acumen, the extent of which is determined by the type of hand on which it is found and its development. Traditionally, this is also said to be the mark of the true spinster or bachelor as it implies little inclination to marry, although normal social relationships with the opposite sex are still carried on.

Ring of Venus

More popularly known as the family ring, this is the dividing line between the second phalange of the thumb and the mount of Venus. When heavy and well marked, it shows strong family ties and loyalty. The fainter the line, the less the owner will care about family relationships.

Loyalty line

A line or series of lines that stems from the family ring across the mount or Mars, inside the line of life, which sometimes touches or cuts through the vitality line. When deeply-etched the owner has strong ties with the circle in which he was raised. It matters little if this was the family, an adopted one or any other early environment. When the line touches or goes through the line of life, much of what the subject does is connected with this early life and may actually promote family inter-relationships or attach great importance to them.

Marriage and children

Traditionally, marriage lines are those small horizontal lines which enter the palm just above the line of heart on the Mercury mount. The stronger lines refer to longer lasting emotional attachments, and the strongest of them all usually denotes marriage. However, these days it is best to interpret them all as lines of strong emotional ties. Children are said to be indicated by little vertical lines which rise from these marriage lines. The most upright or strongly etched are said to indicate boys, the lighter markings or slightly sloping lines are said to refer to girls.

Skin patterns

It is now accepted that the patterns of fine ridges and furrows on the fingers and palmar surfaces of anyone's hands remain constant throughout life. This is a very complex study and should not be glossed over. It is not possible to enter into it here but the following observations may be carried out as part of a general examination.

The skin pattern will seem to be either a 'closed' or 'open' type. The former will look like small finely textured lines which suggest a refined and gentle nature; a wide type of pattern will indicate a person with an open or physical personality.

A hand soft to the touch will reflect these general tendencies for this implies an indolent nature. With a closed, finely textured pattern the character is likely to be quite lazy mentally and physically. A soft hand with the wide pattern will be quite basic in its overall approach and may be inclined to be coarse natured.

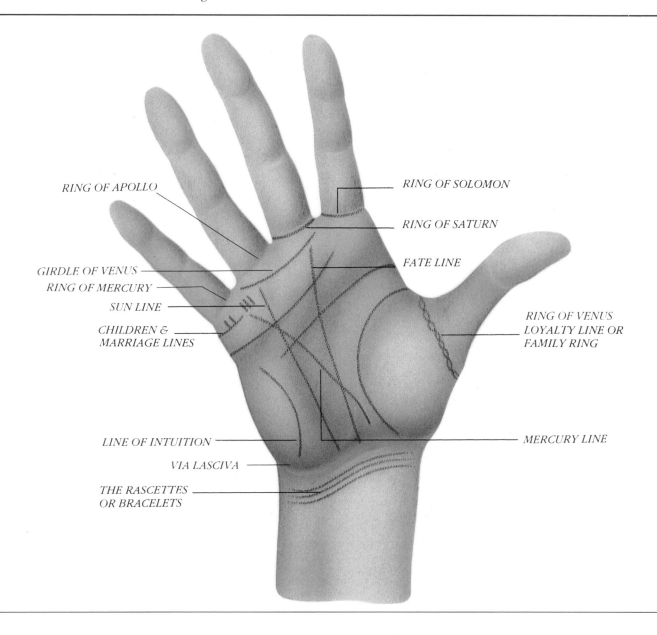

RING OF APOLLO

RING OF SOLOMON

RING OF SATURN

FATE LINE

GIRDLE OF VENUS

RING OF MERCURY

SUN LINE

CHILDREN & MARRIAGE LINES

RING OF VENUS LOYALTY LINE OR FAMILY RING

LINE OF INTUITION

VIA LASCIVA

THE RASCETTES OR BRACELETS

MERCURY LINE

Time on the hands

This is, perhaps, the most difficult area of palmistry and is the most controversial. It is best to refer to the line of life when attempting to date events. Other lines may be used, and the illustration gives guidance for each of them.

This guide will not necessarily coincide with each hand you try to interpret. They should all be read separately and individually, preferably from a print of the hand using a small ruler and dividers for accurate measurement. A question and answer technique is always helpful if your subject is 'live' and each hand thus read gives experience.

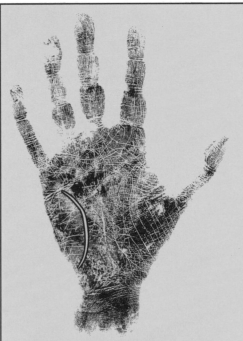

Above: This print shows a good, square hand type. Long, quite well-marked fate and Sun lines; also broken Girdle of Venus.

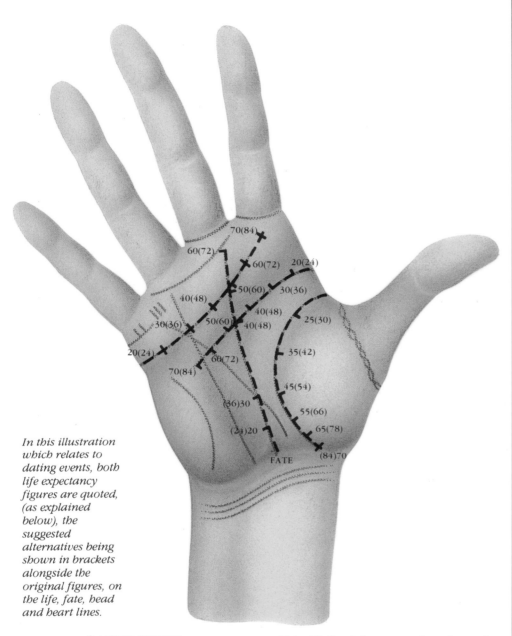

In this illustration which relates to dating events, both life expectancy figures are quoted, (as explained below), the suggested alternatives being shown in brackets alongside the original figures, on the life, fate, head and heart lines.

Below: The FULL hand (the entire palmar surface is criss-crossed with lines so that the skin pattern is virtually obscured). The hand has a long palm and short fingers. Both hands display a good fate line. There is an interesting, well-marked Mercury line on the right side of the hand.

DATING EVENTS

The life line

Assuming that the line sweeps far enough into the palm, the dating method is to draw three imaginary vertical lines down the palm from the centre of the base of the Jupiter finger, the point where Jupiter and Saturn meet, and the centre of the Saturn finger. Where these imaginary lines intersect the life line will represent approximately 10, 20 and 35 years respectively.

These three points enable further calculations to be made. If the start of the life line to the first intersection equates to 10 years, dividing this length by two will indicate the 5 year mark; the halfway point between the 10 and 20 year marks will represent 15 years, and so on.

If the life line is long enough to do so, the 52/53 year point can be obtained by bisecting the distance between the 35 year mark and the end of the line, though this is not likely to prove as accurate a measure as the earlier age points, which is why confirmation is sometimes sought by carrying out a similar exercise on either the fate, head or heart line.

Accuracy

Traditionally, dating systems are based on the biblical life expectancy of three score years and ten. However, in view of the longer life expectancy nowadays, it seems reasonable to extend this allotted span to a more realistic 84 by the simple expedient of allowing 12 instead of 10 years for the traditional divisions.

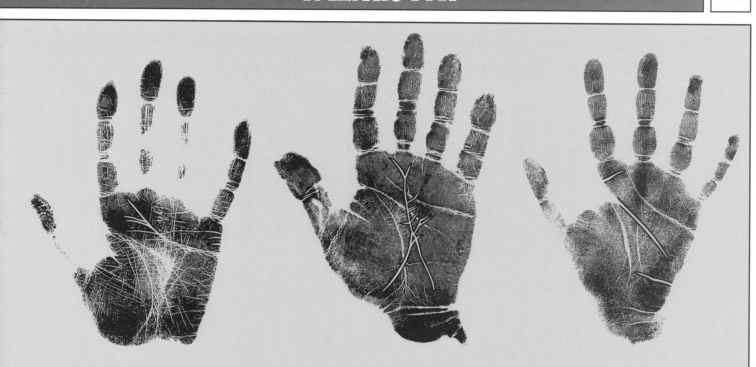

Above: This shows a narrow, cramped hand (the fingers are held 'tightly' together). Note the three 'marriage' lines and obvious Girdle of Venus. There is a triple fork start to the heart line which is also chained.

Above: The fingers are short in proportion to the palm but are set very square on the hand. Note the long fate line which starts with two branches, one from inside the life line, the other from Luna; after they join, there is a period of apparent indecision (small branches and slight zigzag) before the line continues well up the hand to end in a branch.

Above: A strong 'ego' hand: a good, firm head line, almost straight; well-marked Ring of Solomon; also Via Lasciva or 'allergy' line as it is sometimes called.

Below: This print shows a well marked line of intuition and high-set thumb.

Below: A young girl's hand revealing strong personal control in that Mercury stands apart from the other fingers. Opposing thumb. Generally, a good, square shape, although the lines are rather poor.

Below: Good example of a young female's hands. The thumb makes a rather narrow angle to the palm. There are sensitivity pads on all the fingers which is quite unusual.

CHAPTER THIRTEEN

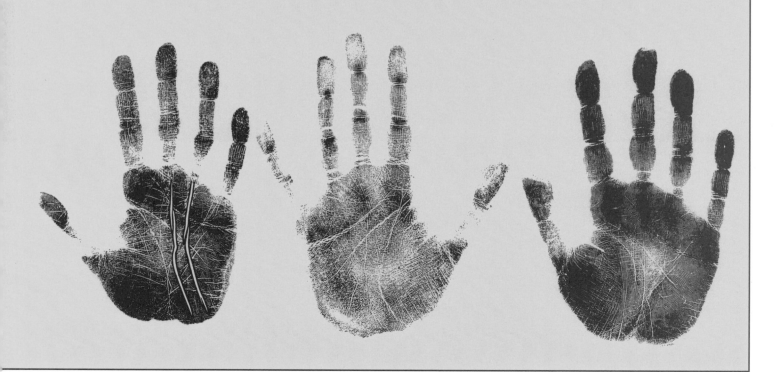

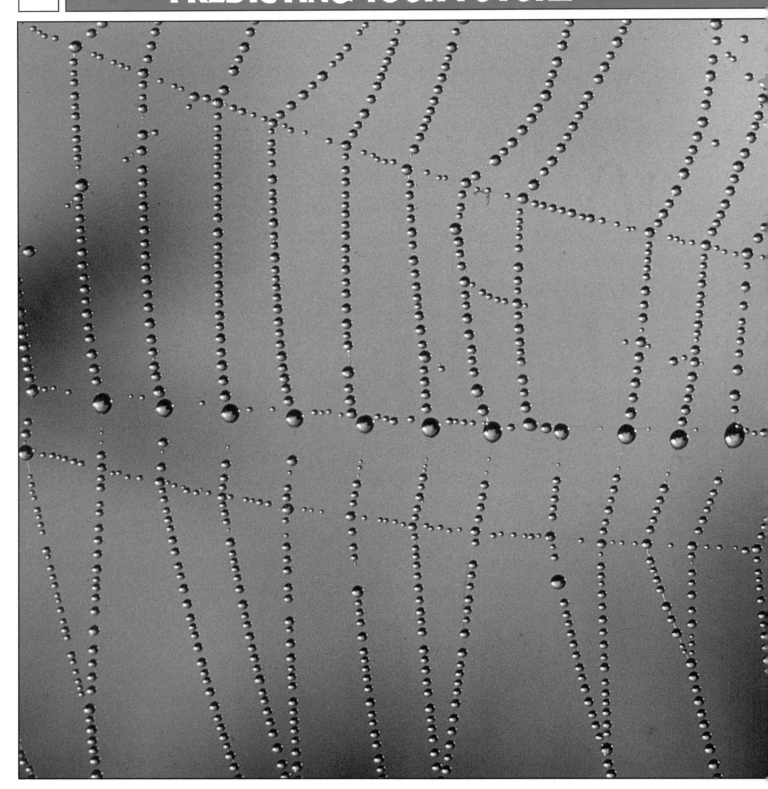

RUNES

The word "rune" means a mystery or a secret, and certainly the twenty-four characters of the runes have exercised a fascination over people's minds for untold time. It is not immediately apparent what meaning lies behind their enigmatic angular shapes. They are popularly associated with the Vikings who came to settle in Britain between 800 AD and 1200 AD yet they were used centuries before by people all over Europe.

Tradition asserts that, unlike our alphabet, it was not just a method of day-to-day communication, the illustrating of the sounds of speech. As the word says, they were secret symbols of knowledge. The runes held the key to universal understanding of the mysteries of life and death.

When a sacred alphabet is written down and used for mundane purposes, that secret knowledge begins to dissipate and may be lost entirely. This, it would appear, is what happened to runes in the last few centuries.

UNDERSTANDING RUNES

Roman letters have a sound; together these sounds can be made into words. They do not, however, have meanings in themselves. This is not so with rune-letters, nor with the 22 letters of the Hebrew alphabet. Each rune has a particular meaning, a particular set of associations and symbolises a particular mode of energy.

This is easier to understand if a further example is suggested: in Chinese, an ideogram is both a letter and a sound, but is also a picture, a tree, for instance. This is obvious because of its pictorial nature. Or take the example of a Tarot card, where the picture is the message. These are both recognisable examples of visual communication of an idea or a concept via a commonly-accepted symbol.

A symbol suggests many meanings which resonate with or speak to the soul, or the higher intelligence, whichever your prefer. It is not obvious to the uninitiated or to those who only think in terms of logic and one half of the brain. To understand a symbol, or a rune, it must be allowed to permeate the intuitive mind and to allow its meanings to subtly unfold, and a connection be made. It cannot be grasped or understood in any other way.

We all have a store of universal experience and knowledge nestling in our subconscious minds. Runes and this store must be allowed to meet. This is a kind of magical meeting, which is why any useful understanding of them or any other symbols must result in a change of consciousness.

Psychologists define learning as a permanent change in behaviour as a result of experience. Ordinary language allows human beings to communicate with each other; the language of symbols allows us to communicate with gods and with other levels of existence in the universe. This is the way of wisdom, and that is why the runes are such potent symbols.

The meanings of runes

What are the meanings of these runes and what has this to do with divination? Everything in the universe is made up of differing energy-forms. These form a pattern of relationships which is ever changing; we do however fit into this pattern in varying ways as we live our lives and time unfolds. Each rune symbolises a kind of archetypal energy or energy-pattern.

In some unknown way, which the psychologist C. G. Jung labelled synchronicity, everything in the universe at a particular moment exhibits the quality of that moment. That is why apparently unrelated events seem to have a connection or link which has meaning, if only we can observe it. In order for the quality of the moment to be perceived, we need a tool or a key which enables the subconscious mind (remember this has a store of universal knowledge) to understand that pattern. The runes, since they themselves are symbols of energy and energy-patterns, are that key.

Right: Runes were mainly inscribed on wood, which is the reason why very few early examples have been preserved. However, runes were inscribed on stone or metal, and there are several stone monuments throughout Europe with legible inscriptions.

The twenty-four runes which comprise the list are known as the *FUTHARK,* from the sound of the first six runes. There are other runic alphabets with sixteen or thirty-three figures, but that need not concern us here. This is the FUTHARK which is in common use.

These are divided into three sets of eight each. The first set is known as Freyr's set and represents the principle of growth and unfolding. Once a seed has germinated, or a process has been set into motion, then it naturally follows that a sequence of events will unfold. We do not have to plan or change things at this stage. Of course, we have to do whatever is necessary if we are an integral part of that process. Thus this can be called the creative, or creating set of runes.

The next eight are known as Haegl's set and these represent the elements and the dance that goes on between them. There is little that we can rely on in this stage. There is always the element of chance at work here, as all is susceptible to change. Matter is not in our control here, so caution and patience, as well as adaptability and flexibility, must be learned in order to understand the nature of Haegl's set of runes.

The final eight are known as Tyr's eight. Tyr is a Norse warrior who represents courage in the face of adversity. At this stage matters may be influenced or even controlled, but it takes a lot of hard work and perhaps sacrifice. However, divine help is also possible because the nature of these runes allows that those who try to do their very best will be given a measure of assistance from the gods.

Right: In recent years, many rune-sets have become available commercially. This set is carved from wood, with the runes inscribed and coloured-in. Note the blank rune. Note also that the shape of some runes differs from those shown below.

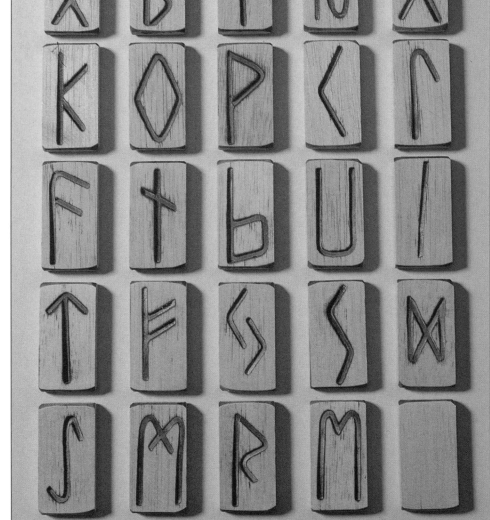

FREYR'S SET

FEOH: Money, possessions and wealth. Success.

UR: The strength to advance. Persistence and patience.

THORN: Protection or defensive action. Test of will and sincerity.

OS: Communications, advice. Wisdom of the creative self.

RAD: Travel, a change is welcomed.

KEN: Illumination. This can be either understanding or new energy.

GYFU: Gift. Sharing. Balance and harmony.

WYN: Joy or happiness.

HAEGL'S SET

HAEGL: Elemental forces may disrupt. Unknown factors.

NYD: Inner power or control. Understanding limitations.

IS: Progress temporarily blocked. Emotional cooling.

GER: A Year. Waiting. Cultivation: first sow, then reap.

EOH: Transformation. Protection is in change.

PEORTH: Secret knowledge. Initiation. Unexpected gains.

EOLH: Protection or healing. Fending off dangers.

SIGEL: Wholeness. The life-force. Achievement/success.

TYR'S SET

TYR: Male power. Courage and self-sacrifice.

BEORC: New beginnings. Birth and growth. Nurturing.

EH: Long journey. Large-scale change.

MAN: Right relationships. Correct behaviour.

LAGU: Emotional understandings. Intuitions/feelings.

ING: Potential energy. Before the beginning of projects.

DAEG: New dawn. Total transformation.

ODAL: Inherited possessions. Ancestral influence. Duties.

USING THE RUNES FOR DIVINATION

The next step is to obtain a set of runes. They can be purchased these days from many shops, or by mail order. They come in various materials, such as wood, inscribed pebbles or stones. Cheaper versions are available in plastic or other artificial materials. They can even be made from metal such as silver. It is best to choose a set yourself, paying attention to your own feelings or instincts in the matter. If a set feels good to you, then they are probably the ones that you should have.

In order to get started though, it is permissible to take pieces of thick card and use a heavy felt pen to inscribe one of the twenty-four runes onto each piece. Do not forget the twenty-fifth blank piece. Another way, if you are feeling adventurous, is to take pieces of soft, flat wood and use the end of a hot poker to burn out the shapes. Care is recommended, of course, but this can be a very satisfying method of obtaining your first working set. The results may be crude but often something that you make yourself can be far more satisfactory than a more commercial set.

Having now a set of runes, the easiest way to commence divination with them is simply to concentrate on the matter in mind, then take one rune at random. If the runes are flat-shaped, they should all be face-down and mixed so that you are unaware of their positions. You may have them in a little bag, or box. If so, just jiggle or shake this around until you feel that you are ready to dip in, then pull one out without looking. This method is best conveyed by an example;

I am asking whether it is a good idea at this moment to begin to look for another place to live because there is not enough room for us all, with our various activities, in the present accommodation. The rune that I drew is ᛁ, IS.

This is from the second set of Haegl, the set of the elements that are in a continual flux. Nothing is stable here, and nothing can be controlled. That is my first intimation. Reading from the list, the rune itself means: "Progress temporarily blocked. Emotional cooling".

One could say that this speaks for itself. It is not a good time to move, everything is against it. This is not the whole story, though. A moment's reflection should take us back to the actual words of the question being asked. It is important to understand that the answer should always be interpreted in the light of the question posed; if the wording is changed, there may well be a different answer.

It is important to be clear in your own mind what it is that you actually want to know. Examples of alternatives to the sample question asked are:
☐ "Is it a good idea for me to consider moving at the moment?"
☐ "Should I stay in my present house?"
☐ "Will I move in the next six months?"
☐ "Should I obtain a job in another area?"

These are ultimately differing forms of the same question although the emphasis is different in each case. You will be able, I'm sure, to add to them.

A further consideration is to use your own reflective mind in order to gain a deeper insight into what the answering rune means. By doing this, you may also receive more specific advice regarding a course of action, rather than the bald statement given in this example, which is fairly negative and uninspiring. This indeed may be the answer to the question but, as I have pointed out above, the runic symbols are enigmatic.

At first sight, therefore, many people are not immediately able to elicit any answer beyond the words stated in a brief key such as the one given previously. The runes, however, are capable of unlocking their powerful energies if you approach them in the spirit of honest enquiry.

Meditation exercise

To continue with the example, it would be much more useful to obtain a more personal insight into what it is that the chosen rune, IS, is saying. This can be done by using a meditation exercise.

Hold the rune in your hand and sit comfortably, minimise distractions as much as possible so that you are not disturbed, then begin to breathe slowly and evenly. Stare at the rune until you feel that you can carry its image into your mind. Close your eyes and keep the image before you. Imagine that you are in a great hall which is carved out of the living rock. Fill in your own details but allow that there are several doorways ahead of you. You must choose one and, when you have done so, will move towards it. First, though, you must cross a narrow bridge.

When you get to the doorway, you knock and say: "I seek the knowledge of this rune. I come in the spirit of honest enquiry." This will allow you to move behind the door and experience the images and associations of this rune. You will be able to understand far more by this method than merely reading a list of attributes. As I have said, the runes demand some extra work. The people who use the runes today tend to have been drawn to them, sensing some affinity or otherwise which aids the opening of the doorway to their secrets.

To give a practical vision to this method, the Is rune was visualised as described. After going through the doorway, I sank into some water which covered me. I was unable to do anything except float; it was a peaceful sinking below the surface. This then became bright blue sky, the kind that you see on a sunny winter's day. I was held by the claws of a great bird which I could not see. It deposited me on the index-finger of a hand which was motionless in the sky. The finger turned and pointed downwards and I saw a large house outlined in the snow; there was nothing else around, just snow.

I was set down in front of the door and was able to open it. I went in and all the furniture was covered in dust-sheets.

The fire-grate was cleaned out, unused. Herbs hung in bunches from the rafters. It had a clean but unusual feel about it. I realised that there was no road or access to the house at this time of year. I understood that I could come back in the spring. The last thing that happened was that the bird took me back to the entrance to the great hall where I had begun my imaginary journey; the meditation was complete.

This exercise helped me to understand much more the meaning of the rune given in answer to my question. Sinking into the water shows powerlessness at this time; I must accept that I must "go with the flow." It would appear that there will be a place available to me, but not at present because there is no path or access to it. However, I now have some hope as it seems that in the spring matters will have changed, the restrictions will have melted away.

Below: 10th century cross-slab at Andreas Church, Isle of Man. Odin, the chief God of Norse myth, is here depicted at the end of the world.

The three-rune lay

A further way to tackle questions in more depth is to use more runes, of course. The following lay uses three runes. It is important that you keep to the order of one, two, three, also that you are consistent in your labelling of the positions as there is a choice here in the three-rune lay;

1) The Past 2) The Present 3) The Future. or
1) A choice 2) The matter considered 3) Alternative choice or
1), 2) and 3) may be seen as a story.

It is important to bear in mind that the order and relationship of the runes will modify or change your reading of them. For example, in respect of a proposed journey, if you draw RAD, then WYN and finally IS, this can be read as the journey itself will be useful and enjoyable. You will get much out of it but the arrival at your destination will be somewhat of a let-down. There are likely to be delays in returning or a sense of being in the wrong place at the wrong time. On the other hand, if IS is drawn first, followed by RAD then WYN, this

would suggest that a much-desired journey will be difficult to make. There might be circumstances that make it impracticable at this time. It may even have to be called off.

It is best to make your own experiments with the various methods. The experience of ordering and noting the relationships are part of the process of learning the runic language. There is no real short-cut to this.

The cross

This another useful lay:
Central position: The matter at hand
To the left: The influence passing
Beneath: Foundation. Useful thing or person germane to the matter
Above: Desired outcome

Putting all these elements together, it will be understood how to move forward in the most useful way; or maybe to desist altogether.

The rune-cast method

This is best left until you are quite familiar with all the runes as it involves mixing the pieces in a bag until ready, then tossing them all onto a table or appropriately-prepared surface. Only the runes that are face-up are read. The ones that are closest to you are more important, while the ones that are furthest away are less

important. Another method of doing this is to lay a cord straight in front of you, about a foot away. After casting, the runes which have fallen nearest to you are read. Any that have fallen over the boundary of the cord are irrelevant and therefore ignored.

A word is necessary here about runes which fall in a reversed position. According to some, if a rune is drawn or cast upside-down, its meaning is either diminished in power or relevance. Others think that the meaning itself is reversed. Put simply, success reversed is failure. My opinion is that your own judgements in the matter are the important factor. If you feel that reversals are useful, then use them. If not, don't. The proximity and relationship of one rune to another is often sufficient to show the nature of what is going on without other complicating factors.

There are many other lays which you will find either in books or, indeed, in the Tarot chapter. Use your own ingenuity in order to find a lay which is most suited to the question and to yourself. Also, why not come up with your own design? The runes' return to popularity in recent years suggests that there is still much to be discovered in this ancient hoard of wisdom.

Deeper meaning

In order to gain more understanding of the runes it is necessary to look at each one in more detail. However, remember also that it is up to you to add or modify meanings from your personal experience. Use the runes, get in touch with them as friends, understand that the benefits will multiply as you increase your efforts to create a working knowledge of the Runeworld.

Left: 11th century stone from Olsa, Uppland, Sweden. It was carved by Asmund Karesson, and his inscription reads: "BJORN, ODULF, GUNNAR AND HOLMDIS RAISED THIS STONE TO ULF, GINLOG'S HUSBAND AND ASMUND HEWED (IT)". It is now in Stockholm.

FEOH

THORN

RAD

*T*his rune signifies wealth and possessions. It is movable in the sense that people in the past used cattle as a measure of someone's value. They could be bought, sold and taken from one place to another. Cattle are a visible display and ownership implies a position of power, including the responsibility that goes with it, and therefore implies being a force in the community. The god Freyr is associated with the F-Rune; he is a fertility god, a god of peace, plenty and abundance.

*W*ith two faces. On the one hand it is the thorn that protects the beauty of the rose from destruction; thorn-thickets were used to surround camps at night, in order to keep out unwelcome guests, both animal and human. It also implies a test for the small wounds of thorns are not in themselves enough reason to give up on a quest; they are the little annoyances of everyday life. On the other hand, this rune can be equated with Thor's Hammer, with which he delights in charging-up a situation or changing it, to see what will happen. Great power, the lightning-flash.

*T*his rune signifies the wheel, the mode of a journey or the journey itself. It is also connected with the round of the seasons and the continual journey of the known stars around the sky. Thus with continuity and change, it symbolizes making the effort to step out of the familiar rut in the search for new experiences. It must always be borne in mind that wherever you travel, you always take yourself with you. The effort involved, however, is transformative. It is also generative because the wheel generates power, which is true for us today with our power-stations and cars.

UR

OS

KEN

*A*urochs, or wild ox, symbolising the wild and untamed side of cattle. There is great strength available but it must be approached with the right attitude; too much force can destroy. Persistent effort is an attribute of these creatures, both in the sense of rushing in to attack a foe and not giving up plus the ability to wait patiently for the right moment, unmoving. There is the idea of sacrifice since oxen can be caught and killed, giving up their lives for others' food, or can be caught and domesticated, thus giving up freedom.

*O*din's rune. He has already been mentioned as he is the subject of the poem illustrating the origin of the runes. OS is also the mouth from which speech, and therefore communication, issues. Odin is called the "Shapeshifter". He is a man dressed in a black cloak; a large-brimmed hat may obscure the fact that he has only one eye, having given the other away in exchange for drinking from the Well of Wisdom. In past times only a few were educated and could write; therefore their knowledge bestowed power.

*T*he creative and transformative fire. It is actually a representation of a pine torch, the flaming brand that is both a light to see by and a protection at night from the dark and prowling animals. It can also be transported from one place to another and can start a cooking-fire. One material transforms another, one element cannot exist without the other; in the process, there is a third effect. This is also the inner light for which one has to overcome many trials and obstacles in order to be illuminated. It can also relate to sexuality.

GYFU

A rune that you should recognise; we still use it today to end our letters — a kiss. It signifies union or sharing, or it may be a gift. This gift may be the gift of the self in love, as in a marriage union. Within this is the idea of mutual support and the following of a joint path. This rune promises peace, often as a result of giving of one's self unstintingly.

HAEGL

T his is the rune of the element of winter. It is the hail and rain of the cold season that may suddenly fall without warning and change the landscape and your plans. You may be forced to shelter, or suffer inconvenience. Sometimes it is impossible to understand the arbitrary nature of the elemental powers, yet they do lead to change and the need for reappraisal. This can be liberating, freeing one from old forms or limitations. After the storm, the Sun melts the hail or snow and it changes to water. HAEGL contains the seed-structure of all forms in the Runeworld.

NYD

F ire is the element of this rune, but it is constrained or bound within limits. This is more a limitation that guides or helps, rather than purely a restriction. Thus, one can see this as a hold-up, an excuse to stop or give up; alternatively, by using thought and effort, obstacles can be overcome and challenges met. This rune may be seen as a pictogram of two sticks being rubbed together to obtain fire. It means to do what needs to be done, even if that isn't exactly what is desired.

WYN

J oy and happiness, harmony and the achievement of balance in all things. Therefore this rune means fulfilment in these matters.

IS

L iterally the principle of solidified water, ice. In Norse myth the universe was created from fire and ice, so ice in this respect is primeval matter. The energy is inert, static, whereas living relationships are dynamic. As in the depths of winter, all is still, life is in hibernation. Thus patience must be cultivated as plans are in cold storage. Meanwhile matters may be understood in crystal clarity through contemplation.

GER

F ruition of efforts and the gathering in of the harvest. However, the work must have been carried out first. In order to reap, you must first attend to the sowing and then cultivate throughout the season. Only then will the order of the natural cycle be appreciated. This rune suggests both an ending and a beginning, as all cycles are cyclic, by their name. This is not always understood. Yet is true of all universal laws, as it is of the Runeworld.

Left: The central region of our galaxy, the Milky Way. Sagittarius is to the left, with the constellation of Centaurus to the right. All galaxies have a recognisable shape but no two are absolutely identical, as astronomers have proved.

Right: The symmetrical pattern in a snowflake. Due to the fixed shape of the water-molecule, a hexagonal shape is the only stable crystal arrangement that can be formed. Despite this, no two are identical. Galaxies, snowflakes and the spider's web all share characteristics which Runemasters discerned long before our scientific age.

EOH

*T*his is a yew tree that lives a long time and it is also an evergreen. It is therefore a symbol of eternal life, which is why it is seen outside graveyards. It also has a connotation of death for this reason; it is often forgotten that time itself is an energy which causes changes, each new moment is the death of the previous one, and so on. In order to truly benefit from this knowledge, it is well to live in the present, accept what comes without clinging to the past or hoping for the future. Letting go is the protection offered by EOH.

EOLH

*T*his is a glyph of an elk's horn and is associated therefore with protection. It is used to defend yourself, family and friends against all hostile forces. Stemming from this is the idea that if one feels able to defend one's self, then confidence and optimism are increased. Also a place of protection is a sanctuary, so this can mean a private retreat. This is a rune to meditate upon. It could certainly be used as a talisman.

TYR

*S*piritual warrior, the man of courage. This rune was seen as a sign of invincibility in battle and therefore of honour and self-sacrifice. Other attributes are tenacity and strength of purpose. In view of all this, it follows that it represents the movement towards a goal, which brooks no interference or obstacle in its achievement.

PEORTH

A rune that demands an explanation but which is not forthcoming if you are not privy to it! In a word, a secret. Appearances are not all they seem: one must seek out what is behind the mask or delve below the surface. If you succeed in this, you will have passed a test, been initiated into another world. Then you will see life differently — only time will tell. In this respect, you could be better off but your ideals will have changed, so you won't know till you are there.

SIGEL

*B*ecause this is the rune of the Sun, it is connected with the life-force, with energy, with healing and health. Wholeness, power and self-regeneration. It is victory and success. Check the astrology section for further images. Feel or imagine the power of the Sun's rays.

BEORC

*B*irch tree. This is a symbol of birth and the nurturing that comes afterwards, thus it is birth and growth. Life is a gradual unfolding, the seed splits open and pushes up through the earth, seeking the light of day. The Earth goddess may be envisaged as dressed in green; she is fertile, has a healing touch and a day of her celebration is May Day. New beginnings should be monitored with care and attention, not to mention love.

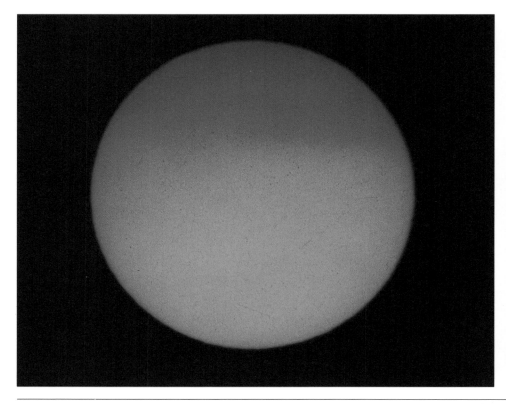

EH

LAGU

ODAL

*T*his rune symbolises a horse. Although this animal was a means of making a journey, the horse and rider bear a special relationship based on trust, affection and mutual respect. It was also sacred to the gods, particularly Odin. Therefore it can be said to have some magical attributes. While it does signify a journey to another place, perhaps as in moving to take up a new job, it also refers to journeys of the mind. This means a change in consciousness, which can only be attempted if there is harmony, self-control and direction within one's self. A rune of large-scale changes.

*T*he Moon and water. Thus it is fluidity, change, impressionability, the use of the intuitive or psychic mode of perception. This cannot be achieved directly but must be allowed to flood the consciousness, which is fearful of those of sharp logical minds. Water separates, but also joins; dreams of connections and connections of dreams. It is the unconscious mind, that which we all share. Physically, water sustains life: we can live for quite a while without food but only a short time without water. The waters of life; the cycle of the tides. This is a very powerful rune, rightly understood.

*P*roperty which is immovable, such as the home. Inheritances of personal qualities and characteristics also belong here. The link with the ancestors was very strong in the peoples of the Runeworld, giving a sense of continuity and responsibility. A home is also a place of retreat, an enclosure from the world where you can be alone or entertain family and guests of your choice. It is also the inner sanctum, the private place within yourself which you know is your measure of worth, your self-evaluation. As you proceed through the trials of life, its successes and failures become part of this measure.

MAN

ING

BLANK

A person, a human. Not just every man though, it is that part of us which can perceive and put into action the right things in the right order, at the right time. The key-word is relationship; these must be correctly maintained and understood. In that sense it refers not to what we do or who we are, but our attitudes towards self, tasks, others and the world. This would include co-operation, professionalism and self-examination.

*O*ne of the fertility gods. It is he who transmutes energy which he first stores up, then waits for the right time and place before releasing it. Thus this rune symbolises potential energy for change. It also refers to that point before actually beginning a project: the seed-thought, the germ of an idea.

*T*his is always included in a rune-set because it represents that which is unformed or unseen in its meaning as yet. This means that the issue at hand is either too fresh to be judged or that its part in the unfolding patterns is not yet discerned. There may be too many variables as yet for any sensible prognostications to be made; or it may be the unexpected or the unknown that dashes in. The web of events is woven and everyone is affected by, or caught up in it. Hence it is our fate or destiny. This is not to deny choice; the blank rune is suggesting that there are powerful forces at work. The weaving of the wyrd, as it was called, offers you fate or free-will, destiny or choice. The runes nearby will be a clue as to which way you go.

DAEG

*D*awn of a new day. It is the change from darkness to light, that magic moment just before the Sun tips the horizon. It shows polarity; without the one state, the other could not be experienced. So it can be a breakthrough, the arrival of the change one has been patiently waiting for. New dawn is the opportunity for new growth. But remember that things look different in the light of day. Clarity goes with this new viewpoint and this should lead to fresh understandings.

Far left: The cosmology which underlies runes is based on the polarity of fire and ice. Fire is expansive energy, so the day is for action; sunset is for contemplation.

Left: A 12th century Swedish wallhanging depicting Odin, Thor and Freyr.

This completes the tour of the Runic symbols. May they help you to understand your life in all its aspects: physical, emotional, mental and spiritual.

Whether it is a simple issue, such as choosing between buying this car or that, or a more serious issue, concerned with your self-development, the runes, if you have studied them and allowed them to become part of your world, will always come up with an answer. If it is an answer that you did not want or were not expecting, then pay attention to it: let its meaning add to your experience and broaden your vision. Sometimes we are not always aware of what we really want; the runes are good at encouraging us to look in the mirror honestly. If you receive your desired answer, then all well and good. Proceed: may the WYRD treat you well!

CHAPTER FOURTEEN

SCRYING

Scrying enables the prediction of future events by gazing at or into reflective surfaces. This ancient art probably predates written history to the days when early man first looked into a pool or stream and saw the changing patterns made by the passing clouds, shifting light and shadows of the Moon and stars on the water surface. This would have triggered off a visionary response in those sensitive enough to interpret these moving shapes into information that would help the rest of their clan or tribe in the struggle to survive. Because the unknown was also feared in these primitive societies, anyone capable of demonstrating such a useful talent would have been regarded both with respect and awe. Thus the seer — literally someone who sees visions or has insight — would have been held in high esteem. Probably excused the mundane duties of the other members of the clan, such a person would then have the time to devote themself to the more important role of guide or adviser: shaman, wiseman or high priest.

Nowadays, of course, a person with the ability to predict future events is called a psychic or clairvoyant and uses his or her skill to help guide those who come for advice on such things as whether or not to change jobs, become engaged, seek medical advice, or achieve that long-coveted promotion! Even so, the roles are not so far apart despite the aeons that have passed since the first scryer interpreted the signs.

Most people incorrectly associate scrying solely with crystal-gazing (crystalomancy), when it in fact also refers to mirror-gazing (catoptromancy or catoxtromancy) and has strong links with certain forms of hydromancy. It is a comprehensive subject encompassing many differing methods of divination but probably the most rewarding is crystal gazing as this allows the scryer to give full rein to his or her psychic capabilities.

CRYSTAL GAZING
If you wish to try it yourself you may not have successful results no matter how hard or long you try. Scrying is wholly dependent on the individual's sensitivity and many may find other forms of divination easier to practise. Others, though, may find they have a natural talent which enables them to scry successfully after only a few practice sessions; so it is at least worth while finding out.

The tools
You will need a crystal-ball (usually glass is used nowadays, and it is much cheaper to buy), a dark cloth to lay beneath the crystal or in which to hold the sphere in your hands; perhaps a stand on which to rest the crystal should you so prefer.

Preparation
This will depend largely on personal taste and inclination but, if you are someone who can only embark on psychic work when in tranquil surroundings, then follow your normal routine for creating the atmosphere you require — soft background music, subdued lighting, a lighted joss-stick perhaps.

Once the area in which you are to work feels right for you, sit yourself comfortably in a chair with the crystal on a table in front of you or held loosely in your hands on your lap. Relax; make sure you feel completely at ease and, if you think it would help, do a few deep-breathing exercises to set the mood.

Using the crystal
Concentrate on the crystal and try to put all other thoughts from your mind. Let your eyes focus on the sphere for a short while then shift your gaze slightly. Do not stare at the ball or you will get eye-strain and will not be able to see anything in its surface.

After a few minutes you may find your gaze being drawn *into* the crystal's depths; its edges begin to blur and you will be on the verge of seeing within.

What happens next varies from person to person. Some people report that the crystal seems to cloud over or becomes milky-white; others state that the crystal changes colour, perhaps from red to green to black; others still explain the phenomenom as a sense of the crystal dispersing into a swirling mist. No two

people are likely to experience exactly the same effects, so don't worry too much if your experiment has a different outcome.

It is also possible that nothing will happen at your first attempt. The crystal may remain a lifeless sphere of glass and all you can see is your own reflection on its surface. Don't despair if so, only a very few people succeed in-scrying straight away, most need to practise for several weeks or months, perhaps even years, before the breakthrough occurs. And some, as I mentioned earlier, may not find scrying a suitable medium for their psychic potential.

Whatever happens, do not persevere for more than a few minutes the first time; it is best to repeat the exercise again another day rather than be put off right at the start because your eyes and back ache, you've got cramp in your legs, or whatever. You never know, you may after all develop into a natural scryer if you approach the subject sensibly, take one step at a time, don't try to hurry things along by taking short-cuts or spending too long hunched up over a crystal ball.

Results
If all goes well and your psychic eye does begin to observe changes in the crystal, what next? Again, experiences differ in this respect but basically they fall into two main categories: those who "see" actual pictures — people, places and events — and those who see symbols that can be interpreted either by the scryer or, if doing a reading for someone else, the querent.

It matters not at all which category you fall in, or perhaps your experiences will be different again; what is important is that the crystal's message should be received and understood. Psychic development is a slow process, it needs time and patience, but the results can be infinitely rewarding.

Alternatives
Perhaps you feel that you would like to test out your scrying skills before buying a crystal ball. If so, there are numerous alternatives to choose from and everyone will have at least one suitable scrying vehicle to hand in their homes.

For instance, remembering that the earliest seers obtained their visions when peering into watery depths, you may care to experiment with a receptable filled with liquid of some kind. Beginners usually find a dark surface easiest, so a shallow bowl or saucer containing ink or a dark coloured glazed pottery dish filled with tap-water will suffice.

Highly reflective surfaces, such as burnished brass, copper or bronze, offer suitable alternatives, especially when covered by water; some people though have great success simply by using the metallic surface itself. Old silvered mirrors are sometimes used too although it may be difficult for the novice to 'see' beyond his or her own reflection.

A very simple method of making your own scrying mirror is to take any slightly convex, circular piece of glass — an unwanted clock or watch face perhaps — and paint the convex side matt black. As usual, scry by looking into the unpainted, concave surface. There is really no limit to what can be used given a little imagination and determination: two qualities vital to successful scrying.

CHAPTER FIFTEEN

SELENOMANCY

Mankind has always been fascinated by the heavens and in particular with the mysterious Moon whose ever-changing appearance can be discerned so clearly in the dark night sky. This silvery orb was soon credited with feminine attributes and defined as the Queen of the Night, consort to the Sun whose warmth and light enabled early man to survive in an otherwise hostile environment. The Sun held sway over the daylight hours but at night the Moon ruled supreme.

Despite the Moon's predictable cycle, she still retains her aura of mystery because she always keeps one face hidden from observers on Earth.She has therefore come to be associated with the more subtle forces of nature: the inner self, the subconscious, psychic powers and, above all else, with divination itself. So it is not surprising to discover that there is one form of divination, Selenomancy, which is based on the Moon's changing shape as she completes her cycle.

Selenomancy is divination by the phases and various aspects of the Moon whose changing appearance is caused by its angular relationship to the Earth and the Sun. These phases can, of course, be used as transits to an individual birth-chart, but one can also obtain a fair indication of prevalent moods and trends simply by considering the current Moon phase on any particular day of the month.

As a general rule it should be remembered that Lunations (New and Full Moons) will hold more power than any other phase and that the effects of these will be intensified at the time of an eclipse. Aspects formed between the Moon and other planets will also be effective; by studying the nature of any aspect (see Astrology) and considering these in connection with the planetary keywords you may be able to judge the likely outcome of Lunar aspects.

Raphael's Ephemeris provides information on the times of Lunations, aspects from the Moon and the sign that it is in each day.

But even if you do not wish to study astrology, you can still make use of Selenomancy simply by observing the night-sky and noting the changing shape of the Moon. The times of actual Lunations and eclipses are recorded in almanacs, many diaries and some publications.

It should be remembered that the apparently changing shape of the Moon only occurs because of the light that it receives from the Sun, therefore one can easily ascertain the Moon's sign at the time of Lunation by knowing which Sun-sign rules the period in question. At New Moon both lights will be together in the same sign and at Full Moon they will be exactly opposite each other: if a Full Moon occurs on May 16th, the Sun will be in Taurus, therefore the Moon must be in Scorpio.

Before studying the meaning of each individual Moon phase you should first consider the nature of the sign(s) involved as these may either intensify, modify or even nullify the intended action of any phase. In the pages that follow you will find keywords that suggest the possible influence of each sign; these should always be taken into consideration when reading the more detailed descriptions given to the Moon phases.

But, as with any other form of divination, experience is always the best teacher. Try not to assume a fatalistic attitude, especially when contemplating eclipses.

Although the Sun takes a whole year to pass through the zodiac, the Moon makes this same journey in one Lunar month. Thus, in the period between one New Moon and the next, the Moon will transit all 12 signs in turn, spending approximately 2½ days in each.

On the next two pages you will find keywords associated with the Moon's occupation of the 12 zodiacal signs. These will give an indication of those issues, feelings or aspirations which are most likely to be emphasised during each stage of the Moon's monthly cycle.

MOON IN ARIES

Beginnings; openings; action; assertiveness; energy; leadership; impatience; quick-temper; conquest; challenge; enterprise; will; selfishness; naivete; open-mindedness; introduction; fervour; thoughtlessness; liberty; whims; self-reliance; provocation; inspirations; excitement; announcements; invigoration; release; speed.

MOON IN CANCER

Fecundation; fertilisation; feeling; receptivity; sensitivity; fidelity; tenacity; conclusion; heredity; memory; absorption; retaining; clannishness; patriotism; nurturing; residence; family; possessiveness; protection; provision; defensiveness; empathy; environment; feelings; hospitality; protection; reminiscence; security; storage.

MOON IN LIBRA

Peace; harmony; diplomacy; tact; balance; beautification; agreement; partnership; contradiction; arbitration; comparision; conciliation; compromise; justice; litigation; manoeuvre; manipulation; matrimony; mediation; reconciliation; ultimatum; vacillation; reason; logic; complacency; contradiction; co-operation; rivalry.

MOON IN TAURUS

Consolidation; support; perseverance; endurance; stamina; construction; abundance; calmness; evaluation; materialism; investment; recompense; merchandise; artistry; comfort; stability; thoroughness; obstinacy; satisfaction; inflexibility; greed; acquisition; affluence; capability; bluntness; constancy; conservatism; inertia; propriety.

MOON IN LEO

Creation; self-confidence; self-reliance; arrogance; aggrandisement; amusement; display; glorification; attention; ornamentation; pageantry; revelry; speculation; pleasure; pride; flamboyance; dominance; ostentation; dramatisation; celebrity; adoration; warmth; exhilaration; romance; happiness; demonstration; procreation; benevolence.

MOON IN SCORPIO

Endings; birth; regeneration; passion; intensity; compulsion; concentration; removal; revitalisation; rejuvenation; destruction; research; secrecy; re-evaluation; fascination; jealousy; dissolution; redress; renovation; transformation; sensuality; elimination; obsession; bequests; denunciation; inheritance; investigation; revenge.

MOON IN GEMINI

Diversity; duality; versatility; adaptability; mobility; communication; geniality; flexibility; cleverness; eloquence; learning; shallowness; ambivalence; congeniality; dexterity; changes; ingenuity; superficiality; pliability; playfulness; malleability; restlessness; rumour; gossip; quick-wittedness; fickleness; adeptness; information.

MOON IN VIRGO

Diligence; tidiness; correctness; criticism; discernment; categorisation; discrimination; examination; fastidiousness; modesty; hypochondria; inspection; preparation; pettiness; regimentation; pertinence; prudence; meticulousness; simplicity; service; technique; utilisation; workmanship; virtuosity; trivialities.

MOON IN SAGITTARIUS

Hopes; dreams; forward-planning; striving; optimism; expansion; foreign affairs; bravery; chivalry; honesty; dogma; pomp; ceremony; truth; vision; wisdom; audacity; generosity; luck; imprudence; embellishment; exaggeration; scholarship; prophecy; sanctimoniousness; thanksgiving; understanding; adventure.

MOON IN CAPRICORN

Industry; patience; consideration; achievement; honour; coldness; determination; authority; cynicism; alienation; composure; integrity; monopoly; obedience; organisation; prestige; promotion; respectability; sagacity; shrewdness; caution; superiority; tradition; reserve; officiousness; order; structure; merit; reputation.

MOON IN AQUARIUS

Rebellion, sociability; humanitarianism; camaraderie; chaos; independence; eccentricity; originality; expectation; freedom; brotherhood; meetings; representation; conspiracy; experimentation; futuristic; inventive; open-minded; modern; shocking; team-work; amalgamation; unity; conviviality; diversity; diffusion; friendship.

MOON IN PISCES

Ethereal; elusive; intangible, devoted; dreamy; imaginative; repentant; self-sacrificing; solitary; surreptitious; sympathetic; mystical; telepathic; psychic; tranquil; martyrish; retiring; superstitious; muddled; confused; mysterious; hypnotic; corrupt; bewitching; compassionate; cryptic; remorseful; escapist; merciful; observant; weird.

WAXING GIBBOUS MOON: In some ways this may be a period of comfort and ease when things seem to be working out right; or it could be a time of laziness. Whatever, we should not let this deliciously relaxed feeling blind us to any need to take on extra work or rearrange things. In areas where there has been slackness, this could be our last chance to attend to the details that conclude a project; so do watch out for unwarranted complacency under this phase. More usually, this is a period for winning support where this has been absent or for reconciliation or compromise where there has been argument. It may be advisable to remember that other people are experiencing this easy phase as well! Should either your own or anyone else's health have been problematic, this may be a good period for rest and recuperation.

FULL MOON: This may be the time for completion of projects or it may indicate the first real signs from others. Life will probably be quite challenging at the moment and something may provoke an extremely emotional reaction. But, if you made the correct moves earlier in the cycle, it could be that the auspices are in your favour; when this occurs, now may bring very definite signs of approval or appreciation from other people. Contacts with others will almost certainly assume more importance than usual, whether these be encouraging or antagonistic. Sometimes at this phase there may be a very strong attraction to someone you would not usually consider a suitable partner, so take note of who is around you. Consider the signs that hold the Sun and Moon, as these may suggest likely effects.

WANING GIBBOUS MOON: As the Moon begins to wane there may be a feeling of euphoria that you wish to share with other people; conversely, you may be feeling slightly depressed over failure. You may need to disseminate information at the moment and to discuss what was right or what went wrong: such inquests may be useful in the future, whatever your current success rate. It may be necessary to understand that the present is not ripe for changes, one can only analyse past experience and learn from this, whether this was good or bad. This may also be a sensible period to catch up on mundane chores or to attend to matters that have been left pending. There is still energy to spare before the closing cycle. You may have perverse ideas to become a crusader, but remember this is no time for action, it is a time for the formulation of ideas.

FIRST QUARTER: *This occurs 7-8 days after the New Moon and is a time for settlements or conclusions. Any new projects should be well in hand at the moment and one should be in a position to make definite statements or commitments about these. Home life might become more important at present and there may be a reluctance to spend too much time on aimless pleasure. One needs to get life into perspective and create order just now and often a set routine is attractive. This is often a good time to buy property as you are likely to be very sure of your own mind. There is little danger of taking miscalculated chances and you may even become overly cautious. This is often a time for hard work and effort and for laying down firm foundations for the future: everything must be tangible and real.*

WAXING CRESCENT MOON: *Around the 3rd-4th day after the New Moon, the first crescent will become visible. This may indicate that a desired project is just beginning to take shape or may even present the first hint of choices or changes that must be made in order to arrive at completion. Now may be a good time to discuss ideas with other people or even to travel around more than usual to bring some variety into your life. You may be more gregarious than normal and desire to improve your social life; there may be more post to attend to than at other times or you may spend a lot of time on the telephone. The main thing to avoid at the moment is harping on the past; it is important to move forward somehow. Everything begins to take shape at the first crescent and you should use this to your advantage*

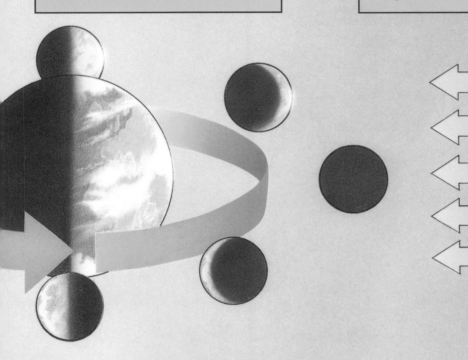

NEW MOON: *One can never see the New Moon as it is so close to the Sun, causing them to rise and set together. When these two lights are in conjunction, it is a time for beginnings. Now is the time to initiate new activities, create a different image or cultivate new ideas. To some this may be an emotional period when feelings are more sensitive and acute; if so, some time should be set aside to reflect on hoped-for achievements that you wish to make during the coming month. You may tend to react instinctively at the moment, so this may be a good time to tell others of your wants and your needs. Always consider the nature of the sign that the New Moon falls in, for this may tell you something about your best courses of action or the area of your life you should concentrate upon.*

LAST QUARTER: *This may be a period of responsibility and for carrying out obligations; often time is wasted in bemoaning the lack of co-operation or ethics of other people. Duty will invariably figure in one's life at the moment and pleasure may only be conspicuous by its absence. Other people may be difficult to deal with or even impossible to contact. But impatience is a useless waste of energy now and will not achieve any desired results. You may tend to be rather inflexible and inclined to lay down your own mode of law; try to avoid issuing ultimatums, they will be difficult to escape from when you later change your mind. This may be a good period for limiting social interaction unless it is in the line of duty. Solitude may benefit, especially when reflecting on a better future, which isn't very far away.*

WANING CRESCENT: *More optimism is around at the moment as you sense that the Moon is close to approaching its next beginning. This may be the time to make secret plans and for getting wants and needs into practical perspective. You know another opportunity will soon present itself. Clear something from your life during this phase, whether you relinquish a grudge or physically get rid of an accumulation of rubbish. You may be very sensitive or intuitive just now and may have a subconscious feeling that something is about to happen. This is the best time to take note of the signs in which the imminent New Moon is about to fall and then to get into a positive frame of mind and make your plans accordingly in order to cultivate success in the future; better still, look at Lunations for at least 3 months ahead and plan a definite campaign of action now.*

CHAPTER SIXTEEN

SORTILEGE

Sortilege involves the casting or drawing of lots. These may be any small objects that can be scattered onto a prepared surface or randomly selected to give an answer to a specific query. Dice, dominoes and runes are examples of how sortilege has been developed and refined over the centuries to emerge as distinct and separate forms of divination. Perhaps not so obvious is the practice of choosing someone to undertake a specific task by tossing a coin or asking several people to draw a straw, one of which is shorter than the rest; whoever gets the short straw or wins the toss is of course the winner or loser depending on the ultimate goal of the exercise. Sortilege is therefore one of the cornerstones of divination from which the vast majority of practices currently in use today derive. All manner of artefacts and a variety of both natural and man-made materials can be used for this purpose; slivers of wood; inscribed pieces of parchment, skin or paper; small bones, pebbles or shells; seeds and berries; the list is endless.

Most of the earlier forms of divination by drawing lots have now fallen into disuse. However, some practices retain strong and obvious links with their forerunners and still provide simple and effective ways of solving a dilemma or answering a question. One of these you may care to try out for yourself is stone divination, sometimes referred to as "talking stones".

USING STONES

There are several alternative ways of using small stones or pebbles, so choose whichever appeals to you most. The number of stones required may vary according to the method chosen but I would suggest that 12 would be the maximum number anyone might need. If possible collect only those pebbles which are nicely rounded at the edges, but preferably with flattish sides so that a symbolic design can be painted on one of their surfaces. The stones should be no larger than 1-1½ inches (3-4cm) in length, perhaps ⅞ inch (2cm) wide at the broadest point, otherwise you will not be able to hold them all in your cupped hands at one time.

The painted symbols should represent specific areas of life which are important to you: the Sun for health and happiness; an aeroplane for long-distance travel; parallel lines for a journey by road or train; a flower or heart for romance; and so on. There are no hard and fast rules, what matters is that the symbols should convey to you, the person reading the stones, whatever you consider are the major aspects in your life and of those around you.

If you like the idea, you may prefer to dispense with such symbols and instead carefully select a set of 7 or 10 stones of differing hues to represent each of the planets. In the Astrology Chapter you will find reference to each planet's domain so it should be relatively simple to associate each coloured stone with specific spheres of everyday living. Or you may perhaps collect 12 stones, one for each month of the year, which can be numbered for easy identification.

Whatever you decide, the important point is to use symbols that will help you quickly recognise what any particular stone represents, no matter how many you use. You will next need to find a convenient surface for the stone-casting. This may be anywhere, indoors or out, as long as it is relatively clear of obstructions and level.

If working outdoors, a patch of bare earth, a path or area of fine sand may prove suitable; a table-top, tiled floor or large tray may suffice in the home. Again, it does not matter what you use as long as it is smooth enough to allow the stones to roll a little way when they are cast but not so slippery that they disappear into the bushes or fall on the floor from the table.

Depending on what your stones symbolise, you can mark out your surface into specific areas to represent associated concepts. The 12 houses of a horoscope wheel could, for example, be used in conjunction with planetary stones; each stone that landed in a house would then be interpreted in exactly the same way as would a planet in a birth chart. Or you could decide to draw 8 numbered squares on a large sheet of paper to represent different things such as work, love, health, family and so

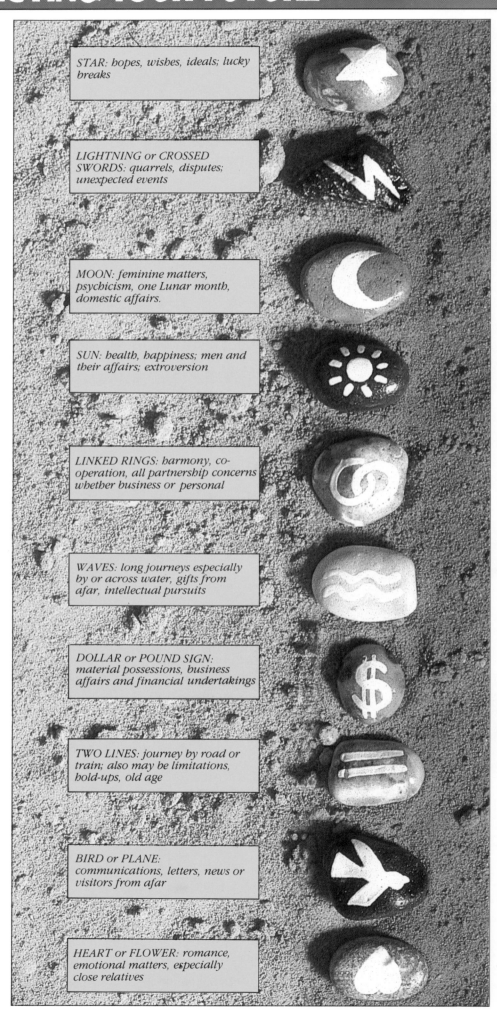

STAR: *hopes, wishes, ideals; lucky breaks*

LIGHTNING or CROSSED SWORDS: *quarrels, disputes; unexpected events*

MOON: *feminine matters, psychicism, one Lunar month, domestic affairs.*

SUN: *health, happiness; men and their affairs; extroversion*

LINKED RINGS: *harmony, co-operation, all partnership concerns whether business or personal*

WAVES: *long journeys especially by or across water, gifts from afar, intellectual pursuits*

DOLLAR or POUND SIGN: *material possessions, business affairs and financial undertakings*

TWO LINES: *journey by road or train; also may be limitations, hold-ups, old age*

BIRD or PLANE: *communications, letters, news or visitors from afar*

HEART or FLOWER: *romance, emotional matters, especially close relatives*

on, then cast your calendrical stones on to the paper; any stone that came to rest in a numbered square would then signify the month when that particular facet of life would be emphasised. If working outside, a sharp stick could be used to scratch a design into the earth to represent specific areas of existence, perhaps. The possible permutations that you will find with this exercise are limited only by your own creative imagination: you can use any method you choose.

Reading stones

In practical terms, the usual procedure is to cup all the stones loosely in both hands, concentrate on the problem or query uppermost in your mind at the time of the reading, then simply scatter the stones on to whatever surface you are using. Only those stones that fall within the confines of the chosen design are read; if using decorated stones, this is further limited to reading only those that display their painted or numbered faces.

For a quick reading where a fairly simple response will suffice, the stones could be placed in a pouch or small bag which is then turned over a few times while concentrating on your query. One, two or three stones are then selected at random, without looking, to obtain a solution. This can work very well for a "Shall I, Shan't I?" situation but will not, of course, provide sufficient information which you will usually require for a comprehensive reading. So, let the stones talk.

CHAPTER SEVENTEEN

TEALEAVES

Tea drinking goes back thousands of years in the Far East, yet it was not until the 15th century that it became a common practice in Europe. Then, tea was an expensive luxury as it had to be transported many hundreds of miles in slow sailing-vessels along with other costly items that made up the rich cargoes from China and India. This made it a very precious commodity which was kept locked up in specially made tea-caddies, away from the eager hands of the serving classes. Gradually, as trade increased, its price became more competitive and the less wealthy were able to enjoy the delights of drinking tea, until it became a national pastime.

Soon, people began to notice that dregs left in a cup after the tea was drunk formed patterns which could, through half-closed eyes, be seen as everyday images; symbolic shapes ripe for the interpretation of character and destiny. And thus the art of tasseomancy, or tealeaf reading, developed; a practice still much in evidence today despite the advent of the tea-bag.

Ideally, boiling water poured onto two spoonfuls of large leaf tea dropped into a preheated teapot will produce a good cup of tea and provide the best grounds for interpretation. Tea-bags, too, can be used; simply break the bag and shake the loose tea into the cup before pouring on boiling water, and then proceed as usual. Obviously, a plain cup or shallow bowl is needed, preferably white or cream as this will allow the leaves to show up to best advantage. Swirl the dregs three times towards you, then turn the cup upside down on a saucer quickly for the liquid to drain off. Invert the cup and you are ready to begin your reading.

Remember though, these are mere tools; the secret of a successful reading lies in your ability to recognise the symbols seen in the cup; and this will only come with practice. Concentration will help, especially at first, as this will enable your inherent psychic abilities to gradually emerge before long.

Before starting to read the leaves there are one or two points that should be noted, such as whether any symbols stand out more prominently than others. If so, consider these to be more important than less well-defined shapes. Also, the position of the leaves will provide an indication of the timing of events; those closest to the rim indicate immediate occurrences and those at the bottom of the cup refer to future happenings.

The cup handle represents your home and close family, so symbols here will refer to your domestic environment and family affairs, whereas those at the opposite side of the cup relate to your work situation and business matters generally.

Often, two or more distinct symbols will appear in close proximity, in which case they should be interpreted in conjunction. For instance, a human figure or face next to a letter would be identified as a person known or shortly to be known to you, and the initial letter of that person's name. Similarly, a number next to a plane could indicate the number of days or weeks which are likely to elapse before you take a trip; and so on.

It is worth taking your time to note such points before commencing to interpret the individual symbols from the following list as it will help you gain a fuller picture and thus get a more accurate reading. In time, you will find the whole process becomes much easier.

READING THE SHAPES

A

ACORN A lucky omen meaning success; sometimes denotes a pregnancy.
AIRCRAFT Unexpected journey.
ANCHOR A positive sign; career improvement.
ANGEL Unexpected good news; rejoicing.
ANVIL A sign of strength.
APPLE The fulfilment of material desires.
ARCH The start of a new and profitable friendship.
ARROW News concerning career.
AXE A warning of obstacles ahead.

B

BABY Financial problems of a minor nature.
BALL Changes are imminent.
BASKET A tip-off brings success.
BAT Rivalry; unforeseen problems.
BEAR A warning against taking unnecessary risks.
BED Subconscious worry.
BEE Good news; an important document to be signed.
BELL Welcome news.
BIRD A good luck omen signifying improved circumstances.
BOAT A change of plans or unexpected trip; successful business negotiations.
BOOK If closed, the end of a relationship; if open, proceed with your plans.
BOOT Protection from danger.
BOTTLE Warning against over-indulgence.
BOUQUET Happiness in love.
BOW A symbol of hope.
BRANCH A birth in the family.
BROOM The start of a new project or scheme.
BULL Sudden gain and prosperity.
BUTTERFLY A frivolous occasion.

C

CABBAGE A time of change, usually for the better.
CACTUS Courage and perseverance.
CAMEL Progress.
CANDLE A new friendship.
CAPE/CLOAK A warning against deception.
CAR A change for the better.
CASTLE Strength and endurance; an unexpected inheritance.
CAT Guard against deception and avoid doubtful deals.

CHAIN A symbol of love or marriage
CHAIR An unexpected visitor.
CHILD An omen of hope and fruitful endeavour.
CHURCH An invitation to a formal occasion.
CIRCLE Successful conclusion to a project.
CLOCK A time of reassessment; plan ahead more carefully.
CLOVER Good future prospects.
COFFIN Failure in business.
COMET An unexpected visitor or news from afar.
CONCH SHELL News from abroad brings improvements.
CORN Prosperity.
CORONET Success and high honours.
COT A fresh enterprise.
COW Wealth and prosperity.
CRESCENT MOON A friend's advice proves helpful.
CROSS A sacrifice.
CROWN Success and good fortune.
CUP A good omen denoting bounty; a new friendship.

D

DAGGER Warning to beware of false friends.
DAISY An enjoyable romance.
DEER Victory over a rival.
DEVIL A danger of extravagance.
DOG A trustworthy friend, fidelity.
DOVE Peace and happiness.
DRAGON Important changes.
DRUM An exciting and unexpected invitation.
DUCK Financial help from a friend.

E

EAGLE A fortunate symbol denoting status and prosperity.
EGG Beneficial change and new projects.
ELEPHANT Strength and bright prospects.
EYE Careful planning will pay dividends.

F

FAN Guard against indiscretion.
FEATHER Inconstancy.
FIR TREE Prosperity and success.
FISH An omen of good luck.
FLAMES Hasty news brings opportunity but think before you act.
FLOWER Festivity and celebration.
FOUNTAIN The completion of plans.
FOX Beware deception, specially regarding legal documents.

FROG Look before you leap in business matters.
FRUIT Always a symbol of increase and plenty.

G

GALLOWS A change of attitude is needed.
GATE Matters are satisfactorily resolved.
GLASSES (EYE) A surprise.
GOAT A conflict of ideas.
GRAPES A fortunate omen showing increase and prosperity.
GUITAR Ardent love and affection.
GUN A warning.

H

HAMMER A challenging situation that demands strength.
HAND Help is available.
HAT Your plans succeed.
HEART Reliable friend or, where applicable, a proposal of marriage.
HEN Take care of your money.
HOLLY A crossroads has been reached.
HORN A symbol of good fortune.
HORSE A faithful and loyal friend.
HORSESHOE The promise of good fortune.
HOUR-GLASS Danger is imminent; do not make hasty decisions.
HOUSE A symbol of protection.

I

INITIALS Letters of the alphabet refer to people you already know or are about to meet.
INSECT Small irritations or minor difficulties.
IVY Loss through misplaced trust.

J

JESTER Don't trust too much to first impressions.
JUG Guard against excess.

K

KETTLE Domestic harmony and happiness.
KEY Important decisions must be made; a new start.
KITE Unexpected opportunities.
KNIFE Caution is advised, especially in relationships.

L

LADDER A new venture will prove successful.
LAMB Good news concerning a child.

LAMP A family celebration, perhaps a wedding.

LEAVES Omens of hope.

LEG Strength and fortitude.

LiLY Faithful friend.

LINES If straight and unbroken, success; wavy or broken, disruption; two parallel lines, an important journey.

LION Honour and respect.

LOBSTER Unexpected gains.

LOCK Obstacles.

LOOP Confusion or entrapment.

LUGGAGE Changes are imminent.

MASK Guard your innermost thoughts and secrets.

MERMAID Temptation.

MONK Beware of deception.

MONKEY A mischief-maker.

MONSTER Unpleasant shock.

MOUSE This animal represents neglected opportunities or loss.

MUSHROOM A lovers' tiff.

NAIL Wounded feelings.

NECKLACE A conquest or admirer.

NET Problems can be overcome if caution is exercised.

NUMBERS These represent days or weeks, or may refer to addresses; should be read with adjacent symbols.

ʻNUN/NURSE A family illness.

OAR A time to change course.

OCTOPUS An unwelcome but temporary task.

OWL An unfortunate omen denoting failure or illness.

PAGODA Unfamiliar territory provides inspiration.

PALM TREE Health, wealth and happiness.

PARACHUTE Providential intervention.

PARCEL A surprise.

PARROT Scandal or mischief-making is in the offing.

PEACOCK Vanity and luxury.

PIANO Harmony and domestic happiness.

PIG Expected help doesn't arrive.

PIGEON Surprising news; perhaps a long journey.

PIPE A thoughtful period.

PRAM New projects.

PURSE Financial gain.

PYRAMID A revelation brings great improvement.

QUESTION MARK Better safe than sorry.

RABBIT You need more confidence.

RAINBOW An excellent omen denoting success.

REPTILE Symbol of deceit and treachery.

RING The completion of projects; enduring friendship.

ROSE A forthcoming engagement or likely marriage.

SAILOR News from abroad.

SAW Hard work or interference from others.

SCALES A difficult decision must be made.

SCORPION Vindictive or malicious behaviour; beware.

SCYTHE Projects come to an untimely end.

SEAGULL Presages problems ahead.

SHOE Beware self-indulgence.

SNAKE A hidden enemy.

SOLDIER Courage and enterprise will win rewards.

SPADE Hard work will pay dividends and bring riches.

SPIDER Unexpected gifts.

SPOON Good luck; a frivolous invitation.

STAR A dramatic improvement in circumstances.

SWAN A wish is fulfilled unexpectedly.

SUN Complete success; achievement.

T

TABLE Business negotiations.

TAP Political involvement.

TASSLE Entertainment.

TEA POT Business meetings; consultation.

TELEPHONE Important news.

TORTOISE Future riches and comfort; triumph after troubles.

TRAIN Impending change.

TREE A symbol of protection and good health.

TRIANGLE Always a sign of good luck if the apex is uppermost; if reversed, then a disappointment.

TRIDENT Authority and leadership.

U

UMBRELLA If open, friends help your aims; if closed, adverse circumstances.

W

WAND Delegate authority.

WHALE Strength and persistence bring social acclaim.

WHEEL Achievement.

WINDMILL Be cautious and you will win your goal.

WINGS Messages.

WOLF Envy and intrigue at work, take care!

Y

YACHT A surprise gift.

Z

ZEBRA A rich suitor.

In the 18th century China led the world in both the production and export of tea. Unfermented green tea was preferred, leaving a more delicate flavour. Britain and the rest of the world preferred stronger black tea. Here, the skilled art of tea sampling is in progress. The art of tasseomancy is easier performed with larger-leaved green tea rather than dark blends provided for mass consumption.

THE MANTIC ARTS

The term Mantic Arts encompasses all forms of divination or prediction, many of which are so specialised that they have warranted whole chapters to themselves in this book. Some have been modified continuously over the centuries and are no longer recognisable in their original form or follow such similar lines that they have fallen into disuse. This picture, for example, is a painted terracotta of Greek women playing knuc-klebones in the 3rd century, a forerunner to the dice and dominoes that are in popular use today.

There are though a considerable number of lesser known methods that can be adapted easily to modern usage and these are beginning to gain in popularity once more.

Based on sound esoteric principles, they provide a variety of effective means of discovering more about yourself and your expectations.

ACUTO-MANZIA

Divination using dressmaker's pins. You need 13 pins, 3 of which should be bent round to form a horseshoe. Arrange the straight pins on a cork tile in the same positions as the Sephiroth on the Tree of Life. Put the three bent pins into an egg-cup and shake them while thinking of your question or problem; hold the egg-cup about 6 inches above the board, tip it and see if any of the bent pins hook themselves around the pins in the board. If they do, the hooked pin will indicate the answer to your query.

AEROMANCY

Once a popular form of divination, this entails predicting future events through the study of atmospheric conditions, such as air currents, winds, and cloud formations. In many ways this is similar to Scrying and Tasseomancy where the reader's imagination and intuition allows him or her to interpret the changing shapes of the cloud formations into symbolic pictures.

ALECTROMANCY/ALECTRYOMANCY

Originally a protracted and complicated process involving a cockerel, grains of corn and the letters of the alphabet written on pieces of paper, to spell out the answer to a query. Modern variations based on identical principles include a ouija board and upturned glass; roulette wheel where the alphabet has been allocated numerical value; or any other lettered circular shape that can be spun until a pointer indicates an individual letter.

ALEUROMANCY

Traditionally this involved the use of various cereal crops but nowadays a convenient method would employ the use of flour and water. Simply quarter-fill a coloured basin or bowl with cold water to which a small quantity of flour has been added; turn the bowl 3 times while concentrating on the question, then tip the liquid away quickly down the sink and read the pattern of shapes left in the bowl.

ALOMANCY/HALOMANCY

This dates back to ancient times when salt was a precious commodity and was used as an offering to Pagan gods. This led to the practice of throwing salt into a fire in order to read the patterns made by the ensuing smoke. This developed into the modern practice of throwing a spoonful of salt on to a level surface and then reading the random patterns this makes.

ARITHMANCY

This is another name for numerology but some of its more diverse forms include other methods of using numbers for predictive purposes. A few of the more interesting variations follow.

The Mystic Triangle

Using the diagram above take a pencil in your left hand and with your eyes closed bring the point of the pencil down on to the triangle. Without moving the pencil, open your eyes and note on which number its point lies. If it falls outside the figure try again; if the same thing happens a second time, abandon the reading until a more favourable time.

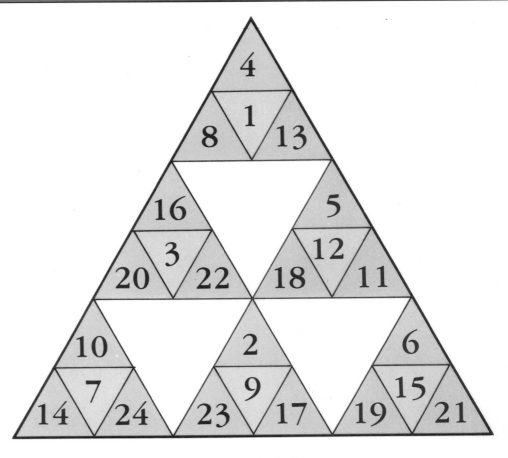

Assuming the time to be auspicious, note the numbered triangle on which the pencil point rests and read the interpretation from the following list.

The Meanings

1. If you do not allow yourself to be swayed from your purpose by others, you will succeed.
2. If you neglect an important duty, things will go wrong.
3. Happiness is coming your way. If there are difficulties at present they will soon vanish.
4. You will suffer a small loss.
5. Business opportunities may come your way. Take advantage of these.
6. You will receive a rise in pay or a gift.
7. This is no time to speculate or take chances.
8. There may be a quiet period ahead.
9. You can expect financial gain, or even a legacy.
10. Your fortunes will change shortly.
11. You are aiming too high. Your ambitions are unlikely to be fulfilled.
12. The time is ripe to pursue your plans with all your might.
13. You may be due for a disappointment.
14. Avoid quarrels in order to avoid unnecessary difficulty.
15. Be self-reliant.
16. Beware of gossip or scandal.
17. Do not lend money.
18. A long period of good fortune is ahead.
19. Do not ignore an opportunity to travel.
20. You should take better care of your health.
21. A surprise awaits you.
22. You will reach success after a long period of effort.
23. Be loyal and spurn all thoughts of deceit.
24. Patience is needed. Do not rush into anything without careful thought.

Lucky Dip

This is a very simple method of obtaining an answer to a question; but it will only give good results as long as it is not used too often. Cut slips of paper, each two inches square. Number the slips from 1 to 50 and place in an empty box. Shake the box and pick out three slips at random. Note the numbers and read the delineations below.

1. Obstacles are blocking your path.
2. Important news is on the way.
3. A good period for new undertakings.
4. Change is around you.
5. Luck is with you.
6. Accept an offer, as long as your conscience can also do so.
7. Good health and happiness.
8. Scandal and gossip.
9. Your wish will be fulfilled.
10. The possibility of romance or perhaps even marriage.
11. Financial gain.
12. Look out for a surprise.
13. Success in business.
14. Be on your guard.
15. There may be a quarrel.
16. Beware of dishonesty or treachery.
17. Happiness in love.
18. Irritating news.
19. Troubles through the fair sex.
20. Hard work and effort will bring reward.
21. Beware of false friends.
22. Guard against losses, especially important papers.
23. A journey will be successful.
24. Accept an invitation, it may lead to important events.
25. Family problems.
26. Financial success, perhaps through investment.

27. *Keep your promises.*
28. *A surprise offer will please you.*
29. *There may be difficulty in the immediate future.*
30. *A party or a social gathering.*
31. *A meeting with an old friend.*
32. *You may have success in a competition.*
33. *Changes are indicated.*
34. *The next 7 days will be lucky.*
35. *Money worries.*
36. *Take care of your health.*
37. *You have nothing to worry about.*
38. *Keep away from dubious situations.*
39. *Care needed in legal matters.*
40. *Prosperity.*
41. *Friends may be useful.*
42. *Good fortune.*
43. *Selfishness does not pay.*
44. *A peaceful, comfortable period lies ahead of you.*
45. *Difficulties will soon pass.*
46. *Honesty is the best policy.*
47. *Count your blessings.*
48. *Guard your tongue.*
49. *Accept an offer of friendship.*
50. *Great achievements.*

The Square of Nine
First take a large sheet of clean white paper and copy the diagram below, making sure that each of the squares within this measure is exactly 3 inches. Place a small coin or pebble in an egg-cup and shake three times while concentrating on your question, then close your eyes and tip the coin or pebble on to your diagram. If it falls outside the square you must accept that this is not a propitious time to obtain an answer.

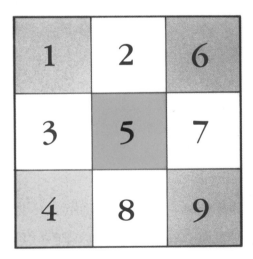

1. *This number requires patience as there will be a delay to the answer to your question. However, the overall prospects are good and you will soon be entering a more favourable period.*

2. *Although there may be a difficult period ahead it is not insurmountable. Hard work and effort will bring the greatest rewards. Take calculated risks as this is a time for boldness.*

3. *Do not expect something for nothing; hesitation may lead to failure. Someone of the opposite sex will have some influence on whether you succeed or fail.*

4. *Accept the help that has been offered to you and you will achieve your heart's desire. Have the confidence to believe in yourself and your own abilities.*

5. *Ultimately you will achieve your aims and realise your dreams, but you may need a little patience at the moment. Unexpected events, sudden friendships and invitations are on the way.*

6. *Refuse to be influenced by others and only depend upon yourself. You have the right attitude about your present situation and this is what will lead to success.*

7. *There may be obstacles in your path, even a reversal of current good fortune, or other people may let you down. This will all pass with time, so have patience.*

8. *As long as you are true to yourself you will succeed in your desires and ambitions. However much the odds seem to be stacked against you, do not deviate from your present path.*

9. *Good luck, financial gain and personal advancement surround you; this will be an extremely successful period. But do not let this good fortune make you neglect those closest to you.*

Wheel of Fate
Take a pin in your left hand, close your eyes, move the pin three times anti-clockwise over the wheel and bring it down on the number of your fate. The number thus indicated may

also prove to be lucky for you and should be used when having anything to do with numbers.

1. *Happiness will be yours in the very near future.*
2. *Your current admirer will not make you happy.*
3. *Eventually you will be prosperous though not immediately.*
4. *You will always be lucky.*
5. *Take care, lest you marry the wrong person.*
6. *Be prepared for a disappointment.*
7. *You will not be married in the immediate future.*
8. *Someone truly loves you.*
9. *Pride goes before a fall!*
10. *Be patient and things will change for the better.*
11. *The one you love is not for you.*
12. *Do not pass by an opportunity for advancement.*
13. *Someone does not have your best interests at heart.*
14. *You will soon receive a gift.*
15. *Your friends may be jealous of you.*
16. *Your present love situation is the right one for you.*

ASTRAGLOMANCY/ASTRAGYROMANCY
This form of divination derived from the ancient practice of casting bones, usually those from sheep. This has developed into the method of using Dice. The underlying principle is that only those bones that fall within the confines of a previously marked out area are read.

AUGURY

This is the general art of divination that uses all forms of prophecy.

AUSTROMANCY

This another form of Aeromancy specifically related to the behaviour of the wind.

BIBLIOMANCY

Opening a book at random in order to obtain a sign will provide guidance that is similar to consulting an oracle. But, unlike the Delphic variety, it is quite simple to practise oneself. The basic technique employed is to allow a book to fall open and to note the first words or phrase on which your eyes focus.

Although in the past it was traditionally a religious book such as the Bible that was used for this purpose, any book with which you feel some form of affinity would be ideal; the classics are often used in such a manner.

It would be unrealistic, however, to expect to receive an instantaneous answer to one's question through this method, yet it will trigger off one's intuitive powers so that a solution will surface from the self at some time in the near future; bibliomancy acts as a bridge between the objective and subjective worlds.

CAPNOMANCY

This is divination that is made by observing the smoke that emits from a fire or bonfire. The omens are fair when the smoke rises straight and true, but when it lies low trouble might be brewing. One could, of course, also study any shapes or patterns that one observes.

CARTOPEDY

An outmoded method of predicting the future and assessing character from the soles of the feet. Later, alternative therapists developed the principle into a form of diagnosing and treating illness from the stimulation of specific areas of the feet; this is known as Reflexology.

CATOPTROMANCY/CATAXTROMANCY

This is a very early form of crystal-gazing which uses a mirror to catch Lunar rays or which is suspended in water when the reflections are read. Magic Mirrors gained popularity in the Middle Ages, although they are still obtainable today. Any form of shining surface could replace a mirror.

CEROMANCY/CEROSCOPY

Originally this was an ancient form of prediction that derives from dripping candle wax into water and studying the shapes and patterns that are thus formed.

Acorn The seed has been planted, now is the time to put ideas into motion.
Anchor Ignore criticism and stand by your decision.
Bat A disappointing period lies ahead.
Bear Listen to your instincts; don't let others con you.
Bell Good luck is in the offing.
Bird Travel beckons.
Boat A need to be more sympathetic.
Boot Long-distance travel.
Butterfly Fickleness; your partner could let you down.
Cat Domestic happiness.

Dragon Keep on your toes, you may have a rival.
Eye A secret is disclosed.
Fish A need to widen your circle of friends.
Flower A fortunate omen.
Frog Imminent changes which prove beneficial.
Heart Romance is in the air.
Key New opportunities.
Leaf You are out of step with your colleagues.
Man An admirer.
Motor Car A romantic encounter while on a journey.
Numbers This may indicate a date or a time period.
Owl Don't allow others to interfere in your life.
Pig Perfect contentment.
Pipe Your partner may be unfaithful.
Rose True love.
Shoe You will change your job or place of residence.
Snake Use your knowledge wisely.
Spider Good luck is coming your way, probably financially.

Sun Health, wealth and happiness.
Tree All plans come to fruition.
Umbrella Make no rash moves, think before you act.
Vase Someone goes out of your life.
Wheel Your fortunes are changing.

CLAIRVOYANCE

The faculty of seeing mentally what happens or exists out of sight.

CLEIDOMANCY/CLIDOMANCY

This is an offshoot of Bibliomancy entailing the use of a book with a key. The key was suspended over a book to answer a simple 'Yes' or 'No' question and the answer could be

obtained by observing whether the key spun or not. There are several variations of this theme including that of suspending a ring on a thread over a bowl of water; nowadays this would be termed dowsing.

CLEROMANCY

This is a generic term to describe sortilege or divination by the use of small objects such as stones, sticks, bones, pebbles, shells, etc.

COSCINOMANCY

Another form of Cleidomancy using scissors and a sieve.

CRYSTLOMANCY

A form of scrying which specifically uses the crystal.

CYCLOMANCY

As its name implies, this method of divination depends on spinning an object in order to select a written answer to a question. Remnants of this form of augury can be seen in the Wheel of Fortune at fun-fairs and the party game 'Spinning the Bottle'.

DICE/DOMINOES

See Cleromancy.

ESP

Extra-sensory perception. The faculty of receiving or transmitting information through means other than the known senses; clairvoyance, clairaudience and telepathy are examples of this.

FLOROMANCY

The language of flowers; a symbolic method of conveying messages to others and of foretelling future trends. Some of the more popular meanings are listed below.

Amaranth Faith, fidelity and immortality; my love for you will never fade or die.
Anenome A mild flirtation.
Apple Blossom Weddings and romantic occasions. Eternal youth.
Bluebell Constancy in love.
Broom Peace and tranquillity.
Buttercup Abundance and happiness.
Camelia Beauty and opulence.
Canterbury Bell A secret admirer.
Carnation Good fortune, especially for a female. An unexpected gift.
Celandine Legal disputes; unhappy love affair.
Cherry Blossom Early disappointment, but abundance later in life.
Chrysanthemum Optimism under adversity; long life and happiness.
Clematis Beauty and truth; a love token.
Clover Luck and good fortune.
Coltsfoot Ease and comfort; improvement in health, justice.
Cowslip Feminine charm; the admiration of others.
Crocus Hope springs anew.
Daffodil Financial success.
Daisy Fidelity and innocence; also means 'I share your sentiments'.
Dandelion Pleasant thought about one's loved one.
Ferns Protection and healing.
Forget-me-not Constant love.

Gardenia *A secret love.*

Geranium *Unexpected meetings.*

Gorse *'I am thinking of you'; a good luck gift for a woman.*

Hazel *Wisdom.*

Heather *Good luck.*

Heliotrope *Dedication and devotion.*

Holly *Eternal life; the fulfilment of plans.*

Hollyhock *Fecundity.*

Honesty *Sincerity; strong intuitive powers.*

Honeysuckle: *Generosity and fidelity; we belong to each other.*

Hyacinth *Frivolity and enjoyment.*

Iris *Protection from above.*

Ivy *Love will soon come to you.*

Jasmine *Joy; an ardent attachment.*

Larkspur *Fickleness.*

Lavender *Calmness; also undying love.*

Lilac *Innocence; first dreams of love.*

Lily *Purity and humility.*

Lily-of-the-Valley *Reconciliation; return to happiness.*

London Pride *Eloquence; others admire your charm.*

Love-in-a-Mist *Perplexity.*

Lupin *Grace and elegance.*

Magnolia *A pleasant courtship.*

Marigold *Adoration, constancy and endurance; a love charm.*

May Blossom *Unlucky in love.*

Milkwort *Isolation; a love of the countryside.*

Mimosa *Friendship; idealistic love.*

Myrtle *Domestic bliss and happiness; a legacy.*

Narcissus *Fertility and abundance.*

Nasturtium *Victory over one's enemies.*

Night-Scented Stock *A sweet nature; enduring affection.*

Orange Blossom *A happy and prosperous marriage.*

Orchid *An expensive gift; an ardent admirer.*

Pansy *Changing fortunes.*

Peony *Fruitful marriage and prosperity.*

Periwinkle *Happy thoughts of the past.*

Petunia *Discretion.*

Poppy *Remembrance; consolation.*

Primrose *Protection; a well deserved rest.*

Rose *Pleasure; love and desire.*

Rosemary *Protection; an aid to memory.*

Sage *Expansion and prosperity.*

Scarlet Pimpernel *Change; a secret assignation.*

Snowdrop *Hope and consolation; purity.*

Soloman's Seal *Wisdom, endurance and perseverance.*

Sunflower *Adoration and devotion.*

Sweet Pea *Modesty, simplicity and fidelity.*

Sweet William *Protection for the home.*

Tamarisk *A challenging situation.*

Teasel *A tantalising secret.*

Thistle *Interesting news is on its way.*

Thyme *Courage and activity.*

Traveller's Joy *Safety while journeying.*

Tulip *Fame and good fortune.*

Venus' Looking Glass *Unity; an enchanting love affair.*

Vervain *A revitalising force.*

Violet *Mutual love and respect; modesty.*

Water Lily *Purity of heart.*

Woodbine *Wit and eloquence.*

HYDROMANCY

Quite literally divination by water. One can either use a pool or bowl of water as a form of scrying mirror or drop pebbles in the water and observe the patterns made by the ripples. Another version is really a form of sortilege in that all possible answers to a carefully thought-out question are written on to separate pieces of paper; these are then dropped into a bowl of water which is turned 3 times. The first answer to rise to the surface becomes the answer to the question. It is also said that one can use this method to enable one to choose a winning horse!

LECANOMANCY

This is a form of Hydromancy, except that gems of different colours are used. Keeping one's eyes tightly closed, one drops the gems into the water (having carefully framed the question beforehand); the ensuing patterns made by the different colours are then divined for answers.

LIBANOMANCY/LIVANOMANCY

Another form of reading patterns made by smoke, but this time incense is used. This works especially well if it is combined with meditation.

LITHOMANCY/LETHOMANCY

Divination by precious or semi-precious stones. One form of lithomancy involves the use of a candle and relies on the colour of the stone for an interpretation. The candle should be lit and placed on a table in a darkened room, a selection of stones or coloured beads (preferably glass) are then scattered on the surface around the candle. Whichever stone/bead first reflects the light of the candle will denote the answer to your query according to its colour.

Black *A run of bad luck, a disappointment; a long journey.*

Blue *Good fortune and happiness in love.*

Brown *Health, wealth and happiness.*

Colourless *Happiness and success; health improvement.*

Cream *Arranging a social function, perhaps a wedding.*

Green *Hopes fulfilled; cessation of domestic problems.*

Grey *A setback to plans; a broken relationship; money worries.*

Mauve *Petty annoyances; gossip; an onerous task.*

Orange *Achievement of an ambition; promotion.*

Pink *Eternal love; birth of a child.*

Purple *A separation; a disagreement; financial outlay.*

Red *A conquest; cash gain; exciting new love.*

Turquoise *A delightful journey, perhaps a holiday; opportunity.*

Violet *A need to extricate oneself from a difficult situation.*

White *A wish fulfilled; the beginning of a successful enterprise.*

Yellow *Unhappy love affair.*

Another very simple but effective means of divination involves the use of 24 stones or semi-precious stones and a pouch. Simply select any 24 from the following list — you may have some of these already or most are fairly cheap to buy — and place these in a bag or pouch with a draw-string top. Think of a question or problem that is worrying you while gently turning the pouch in order to mix up the stones inside. When you feel the question is firmly in your mind put your hand into the pouch and without looking pull out three stones. Combine their three meanings from the definitions given below and you should find that this will answer your query.

Agate *Promotes good health and increases physical stamina; sometimes indicates benefits through wills or legacies.*

Almandine *Clarifies existing problems or difficulties by instilling self-confidence and determination. May enhance psychic abilities.*

Amber *Induces courage, virility, fertility and fitness. Brings the promise of career or business success and marital happiness.*

Amethyst *Inspires confidence, admiration and respect; sharpens intellect and acumen; increases strength and resilience.*

Amosite *Helps expand consciousness and develop deeper understanding. Can denote a rise in social prestige and personal fulfilment.*

Andratite *Emphasises sincerity, honesty, integrity and good judgement. Enhances social standing and business prestige.*

Aquamarine *Betokens love and friendship and promotes youthfulness and physical fitness. Renews confidence and revives flagging energies.*

Aventurine *Promotes health, vigour and cheerfulness; promises emotional and moral support in any new commercial undertaking.*

Azurite *Commands social success, friendship and constancy in love. Helps raise consciousness and improves psychic abilities.*

Beryl *Symbolises hope, honour, friendship and domestic harmony. Sharpens the intellect and favours new commercial projects.*

Bloodstone *Denotes trust, loyalty and devotion. Boosts courage and vitality and helps promote eloquence which can lead to an increase in earnings.*

Blue John *Offers protection against injury or accident while travelling. Also attracts honours and prestige as well as improving business and personal relationships.*

Carbuncle *Increases energy, determination and confidence. Indicates a reconciliation of differences between friends.*

Cat's Eye *Encourages success in speculative ventures or competitive sports. Strengthens ties of love or affection and protects the home from intruders.*

Chalcedony *Attracts public favour, recognition and financial reward; increases popularity, enthusiasm and physical fitness.*

Chrysoberyl *Dispels doubt, diminishes anxiety and helps ease bodily aches and pains. Strengthens resolve in times of hardship.*

Chyrsolite *Affords relief from mental or emotional stress, confounds enmity and encourages good health.*

Chrysoprase *A harbinger of gaiety and joy. Sharpens the intellect, rewards initiative and opens up new vistas.*

Citrine *Associated with courage, boldness and mastery; promises victory over sporting, business or romantic rivals.*

Coral *Promotes vitality, good humour and harmonious relationships. Expands horizons and encourages personal development.*

Cornelian *Affords peace, pleasure and prosperity. Brings joy to those embarking on a long journey or moving home.*

Diamond *Heightens awareness, encourages enterprise and strengthens resolve. May bring personal preferment and acclaim.*

Emerald *Favours love and lovers as it promises constancy and fidelity. Inspires confidence and emotional fulfilment.*

Feldspar *Associated with fertility and fecundity, this strengthens bonds of affection and promotes marital happiness.*

Garnet *Denotes devotion, loyalty and good humour. Increases drive, determination and physical fitness.*

Heliodor *Brings good fortune to speculators, gamblers, sportsmen and athletes; promotes prosperity and happiness.*

Jade *Promises good health and improved circumstances; in particular, favours artistic or musical endeavours and public figures.*

Jasper *A great aid to psychic development. Signifies increased confidence, friendship and loyalty.*

Jet *Strengthens determination and drive; affords success to those seeking to establish themselves in business.*

Labradorite *Expands consciousness and can help bring prophetic visions. Promotes harmonious relationships and marital bliss.*

Lapis Lazuli *Inspires confidence, courage and friendship. Favours those about to undertake new commercial ventures.*

Lodestone *Denotes that the querent will earn the respect, loyalty and devotion of others. Increases stamina and virility.*

Malachite *Lifts depression and brings relief from stressful or embittered situations. Promises favourable judgements in law suits or civil actions.*

Moonstone *Awards success to those involved in artistic and creative efforts and new commercial projects.*

Morganite *Reconciles difference of opinion and dispels anger. Offers safety to travellers in any dimension.*

Obsidian *Encourages boldness, determination and vigour; overwhelms opposition and promotes personal achievement.*

Onyx *Focuses attention on business acumen and perspicacity; revitalises flagging spirits and encourages creative imagination.*

Opal *Signifies fidelity and friendship. Accentuates psychicism and prophetic capacity; stimulates memory and intellect.*

Pearl *Highlights charitable deeds and selfless actions which will be rewarded by love and respect.*

Peridot *Bestows success on long-term schemes or any form of speculation.*

Rose Quartz *Enhances psychic awareness and creative talents. Promises progress to new ventures.*

Ruby *Accentuates vitality and virility, bringing pleasure and prosperity. Beneficial for property development or those considering moving home.*

Sapphire *Heightens perception and rewards commercial or social efforts. Denotes the overcoming of business rivalry or jealousy.*

Sardonyx *Inspires love, romance, vitality, confidence and fitness. Ensures a satisfactory outcome to legal or contractual difficulties.*

Scheelite *Emphasises diplomacy, business acumen and self-assurance, promising commercial success and domestic harmony.*

Schist *Brings relief from nervous tension or irritability. Encourages those about to embark on business ventures of their own.*

Serpentine *Rewards innovative or creative endeavours with the respect and admiration of others.*

Smithsonite *Favours visionary or humanitarian undertakings; affords success to co-operative ventures, especially overseas.*

Spinel *Enhances speculative powers and creativity; promises financial prosperity and social prestige for efforts made.*

Tiger's Eye *Ensures victory in any competitive venture; defeats opposition of any kind.*

Topaz *Bestows courage, determination, confidence and judgement. Heralds joy and prosperity.*

Tormaline *Stimulates the imagination and sharpens the intellect. Promises financial benefit from efforts made.*

Turquoise *Signifies an improvement to health and financial standing; affords a successful conclusion to any constructive enterprise that you undertake.*

Zircon *Denotes the overcoming of obstacles or opposition. Safeguards travellers and signals property.*

LYNCHNOMANCY

Divination from the behaviour of candle flames. One method is to stand three new, lighted candles on saucers on a flat surface such as a table top. These should be placed at equal distances from one another to form a triangle.

The diviner then sits quietly at the table, being sure not to make a sudden movement that can disturb the candles, and watches the behaviour of the flames to ascertain what is in store for him/her as follows.

1. One flame brighter than the others: good fortune in the offing.

2. One spluttering flame: a minor material or emotional loss.

3. One flame extinguished: severe loss, disappointment or depression.

4. Three flames wavering back and forth: a sudden but beneficial change of circumstances.

5. Three flames rising and falling abruptly: over-confidence can lead to loss of respect.

6. Three flames burning steadily: good progress will be made in the matter under consideration.

7. Three bright flames at their tips: increased success and prosperity; the achievement of aims.

Another method, this time involving the use of 12 candles, is the forerunner of the birthday practice of blowing out the candles on a cake 'for luck'.

Stand 12 candles in a circle on a steady flat surface (a metal tray would be ideal and ensures safety in case one of the candles falls over accidentally) and light them one at a time, moving in a clockwise direction. Then, starting at the 12 o'clock position, try to blow out all the candles with one breath by moving around the circle in the same direction as they were lit. Do not take another breath, just note which candles remain alight and which have been extinguished.

Again starting at the 12 o'clock position, imagine that each candle represents a calendar month: 12 o'clock denotes whatever month (irrespective of date) the reading takes place; 1 o'clock represents the following month; 2 o'clock the one after, and so on. Each extinguished candle marks a fortunate period when steady progress will be made; whereas those which remain alight mark an uneventful period.

MAGIC TABLES

This ancient means of predicting future trends has numerological and astrological derivations. In each case the principle remains the same; the idea is to randomly select a number contained within a geometric figure either by the tossing of a stone or a small coin or by the use of a pointer. The number selected is then looked up in a key which will denote the answer to a specific query.

Circle of the Sun

This figure is designed to provide an answer to those querents who wish to know what their financial fortunes are likely to be in the next few weeks.

Key:
  1. You will receive an unexpected sum of money.
  2. You will be rewarded for the return of a valuable item which you find.
  3. A business gain is imminent.
  4. A loss of money or jewellery is likely.
  5. Unexpected money will come to you from a distant relative or friend.
  6. You will receive a surprise gift.
  7. You may suffer loss by theft but the stolen item will be returned to you in due course.
  8. Expect a bonus or raise in pay.
  9. A sudden increase in wealth.
  10. A loss through investment.
  11. A letter brings news of money coming your way.
  12. You will suffer financial setbacks unless you alter your plans.

The Diamond of Mercury

The diamond has long been associated with the mind as a symbol of intellectual powers so it will come as no surprise to see that the diamond shape should be used to answer questions relating to matters of the mind, thought and the making of decisions.

Key:
  1. A sudden inspiration will mark a turning point in your life.
  2. You have unsuspected talents which you should develop.
  3. You need to discipline yourself more in order to achieve your objectives.
  4. You must not allow feelings of inferiority to handicap your progress.
  5. You need to broaden your area of studies.
  6. Do not underestimate your creative abilities; try putting ideas to practical use.
  7. Keep your opinions more to yourself or you may arouse the antagonism or jealousy of others.
  8. Be honest with those who approach you for advice.
  9. Beware of deception.
  10. You have great powers of concentration and should use these to further your aims.
  11. Stick to your decision; you know you are right.
  12. Now is a good time to further your studies.
  13. Do not allow others to distract you.
  14. You have a brilliant mind — use it!
  15. A successful exam result.
  16. A good time to follow or take up specialist training.

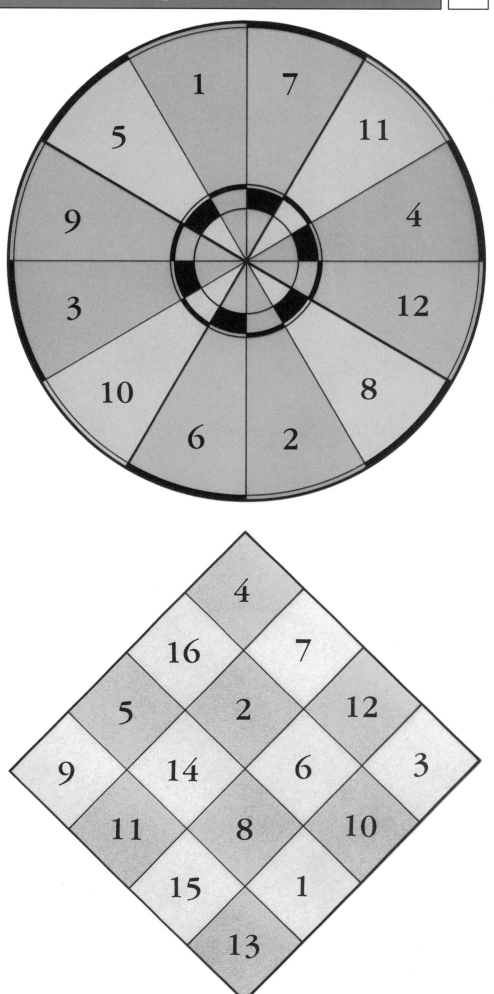

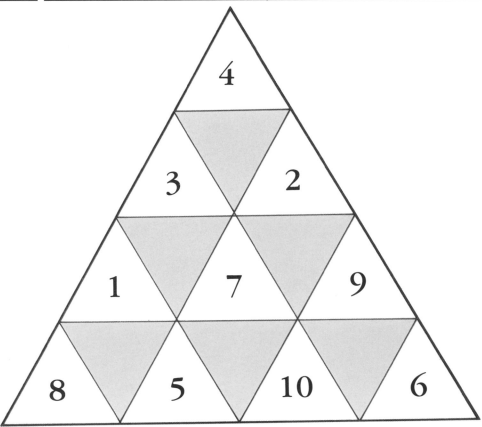

Pyramid of Venus

This relates to matters of love, friendship and the affections.

Key:

1. You are about to embark on a new romance.

2. A quarrel with your loved one.

3. Expect a surprise in connection with a love affair.

4. Be on your guard against jealousy.

5. News of a wedding in the near future.

6. Beware lest you reveal a confidence and ruin another's romance.

7. You will soon find true love and happiness.

8. A passing infatuation.

9. A reconciliation with your beloved.

10. You will meet a stranger at a social gathering; it will be love at first sight.

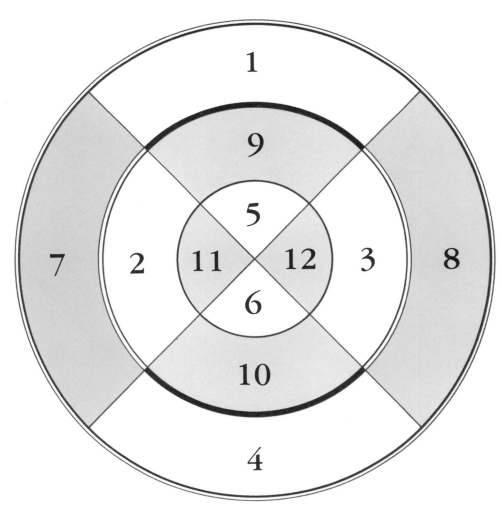

The Mystic Circle of Neptune

Mysterious Neptune, the planet of dreams, fantasies, ideals and intuition will answer your occult questions.

Key:

1. A flash of inspiration will solve your current problems.

2. You will receive a warning in a dream; ignore it at your peril.

3. This would be a good opportunity to join a group that would help you with your occult studies.

4. A time to rest and to recharge your batteries.

5. You should follow the strong hunch that will shortly come to you, as it will pay dividends.

6. Consult a professional reader as an important message awaits you.

7. This will be a period of meaningful coincidence.

8. Listen to that inner voice.

9. You need to expand your horizons and broaden the scope of your studies.

10. A dream will be realised.

11. Have faith in yourself, you have greater abilities than you think.

12. A trip to the countryside could uplift your spirits.

The Cross of the Moon

This figure relates to queries concerning the home and family.

1. A visit from a distant relative or friend you have not seen for a long while.
2. An addition to the family: by marriage or birth.
3. Unless you act hastily to prevent it there will be a family dispute.
4. News of a wedding.
5. Trouble with the in-laws.
6. Guard against jealousy.
7. You will hear of a romantic split.
8. Extra responsibility in family affairs.
9. Change of residence or improvements to the home.
10. Problems with the neighbours.
11. A visitor will remain longer than expected.
12. A happy family outing.
13. A family celebration through a youngster's achievement.

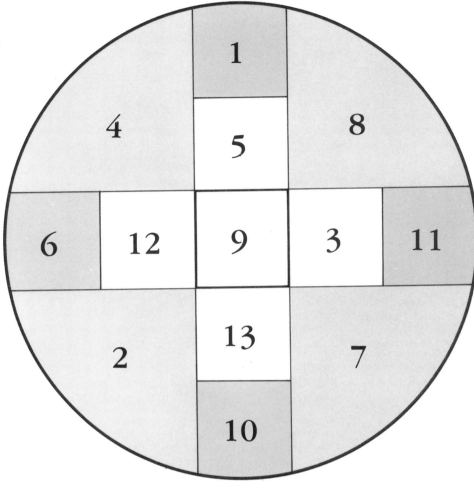

The Star of Jupiter

Jupiter, planet of expansion, is regarded as a harbinger of luck; consult this oracle to see if you will obtain your wish.

Key:
1. An unexpected stroke of good fortune.
2. You will meet with disappointment.
3. You will have a lucky windfall or small legacy.
4. An acquaintance is standing between you and your desire.
5. Talk to those in authority, you could be pleasantly surprised at the result.
6. A great improvement in personal circumstances.
7. You may have to wait a long time before your aims are realised.
8. Factors outside your control are inhibiting your progress.
9. If worried about someone's health you will receive heartening news.
10. Listen to a friend's advice, it could prove profitable.
11. A temporary setback followed by complete success.

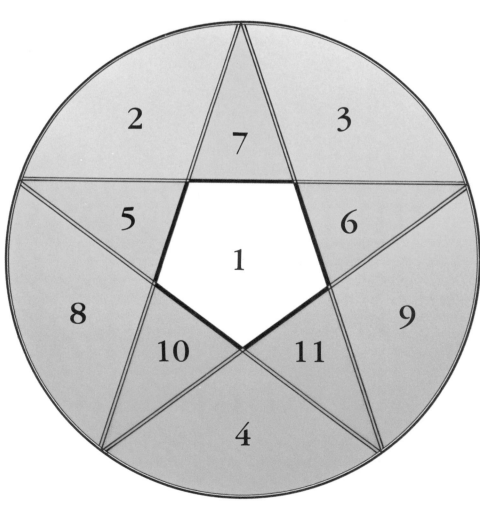

ONYCHOMANCY/ONYOMANCY

A term applied to a method of divination from the nails on a human hand, involving interpretation of the reflections of a bright light on their surface. This is really a form of scrying.

PSYCHOMETRY

This is a technique which allows one to pick up psychic impressions from an object which either belongs to someone else or has been found.

PYROMANCY

If you chance to live in a cold place where a real coal fire is used in winter, here is a method for reading the future. If, however, no fire-places exist in your abode, go out into the country at night, collect some dry branches and twigs of trees, and make a good fire with them.

Sprinkle some salt on to the fire, and wait until the wood is well alight .and glowing. There should be no smoke. If indoors, put out all the other lights in the room and sit on the floor or ground opposite to the fire and gaze steadily into it. Try to see pictures in the burning embers. Sometimes you will have to use a little imagination to identify the different shapes which are to be seen.

SAND READING

This method of divination derives from geomancy, but like scrying, it is not based on a set of rules but on the psychic ability of the reader.

The equipment is very simply obtained: all that is needed is a small quantity of silver sand, a tin or wooden tray. Make sure the sand is dry before placing it in the tray, if it feels damp, place it in a cool oven or warm place until it is dry or crisp, then fill the tray two to three inches deep. Ask the querent to handle the sand for a minute or two, with eyes closed, while concentrating upon his/her question, the diviner must then use intuition to study the resulting patterns.

It is important to note that the soonest events will appear in the sand closest to the querent, those shown nearest the diviner will take greater length of time to come to pass.

Easily recognisable symbols may be visible but, generally speaking, the interpretations of the marks in the sand must be left to the diviner's intuition. However, the following list contains traditional meanings for some of the marks that most commonly occur.

1. One long, deep line: A journey.
2. One short, deep line: An unexpected visitor.
3. A small circle: Marriage.
4. A large circle: Disappointment.
5. A cross: An obstacle to overcome.
6. A cross made diagonally: A happy love affair.
7. A triangle: Success with money or career. Initials may also have special meaning for the querent, as might numbers.

SYMBOLS

This list of symbols can be used in connection with any method of divination that employs the use of specific shapes or patterns in order to predict future trends.

Abbey *You will receive an invitation to a wedding.*
Acorn *News of a birth or pregnancy; if this combines with an initial it may be an indication of to whom this applies.*
Adder *The termination of an unwanted friendship.*
Aeroplane *An unexpected journey.*
Alien *You feel threatened in some way.*
Almond *Someone will help you achieve an ambition.*
Ambulance *Distressing news.*
America *News about a group involvement; perhaps political.*
Anchor *A change is in the offing.*
Angel *Someone may need your help.*
Animals *An unexpected admirer.*
Anvil *You may be doubtful about a forthcoming marriage.*
Apples *A tempting offer.*
Archer *Be wary of a newcomer.*
Archway *Reconciliation or a new relationship.*
Arrow *Good news is on the way.*
Asteroid *You need to come down to earth.*
Athlete *There may be a minor health problem.*
Axe *An approaching quarrel.*

Baby *Sickness in the family.*
Balcony *Danger of a fall.*
Ball *A friend may let you down.*
Ballerina *A longing for freedom.*
Balloon *Promotion at work.*
Banana *Stomach trouble.*
Bandage *Peace within the family; healing.*
Bank *Caution; there are hard times ahead.*
Banner *Victory over problems; a superior may be helpful.*
Banquet *The future looks bright.*
Bar *An active social life.*
Barn *Prosperity.*
Basket *Good luck is on its way.*
Bath *Bad news.*
Bathroom *If clean, exciting changes; if dirty; something to hide.*
Bats *Delay your present intentions.*
Bear *An older and wiser person will be of assistance.*
Beaver *Team-work is essential.*
Beds *A move of house.*
Bees *A legal matter will work in your favour.*
Beetles *Money luck.*
Bellows *A recent disappointment will prove to be a blessing in disguise.*
Bells *News of a wedding.*
Bible *You may have been acting unfairly.*
Bicycle *A short journey.*
Birds *Unexpected news; but if on a branch, plans need changing.*
Bird's Nest *Good news of a child; security.*
Blacksmith *Success through effort and endeavour.*
Bluebell *You are surrounded by love.*
Boat *Material rewards.*
Bomb *Domestic problems.*
Books *Study could improve your circumstances.*
Bottle *Success and happiness.*
Bow and Arrow *You are right on target.*
Box *The future is as yet unknown.*
Bracelet *Love from a stranger.*
Branch *A fruitful period.*
Bread *Be cautious.*
Bridge *A sense of loss.*

Broom *You need to reconcile a difference of opinion.*
Buckle *A need to defend your actions.*
Bull *A promising love affair.*
Butterfly *A flirtation.*

Cabbage *A change of direction is needed.*
Cactus *Ignore demands from others.*
Cage *You feel trapped.*
Cake *Health, wealth and prosperity.*
Calendar *A friend will ask your advice.*
Camel *You will take on a new responsibility.*
Camera *Your job will change for the better.*
Camp *Success in love.*
Canary *A happy home life.*
Candelabra *There will be a connection with music.*
Candles *Good fortune.*
Cannon *A friend will come to your aid.*
Canoe *A flirtation may cause problems.*
Car *An exciting journey.*
Cards *Sorrow.*
Carnation *Closeness with another.*
Carpet *A change of residence.*
Carpenter *An opportunity to brighten up your surroundings.*
Carriage *A visit to a hospital.*
Castle *A worrying experience.*
Cat *Fame and fortune.*
Caterpillar *A rival will wreck your plans.*
Cathedral *Metaphysical studies.*
Cemetary *News of a birth.*
Chains *You will soon be free of a worry.*
Chair *An invitation from a friend.*
Chariot *Have confidence in a financial scheme.*
Cherry *A secret love affair.*
Cherubs *A new romance.*
Chickens *Impending change.*
Children *Business success and a happy marriage.*
Christmas Tree *A gift will speak from the heart.*
Church *A discussion may become heated.*
Circles *You are not happy with the state of your life.*
Clock *Disturbing news.*
Clothing *A worry will disappear.*
Clouds *A disagreement will soon be resolved.*
Clover *Your patience will be rewarded.*
Cobblestones *Expect trouble with your car.*
Comet *A warning that trouble is brewing.*
Crab *Avoid travel by water.*
Cradle *An unexpected pregnancy.*
Cross *This signifies the need for sacrifice.*
Crow *A close relative may become ill.*
Crown *Promotion.*
Cuckoo *A disappointing love.*
Cupboard *Money troubles.*
Curtains *The end of a friendship.*
Cushion *Comfort and material gain.*

Daffodils *Someone of the opposite sex is being selfish.*
Dagger *Keep a secret to yourself.*
Daisy *You will solve a mystery.*
Dancer *An unexpected windfall.*
Dandelion *News from a distant friend.*
Darts *An argument at work.*
Decanter *A change of surroundings.*
Decorations *Favourable news regarding property.*
Deer *News of an old friend.*
Dentist *Your doubts will be proved correct.*

Desert *A difficult journey.*
Desk *The signing of a legal document.*
Devil *Temptation.*
Diamonds *Cross words.*
Dice *Speculation could prove profitable.*
Ditch *Careful planning is needed.*
Diver *You are running away from reality.*
Doctor *A friend needs help.*
Dog *A favour from a friend.*
Dolphin *Excitement over a child's achievement.*
Donkey *A decision will be proved correct.*
Doves *Peace within the home.*
Dragon *Dramatic changes with a favourable outcome.*
Dragonfly *Bad news concerning someone's health.*
Dress *Someone will leave the home environment.*
Drill *You are too inquisitive.*
Drum *An invitation from a secret admirer.*
Duck *Peace and contentment.*

Eagle *You will reach your objective.*
Ears *Interesting news that solves a mystery.*
Earthquake *A business may go into liquidation.*
Eclipse *A happy marriage for the fancy-free.*
Eel *A secret enemy will come out in the open.*
Effigy *A business rival.*
Egg *Money in the mail.*
Elephant *Discussion regarding a new partnership.*
Elevator *Promotion.*
Elves *Disregard rumour.*
Emerald *A new romance.*
Emperor *Contact with an important personage.*
Engine *A business loss.*
Eye *Your future is in the hands of others.*
Eye Brows *You are behaving out of character.*

Face *If you recognise this, you will hear news of the person; a stranger suggests a meeting in the near future.*
Factory *Your financial worries are over.*
Fairy *An omen of joy.*
Falcon *Accept guidance from an influential person.*
Fan *A holiday romance.*
Farm *Recovery from sickness.*
Feast *A celebration.*
Feather *A financial boost.*
Fence *You must face up to responsibility.*
Fender *Stress will ease.*
Fern *Love at first sight.*
Ferret *Embarrassment.*
Ferryboat *Reminiscing over past happiness.*
Fields *Someone is taking advantage of your good nature.*
Fig Tree *Domestic happiness; a celebration.*
Fir Tree *An anonymous gift.*
Fire *Beware of impulsive acts.*
Fish *Relationships improve beyond your dreams.*
Fist *Listen to advice.*
Flag *A need to stick by your principles.*
Flies *A minor irritation.*
Floods *Disruption in the home.*
Flowers *Accept an invitation.*
Flute *A reunion.*
Food *Prosperity and joy.*
Football *A chance for revenge.*

Fort *Strength and determination.*
Fountain *You can be optimistic about the future.*
Fox *Care is needed with finance, also in legal affairs.*
Frogs *Seek professional counsel.*
Fruit *An inheritance.*
Furs *Take care of your pets.*

Gallows *You need to analyse your motives.*
Garden *Peace after a long period of trouble.*
Garter *Petty problems.*
Gate *The beginning of a new enterprise.*
Geese *An irritating visitor.*
Gems *News of an engagement.*
Ghost *A need for more self-confidence.*
Giant *Don't make a mountain out of a molehill.*
Gipsy *A desire for freedom.*
Giraffe *Your affairs will prosper.*
Girl *Happiness in the immediate future.*
Gladioli *Think carefully about making a decision.*
Gloves *You are afraid to deal with a problem.*
Gnome *An odd character may make a wise suggestion.*
Goat *Keep to your chosen path against all obstacles.*
Gold *Success in a new venture.*
Golf Club *You meet an interesting story-teller.*
Gondola *An exciting period is about to begin.*
Gong *Caution.*
Gooseberries *Someone is being uncharitable.*
Grapes *Don't trust a flatterer.*
Grass *Give a friend practical advice.*
Greece *Watch out! There's a thief about.*
Greyhound *A small windfall.*
Guillotine *The cutting of the ties of friendship.*
Guitar *An invitation to a party.*
Gun *Don't accept unjust criticism.*

Hair *You are too concerned with your appearance.*
Halo *Someone will fall from their pedestal.*
Hammer *Accepting a challenge will prove your worth.*
Hammock *A chance for a short break.*
Hand *Help is available.*
Handwriting *News of a legacy.*
Hanging *Money is on the way.*
Harp *A love that grows.*
Harvest *Prosperity in many areas.*
Hat *Business gains.*
Hawk *Be careful you are not cheated.*
Hay *Steady progress.*
Heart *Burning desire.*
Heather *Good luck.*
Hedgehog *Speak your mind.*
Hedges *Beware a possessive person.*
Helmet *Literally wear a crash helmet.*
Hen *Information you receive will be useless, don't rely on it.*
Herd *Gathering in of resources.*
Hermit *Losses followed by enormous gains.*
Hills *A need to escape from mundane reality.*
Holly *You may be at a crossroads or a turning point.*
Home *Unsettled monetary affairs.*
Hood *A need to take care of your health.*
Hook *Guard against accident.*
Hoop *Someone will pry into your affairs.*
Horizon *A disappointment over property.*

Horn *Important news, perhaps regarding an eminent person.*
Horse *A faithful and loyal friend.*
Horseshoe *A visit to a new location may cause a hint of romance.*
Hospital *Business promotion.*
Hotel *Unexpected visitors.*
Hounds *A failed relationship.*
House *Changes that work in your favour.*
Humming-Birds *Travel.*

Iceberg *Difficulties and hardship.*
Icicles *Happy marriage and children.*
Idols *A need to decide on your objective.*
Image (own) *An unsuccessful relationship.*
Incense *Bad news.*
Inn *A happy relationship.*
Invalid *Your health needs attention.*
Iris *Upsetting news.*
Iron *You should compromise and smooth out any differences.*
Island *A fear of isolation.*
Ivy *The good things of life will cling to you.*

Jackdaw *Keep an eye on your wallet.*
Jail *You need some privacy.*
Jar *An opportunity.*
Jaws *Guard against taking risks.*
Jelly *You feel insecure.*
Jester *Don't place too much faith in first impressions.*
Jewellery *You should try to create a new image. Be sure that it is the correct one.*
Jockey *An important decision will have far-reaching effects.*
Jug *News of a friend.*
Jungle *You crave more exictment.*
Jury *Don't heedlessly judge others.*

Kangaroo *Try to be more organised.*
Kettle *Harmony and happiness.*
Key *May be the key to a door or the start of a new venture.*
King *You are pushing your partner too far.*
Kitchen *A difficult responsibility.*
Kite *Be quick to grasp a new opportunity.*
Kitten *Great happiness.*
Kneeling figure *Someone will beg forgiveness — listen.*
Knife *Sharp words may clear the air.*
Knight *A charmer with dishonourable intentions.*
Knitting *An untrustworthy person is around you.*
Knocker *An invitation to a house-warming party.*

Label *You feel deservedly guilty.*
Ladder *A sudden rise in life.*
Lake *A happy marriage and business success.*
Lamb *Prepare to take a gamble.*
Lamp *Listen to helpful advice.*
Lantern *An inner fear is revealed.*
Lark *Good news for a friend.*
Laurel *Victory.*
Leaves *A fruitful marriage.*
Legs *You should face up to a challenge.*
Lemons *Beware of a business colleague.*
Leopard *Resist trying to change your partner, respect their ways.*
Letter *Try to get in touch with someone from the past.*
Lettuce *Happiness from a new pet.*
Library *Continue with your studies.*

Lighthouse *Guard against accident.*
Lightning *Unexpected advancement.*
Lilac *Good fortune.*
Lily *An exceptionally happy marriage.*
Lion *An acquaintance may cause confusion.*
Lobster *An idea that is in its initial stages will be successful.*
Lock *You should pursue a new interest.*
Luggage *All-round changes or the need for a hasty journey.*

Machinery *Stop causing complications!*
Magnolia *The chance to revive an old love — resist it.*
Magpie *One for trouble — more cancel it out.*
Mallet *Be firm and get what you want.*
Man *Someone you like will surprise you.*
Mansion *You are trying to live above your station.*
Map *Changes in the home life.*
Maple Leaf *You will have mixed feelings about news that arrives.*
Marble *Financial success.*
Marigold *You can expect a snub or rejection.*
Mars *Strife.*
Mask *You have something to hide.*
May-Pole *A sign of great joy: widows will remarry.*
Meadow *A happy reunion.*
Medal *Pride in achievement; an honour.*
Melons *Overseas travel.*
Mercury *A quest for knowledge.*
Mice *Domestic troubles concerning children.*
Microscope *A friend is deceitful.*
Midget *You will soon have independent means.*
Mill *A new idea should be put into practice.*
Mine *A financial scheme is doomed to failure.*
Mirror *You are at a major crossroads.*
Mistletoe *A new romance which may lead to marriage.*
Monastery *Freedom from fears and worries.*
Money *Guard your savings.*
Monk *You are being too secretive.*
Monkey *Someone will try to undermine your confidence.*
Monster *You may be nervous about impending marriage.*
Moon *Love and domestic bliss.*
Moth *Be careful whom you trust in business.*
Mountain *An onerous task is ahead.*

Mushrooms *Gradual financial progress.*
Myrtle *Comfortable circumstances; a contented second marriage.*

Nails *You should demand a rise in pay.*
Necklace *You will soon be married to a wealthy person.*
Needle *You should try to be less arrogant.*
Nets *You will capture the attention of one you admire.*
Nettles *Good health.*
Newspaper *A desire to keep one's business private.*
Nun *A helping hand.*
Nurse *Seek medical advice.*
Nuts *Happiness and success.*

Oak Tree *An increase in security.*
Oar *Disappointments.*
Ocean *A sudden urge to travel.*
Octopus *You should escape from a misguided love affair.*
Office *New responsibility.*
Old Man *A sign of financial success.*
Old Woman *Achievement of ambition.*
Olives *A beneficial change of job.*
Onions *Recovery of a treasured lost object.*
Oranges *A pleasant outing with friends.*
Orchard *A substantial inheritance.*
Organ *A very fortunate liason.*
Otter *Delightful news about a youngster.*
Oven *Instant success.*
Owl *Someone is watching your progress with interest.*
Oyster *Your plans will be slow to mature.*

Package *A pleasant surprise.*
Padlock *Don't let anyone try to restrict your freedom.*
Page *You lack attention from the one you love.*
Pagoda *A long anticipated journey.*
Pail *A pleasant meeting.*
Palace *An improvement in financial standing.*
Palm Tree *Good news from a surprising source.*
Panther *Someone is being unfaithful.*
Parachute *You will learn something at just the right moment to prevent you from making a mistake.*
Party *An exciting invitation.*
Path *The tide is about to turn in your favour.*

Peaches *A rewarding friendship.*
Peacock *Jealous friends may undermine your progress.*
Pearls *True love and elevation in business matters.*
Pears *News of a welcome windfall.*
Peas *Good fortune in affairs of the heart.*
Pebbles *Keep on your toes — you have a rival at work.*
Pen *An important paper to be signed.*
Pencil *An instant change of plan.*
Penny *Financial loss.*
Pheasants *A gift of money.*
Photograph *Contact with the past.*
Piano *A joyful occasion.*
Pig *Someone will play a dirty trick on you.*
Pigeon *Surprise news may cause a journey.*
Pillow *An unusual gift.*
Pineapples *You will soon meet your soulmate.*
Pipe *Someone will act as peacemaker.*
Pistol *Bad luck.*
Plate *A need to curb extravagance.*
Plums *Better things are ahead.*
Policeman *Attendance at a court.*
Poppies *Avoid self-indulgence.*
Pot *Unwanted guests prove expensive.*
Prison *You will soon be free from restrictions.*
Pyramid *You will achieve something no one thought possible.*

Quay *Hesitate before taking an opportunity to travel.*
Queen *News of one's mother.*
Question Mark *Look before you leap.*

Rabbit *An addition to the family.*
Raft *You will be prevented from making a rash mistake.*
Railway *A long awaited quest.*
Rainbow *An unusual occurrence.*
Rake *Nagging worries.*
Rat *Someone is stirring up trouble.*
Rattle *News regarding a child.*
Rattlesnake *Tread carefully.*
Raven *An injustice.*
Razor *A rift in friendship.*
Restaurant *Be wary over flattery.*
Ribbon *A frivolous occasion.*
River *A way through difficulty.*
Road *Don't rush into a new change of job.*

Robin *A change of luck.*
Rocket *An unexpected increase in income.*
Rocking Chair *News of an elderly person.*
Rocks *You need to make more effort to instigate changes.*
Roof *A dominating figure is blocking progress.*
Ropes *Complications in your affairs.*
Roses *Happy family life.*
Rubbish *A need to change your lifestyle.*
Ruins *A broken romance.*

Saddle *Unexpected visitors.*
Safe *A need to protect your interests.*
Sage *Wise advice.*
Sailor *A delightful flirtation.*
Salmon *An invitation to a grand occasion.*
Sand *You should curtail spending.*
Sapphire *Surprise gains.*
Sardines *Sudden illness.*
Sash *An illicit affair.*
Saw *A welcome ending to a friendship.*
Scaffold *Let-down over a property deal.*
Scales *Your judgement was too hasty.*
School *Don't underestimate talent or ability.*
Scissors *The breaking of a friendship or relationship.*
Scorpion *Power struggles.*
Screw *Someone will leave home.*
Scythe *Disappointment in love.*
Sea *News is on the way.*
Seagull *Speak your mind before it is too late to change it.*
Seal *You are working your way to success.*
Seat *Someone will go out of your life.*
Seed *Bright hopes for a new project.*
Serpents *Someone hopes for your downfall.*
Shark *Be careful whom you trust.*
Shawl *You will be hurt because you are excluded from an invitation.*
Shears *A disagreement over finance.*
Sheaves *Well deserved wealth.*
Sheep *Try to be more forthcoming.*
Shells *Criticism over an extravagance.*
Shelves *A secret will come out in the open.*
Shepherd *Protect yourself against illness.*
Ship *Your troubles are coming to an end.*
Shirt *You should try to avoid a gamble.*
Shoes *An argument over possessions.*
Shotgun *An unexpected pregnancy.*

Shovel *Rewards for efforts made.*

Shower *Excellent prospects for health improvement.*

Shroud *You need to update the outfits in your wardrobe.*

Sieve *You feel that life is passing you by — change it.*

Silver *Bad luck is in its final stages.*

Skater *Try to work harder.*

Skeleton *A secret is best left unrevealed.*

Skull *Eavesdroppers never hear good of themselves.*

Sleigh *An exciting adventure.*

Slippers *Your home life needs improving.*

Snakes *A barbed remark from a comparative stranger hurts.*

Snail *Someone's health needs attention.*

Snow *You are anxious about a secret.*

Snowdrop *A change of heart leads to happiness in love.*

Soap *A reward for being honest.*

Sovereign *Increasing prosperity.*

Sparrow *An expensive outlay.*

Spider *Good luck is coming your way.*

Sponge *Money loss.*

Spoon *Contentment in family affairs.*

Spring *A new beginning.*

Stable *A visit from an old and valued friend.*

Stag *Don't let others tie you down.*

Stairs *Take heed while travelling.*

Stallion *Good health and prosperity.*

Star *Dramatic improvement in circumstances.*

Statue *You need to rest.*

Steeple *An attempt to keep up with the Jones'.*

Stone *Develop a new interest.*

Sun *You need to escape from your present way of life and will succeed.*

Swallow *Peace in the home at last.*

Swan *You will achieve a secret desire in an unexpected way.*

Sword *Public acclaim.*

Table *A happy reunion.*

Tail *A petty annoyance.*

Taxi *A complicated journey.*

Telephone *A message from the past.*

Telescope *Your plans can proceed; go ahead with confidence.*

Tent *A temporary change of address.*

Theatre *Great happiness is in store for you.*

Thimble *An unsettling influence in a group of friends.*

Thorn *Look after physical wellbeing.*

Tiger *Infuriating delays in travel.*

Toad *A minor misadventure.*

Torch *Someone will stand up for your rights.*

Train *A hasty journey.*

Tramp *A request for a loan of money.*

Treasure *Keep your goals in perspective.*

Trees *A new door will open.*

Triangle *A mistaken romantic alliance.*

Trumpet *Official news.*

Turkey *Instability in business matters.*

Umbrella *Great protection.*

Unicorn *Your dearest dreams could come true.*

Uniform *Try to take control of a situation.*

University *Scholarly achievements.*

Vampire *You have a fear of authority.*

Vase *A pleasant surprise from a lover.*

Vatican *You desire a more protective partner.*

Veil *You are trying to disregard lack of compatability in a relationship.*

Vestry *Someone will try to persuade you to adopt their views.*

Viaduct *Bad news.*

Vicar *You need to be more moderate in your habits.*

Vine *Success in a business venture.*

Violin *You should face up to reality.*

Volcano *There may be a need to consult a solicitor.*

Wagon *An unhappy relationship.*

Waiter *An invitation from a charming person.*

Wall *You must break down a barrier.*

Wallet *An unexpected gift of money.*

Walnut *Let your hair down and enjoy yourself for a change.*

Warehouse *Great wealth.*

Wasp *A friend envies your assets.*

Watch *Your aims are slow to materialise.*

Water *A message.*

Water Lily *You are tempted to get involved romantically with a friend.*

Waves *A snap decision creates sudden change.*

Web *Try to be a little more forceful.*

Wedding *Misfortune.*

Well *A wish you have made will come true.*

Whale *Absence of someone you care for.*

Wharf *Good news from abroad.*

Wheat *A happy retirement.*

Wheel *A change of heart that confuses others.*

Whip *Sharp words in a friendship.*

Whirlpool *A court case.*

Whisk *A carefree break from routine.*

Willow *Tears.*

Windmill *A solution to a problem.*

Window *You are barking up the wrong tree.*

Wine Glass *You are nervous about a social gathering.*

Witch *You are well protected.*

Wolf *Protect your property.*

Wool *A sign of prosperity.*

Wreath *Prominence and recognition.*

Wren *Good news from afar.*

Writing *Try to avoid an expensive mistake.*

Yacht *A happy reconciliation.*

Zebra *You have too many irons in the fire.*

Zodiac *Think positively about changing your lifestyle.*

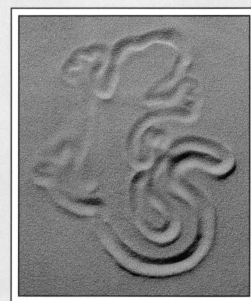
PICTURE CREDITS

The author and publishers would like to thank everyone, as credited here, who kindly supplied pictures for inclusion in this book. Particular thanks go to Frances Cartes — Grimaud, who allowed us to reproduce their splendid tarot card designs on pp. 78-87. We would also like to acknowledge the co-operation of W. Foulsham & Co. Ltd. who allowed us to reproduce extracts from the Raphael's Ephemeris for October 1963 on pp. 20-23. The British Summer Time Listing and World Time Zone Map on pp. 25 & 26 are reproduced with kind permission from data supplied by the Science and Engineering Research Council. The photographs are credited by page number.

Aldus Archive: 6/7
Bodleian Library: 28-39 inclusive, 111, 115, 116/7, 132, 133
C.M. Dixon: 122, 125, 148, 150, 151, 154/5, 174/5,

Rod Ferring: 100/1
Ian Hunt (commissioned photography): 1, 88/9, 90, 92, 93 upper & lower
Michael Little (commissioned photography): 8/9, 58/9 (computerised graphically by Kentscan), 66/7, 72 upper & lower, 73 upper & lower, 74 upper & lower, 75 upper & lower, 77, 96/7, 98 upper, middle & lower, 99 left, 106/7, 118/9, 121, 126/7, 134/5, 136, 149, 152, 158/9, 166/7, 168, 169, 170/1, back jacket
National Film Archive: 102/3, 105
Science Photo Library: ⅔ title, title, 10/11, 13 left & right, 14 right, 15 left & right, 16 left & right, 17 right, 45, 120, 146/7, 152, 153, 154, 160/1, 162, 178, 180
Agence Vandystadt: 185
Victoria & Albert Museum: 173